Visual Basic

A complete course

Phil Jones

CONTINUUM
London • New York

1998

Dedicated to

John Gordon Jones and Nancy Jones

Continuum
The Tower Building, 11 York Road, London SE1 7NX
570 Lexington Avenue, New York, NY 10017-6503

A CIP catalogue record for this book is available from the British Library

ISBN 0-8264-5405-4
Copyright Phil Jones © 1998

First Edition 1998
Reprinted 1999, 2000, 2001

Printed in Great Britain by Martins the Printers Ltd, Berwick upon Tweed

Contents

Preface

How to use this book

It is not possible to learn how to play the piano by reading about it, you have to practise at the piano. Progress is made by practising easy pieces of music until they are played correctly. Then harder pieces are practised until they too are played correctly. Likewise it is not possible to learn a programming language by reading a textbook. **To learn a programming language requires that you practise what you have just read, at the computer**. This textbook introduces you to aspects of programming then advises that you practise them **at the computer** before moving on.

I have introduced new aspects of programming through a *specification* that defines a problem to be solved. The text then describes a solution to this problem and you are then directed to implement this solution **at the computer**. As you progress through the book the specifications become more involved and difficult. **You should not move on to the next specification until you have implemented (and understood) the solution to the specification** *at the computer.*

Icons are used to direct your study

The book supports **student-centred learning** by using icons to direct students' activities, and as such, would make an ideal course text for GNVQ, HND/HNC, OND/ONC and first-year degree students in Computing, Software Engineering and Information Technology courses.

The book has also been developed with the sole user in mind. Individuals who wish to learn about Visual Basic, without attending a course, will find the material useful and the layout of the book will encourage an interactive approach that is ideal for learning a programming language.

There are two icons used to direct study throughout this book; they are listed below with an explanation of their meaning.

 Adjacent to this icon will be one of two types of questions.

1. Revision Question

2. Development Question

Every question will be numbered. A revision and development question will be specifically identified by the words Revision or Development appearing in parentheses after the question number. Two examples are shown below

QUESTION 2.1 (DEVELOPMENT)

Learn how to run the executable files, produced during Practical activity 2.4, from the Windows operating system. That is, run them outside of the Visual Basic design environment.

Question 2.2 (REVISION)

Suggest suitable project names for the following:

(a) A database is being developed for a local hospital.

(b) A multimedia CD is to be produced for a local Rugby club that charts their history during the last decade.

A Revision Question is designed to test the students' understanding of what they have just read or it will test their understanding of a Practical activity they have just completed.

A Development Question differs from a Revision in that it is not designed to check the students' understanding of what they have just done. Instead a Development Question is designed to encourage the student to develop further understanding of the subject by utilising the Visual Basic comprehensive help database.

A Practical activity icon usually follows a section of text that showed the steps involved in performing a practical task with Visual Basic (e.g,. how to save a file). Adjacent to the icon is the description of a Practical activity the student is to undertake and is always related to the text just read. The Practical activity directs the reader to **practise at the computer**.

Direction of the book

Visual Basic is a vast product. Its language alone has numerous functions and operators, together with over a hundred methods. It also has over forty categories of controls and insertable objects, etc. All of these cannot possibly be covered in one relatively small textbook.

The book has concentrated on the 'core of the language' and its data processing abilities. It has not, for example, considered the multimedia capabilities of the language. This is not to underestimate Visual Basic use in this and other areas, but more a decision to concentrate on the following topics:

- How to build the graphical user interface (GUI).

- The fundamental building blocks of the language, i.e., sequence, selection and repetition.

- The imposition of structure through the use of procedures, data and control arrays.

- How to manage a Visual Basic project.

- The graphical co-ordinate system, graphical methods, graphical controls and how they assist in using Window resources efficiently, i.e., by loading and positioning controls at run-time when they are required.

- Files and how program data is read from and written to them.

- How Visual Basic can be used as a database development tool.

- How Visual Basic can interact with its operating environment.

What is in the book?

Visual Basic is used to develop a vast range of software products. It is used to build graphical user interfaces (front ends) and for database products, spreadsheets products, integrated office products, etc., but it is much more than a language that just builds front ends. It is a comprehensive and powerful programming language that can be used to develop multimedia products, computer-aided learning products, computer games, an interface to music keyboards, etc. However, possibly the most useful and powerful feature of Visual Basic is its ability to develop fully functioning databases. The book can be regarded as being in eight sections: Chapters 1 to 6, Chapters 7 to 11, Chapters 12 to 14, Chapter 15, Chapter 16, Chapters 17 to 20, Chapter 21 and Chapters 22 to 24. Each section and chapter is briefly described on the following pages.

Chapters 1 to 6

These chapters concentrate on the Visual aspect of Visual Basic with some reference to coding.

Chapter 1 is an introduction to Visual Basic that emphasises the event driven nature of the language. It also introduces a simple definition of an object.

Chapter 2 introduces the Visual Basic environment and shows how to load and run a project.

Chapter 3 shows how to build a graphical user interface and in doing so it introduces the form plus commonly used controls and some of their properties.

Chapter 4 shows how an application is coded. It introduces variables and event and general procedures.

Chapter 5 acts as a summary to the techniques learnt in the first four chapters. It shows how to develop a simple application that requires the building of a GUI and its coding using event and general procedures. It also shows how an applications code can be printed. There are four practical activities that allow for **practice at the computer**.

Chapter 6 introduces some frequently used controls and how they are used. In particular it covers the important **properties**, **events** and **methods** associated with a command button and text box.

Chapters 7 to 11

These chapters concentrate on the fundamental 'building blocks' of all programming languages, that is, program data, making decisions, sequence, selection and repetition.

Chapter 7 deals with program data, what it is, how it is supplied to the program, how it is processed, and where it is stored when processed. It covers Visual Basic variables, their data types, scope, lifetime and their implicit and explicit declaration. It also introduces the use of constants and the assignment statement.

Chapter 8 introduces the three fundamental program logic structures sequence, selection, iteration and how they can be represented by flowcharts, N-S Charts and Structured English. It then shows how to implement two sequential programs and in the process it introduces the important ideas of data tables and test plans.

Chapter 9 shows how a computer program can make a decision.

Chapter 10 is devoted to the selection construct and shows four Visual Basic structures that implement selection.

Chapter 11 is devoted to the repetition construct and shows six Visual Basic structures that implement repetition.

Chapters 12 to 14

These chapters look at the benefits that can be obtained from the **'imposition of structure'** on program data, Visual Basic controls and program code.

Chapter 12 looks at data arrays and how they can be used to structure program data. Structured data is easier to access and process.

Chapter 13 introduces control arrays and shows how they can improve program design.

Chapter 14 shows the benefits that derive from structuring program code into 'small manageable chunks' called procedures.

Chapter 15

Chapter 15 shows how the development of a Visual Basic project is managed.

Chapter 16

Chapter 16 introduces the graphical co-ordinate system, graphical methods and graphical controls.

Windows is memory intensive and many applications save memory by loading controls only when they are required. Once a control is loaded it needs to be positioned; this chapter shows how a control can be positioned on a form at run-time. (Chapter 13 showed how to load a control at run-time.)

This chapter also shows the important technique of passing an object as an argument (parameter) to a procedure.

Chapters 17 to 20

These chapters deal with how program data is read from and written to files. All of the chapters to date have dealt with program data being supplied from the keyboard and output to the VDU; this is adequate for the purposes of learning a language. However, commercial software use files for inputting and outputting data.

Chapter 17 deals with records. Data read from and written to files are usually in a structured format. A record is an example of a structured data type that can be defined by the programmer.

Chapter 18 introduces the concept of the file system and all types of files. It concentrates in particular on how data is input and output to and from **text** files.

Chapter 19 deals with how records (structured data) is input and output to and from **binary** files.

Chapter 20 deals with all types of list boxes. List boxes enable a professional-looking graphical user interface to front the accessing of files.

Chapter 21

As well as being a comprehensive and powerful programming language, in its own right, Visual Basic is a very powerful database development tool. All of the chapters to date have dealt with techniques that in the main can be applied to many other programming languages. This chapter is different. It deals with techniques that are unique to Visual Basic and shows how Visual Basic can be used as a database development tool.

Chapter 21 shows how Visual Basic can, through its data control, manipulate Microsoft Access databases. It deals with both the navigational and relational database model.

Chapters 22 to 24

These chapters show how Visual Basic can interact with its operating environment.

Chapter 22 shows how mouse events enable an application to respond to the location and state of the mouse.

Chapter 23 shows how an application can respond to keyboard input events.

Chapter 24 shows how an application can respond to the passage of time.

Appendix

This deals with the fundamental knowledge required by a computer programmer. If you are new to programming then you should read this appendix before starting Chapter 1.

What you should study next

This book has concentrated on the fundamental core of the Visual Basic language and product. The approach of the book is to encourage the reader to practise at the computer. An important aspect of this practice is the use of the comprehensive on-line help facility. Once you have finished all of the practical activities in this book I recommend that you learn the rest of the language from the on-line help and the Visual Basic knowledge base supplied by Microsoft (there are over 600 categorised articles in the Visual Basic Windows collection).

A copy of the Visual Basic knowledge base can be obtained from the following sources.

- CompuServe
- Microsoft Download Service (MSDL)
- Internet (anonymous FTP)

There are two files VBKB.EXE and VBKB_FT.EXE both are self extracting. The latter file (VBKB_FT.EXE) is the better because it includes a full text search engine that allows you to query the knowledge base.

To obtain the VBKB_FT.EXE file from CompuServe perform the following:

 GO MSL

 Search for and download VBKB_FT.EXE

To obtain the VBKB_FT.EXE file from the Internet perform the following:

ftp ftp.microsoft.com

Change to the \softlib\mslfiles directory

Get VBKB_FT.EXE

I recommend that you should study the following aspects of the language first: How to use menus, dialog boxes, the grid control, MDI forms, debugging and handling run-time errors.

Who should use this book?

The book is a course in Visual Basic that covers introductory to advanced topics. It is suitable for individuals who wish to learn a programming language for the first time. However, it does assume that you have a working knowledge of the Windows environment.

A word to the beginner: if you have never programmed before please use the book in the way it is intended. Read a section and practise at the computer (by completing the practical activities). Do not move on until you have successfully completed all the practical activities associated with each section of text. **If you are completely new to programming then please read Appendix A** *before* **you start Chapter 1**.

1 Introduction to Visual Basic

Visual Basic is the easiest and quickest way to develop fully functioning applications for Windows 3.1, Windows 95 and Windows NT operating systems. It allows developers to make full use of the graphical user interface (GUI).

Visual Basic provides numerous tools for developing the different aspects of applications that use the GUI interface. A Visual Basic programmer develops an application in three main stages. These are:

1. Produce the graphical user interface by drawing objects onto forms.
2. Refine the appearance and behaviour of these objects by setting their properties.
3. Identify the actions of the user in using the graphical interface and attach code to the events that can subsequently occur.

Comparison of event-driven and procedural programming

Visual Basic is referred to as an event-driven programming language. Traditional programming (e.g. Pascal) is referred to as procedural programming. **Procedural** code consists of sequence, selection and repetition. All program actions are dictated by the execution of program statements. To enable a comparison to be made and to understand the operation of an event-driven application consider the examples described below.

Procedural example

Consider the installation of a software package in a procedural MSDOS environment. The user would typically type an instruction at the DOS prompt as illustrated next:

    C:\ > a:\install.exe

The install program runs with the co-operation of the MSDOS operating system. It will read files off the floppy disk (in drive a) and write them to the computer's hard disk (drive c). It is highly likely that the program will require the user (the individual who launches and uses an application) to enter the path name of the directory where the software package is to be installed. The user would then enter the path name. This is illustrated below:

Please enter the destination path name for the software package.

    C:\PACKAGE

Upon entering the path name each instruction in the installation program will execute in turn until the application is installed. This describes a typical execution of a procedural program. However, what happens if the user has a change of mind and decides not to proceed with the installation because there is not enough disk space on the system? The answer is that the user would have little choice but to reset the computer to halt the installation program. The procedural program is in complete control over the computer and the user is unable to interrupt its process – apart from the crude method of resetting the computer.

Event-driven example

An **event** is an action to which an application responds. For example, a keypress or mouse move. Event-driven programs, like procedural programs, consist of sequence, selection and repetition. However, program statements are executed only upon the occurrence of an event. An event-driven installation program allows the user to interrupt the installation process. The installation program is no longer in total control of what happens because it allows the user to interrupt, i.e., the program will respond to outside *events*. Consider the following event-driven installation program. A user is asked to enter a path name and is given choices. The user can enter the path name and select OK or cancel the choice by selecting Cancel. This is illustrated in Figure 1.1

Figure 1.1 An event-driven example

The fundamental difference between this and procedural coding is that the user is given the chance to interrupt the operation of the program. At its simplest level this describes an event-driven program.

When writing an event-driven program the programmer doesn't know in advance which option a user will choose (a **programmer** is the individual who writes the code to perform the functions of the application). The programmer's responsibility is to attach appropriate code to all of the *possible* events. For the example shown in Figure 1.1 the user will do one of the following:

- Enter the path name and select OK.
- Enter the path name and select Cancel.
- Select OK (without entering a path name).
- Select Cancel.

With event-driven coding, code must be attached to control each of the following:

- The entering of text (i.e., the path name).
- The selecting of OK
- The selecting of Cancel.

The code attached to the selecting of OK must be able to accept the path name or report back to the user that they forgot to enter the path name.

When the installation program is running what code actually executes will depend upon what the user does. Figure 1.2 illustrates code attached to all the possible events.

Figure 1.2 Code attached to events.

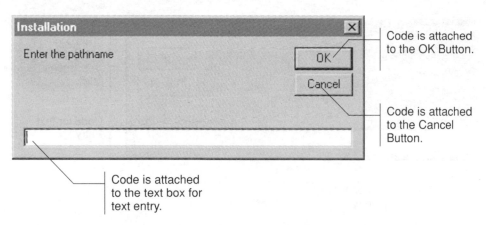

If the user selects Cancel then the code attached to the Cancel button will execute. This is illustrated in Figure 1.3 by the shading.

Figure 1.3 This illustrates the application responding to a click event.
The user positions the cursor over the Cancel command button using the mouse.
The user then clicks the left-most button on the mouse, i.e., a click event.

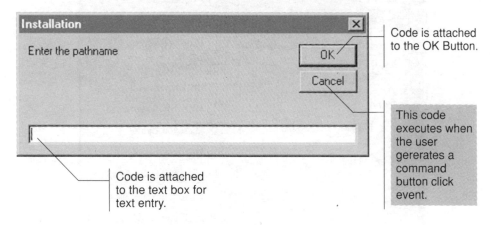

If the user selects OK then the code attached to the OK button will execute. This is illustrated in Figure 1.4 by the shading.

QUESTION 1.1 (DEVELOPMENT)

The 'screen shot' in Figure 1.5 illustrates a typical scene from Windows 95. List the type of events attached to the scene shown and state what you think each event will activate.

Figure 1.4 Another example of an application responding to an event.

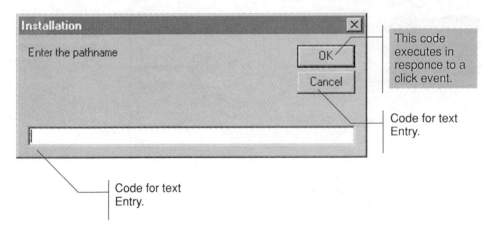

Figure 1.5

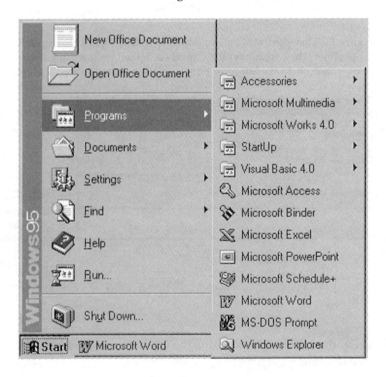

Objects

All modern programming languages are moving towards object-orientated programming and Visual Basic is no exception. When programmers develop an application using Visual Basic they are working with objects. These objects are forms, controls (Command Buttons, Picture Boxes, etc.) and data-access objects. From Visual Basic it is also possible to control the objects of other applications. Programmers can also create their own objects and define additional properties and methods for them.

Definition of an object

An object is a self-contained combination of code and data that can be treated as a unit. Within Visual Basic an object can be a form, a control or an entire application. Figure 1.6 'graphically describes' an object.

Figure 1.6 A 'graphical description' of an object.

Program code

Program data

An object containing code and data.

A form as an object

A design-time form is referred to as a Window at run-time. A form will have associated code and data, it also has associated properties, events to which it will respond and methods. The properties of a form are responsible for changing its appearance (e.g. its background colour) and other features of the form (e.g., whether the form is visible on the VDU). Associated with a form are methods that can act upon it. Hide is an example of a method. The Hide method removes the form from view by setting its visible property to false. The Click and Double Click (DblClick) event are examples of events to which a Window (Form) will respond.

It is necessary therefore to redefine the graphical description of a Visual Basic object – refer to Figure 1.7.

NOTE: The Methods, Properties and Events 'come with' a Visual Basic object. The programmer is responsible for adding the code and data. **Therefore a Visual Basic object is defined by its Properties, Methods and Events.**

Figure 1.7 A 'graphical description' of a Visual Basic object.

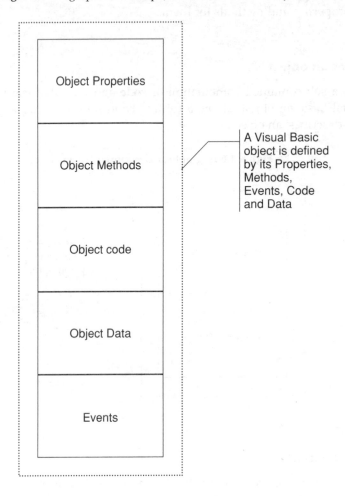

2 The Visual Basic environment

To open Visual Basic the user issues appropriate mouse moves and clicks as illustrated by Figure 2.1 (which shows a typical Windows 95 environment).

Figure 2.1 Click onto Visual Basic 4.0. What you see on your VDU screen will be dependent upon the applications installed on your system. Consequently, it may not be exactly as shown here.

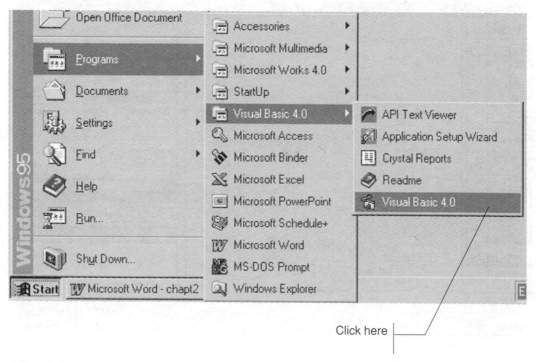

Click here

After clicking Visual Basic 4.0 you should see something similar to the illustration shown by Figure 2.2.

Interface elements of the VB design environment

Figure 2.2 illustrates the VB environment, which shows six of the main eight interface elements. These six elements are:

1. Menu bar
2. Toolbar
3. Toolbox
4. Form
5. Project Window
6. Properties Window

Figure 2.2 This illustrates the main interface elements of the Visual Basic environment
after user arrangement. It is usual for all the interface elements to be overlapping each other.
Each interface element can be closed until required by the programmer – by clicking the x in the top
right corner of each element.

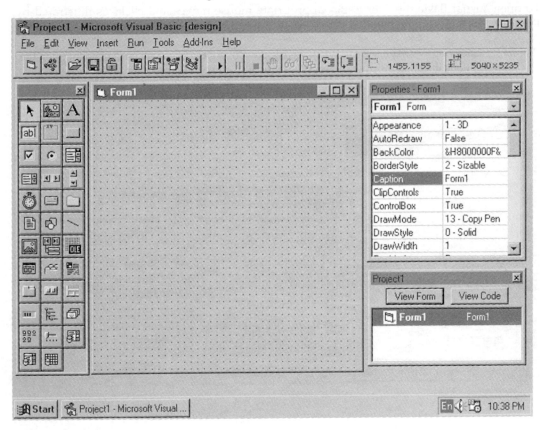

The seventh element is the object browser (shown in Figure 2.12). The content menus comprise the eighth interface element (examples are shown in Figures 2.13 and 2.14).

Each component will be considered in turn.

1. Menu bar

The menu bar is illustrated in Figure 2.3.

The menu bar displays the commands used to build an application. There are eight main menu headings:

- File
- Edit
- View
- Insert
- Run
- Tools
- Add-Ins
- Help

Figure 2.3 The menu bar.

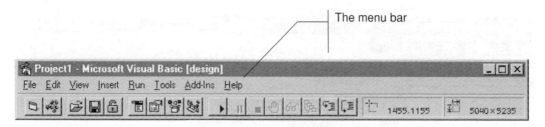

The menu bar

PRACTICAL ACTIVITY 2.1

It is not advisable to discuss the details of the menu bar at this stage. They will be covered, where appropriate, throughout the text. However, before you continue with this book you are strongly advised to take note of the help menu and in particular the tutorial. I suggest you run the tutorial before continuing. Figure 2.4 illustrates how you start the tutorial and Figure 2.5 illustrates how to activate a section of the tutorial. After performing the task 'described' by Figure 2.4 Visual Basic will respond by displaying the Window illustrated in Figure 2.5.

2. Toolbar

The toolbar is labelled in Figure 2.6.

Figure 2.7 illustrates the main groups of the toolbar.

The function of most of the buttons will be explained in more detail throughout this book as appropriate.

PRACTICAL ACTIVITY 2.2

Allow the cursor to 'rest' on each of the buttons in turn and wait a short while. A label (tool tip) will appear to indicate the function of the button. An example of this is illustrated in Figure 2.8.

3. Toolbox

Figure 2.9 illustrates the Visual Basic toolbox (there are other controls that can be added, this will be dealt with in a later chapter). The toolbox provides a set of tools that the programmer can use when designing the graphical user interface for an application. These tools can be used to draw controls on a form, such as buttons, labels, text boxes, etc.

Figure 2.4 How to run the tutorial.

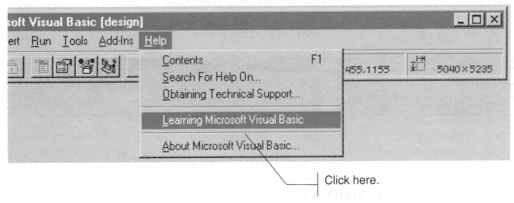

Click here.

Figure 2.5 The help tutorial.

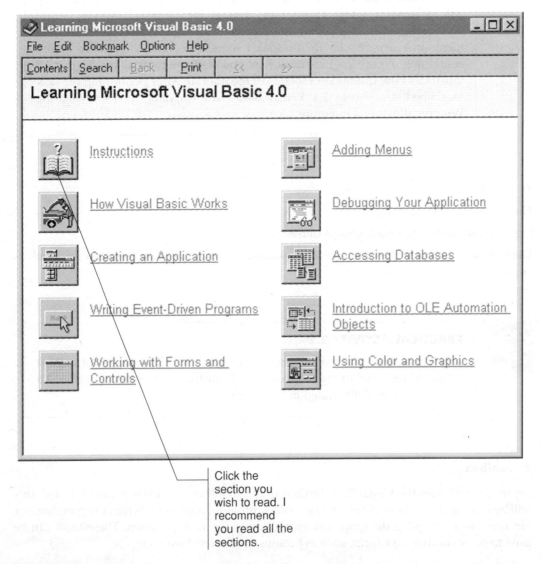

Click the
section you
wish to read. I
recommend
you read all the
sections.

Figure 2.6 The toolbar allows for quick access to the more commonly used commands in the Visual Basic design environment. Click on a button to carry out the action it represents.

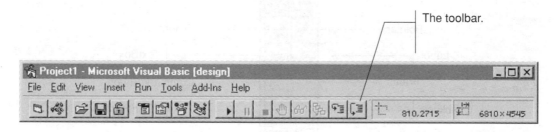

The toolbar.

Figure 2.7 The main groupings of the toolbar.

Open or save a project.

Display the Menu Editor, Properties window, Object Browser, or Project windows.

Set breakpoints, display the Instant Watch dialog, open the Calls dialog, or step through code.

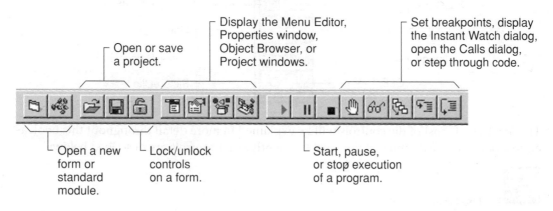

Open a new form or standard module.

Lock/unlock controls on a form.

Start, pause, or stop execution of a program.

Figure 2.8 The automatic appearance of a label.

cursor

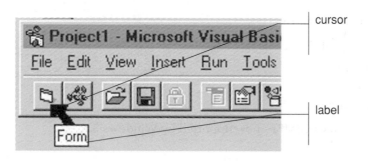

label

11

Figure 2.9 The toolbox; all controls are suitably labelled with their Visual Basic control name.

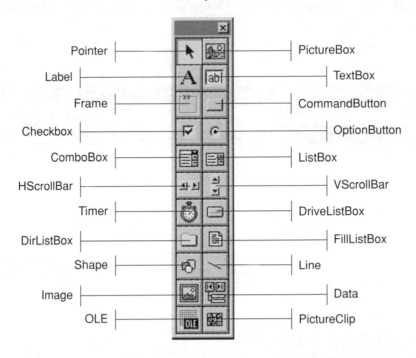

Pointer	PictureBox
Label	TextBox
Frame	CommandButton
Checkbox	OptionButton
ComboBox	ListBox
HScrollBar	VScrollBar
Timer	DriveListBox
DirListBox	FillListBox
Shape	Line
Image	Data
OLE	PictureClip

The function of most of the controls will be explained in more detail throughout this book as appropriate. However, three of the most frequently used controls are described below:

    The label control.

A label is a *graphical* control you can use to display text that the user **cannot** change directly. However, code can be written that changes a label in response to events at run-time. For example, if an application takes a while to process data you could display a processing-status message.

    The picture control.

A picture box can display a graphic from one of the following formats.

- Bitmap (*.BMP)
- Icon (*.ICO)
- Metafile (*.WMF)
- Enhanced Metafile (*.EMF) – not supported by Windows 3.1.

    The Command button

A Command button is chosen (clicked) by the user to begin, interrupt or end a process. When chosen a Command button appears to be pushed in, consequently, it is often called a push button.

How to use the Visual Basic online help

In the application developed during Practical activity 4.1 the programmer (you) entered two lines of code, Unload Me and End. These are examples of Visual Basic statements. Both of these statements perform a specific task and the Visual Basic online help can be used to discover the action performed by these and any other Visual Basic statement. To obtain help on any VB statement involves positioning the cursor over the statement and pressing the F1 key. Visual Basic responds to the F1 key press by displaying the appropriate help screen. This sequence of actions is illustrated in Figure 4.9.

Alternatively, select *Search for Help on ..* from the <u>Help</u> menu.

Figure 4.9 Using the Visual Basic online help.

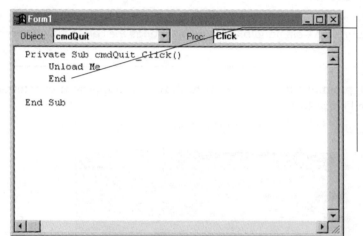

Position the cursor over the statement on which help is required and then press the F1 key. VB will respond by displaying the relevant help screen as shown below.

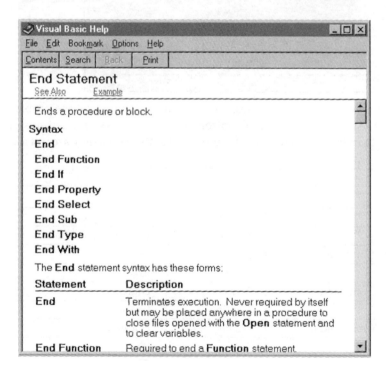

QUESTION 4.3 (DEVELOPMENT)

Discover the action performed by the End statement by using the online help facility.

A simple program (Specification 4.1)

A program is developed on the following pages that meets the requirements of the following specification.

SPECIFICATION 4.1

Write a program that uses three command buttons to change the background colour of a form. The Command buttons are to change the colour to Red, Green or Blue.

As with all Visual Basic programs the first step is to draw the graphical user interface. A suitable GUI is shown in Figure 4.10.

Figure 4.10 A suitable GUI **before** the appropriate properties have been set.

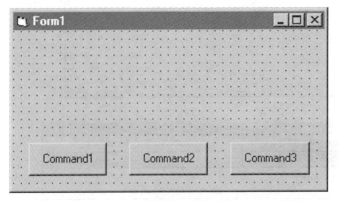

Once the GUI has been drawn, as shown in Figure 4.10, the next step is to set the properties of the form and the controls. Table 4.1 lists the controls, their properties and settings. **Those properties *not* referred to in the table are left at their default setting (i.e., they are not altered).**

Table 4.1 Controls and their property settings.

Control	Property	Setting
Form (Form1)	Name	frmColourDemo
	Caption	Colour Demonstration
Command Button (Command1)	Name	cmdRed
	Caption	Red
Command Button (Command2)	Name	cmdGreen
	Caption	Green
Command Button (Command3)	Name	cmdBlue
	Caption	Blue

Once the properties have been set, as indicated by Table 4.1, the GUI of Figure 4.10 will look like the GUI illustrated in Figure 4.11.

Figure 4.11 The GUI **after** its properties have been set.

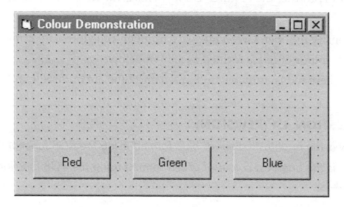

Having completed the GUI the next step is to attach an event procedure to each command button. The event procedures for this simple program are graphically represented by Figure 4.12.

Figure 4.12 The three event procedures. All invoked by their associated command button being clicked.

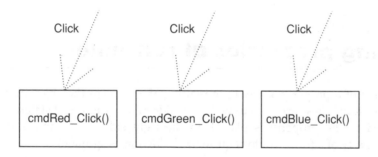

When the user clicks the Red Command button (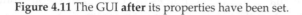) the form's background colour must change to red and clicking the green must change it to green and obviously clicking the blue must change it to blue. Therefore, code must be inserted into each of the event procedures to perform the desired function – change the colour of the forms background at **run-time**. *Before the code used to achieve this is considered it is necessary to understand how colours are formed.*

Forming colours in Visual Basic applications

All colours on a VDU are formed from three basic colours, red, green and blue. Each of these basic colours can 'shine' with a range of intensity. This range is represented by a number between 0 and 255. If the red component is assigned the intensity number 255 then it is 'fully

47

on' and if it is assigned the number 0 then it is 'fully off' (i.e., not 'shining' at all). This number range applies in the same way to green and blue.

A function exists in Visual Basic that combines the three basic colour components with their intensity number to produce the required colour. This is the RGB function. The format for this function is as follows:

RGB(Red intensity number, Green intensity number, Blue intensity number)

The 'brightest' colour of red is formed as shown below:

RGB(255, 0, 0) here red is 'fully on' and green and blue are both 'fully off'.

QUESTION 4.4 (REVISION)

How is the brightest colour of blue formed using the RGB function?

How is the brightest colour of green formed using the RGB function?

NOTE: If all the colour intensity numbers in an RGB function are set to 255 then white is formed and if all these numbers are zero then black is formed.

Changing properties at run-time

To set the value of a property at run-time requires the name of the object and its property linked by a full stop. These are placed on the left side of an assignment statement. The value to be assigned to the property is placed on the right side. For example to change the BackColor property of a form would require the following assignment:

frmColourDemo.BackColor = RGB(255, 0, 0)

To the left of the full stop is the name of the object (in this case a form). To the right of the full stop is the property of the object (in this case the BackColor) that is to be altered by the value on the right of the assignment sign (i.e., the equals sign). On the right-hand side of the equals sign is the formation of the colour red using the RGB function. This is illustrated in Figure 4.13.

An assignment statement **copies** the value on the right-hand side of an equals sign to the variable or property on the left-hand side. Assignment statements are fully covered in a later chapter.

The code that is inserted in the cmdRed_Click() event procedure is therefore:

frmColourDemo.BackColor = RGB(255, 0, 0)

The code that is inserted in the cmdGreen_Click event procedure is:

frmColourDemo.BackColor = RGB(0, 255, 0)

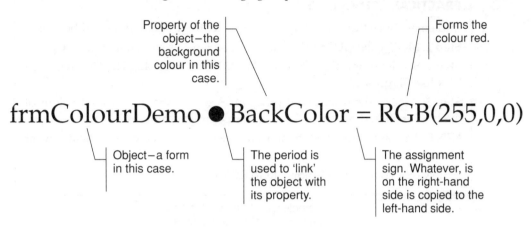

Figure 4.13 Changing Properties at run-time.

Property of the object–the background colour in this case.

Forms the colour red.

frmColourDemo ● BackColor = RGB(255,0,0)

Object–a form in this case.

The period is used to 'link' the object with its property.

The assignment sign. Whatever, is on the right-hand side is copied to the left-hand side.

QUESTION 4.5 (REVISION)

What assignment statement is inserted in the cmdBlue_Click() event procedure?

PRACTICAL ACTIVITY 4.2

Develop the simple program represented by Figure 4.11. Set the properties as defined by Table 4.1 and code the three event procedures with the assignment statements discussed, that is:

frmColourDemo.BackColor = RGB(255, 0, 0)

frmColourDemo.BackColor = RGB(0, 255, 0)

and the assignment statement that is the answer to Question 4.5 (revision).

Another simple program (Specification 4.2)

Specification 4.2 involves a modification to the program developed during Practical activity 4.2.

SPECIFICATION 4.2

*Write a program that uses three command buttons to change the back ground colour of a **label** (not the form). The Command buttons are to change the colour to Red, Green or Blue.*

PRACTICAL ACTIVITY 4.3

Implement Specification 4.2 by following the three steps suggested below:

Step 1: Modify the GUI by the addition of a label as shown in Figure 4.14.

Step 2: Set the properties of the label as listed in Table 4.2. The GUI will then look like Figure 4.15.

Step 3: Amend the three event procedures so that the background colour of the label is altered by the clicking of the Command buttons.

HINT The assignment statement inserted in the cmdRed_Click() event procedure is:

lblColourDemo.BackColor = RGB (255, 0, 0)

The object is changed; it is now the name of the label not the form.

Figure 4.14 Amending the GUI that implemented Specification 4.1 by the addition of label.

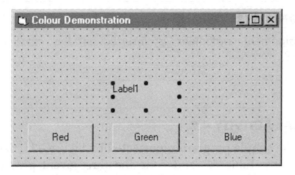

Table 4.2 Set the values of the label properties as listed.

Control	Property	Setting
Label(Label1)	Name	lblColourDemo
	Caption	<empty>
	BorderStyle	Fixed Single

Figure 4.15 The GUI **after** the properties of the label have been set according to Table 4.2.

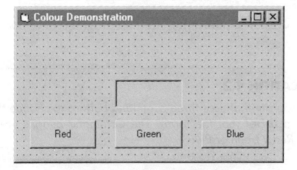

Horizontal scroll bars

A scroll bar can be used as an input device to, for example, control the volume of multimedia speakers. Figure 4.16 illustrates a typical use for a scroll bar.

Figure 4.16 A typical use of a horizontal scroll bar.
As the slider is moved to the right the volume of the speakers increases.

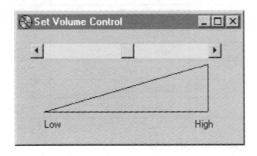

When a scroll bar is used as an input device its Max and Min properties are set to the appropriate range for the control. The slider can be moved in one of three ways:

1. By dragging the slider.
2. By clicking on the arrows at the edge of the bar – called the small change.
3. By clicking on the space between the arrows and the slider – referred to as the large change.

A simple program using a scroll bar

A program will be implemented to meet the following specification.

> **SPECIFICATION 4.3**
>
> *A horizontal scroll bar controls the intensity of the colour red displayed in a label. That is, the background colour of the label is controlled by the position of the slider on the horizontal scroll bar.*

Step 1: Draw the interface as shown in Figure 4.17.

Step 2: Set the properties as listed in Table 4.3

Step 3: Attach the event procedure.

Figure 4.17 The GUI **before** the properties are set.

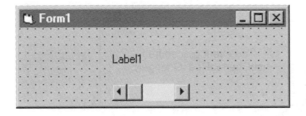

51

Table 4.3 The settings required for the form, label and horizontal scroll bar.

Control	Property	Setting
Form (Form1)	Name	frmHorScrollBarDemo
	Caption	Horizontal Scroll Bar Demonstration
Label (Label1)	Name	lblRed
	Caption	\<empty\>
	BorderStyle	1 – Fixed Single
Horizontal Scroll Bar (Hscroll1)	Name	hsbChangeRed
	Min	0
	Max	255
	LargeChange	32
	MousePointer	9 – Size WE

Properties of the horizontal scroll bar

The position of the slider on the scroll bar is represented by a number that is supplied via the controls *Value* property. This number can reside within a range that is dictated by the Min and Max properties. Consequently, for the example of Figure 4.18 the setting of the Value property can be between 0 and 255 (the Min and Max property settings). The values of the Min and Max properties were chosen to reflect the range of the colour red that can be supplied to the RGB function.

Figure 4.18 After the properties were set and the controls were dragged to the appropriate size.

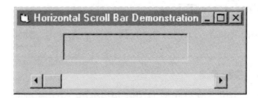

The event procedure for Figure 4.18 is graphically represented by Figure 4.19. The default event for a horizontal scroll bar is the *Change* event and it is activated when the user moves the slider using any one of the three ways previously indicated.

Figure 4.19 The Change event procedure for the horizontal scroll bar.

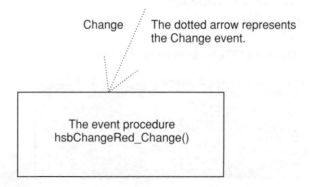

Change / The dotted arrow represents the Change event.

The event procedure
hsbChangeRed_Change()

The code for the Change event procedure is shown in Figure 4.20.

Figure 4.20 The event procedure.

```
Private Sub hsbChangeRed_Change()
Dim Red As Integer
    Red = hsbChangeRed.Value
    lblRed.BackColor = RGB(Red, 0, 0)
End Sub
```

This procedure has a local variable Red declared as an integer. In this code, Red is assigned the number stored in the horizontal scroll bar's Value property. This number is then used in the RGB function to set the intensity of the colour red. As the user drags the slider to the right the Value property of the horizontal scroll bar increases, consequently, the intensity of the colour red increases. When the slider is dragged to the left the number in the Value property reduces and the 'amount' of red displayed in the label reduces.

PRACTICAL ACTIVITY 4.4

Develop the program to meet the requirement of specification 4.3. When the program is running move the slider in all the three ways listed below:

1. By dragging the slider.
2. By clicking on the arrows at the edge of the bar.
3. By clicking on the space between the arrows and the slider.

Carefully observe the effect of the three methods for moving the slider. Experiment with the SmallChange and LargeChange properties, i.e., set them to different values from within the property window and observe the effect when the program is run. Also observe the change in the mouse pointer when it is moved from the form to over the horizontal scroll bar. Again change the setting of the MousePointer property and observe the effect when the program is run.

PRACTICAL ACTIVITY 4.5

Amend the program developed during Practical activity 4.4 so that it includes another label. Arrange for the Value property of the horizontal Scroll bar to be displayed in this label when the user moves the slider.

QUESTION 4.6 (DEVELOPMENT)

Review all of the windows software you have used and reflect on all of the uses of a scroll bar. Make a short list, you will find it a useful resource for ideas for any future projects you may develop.

5 Developing an application

This chapter shows how to develop a simple application that meets the following specification.

SPECIFICATION 5.1

Develop an application that controls the background and foreground colours of a text box, i.e., allows the user to choose the colour of the text and its background.

Steps 1 and 2: draw the interface and set the properties

Figure 5.1 illustrates the graphical user interface designed to implement the specification. The interface has been built from one text box, six horizontal scroll bars and thirteen labels.

Figure 5.1 The Graphical User Interface **after** the properties have been set.

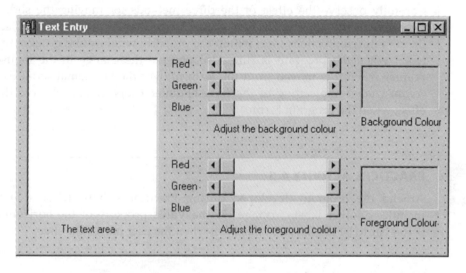

Table 5.1 lists all the controls, their properties and settings.

 NOTE: Table 5.1 lists only the properties that have been changed; all the other properties remain set at their default values.

Table 5.1 Property settings for the application. Again, all positional properties have not been included because all the controls have been dragged into position.

Control	Property	Setting
Form1	Name	frmTextEntry
	Caption	Text Entry
	Icon	c:\vb\icons\writing\pens03
Text1	Name	txtTextArea
	Text	<empty>
	MultiLine	-1 'True
Label1	Name	lblForegroundColour
	Caption	Foreground Colour
	AutoSize	-1 'True
Label2	Name	lblBackgroundColour
	Caption	Background Colour
	AutoSize	-1 'True
Label3	Name	lblTextArea
	Caption	The text area
	AutoSize	-1 'True
Label4	Name	lblBackGround
	Caption	Adjust the background colour
	AutoSize	-1 'True
Label5	Name	lblForeground
	Caption	Adjust the foreground colour
	AutoSize	-1 'True
Label6	Name	lblBlueForeground
	Caption	Blue
	AutoSize	-1 'True
Label7	Name	lblGreenForeground
	Caption	Green
	AutoSize	-1 'True
Label8	Name	lblRedForeground
	Caption	Red
	AutoSize	-1 'True
Label9	Name	lblBlueBackground
	Caption	Blue
	AutoSize	-1 'True
Label10	Name	lblGreenBackground
	Caption	Green
	AutoSize	-1 'True
Label11	Name	lblRedBackground
	Caption	Red
	AutoSize	-1 'True
Label12	Name	lblShowForeColour
	Caption	<empty>
	BorderStyle	1 'Fixed Single

Table 5.1 (cont.)

Control	Property	Setting
Label13	Name	lblShowBackColour
	Caption	<empty>
	BorderStyle	1 'Fixed Single
Hscroll1	Name	hsbRedBackground
	Max	255
	MousePointer	9 'Size W E
	LargeChange	32
Hscroll2	Name	hsbGreenBackGround
	Max	255
	MousePointer	9 'Size W E
	LargeChange	32
Hscroll3	Name	hsbBlueBackground
	Max	255
	MousePointer	9 'Size W E
	LargeChange	32
Hscroll4	Name	hsbRedForeground
	Max	255
	MousePointer	9 'Size W E
	LargeChange	32
Hscroll5	Name	hsbBlueForeground
	Max	255
	MousePointer	9 'Size W E
	LargeChange	32
Hscroll6	Name	hsbGreenForeground
	Max	255
	MousePointer	9 'Size W E
	LargeChange	32

Step 3: write the code

Once the interface is developed the next step is to attach the code to all of the events, i.e., to write the event procedures. Consequently, it is necessary that all of the possible events are identified. Some of the events are obvious but some are more subtle. Indeed, it is often difficult to anticipate all of the events that are required for an application. It is only during development that the more subtle events become apparent. However, with experience most events can be predicted.

The question is, to what events does this application respond? Events come from two main sources, the user and the system. It is usual practice firstly to identify the events generated by the user.

In this application the user will alter the colour of the background and foreground using the six horizontal scroll bars. The user will also enter text in the text box, however, in this simplified application there will be no attempt to process this data – the text box is just used to display the effect of changing the colours.

There will be six event procedures for the six horizontal scroll bars. Each event procedure will be associated with the scroll bar change event.

QUESTION 5.1 (REVISION)

Table 5.1 lists the Name property for each of the horizontal scroll bars. Compose the name for the change event procedure associated with each of the six scroll bars, e.g., the Name property of one of the scroll bars is: hsbRedBackground, consequently, the name of the change event procedure will be:

hsbRedBackground_Change()

You work out the name for the remaining five event procedures!

Figure 5.2 illustrates the 'graphical description', of the calling, of the event procedures, by the change event of all six horizontal scroll bars.

Figure 5.2 Calling all the event procedures.

Change event

Change event

hsbRedBackground_Change()

hsbGreenBackground_Change()

Change event

Change event

hsbBlueBackground_Change()

hsbRedForeground_Change()

Change event

Change event

hsbGreenForeground_Change()

hsbBlueForeground_Change()

The first three event procedures, shown in Figure 5.2, are all responsible for setting the background colour of the text box and the last three are responsible for setting the foreground colour. Consequently, a general procedure can be written to set the background colour and another general procedure can be written to set the foreground colour. Three of the event procedures, therefore, can *call* the general procedure responsible for setting the background colour and the other three can *call* the procedure responsible for setting the foreground colour.

QUESTION 5.2 (REVISION)

1. Suggest a suitable name for a general procedure that will set the **background** colour of a text box.

2. Suggest a suitable name for a general procedure that will set the **foreground** colour of a text box.

The relationship between the event procedures and the general procedures used to code the application, represented by Figure 5.1, are illustrated in Figure 5.3.

Creating a general procedure

A general procedure contains code that performs a common function that can be used by other procedures. Figure 5.3 shows two general procedures SetBackGroundColour() and SetForeGroundColour(), the former is used to set the background colour of the text box and the latter to set the foreground colour.

NOTE: Procedures that execute a common function can be implemented, within Visual Basic, in a number of ways. A later chapter deals with procedures in detail. For the application being developed in this chapter one type of general procedure is used – a form level procedure.

A new procedure can be created in one of two ways. Choose *Procedure* from the *Insert* menu **or** follow the steps illustrated by Figure 5.4.

General procedure for setting the background colour

The code for setting the background colour of the text box is shown in Figure 5.5.

Figure 5.3 The 'graphical representation' of the relationship between the event and general procedures of the application under development.

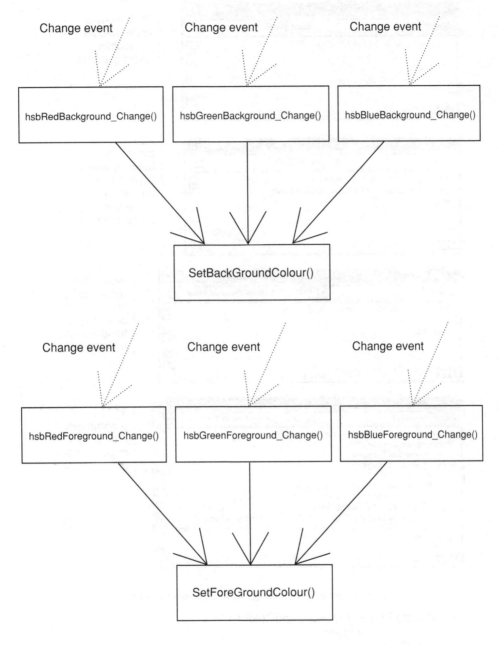

Figure 5.4 Creating a new procedure.

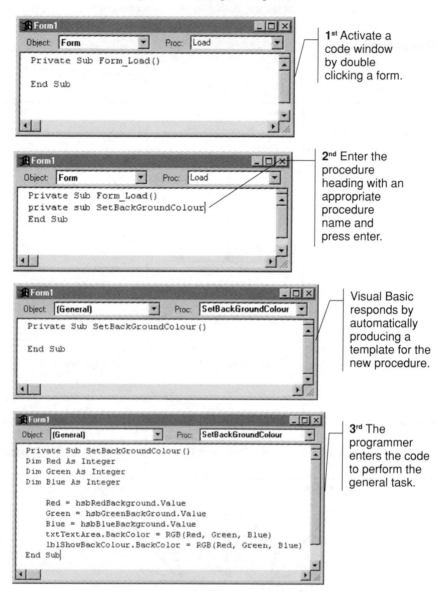

1st Activate a code window by double clicking a form.

2nd Enter the procedure heading with an appropriate procedure name and press enter.

Visual Basic responds by automatically producing a template for the new procedure.

3rd The programmer enters the code to perform the general task.

Figure 5.5 Code for setting the background colour.

```
Private Sub SetBackGroundColour()
Dim Red As Integer
Dim Green As Integer
Dim Blue As Integer

    Red = hsbRedBackground.Value
    Green = hsbGreenBackGround.Value
    Blue = hsbBlueBackground.Value
    txtTextArea.BackColor = RGB(Red, Green, Blue)
    lblShowBackColour.BackColor = RGB(Red, Green, Blue)
End Sub
```

This procedure consists of three local integer variables; Red, Green and Blue. These variables are used within the procedure to store the setting of the *Value* property of the horizontal scroll bars. In the context of the procedure these variables are used as the 'intensity number' for the colour components of the RGB function. (Local variables have a 'life time' for the duration of the procedure. Once the procedure finishes executing, the values in local variables are lost).

IMPORTANT: The operation of the procedure will be described using a 'description trace table'. A description trace is a table with two columns, the first column lists the *order* in which the Visual Basic statements execute and the second column describes the actions performed by each statement. Trace tables will be used throughout the book to describe the operation of Visual Basic code. **NOTE**: The limitations of the table result in a statement crossing onto several lines. VB code **does not** cross over lines in this way.

Description trace table for SetBackGroundColor()

Statement	*Description*
Red = hsbRedBackground.Value	The local variable Red is assigned the setting of the *Value* property of the horizontal scroll bar hsbRedBackground. The value assigned to the variable Red will depend upon the position of the slider on the scroll bar, which is controlled by the user of the application. The variable Red is used in the RGB function to 'fix' the intensity of the red colour component.
Green = hsbGreenBackGround.Value	This assignment statement is used to set the local variable Green to the 'intensity number' for the colour green, in the same way the Red component was set. However, in this case a different horizontal scroll bar is responsible for setting the green component.
Blue = hsbBlueBackground.Value	The hsbBlueBackground horizontal scroll bar sets the Blue variable to the 'intensity number' for the blue component of the colour produced by the RGB function.
txtTextArea.BackColor = RGB(Red, Green, Blue)	The RGB function uses the values stored in the local variables Red, Green and Blue to produce the desired colour. The colour formed is assigned to the BackColor property of the text box txtTextArea, thus setting the background colour of the text box.
lblShowBackColour.BackColor = RGB(Red, Green, Blue)	The RGB function is used again but this time the colour it forms is assigned to the BackColor property of the label lblShowBackColour.

General procedure for setting the foreground colour

Figure 5.6 lists the code for setting the foreground colour of the text box (i.e., the colour of the text entered in the text box).

Figure 5.6 The procedure for setting the foreground colour of the text box.

```
Private Sub SetForeGroundColour()
Dim Red As Integer
Dim Green As Integer
Dim Blue As Integer

    Red = hsbRedForeground.Value
    Green = hsbGreenForeground.Value
    Blue = hsbBlueForeground.Value
    txtTextArea.ForeColor = RGB(Red, Green, Blue)
    lblShowForeColour.BackColor = RGB(Red, Green, Blue)
End Sub
```

This procedure also uses three integer variables and these too are named Red, Green and Blue. However, these variables are local to this procedure and the run-time of the application does not get them 'muddled up' (the local variables of this and the previous procedure are located in different areas of the memory data area, again these three variables only last the 'life time' of the procedure).

QUESTION 5.3 (REVISION)

Produce a description trace table for the SetForeGroundColour() procedure.

Calling a general procedure

Three of the event procedures identified by Figure 5.3 call the SetBackGroundColour() procedure and the other three call the SetForeGroundColour() procedure. A general procedure is called from an event procedure by using the reserved word *Call* and the **name** of the procedure to be called. For example, a call to the SetBackGroundColour() procedure is illustrated in Figure 5.7. Note that the brackets are **not** included in the name of the procedure when it is invoked! If a procedure is declared with parameters (arguments) then the brackets together with its argument list must be included. However, the keyword *Call* need not be used and when it is not used the syntax obeys different rules. It is good programming practice to include the keyword *Call* because it makes the code more readable. A full description of the nuances of the VB procedure *Call* syntax is covered in a later chapter.

Figure 5.7 Calling a procedure.

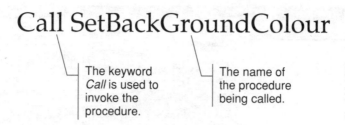

The code for the change event procedure attached to the hsbRedBackground horizontal scroll bar is shown in Figure 5.8. It can be seen that the event procedure consists of one VB statement that simply invokes the general procedure. The other two procedures responsible for setting the background contain the same statement.

Figure 5.8 The event procedure attached to a horizontal scroll bar.

```
Private Sub hsbRedBackground_Change()
    Call SetBackGroundColour
End Sub
```

QUESTION 5.4 (REVISION)

What statement would appear in the change event procedures for the horizontal scroll bars that are responsible for setting the foreground colour of the text box?

PRACTICAL ACTIVITY 5.1

Code the interface of Figure 5.1. This will involve writing two general procedures and six event procedures.

The run-time of the application developed in Practical activity 5.1 should initially look like Figure 5.9.

At run-time the background and foreground labels do not reflect the background and foreground of the text box (which are white and black). They will not reflect the colours until their associated scroll bars have been altered by the user, thus invoking the change event procedure. This is not a desirable feature of the application, the labels should reflect the colours immediately the application is launched.

Earlier in this chapter it was mentioned that it is difficult to anticipate all of the events that are required for an application and that it is only during development that the more subtle events become apparent. The problem associated with the incorrect colour of the labels is an example of the need for an event procedure that was not anticipated.

Associated with every form is a load event and it does not require any user interaction (other than launching the application) it occurs when a form is loaded by the operating system. This

Figure 5.9 Run-time of Practical activity 5.1.

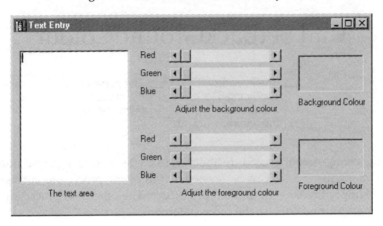

event, like all other events, may or may not have attached code. For the application developed during Practical activity 5.1 no code was attached to this event.

Attaching appropriate code to the load event (i.e. writing a Form_Load event procedure) will solve the problem of the incorrectly coloured labels. The code to solve this problem is shown in Figure 5.10.

PRACTICAL ACTIVITY 5.2

Attach the code of Figure 5.10 to the application developed during Practical activity 5.1. When the application is run its initial state should look like Figure 5.11. The labels now reflect the background and foreground colours of the text box at the application launch.

Description trace for the Form_Load () procedure

Statement	Description
hsbRedBackground.Value = 255	Sets the slider on the 'Red' horizontal scroll bar to the 'maximum position' i.e., the slider is positioned to the right.
hsbGreenBackGround.Value = 255	Sets the slider on the 'Green' horizontal scroll bar to the 'maximum position' i.e., the slider is positioned to the right.
hsbBlueBackground.Value = 255	Sets the slider on the 'Blue' horizontal scroll bar to the 'maximum position' i.e., the slider is positioned to the right.
hsbRedForeground.Value = 0	Sets the Value property of the 'Red' scroll bar to the colour 'intensity number' to be used in the RGB function.
hsbGreenForeground.Value = 0	Sets the Value property of the 'Green' scroll bar to the colour 'intensity number' to be used in the RGB function.
hsbBlueForeground.Value = 0	Sets the Value property of the 'Blue' scroll bar to the colour 'intensity number' to be used in the RGB function.
lblShowForeColour.BackColor = RGB(0, 0, 0)	The foreground colour of the text box is assigned the colour generated by the RGB function (Black in this case).

Figure 5.10 The Form_Load event procedure.

```
Private Sub Form_Load()
    hsbRedBackground.Value = 255
    hsbGreenBackGround.Value = 255
    hsbBlueBackground.Value = 255
    hsbRedForeground.Value = 0
    hsbGreenForeground.Value = 0
    hsbBlueForeground.Value = 0
    lblShowForeColour.BackColor = RGB(0, 0, 0)
End Sub
```

NOTE: The Form_Load event procedure does **not** include an assignment statement to set the background colour of the label whereas the foreground colour is set by an assignment statement. This is because the setting of the *Value* property of the scroll bars to 255 generates a horizontal scroll bar change event. Consequently, the code attached to this event executes and the event procedure includes a call to a general procedure that contains an assignment that sets the background colour.

The Value property of the horizontal scroll bars responsible for controlling the foreground colour is also assigned a number, however, this is zero, which is the default setting for this type of control. Therefore there has been no change and a change event has **not** occurred.

Event-driven programming can result in unexpected effects. These events may be unexpected but they can always be explained if you look long enough. The problem of unexpected effects occurs because the programmer does not consider all of the events that occur during the execution of an application. With experience you will obviously gain more knowledge that will allow you to correctly identify all of the possible events that an application generates. In the meantime, do not panic and always fully test any application you develop.

Figure 5.11 The look of the application at launch (the text is entered by the user).

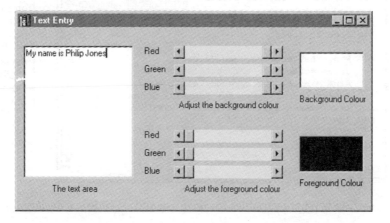

Navigating through an applications code

During the development of code the programmer will, obviously, require to read the procedures written to implement the application. The following sequence of screen shots (Figure 5.12) illustrates methods for navigating through an applications code during its development.

Figure 5.12 Navigating through program code.

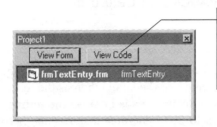

Highlight the form in the project box (there is only one in this case) and click the view code button. VB will respond by displaying the code window shown below.

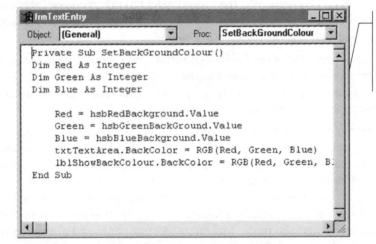

This code Window can **also** be activated by double clicking the form.

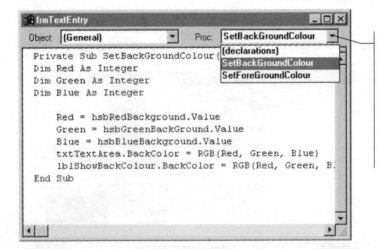

Clicking onto this arrow activates a drop-down list of all the general procedures and the form's declaration section. To view the code select from the list.

A declaration section is where variables for the form and its code are declared.

Figure 5.12 (cont.)

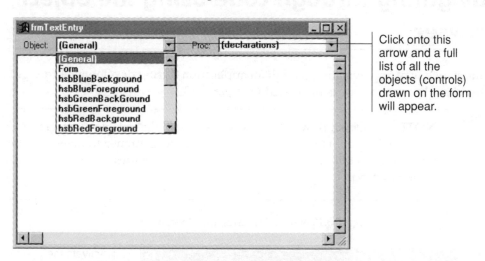

Click onto this arrow and a full list of all the objects (controls) drawn on the form will appear.

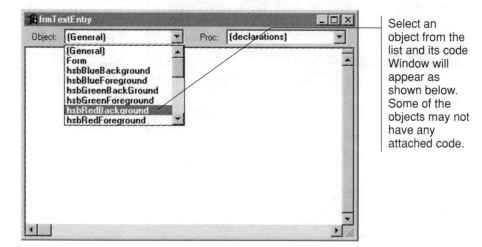

Select an object from the list and its code Window will appear as shown below. Some of the objects may not have any attached code.

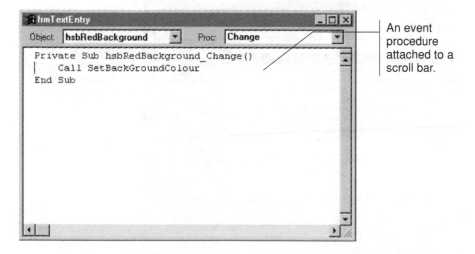

An event procedure attached to a scroll bar.

Navigating through code using the object browser

An alternative way for navigating though an application during development (design) is to use the object browser; its use is illustrated in Figure 5.13.

 NOTE: The Object Browser is a very useful tool that enables a programmer to navigate code. However, it also allows a programmer to determine the types of Object libraries available and which properties and methods exist for their Objects.

Figure 5.13 Navigating using the object browser.

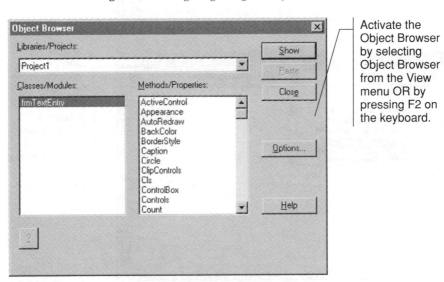

Activate the Object Browser by selecting Object Browser from the View menu OR by pressing F2 on the keyboard.

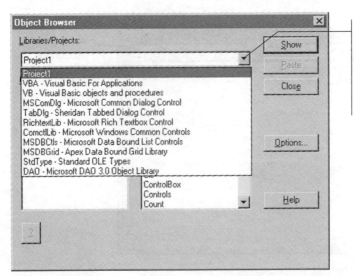

Clicking here displays all the available object libraries including any projects under development.

Figure 5.13 (cont.)

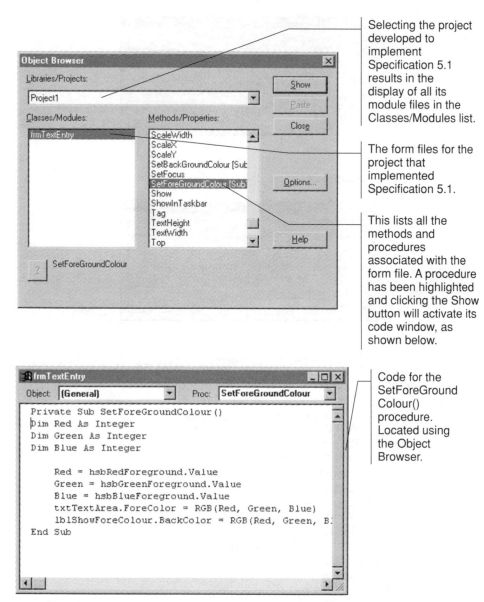

Selecting the project developed to implement Specification 5.1 results in the display of all its module files in the Classes/Modules list.

The form files for the project that implemented Specification 5.1.

This lists all the methods and procedures associated with the form file. A procedure has been highlighted and clicking the Show button will activate its code window, as shown below.

Code for the SetForeGround Colour() procedure. Located using the Object Browser.

Printing an applications code

To print choose *Print* from the *File* menu and the print dialogue box appears (Figure 5.14). There are a number of options that can be set in the dialogue box. It is possible to print just the code for the entire project (i.e., the general and event procedures) or the entire project can be printed as text in which case the code and all the **altered** properties (the default setting for properties is not printed) for all the controls used are printed. It is also possible to print a highlighted section of code or just the information related to the Current module. To print the entire project as text set the options as shown in Figure 5.15 and click OK.

Figure 5.14 The print dialogue box.

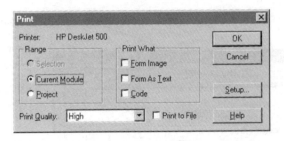

Figure 5.15 Printing the entire project as text.

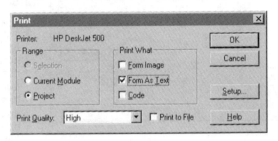

The printout (program listing) for the program implementing Specification 5.1 is shown in Figure 5.16. This print out is achieved by using *Form as text* option.

Figure 5.16 The project listing.

```
VERSION 4.00
Begin VB.Form frmTextEntry
    Caption = "Text Entry"
    ClientHeight = 3615
    ClientLeft = 1725
    ClientTop = 1485
    ClientWidth = 7335
    Height = 4020
    Icon = "frmTextEntry.frx":0000
    Left = 1665
    LinkTopic = "Form1"
    LockControls = -1 'True
    ScaleHeight = 3615
    ScaleWidth = 7335
    Top = 1140
    Width = 7455
    Begin VB.HScrollBar hsbRedBackground
        Height = 255
        LargeChange = 32
        Left = 3240
        Max = 255
        MousePointer = 9 'Size W E
        TabIndex = 6
        Top = 360
```

```
        Width = 2295
End
Begin VB.HScrollBar hsbGreenBackGround
    Height = 255
    LargeChange = 32
    Left = 3240
    Max = 255
    MousePointer = 9 'Size W E
    TabIndex = 5
    Top = 720
    Width = 2295
End
Begin VB.HScrollBar hsbBlueBackground
    Height = 255
    LargeChange = 32
    Left = 3240
    Max = 255
    MousePointer = 9 'Size W E
    TabIndex = 4
    Top = 1080
    Width = 2295
End
Begin VB.HScrollBar hsbRedForeground
    Height = 255
    LargeChange = 32
    Left = 3240
    Max = 255
    MousePointer = 9 'Size W E
    TabIndex = 3
    Top = 2040
    Width = 2295
End
Begin VB.HScrollBar hsbBlueForeground
    Height = 255
    LargeChange = 32
    Left = 3240
    Max = 255
    MousePointer = 9 'Size W E
    TabIndex = 2
    Top = 2760
    Width = 2295
End
Begin VB.HScrollBar hsbGreenForeground
    Height = 255
    LargeChange = 32
    Left = 3240
    Max = 255
    MousePointer = 9 'Size W E
    TabIndex = 1
    Top = 2400
    Width = 2295
End
Begin VB.TextBox txtTextArea
    Height = 2655
```

```
            Left = 120
            MultiLine = -1 'True
            TabIndex = 0
            Top = 360
            Width = 2295
         End
         Begin VB.Label lblForegroundColour
            AutoSize = -1 'True
            Caption = "Foreground Colour"
            Height = 195
            Left = 5880
            TabIndex = 19
            Top = 3000
            Width = 1305
         End
         Begin VB.Label lblBackgroundColour
            AutoSize = -1 'True
            Caption = "Background Colour"
            Height = 195
            Left = 5880
            TabIndex = 18
            Top = 1320
            Width = 1365
         End
         Begin VB.Label lblTextArea
            AutoSize = -1 'True
            Caption = "The text area"
            Height = 195
            Left = 720
            TabIndex = 17
            Top = 3120
            Width = 945
         End
         Begin VB.Label lblShowForeColour
            AutoSize = -1 'True
            BorderStyle = 1 'Fixed Single
            Height = 735
            Left = 5880
            TabIndex = 16
            Top = 2160
            Width = 1335
         End
         Begin VB.Label lblForeground
            AutoSize = -1 'True
            Caption = "Adjust the foreground colour"
            Height = 195
            Left = 3480
            TabIndex = 15
            Top = 3120
            Width = 1995
         End
         Begin VB.Label lblBackGround
            AutoSize = -1 'True
            Caption = "Adjust the background colour"
```

```
          Height = 195
          Left = 3360
          TabIndex = 14
          Top = 1440
          Width = 2085
       End
       Begin VB.Label lblShowBackColour
          BorderStyle = 1 'Fixed Single
          Height = 735
          Left = 5880
          TabIndex = 13
          Top = 480
          Width = 1335
       End
       Begin VB.Label lblBlueForeground
          Caption = "Blue"
          Height = 255
          Left = 2640
          TabIndex = 12
          Top = 2760
          Width = 615
       End
       Begin VB.Label lblGreenForeground
          AutoSize = -1 'True
          Caption = "Green"
          Height = 195
          Left = 2640
          TabIndex = 11
          Top = 2400
          Width = 435
       End
       Begin VB.Label lblRedForeground
          AutoSize = -1 'True
          Caption = "Red"
          Height = 195
          Left = 2640
          TabIndex = 10
          Top = 2040
          Width = 300
       End
       Begin VB.Label lblBlueBackground
          AutoSize = -1 'True
          Caption = "Blue"
          Height = 195
          Left = 2640
          TabIndex = 9
          Top = 1080
          Width = 315
       End
       Begin VB.Label lblGreenBackground
          AutoSize = -1 'True
          Caption = "Green"
          Height = 195
          Left = 2640
```

```
            TabIndex = 8
            Top = 720
            Width = 435
         End
         Begin VB.Label lblRedBackground
            AutoSize = -1 'True
            Caption = "Red"
            Height = 195
            Left = 2640
            TabIndex = 7
            Top = 360
            Width = 300
         End
      End
End
Attribute VB_Name = "frmTextEntry"
Attribute VB_Creatable = False
Attribute VB_Exposed = False
Private Sub SetBackGroundColour()
Dim Red As Integer
Dim Green As Integer
Dim Blue As Integer

      Red = hsbRedBackground.Value
      Green = hsbGreenBackGround.Value
      Blue = hsbBlueBackground.Value
      txtTextArea.BackColor = RGB(Red, Green, Blue)
      lblShowBackColour.BackColor = RGB(Red, Green, Blue)
End Sub
Private Sub SetForeGroundColour()
Dim Red As Integer
Dim Green As Integer
Dim Blue As Integer

      Red = hsbRedForeground.Value
      Green = hsbGreenForeground.Value
      Blue = hsbBlueForeground.Value
      txtTextArea.ForeColor = RGB(Red, Green, Blue)
      lblShowForeColour.BackColor = RGB(Red, Green, Blue)
End Sub

Private Sub Form_Load()
      hsbRedBackground.Value = 255
      hsbGreenBackGround.Value = 255
      hsbBlueBackground.Value = 255
      hsbRedForeground.Value = 0
      hsbGreenForeground.Value = 0
      hsbBlueForeground.Value = 0
      lblShowForeColour.BackColor = RGB(0, 0, 0)
End Sub

Private Sub hsbBlueBackground_Change()
      Call SetBackGroundColour
End Sub

Private Sub hsbBlueForeground_Change()
      Call SetForeGroundColour
End Sub
```

```
        Private Sub hsbGreenBackGround_Change()
            Call SetBackGroundColour
        End Sub

        Private Sub hsbGreenForeground_Change()
            Call SetForeGroundColour
        End Sub

        Private Sub hsbRedBackground_Change()
            Call SetBackGroundColour
        End Sub

        Private Sub hsbRedForeground_Change()
            Call SetForeGroundColour
        End Sub

        Private Sub lblShowBackColour_Click()

        End Sub
```

The listing is arranged as follows:

1. The none default setting of the properties of the form is listed first.

2. The controls drawn on the form and their none default properties are listed next. They are indented indicating that they 'belong' to the form.

3. Following the control definitions are the event procedures.

4. Lastly the general procedures are listed.

NOTE: Scrutinise the listing of Figure 5.16 to identify its 'component areas'. In particular take note of the positional properties of the controls that were dragged into position.

QUESTION 5.5 (DEVELOPMENT)

What are the settings for the positional properties of the horizontal scroll bar whose Name property is hsbRedForeground?

HINT: *The positional properties are Height, Width, Left and Top.*

PRACTICAL ACTIVITY 5.3

Amend the application developed in Practical activity 5.2 so that the background and foreground colour, at the applications launch, are red and blue respectively.

PRACTICAL ACTIVITY 5.3

Amend the application developed in Practical activity 5.2 so that the foreground colour is controlled by three vertical scroll bars (the background remains controlled by the horizontal scroll bars).

6 Creating and using controls

Visual Basic is a collection of program modules that respond to events and procedure calls. Modules communicate with other modules through parameter passing (covered in a later chapter) and they are supplied with the data via the Graphical User Interface (GUI) and supply data to the GUI. All program modules receive input and process it to produce the output. Figure 6.1 illustrates a useful definition of a program module.

Figure 6.1 A definition of a program module.

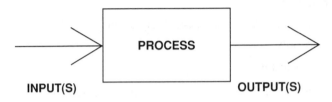

INPUT(S)   OUTPUT(S)

Definition of a program module

A program module is a small number of high-level language statements that process input data to produce output data and in doing so perform one or two functions.

> **NOTE:** A program module may consist of many program statements and perform numerous functions. However, a guiding principle for good program design is that all modules should perform one function on simple input data to produce simple output data. This is the ideal and every attempt should be made to adhere to this principle because code is easier to read and debug if it has been correctly designed.

This chapter will deal with the various ways data is **input** to program modules and **output** from program modules using controls. It will also deal with how the user can generate **events** also using controls. **Later chapters deal with how the data is processed**.

An application developed using Visual Basic involves designing the interface that the user will see by drawing the controls, setting their properties and writing the code to activate the interface.

Controls are used to obtain the user input and to display the output. Typical and frequently used controls for performing input and output are labels, text boxes, list boxes and command buttons.

Other controls in Visual Basic allow a VB application to access and manipulate data from other applications, such as Microsoft Access. The Data Control which 'connects to' Access is dealt with in a later chapter.

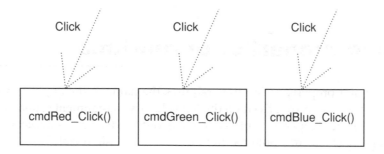

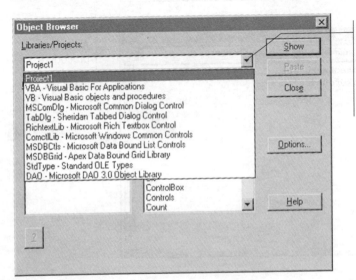

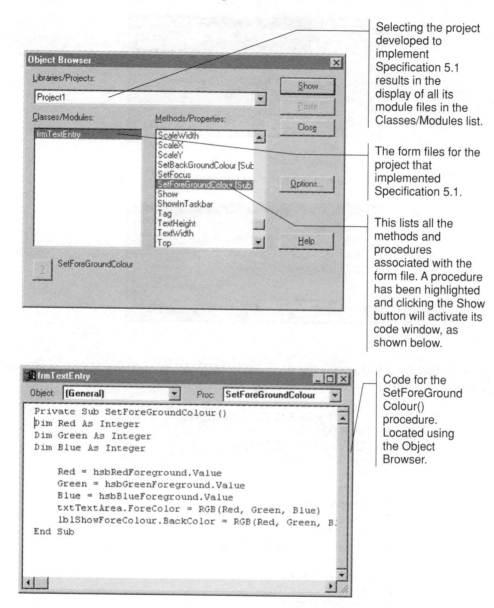

All controls used in Visual Basic have their own set of properties, methods and events. This chapter will look at some of the available controls used in VB, starting with the command button.

Command button

The vast majority of VB applications will contain command buttons that once clicked activate actions within the application. When clicked a command button appears to be pushed in, and therefore, is often referred to as a push button.

Associated with a command button is a set of properties, events and methods.

Properties

A command button has a set of 23 properties listed in its property box. It is not possible within one textbook to describe all of these properties. Instead the common and more frequently used properties will be described and you are left to discover the other properties using the comprehensive Visual Basic online help facility.

Like all controls the most important property is the name property. This is used to identify the command button in the program code. This name is always set by default to Command1 for the first command button drawn and Command2 for the second and so on. However, good programming practice dictates that every control should be renamed to reflect its function and object type. Consequently, a Command button used to quit an application would have its name property set to cmdQuit (refer to Table 3.1).

The caption property of a command button is set to a string to reflect the function of the button. Therefore, for a command button used to quit an application it would, typically, be set to Quit or Quit the Application.

The font property is used to select the appearance of the caption on the button. That is the type of font (System or Times New Roman), its size, whether it is bold or underlined, etc. Figure 6.2 illustrates the appearance of captions on various command buttons.

Figure 6.2 Display of different fonts.

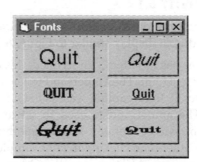

Figure 6.3 illustrates how to change the font setting of a command buttons caption.

Figure 6.3 Altering a captions font.

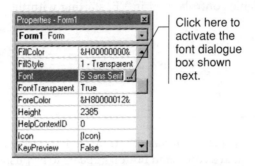

Click here to activate the font dialogue box shown next.

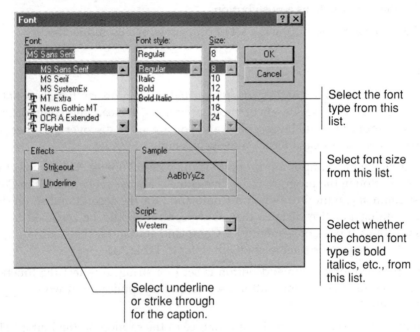

Select the font type from this list.

Select font size from this list.

Select whether the chosen font type is bold italics, etc., from this list.

Select underline or strike through for the caption.

PRACTICAL ACTIVITY 6.1

Draw six command buttons onto a form and set all their caption and font properties to produce a display similar to Figure 6.2.

One of the captions has its letter Q underlined, this is achieved by setting the Caption property to &Quit. The ampersand (&) is not displayed; it is used to underline the letter Q. If the caption was set to Qui&t, then the letter t would be underlined. The ampersand is used to set an accelerator key for the command button. An accelerator key is another way of selecting the command button other than clicking it. For example if the caption was set to &Quit then pressing the ALT key and the Q key at the same time would activate the click event procedure of the command button.

Associated events

A command button is usually clicked by the user. This is a click event and it invokes the click event procedure associated with the command button. Consequently, clicking a command button named cmdQuit would invoke the cmdQuit_Click() event procedure. The code window for this is illustrated in Figure 6.4.

Figure 6.4 A click event procedure.

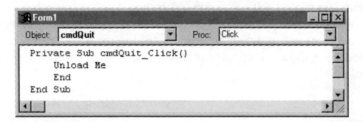

There are, however, another ten events associated with a command button and some are illustrated by Figure 6.5.

Figure 6.5 Events associated with a command button.

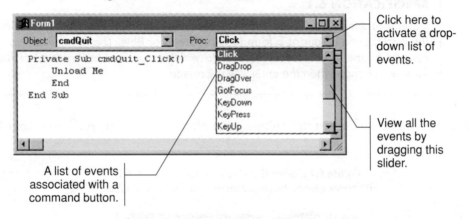

Click here to activate a drop-down list of events.

A list of events associated with a command button.

View all the events by dragging this slider.

Each of the events in this list has a related event procedure whose name is formed from the name of the object and the event. Consequently, the event procedure template associated with the GotFocus event of the cmdQuit command button would appear as shown in Figure 6.6.

Figure 6.6 The GotFocus event procedure template for a command button.

Object name.   Event

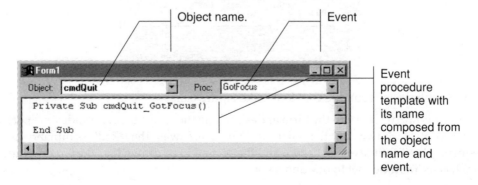

Event procedure template with its name composed from the object name and event.

Focus of an object (control)

Within the Windows operating system environment focus is the ability to receive user input via the mouse or keyboard. When an object has the focus it can receive input from the user. For instance, when a text box has the focus the user can enter text into it. When a command button has the focus it can be selected by pressing the space bar or enter key on the keyboard.

Two of the events associated with a command button (and many other controls) are the GotFocus and LostFocus events. The GotFocus event occurs when an object receives the focus and the LostFocus event occurs when an object loses the focus. A LostFocus event can, for example, be used for validation updates or reversing conditions that were set up by the GotFocus event.

Example of the use of the GotFocus event

> **SPECIFICATION 6.1**
>
> *Develop a simple application that allows three command buttons to change the background colour of a form to Red, Green or Blue. The form should also contain a label that informs the user to which colour the background of the form will change when the enter key is pressed.*

Figure 6.7 illustrates the form at design time **after** all the appropriate properties have been set.

Figure 6.7 Design time GUI for specification 6.1.
It shows a form, three command buttons and a label.

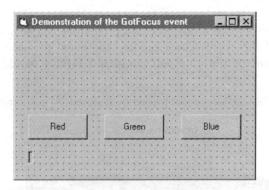

When the application is run the GUI looks like Figure 6.8.

When controls are drawn onto the form at design time they have their TabIndex property set. The first control drawn on the GUI of Figure 6.7 was the 'Red' command button; consequently, its TabIndex is set to zero and the second to be drawn (i.e., the Green command button) has its TabIndex set to one and so on.

Figure 6.8 The GUI at run-time.

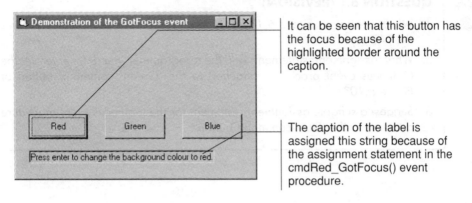

It can be seen that this button has the focus because of the highlighted border around the caption.

The caption of the label is assigned this string because of the assignment statement in the cmdRed_GotFocus() event procedure.

The focus can be changed from one control to another using the TAB key on the keyboard. The order in which the focus moves is dependent upon the TabIndex setting of each control. If the 'Red' command button has the focus then pressing the TAB key will result in the 'Green' command button receiving the focus because the TabIndex of the 'Red' command button is zero and the TabIndex of the 'Green' command button is one.

At launch the 'Red' command button receives the focus which generates a GotFocus event. This event then invokes the cmdRed_GotFocus() event procedure whose code, shown in Figure 6.9, sets the label caption.

Figure 6.9 The GotFocus event procedure associated with the Red command button.

```
Private Sub cmdRed_GotFocus()
    lblDescription.Caption = "Press enter to change the background colour to red."
End Sub
```

Pressing the TAB key moves the focus to the 'Green' command button as illustrated in Figure 6.10.

Figure 6.10 Moving the focus using the TAB key.

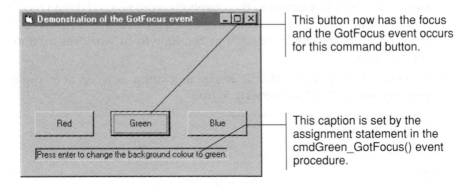

This button now has the focus and the GotFocus event occurs for this command button.

This caption is set by the assignment statement in the cmdGreen_GotFocus() event procedure.

QUESTION 6.1 (REVISION)

1. Which control on Figure 6.10 will receive the focus when the user presses the TAB key?

2. What assignment statement will the programmer need to enter in the GotFocus event procedure attached to the 'Green' command button of Figure 6.10?

3. Suggest a suitable assignment statement for the GotFocus event procedure attached to the 'Blue' command button.

Attaching code to the GotFocus event procedure

Figure 6.11 illustrates the sequence of steps for attaching code to the GotFocus event procedure, associated with the 'Red' command button (cmdRed).

Each of the command buttons shown in Figure 6.8 has eleven possible events, two of them (Click and GotFocus) have code attached, i.e., there are two event procedures for each command button. When navigating through code in an application the events, to which the event procedures are attached, are highlighted in bold; this is illustrated in Figure 6.12.

PRACTICAL ACTIVITY 6.2

Implement Specification 6.1. The settings for all the properties should be obvious from Figure 6.7 with the exception of the AutoSize property of the label.

The label is to be used to display one of three different captions at run-time. How much space is required by these captions is unknown at design time. So rather than drag the label to the size that anticipates the amount of space, the label can automatically be re-sized at run-time to fit whatever caption is assigned to it.

To allow a label to automatically re-size to a string assigned to its caption property, set its AutoSize property to true.

Figure 6.11 Coding an event procedure.

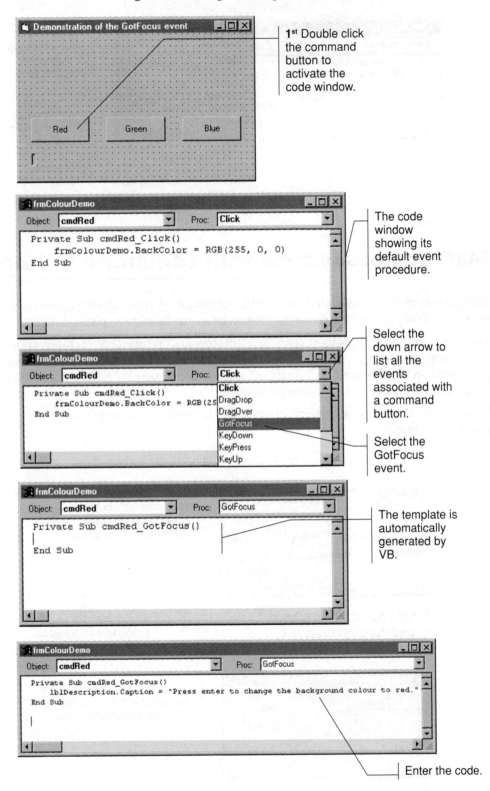

1st Double click the command button to activate the code window.

The code window showing its default event procedure.

Select the down arrow to list all the events associated with a command button.

Select the GotFocus event.

The template is automatically generated by VB.

Enter the code.

Figure 6.12 The event procedures are highlighted in bold.

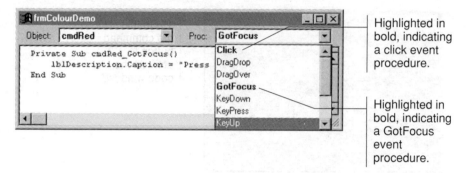

Highlighted in bold, indicating a click event procedure.

Highlighted in bold, indicating a GotFocus event procedure.

Methods associated with command buttons

There are six methods associated with command buttons. A method will perform some action on a control (object), such as move its position or set the focus to a specified object.

The move method can position controls accurately at run-time. For example, consider the positioning of a command button in the top left-hand corner of a form. Controls are positioned on forms according to their left and top properties. When a control's top and left properties are both zero it is positioned in the top left corner of a form.

Figure 6.13 illustrates the effect of a move method on a command button (named cmdMoveDemo).

Figure 6.13 Demonstration of the move method.

The command button is positioned here when the application is launched.

```
Private Sub cmdMoveDemo_Click()
    cmdMoveDemo.Move 0, 0
End Sub
```

This is the click event procedure attached to the command button.

This is the new position of the command button after the user clicks the command button.

Syntax for applying a method to an object

Whenever a method is to be applied to an object, the method and the object name are linked by a period as illustrated in Figure 6.14.

Figure 6.14 A method acting on an object.

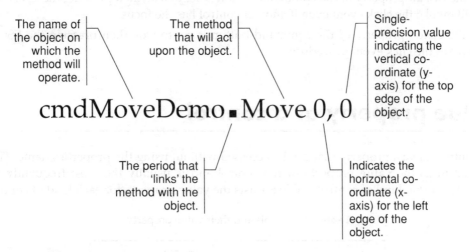

The name of the object on which the method will operate.

The method that will act upon the object.

Single-precision value indicating the vertical co-ordinate (y-axis) for the top edge of the object.

cmdMoveDemo ▪ Move 0, 0

The period that 'links' the method with the object.

Indicates the horizontal co-ordinate (x-axis) for the left edge of the object.

PRACTICAL ACTIVITY 6.3

Make the following amendments to the application developed during Practical activity 6.2.

1. When a command button (Red, Green and Blue) receives the focus it moves to the top left-hand corner of the form.

2. Once the moved command button loses the focus to another control (i.e., another command button). It moves back to its original position.

HINT 1: Attach the following code to the GotFocus event procedure of the 'Red' command button.

    cmdRed.Move 0, 0

and add a similar statement to the GotFocus event procedure of the other two command buttons.

HINT 2: Attach a similar statement to the LostFocus event of each of the command buttons. This time the command buttons are moving back to their original positions. This will involve saving the original top and left properties.

How to select a command button at run-time

There are several ways to select a command button at run-time and each of the ways listed below invokes the click event procedure.

1. Use the mouse to click the button.
2. Press an accelerator key for the command button (i.e., the ALT key plus a letter).
3. Tab to the control using the TAB key and press either the space bar or enter key on the keyboard.
4. Set the command buttons *Value* property to true.
5. If the *Default* property of the command button is set to true then pressing the ENTER key will invoke the click event even if another control has the focus.
6. If the *Cancel* property of the command button is set to true then pressing the ESC key invokes the click event procedure.

Value property of a control

All controls have a property that can be accessed without using the properties name. This is referred to as the **value** property of the control and is usually the most frequently used property for that kind of control. Table 6.1 lists the value property for each kind of control.

Table 6.1 Controls and their value property.

Control	The value property
Check box	Value
Combo box	Text
Command button	Value
Common dialogue	Action
Data	Caption
Drive list box	Drive
File list box	FileName
Frame	Caption
Grid	Text
Horizontal scroll bar	Value
Image	Picture
Label	Caption
Line	Visible
List box	Text
Menu	Enabled
Option button	Value
Picture box	Picture
Shape	Shape
Text box	Text
Timer	Enabled
Vertical scroll bar	Value

When VB code refers to a property of a control, that is the value property of the control, it is not necessary to use the property name. For example, setting the caption property of label can be done as follows:

Label1 = "The disc is not ready"

However, this is not good programming practice because it is always better to fully identify the property; consequently, the above assignment statement is better as follows:

Label1.Caption = "The disc is not ready"

Nevertheless, a knowledge of the value of a control is important because it is often used in program listings that are to be found in magazines, other texts and the online Visual Basic help.

Categories of controls

There are three main categories of controls in Visual Basic, they are:

1. Standard controls.
2. Custom controls.
3. Insertable objects.

Standard controls

This type of control, such as command buttons and labels are contained inside the VB .EXE file (the finished executable file that is the developed application). Standard controls are always included in the toolbox and cannot be removed.

Custom controls

These controls exist in a separate file that has a .VBX or .OCX filename extension. Custom controls include third-party controls, enhanced versions of standard controls and specialised controls such as the common dialogue control. Custom controls can be added and removed from the toolbox and are the foundation of component technology software. If, for example, you wish to include a spell checker in an application then it can be bought from a third-party supplier and added to the toolbox and used like any other control.

Insertable objects

These controls are objects from other Microsoft applications, such as, Excel, Access and Word. These too can be added and removed from the toolbox.

Using text boxes

Text boxes can be used to obtain input from the user and display output from the program process.

SPECIFICATION 6.2

Write an application that allows a user to enter text into a text box. Have a command button click event procedure transfer the contents of the input text box to an output text box.

Figure 6.15 illustrates the GUI for the implementation of Specification 6.2.

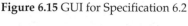

Figure 6.15 GUI for Specification 6.2

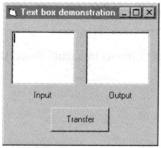

The GUI of Figure 6.15 consists of two text boxes, two labels and one command button. The property of these controls are set as shown in Table 6.2.

The code attached to the command button is shown in Figure 6.16.

Table 6.2 Property settings for the GUI.

Control	Property	Setting
Label1	Name	lblInput
	Caption	Input
Label2	Name	lblOutput
	Caption	Output
Text1	Name	txtInput
	Text	<empty>
	MultiLine	True
Text2	Name	txtOutput
	Text	<empty>
	MultiLine	True
	Locked	True
Command1	Name	cmdTransfer
	Caption	Transfer

Figure 6.16 The click event procedure.

```
Private Sub Command1_Click()
    txtOutput.Text = txtInput.Text
End Sub
```

This assignment statement transfers a **copy** of the text stored in the Text property of the txtInput text box to the Text property of the txtOutput text box.

A user of the application enters text into the text input box and clicks the command button to transfer a **copy** of the text to the output text box. This is illustrated by Figure 6.17.

Figure 6.17 The run-time before and after the command button is clicked.

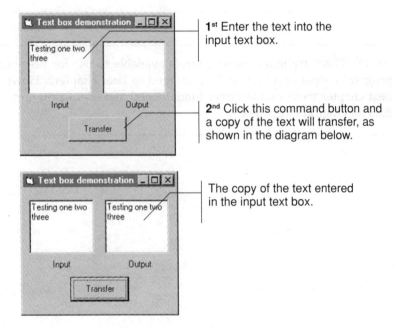

1st Enter the text into the input text box.

2nd Click this command button and a copy of the text will transfer, as shown in the diagram below.

The copy of the text entered in the input text box.

Multiline and locked properties of text boxes

Both of the text boxes had their MultiLine property set to True which allows for text to continue onto the next line. When this property is set to false, the text box ignores the carriage return and restricts data to a single line.

> **NOTE:** You can also add scroll bars to larger TextBox controls using the ScrollBars property. If no HScrollBar control (horizontal scroll bar) is specified, the text in a multiple-line TextBox automatically wraps.

The text box used for the output had its Locked property set to true. This makes the text box read only. It is possible to highlight and scroll through the text but it cannot be edited by the user. However, it is still possible for program code to change the contents of a locked text box by assigning text to its Text property.

PRACTICAL ACTIVITY 6.4

Implement Specification 6.2. Once the application is fully implemented experiment with the properties of the text box and observe the effects, for example, try the following changes.

1. Set the Locked property of txtOutput to false and after text has been transferred highlight the text in the Output text box and press delete. Change the Locked property back to True and attempt to delete the text.

2. Set the MultiLine property of the input text box to false and then enter a very long sentence into the input text box. Click the command button and observe both text boxes.

NOTE: There are many more controls available to use for user input and program output and they will be covered in later chapters. However, the next chapter moves on to cover fundamental aspects of program code, its data and logical structures.

7 Program data

The previous chapter defined a program module as something that receives input data and processes this data to supply the output data. This chapter deals with program data, what it is, and how it is supplied to the program process (input), and where it is stored when processed (output).

Input data

Data supplied as input to a VB program is obtained from files. These files can be:

1. A text file.
2. The Graphical User Interface (GUI).
3. A binary file.
4. Another applications file.

Output data

Output data from the VB program is sent to a file. The file can be:

1. A text file.
2. The Graphical User Interface (GUI).
3. A binary file.
4. Another applications file.

Text file

A text file is a sequence of ASCII (ANSI standard) codes that represent alphanumeric characters. Text files reside on magnetic or optical media, although they can temporarily reside in silicon memory (RAM) for the purpose of being processed.

The GUI

The objects (controls) of the GUI 'connect to' the keyboard, mouse, VDU and the Windows operating system. This connection (interface) allows the user to enter **input data** via the appropriate objects (controls) and **output data** (processed data) is displayed via these objects (controls).

Binary file

A binary file stores data in the internal representation of the computer (not ASCII codes). This internal representation relates to the type of the data. Binary files reside on magnetic media, although they can temporarily reside in silicon memory (RAM) for the purpose of being processed.

Another applications file

Visual Basic is a complete programming language that supports all the same type of data access as all other modern languages, such as C and Pascal. However, it offers more elegant methods for accessing the data of other applications. For example, it easily and directly accesses the data tables of various databases without the programmer needing to worry about the compatibility of this data. Once the VB application has access to this data it can process it. In other words, Visual Basic can input the data of another application, process it and output it back to the other application or to its own files or even its own GUI.

Data types

Every data item (program variable) has a data type and the type indicates:

- The range of possible values the data item can have.
- The way in which the data can be used and processed.
- The memory allocation for the data item.

Visual Basic has eleven fundamental data types; they are shown in Table 7.1.

Integer type

This data type embraces all positive and negative **whole** numbers including zero. Computers cannot cope with infinitely large numbers. Consequently, there is a restriction on the range of numbers the integer type can represent.

An integer can be used to store the number of cars leaving a production line. A variable capable of storing a whole number is ideal because you cannot have half a car.

An integer is an example of an enumerated type. An enumerated value can contain a finite set of unique whole numbers, each of which has special meaning in the context in which it is used. Enumerated values provide a convenient way to select among a known number of choices. For instance, when asking the user to select from a list of items each item can be numbered 0, 1, 2 and so on.

An integer can be processed, for example, by the following operators:

+	addition
-	subtraction
*	multiplication
\	integer division (i.e. 7 \ 3 equals 2, i.e., number 3 goes into 7 twice)
Mod	find the remainder (i.e., 7 MOD 3 equals 1)

Table 7.1 Visual Basic data types.

Type	Memory allocation	Range of values
Integer	2 bytes	-32,768 to +32.767
Long	4 bytes	-2,147,483,648 to 2,147,483,647
Single	4 bytes	-3.402823E+38 to -1.401298E-45 (for negative values). 1.401298E−45 to 3.402823E38 (for positive values)
Double	8 bytes	-1.79769313486231E308 to -4.940665645841247E-324 (negative numbers) 4.94065645841247E-324 to 1.79769313486231E308 (positive numbers)
Currency	8 bytes	-922337203685477.5808 to 922337203685477.5807
String	1 byte per character	0 to approximately 65,000 characters on a 16 bit system 0 to 2E32 on a 32 bit system
Byte	1 byte	0 to 255
Boolean	2 bytes	True or False
Date	8 bytes	January 1, 100 to December 31 9999
Object	4 bytes	Any Object reference
Variant	16 bytes (plus one byte for each character if it is storing a string)	Null or Error Numeric range up to that of a double. Text Arrays

Long type

This is another example of an enumerated data type and is similar to the integer type except it has a larger range, i.e., it can represent bigger numbers. However, it takes up more memory storage than an integer type and consequently takes longer to process than an integer data type.

Single type

A variable of this type can store a single-precision floating point variable, i.e., all positive and negative numbers that have fractional parts. Again there is a restriction on the range of numbers the single type can represent. There is also a restriction on the **precision** with which it can represent a real number. For example, the fraction two-thirds is represented by the recurring decimal fraction 0.666666666666, etc. (i.e., to infinity). A computer cannot represent recurring fractions accurately. Instead it represents so many significant places. Two-thirds can be represented with a precision of six significant places to give 0.666667.

A single number can be used to store the dimensions of a building in metres because it needs to store the fractional numbers that represent the centimetres.

Also an integer can be processed; for example, by the following operators:

- + addition
- - subtraction
- * multiplication
- / floating point division

Double type

A variable of this type can store a double-precision floating point number and is similar to the single type but it takes twice the memory storage and therefore takes longer to process. However, it can represent a larger range of numbers than the single data type.

String type

A variable of this type can represent all the characters present on the computer keyboard plus a few other special characters – referred to as the character set and represented by ANSI codes. A data item of this type is used to store a string of the characters present in the character set. A string variable can be used to store the names and addresses of customers at a bank.

Boolean type

This is the simplest of all the data types and a data item of this type is only capable of storing one of two possible values, **True** or **False**.

A Boolean variable can be used as an indicator. For example, a Boolean variable may be called Overdrawn. If Overdrawn is true then a letter is sent to the customer informing them that they must bring their account up to date. However, if Overdrawn is false the customer is sent a letter asking if they would like a loan.

Variant type

This is a special type that can be very useful in many circumstances. A variable of this type can represent numeric types (i.e., integers, long, single and double), it can also represent strings and all other data types available within Visual Basic. If you do not specify the type of a variable when it is declared then it is a variant by default. A variant variable can be assigned a variable of any other type and Visual Basic automatically performs any necessary conversions.

At this stage no more will be said about the variant data type other than do not use it unless it is absolutely necessary for the functioning of a segment of program code. For example, a binary file may supply a list of integers that represent the sales of widgets. A general procedure can be written to read this file and the integers in the file can be assigned to a variant variable but this is not a good idea, instead assign them to an integer variable. Always use the more obvious data type for variables. There are many good reasons for choosing the integer variable, not least is the fact that the code will execute faster. Although the variant is a very flexible data type it does have overheads that slow down its processing.

> **NOTE:** The data types discussed in this chapter will be used in the following chapters; you are left to research the other data types yourself. If knowledge of other data types is required in later chapters, it will be discussed in the relevant chapter.

Declaration of variables

Variables are used to store values while the program statements are executed. Variables declared within a procedure follow the Keyword **Dim** and precede the Keyword **As**, this is illustrated in Figure 7.1.

Figure 7.1 Declaring a variable.

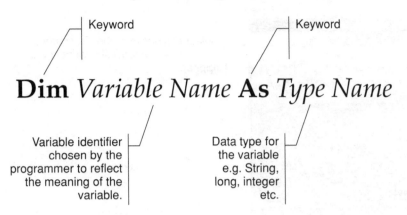

Implicit declaration

Visual Basic allows you to use a variable without having to declare it. However, this is very poor programming practice and can result in bugs that are difficult to correct. *You are strongly advised to declare all variables in your code.*

Explicit declaration

The Visual Basic Environment can be set so that programmers are forced to declare all variables used in an application. *You are strongly recommended to set the Environment to force variable declaration.* Figure 7.2 illustrates the sequence necessary for setting the VB environment to force variable declaration. Setting the environment to force variable declaration causes Visual Basic to automatically add the words **Option Explicit** to all new code modules. If you see these words in your code do not remove them.

Option Explicit can also be added manually to modules to force variable declaration.

Scope of variables

Variables declared inside a procedure can only be accessed by that procedure's code. The variable has a scope *local* to the procedure and is often referred to as a *local variable*.

Figure 7.2 Setting the VB environment.

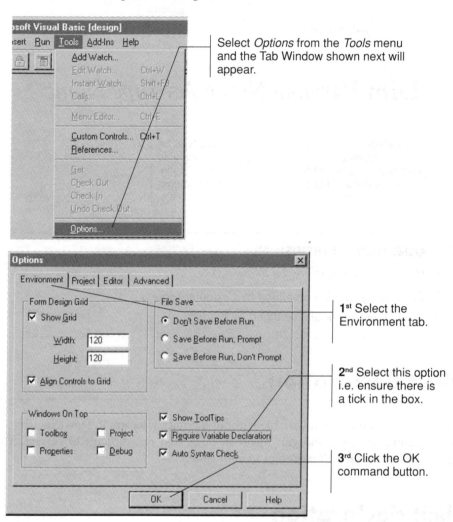

Select *Options* from the *Tools* menu and the Tab Window shown next will appear.

1st Select the Environment tab.

2nd Select this option i.e. ensure there is a tick in the box.

3rd Click the OK command button.

Where and how a variable is declared fixes its scope. Some variables can have a broader scope that allows them to be accessed throughout an application or throughout a subset of the application.

Lifetime of variables

Local variables are usually used to store the intermediate results of calculations. Consequently, the values they store have no long-term use. Therefore, local variables are only valid during the execution of the procedure in which they are declared. The value they store 'disappears' when the procedure finishes executing. They have a lifetime equal to the duration of the procedure execution.

Variables with a broader scope can have a lifetime equal to the duration of the *applications* execution. These variables store information that is needed by program code throughout the application and for all the time the application is running.

Constants

A constant is a meaningful name that takes the place of a number or string that does not change throughout the program code. There are two sources for constants in Visual Basic:

1. System-defined constants.
2. User-defined constants.

System-defined constants

These are constants that are supplied by VB and other applications. A form can be displayed in one of three states, Normal, Minimised and Maximised. The Window state property of a form can be set at run-time with an assignment statement as shown below:

Form1.WindowState = 2

This will set the form (Window at run-time) to its minimised state, i.e., an icon. The assignment statement is simple enough but it is not as readable as it could be. The assignment statement shown below performs the same action but this time uses a *system defined constant*.

Form1.WindowState = vbMinimized

vbMinimized is a constant that stores the value 2. Table 7.2 lists the system constants for the WindowState property of a form.

Table 7.2 System constants for the WindowState properties.

Constant	Value	Description
vbNormal	0	Normal.
vbMinimized	1	Minimized.
vbMaximized	2	Maximized.

User-defined constants

Programmers can create their own constants to improve the readability of their code. An example of declaring a constant is shown in Figure 7.3.

To avoid confusing variables and constants when reading code you are recommended to *prefix* every meaningful constant identifier (name) with lower-case c. Constants can be assigned to variables and properties but they are **not** the same as variables. You **cannot** assign a value to a constant in program code. Once a constant has been declared its value remains fixed.

Scope of a constant

The scope of a constant is dependent, like a variable, upon where it is declared. The scope rules that apply to variables also apply to constants, e.g., a constant declared in a procedure is local to that procedure.

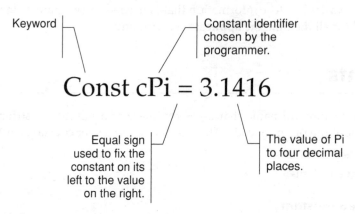

Figure 7.3 Declaring a constant.

Keyword

Constant identifier
chosen by the
programmer.

Const cPi = 3.1416

Equal sign
used to fix the
constant on its
left to the value
on the right.

The value of Pi
to four decimal
places.

Performing calculations and assigning values to variables

The calculation of a worker's gross pay is achieved by the multiplication of the number of hours worked by the rate of pay per hour. Visual Basic would perform this calculation using the following assignment statement:

GrossPay = PayRate * HoursWorked

The contents of the variables PayRate and HoursWorked are multiplied together with the result being assigned (stored in) to the variable GrossPay. This process is illustrated in Figure 7.4.

Figure 7.4 The execution of an assignment statement.

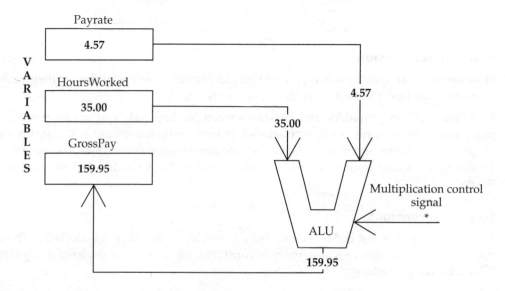

Closer look at an assignment statement

An assignment statement is a way of assigning a value to a variable. The simplest form of an assignment statement is shown below:

Variable = expression

The equals symbol '=' signifies the assignment of the value of the right-hand side to the variable on the left-hand side.

NOTE: A **definition** of an assignment statement is given below:

The expression on the right-hand side is evaluated (worked out) and the resulting value is copied to the variable on the left-hand side.

Consequently, it is acceptable to have an assignment statement of the form shown below:

Count = Count + 1

This assignment statement means take the value of the variable Count, add one to it (i.e., evaluate the right-hand side) and store the result in the variable Count – this will overwrite the original value stored there. Figure 7.5 illustrates how the ALU is used to execute this assignment statement.

Figure 7.5 Execution of the assignment statement.

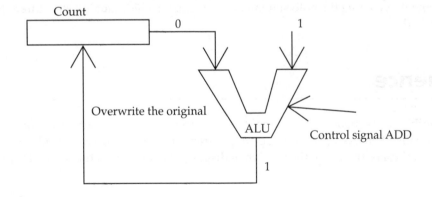

8 Program logic structures

Computer programs are made up of three basic constructs:

- Sequence.
- Selection.
- Repetition (iteration).

This chapter will deal with the sequential construct and following chapters will deal with Selection and Iteration. All of the constructs will be represented by three methods:

- Flow charts.
- Nassi Schneiderman Charts (N-S Charts).
- Structured English.

Structured English and N-S Charts are examples of methods used to express program design. Flow charts are used to express the logic of program constructs and should **never** (except for teaching purposes) be used to express program design. A flow chart represents a 'mental picture' that programmers should carry in their minds as an aid to memorising the logic of the program constructs.

N-S Charts are a graphical representation of program constructs that **ensures** program designers use the constructs that are available to them in the chosen high-level language.

Structured English is a non-graphical method that also ensures that a program designer uses the constructs that are available within the high-level language.

Both Structured English and N-S Charts produce designs that do not require the use of the goto statement. Avoiding the goto statement is essential if a high-quality structured design is to be achieved.

Sequence

This describes a sequence of actions that a program carries out one after another, unconditionally. For example, consider a program that reads in two numbers from the keyboard, multiplies them together and then displays the answer on the Visual Display Unit (VDU).

Flow chart representation

The flow chart representation of a sequence is shown in Figure 8.1.

The flow chart shows the *flow* of control for the program. The first symbol is the START symbol and this is followed by the arrow showing the next action to be performed, which is in turn followed by another arrow showing the next action to be performed and so on until the STOP symbol is reached. Each rectangle symbol represents an action to be performed, for example, Read the first number. Every action shown in a sequence must be completed **before** another action is started. When one action is complete the next action is started and no conditions have to be met before the next action can start. So for the multiplication example

Figure 8.1 Flow chart representation of sequence.

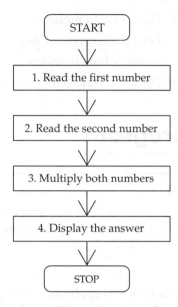

given, the first step (action) of the design will involve the reading of a number from the computer keyboard, the second step will involve the reading of another number from the keyboard. The third step will involve the multiplication of these numbers by the **Arithmetic and Logic Unit** (ALU). The fourth and final step will be to display the product on the VDU.

N-S Chart representation

Figure 8.2 shows the N-S Chart representation of a program sequence.

Figure 8.2 N-S chart representation of sequence.

1. Read the first number
2. Read the second number
3. Multiply both numbers
4. Display the answer

The N-S Chart for sequence essentially lists the sequence of actions to be performed, except that each action within the list has its own separate rectangular box. So for the multiplication example the action of box one is performed first, then the action of box two and so on until the action of the last box (box 4) is performed. At first sight the N-S chart may appear to be very similar to the flow chart and its advantage may not be apparent. However, the way in which N-S charts represent selection and repetition does offer advantages over the flow chart.

Structured English representation

The Structured English representation of a program sequence is shown in Figure 8.3.

The Structured English representation of a sequence is a numbered list of actions that are performed one after another, unconditionally.

Figure 8.3 Structured English representation of a program sequence.

1. Read the first number
2. Read the second number
3. Multiply both numbers
4. Display the answer

Sequential VB program

> **SPECIFICATION 8.1**
>
> *Develop a simple application that will prompt the user (using input boxes) for two numbers and display the product of these numbers in a message box.*

> **NOTE:** The development of this application will ignore the design of a GUI and will attach the code, to implement Specification 8.1, to the click event procedure of a form. This is not the usual way that a Visual Basic application is developed. A GUI is always developed first and the way this specification is implemented does not represent a sensible solution. However, the application developed has been chosen for teaching purposes to **emphasise** the structure of a sequential program and to introduce the Message and Input box.

The solution to Specification 8.1 is derived in five stages:

1. Develop an algorithm represented by an N-S chart (i.e., a design).
2. Produce a data table to identify the variables required.
3. Derive a simple test plan.
4. Convert the design to code and run.
5. Test the run-time against the test plan.

Step 1: develop the algorithm

The N-S chart below represents the solution (i.e. design algorithm) to implement the specification.

1. Read the first number
2. Read the second number
3. Multiply both numbers
4. Display the answer

This design will process two pieces of data to produce a third. The input data to this program will be two variables identified as FirstNumber and SecondNumber. These variables will be processed (i.e., multiplied) to produce the output data (stored in a variable identified as Product). The relationship between the input data, process and output data for this design is illustrated in Figure 8.4.

Figure 8.4 Design 'mapped' onto a program definition.

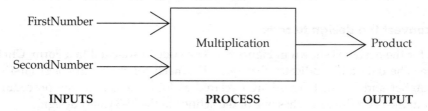

INPUTS PROCESS OUTPUT

Step 2: produce a data table

The production of a data table forces consideration of the variables (and their type) needed to implement the specification. When the specification defines a difficult problem it is often necessary to consider the structure of the variables and their type first – particularly if arrays and user-defined records are to be processed (see later). The data table for this specification and solution is shown below:

Identifier	Type	Description
FirstNumber	INTEGER	Stores the number entered at the keyboard
SecondNumber	INTEGER	Stores the number entered at the keyboard
Product	INTEGER	Stores the product of FirstNumber and SecondNumber and has its contents sent to the VDU

Step 3: derive a simple test plan

A test plan is a table that lists the inputs that should be supplied to the prompts of the code and it indicates the output expected for the supplied input(s).

In the case of this program the user will enter 5 and 20 in response to the prompts and the computer will process this data and produce the expected output, namely 100, the product of 5 and 20.

> **NOTE:** The development of a test plan is an 'acid test' that should not be skipped. If you can derive a test plan for the program you are about to code, then you understand the specification. Consequently, the probability of your design being correct is greatly improved.

Not every test plan will follow the following format, different format test plans will be discussed throughout the text wherever necessary.

Supplied input

User friendly message	Input data (user response)
Enter a number	5
Enter another number	20

Expected output

User friendly message	Output data
The product of the input numbers is	100

Step 4: convert the design to code

The code for the design is shown in Figure 8.5. **The code is attached to a Form_Click event procedure**. The data table indicates that there is a need for three variables, FirstNumber, SecondNumber and Product. These are declared as local integers in the procedure. Each statement in the procedure matches one of the actions in the N-S Chart design.

Figure 8.5 Code for the design.

```
Private Sub Form_Click ()

Dim FirstNumber As Integer
Dim SecondNumber As Integer
Dim Product As Integer

    FirstNumber = InputBox("Enter a number")
    SecondNumber = InputBox("Enter another number")
    Product = FirstNumber * SecondNumber
    MsgBox "The product of the input numbers is " & Product

End Sub
```

PRACTICAL ACTIVITY 8.1

Complete step 4 and step 5, i.e., code, run and test the program against the test plan.

Figure 8.6 illustrates the run-time for this program.

Figure 8.6 Run-time sequence for the sequential program.

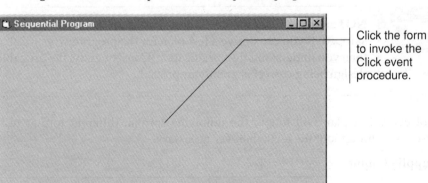

Click the form to invoke the Click event procedure.

Figure 8.6 (cont.)

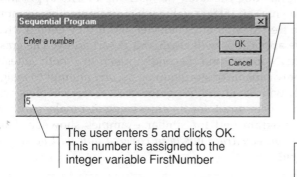

This input box is generated by the following VB statement
FirstNumber = InputBox("Enter a number")
Notice that the string in the box matches the string in the statement.

The user enters 5 and clicks OK. This number is assigned to the integer variable FirstNumber

Avoid clicking the Cancel because the program will crash (see page 156).

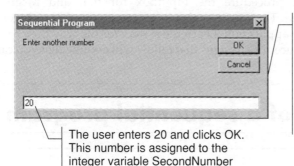

This input box is generated by the following VB statement
SecondNumber = InputBox("Enter another number")
Notice that the string in the box matches the string in the statement.

The user enters 20 and clicks OK. This number is assigned to the integer variable SecondNumber

Product = FirstNumber * SecondNumber

The integer variable Product is assigned the product (multiplication) of the **contents** of the variable FirstNumber and the **contents** of the variable SecondNumber. Consequently, 100 is assigned to the variable Product,

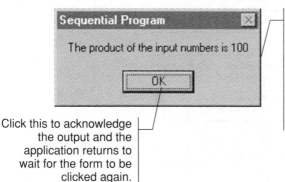

This output box is generated by the following VB statement.

MsgBox "The product of the input numbers is" & Product.

The string and (&) the contents of the variable Product are displayed as shown.

Click this to acknowledge the output and the application returns to wait for the form to be clicked again.

NOTE: This application has **not** validated the user input. The application only requires the user to enter an integer value when prompted by an input box. However, users are free to enter any character and if they enter a letter instead of an integer the application will crash and report a bug. The crash will occur because FirstNumber and SecondNumber are both integer variables and they are only capable of storing integers, any attempt to assign them non-integer values will result in a program crash. Later chapters will deal with the validation of user input, for the time being just make sure you enter integers for this program and for similar examples shown in later chapters. *Once the selection construct has been covered you will be shown how to validate user input.*

NOTE: For this event procedure the InputBox function and MsgBox statement have been used. The way in which they operate should be obvious from the run-time of the application. Learn the syntax for the way they have been used in this procedure. The designs that follow will assume that you can use these statements.

Another example of a sequential program

SPECIFICATION 8.2

Write a Form_Click event procedure that draws a circle in the centre of a form. The various ways for representing the design for this program are shown in Figures 8.7, 8.8 and 8.9.

Figure 8.7 Flow chart representation of a design for drawing a circle on a form.

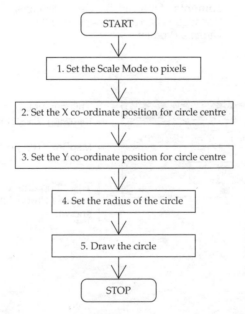

Figure 8.8 The N-S chart representation for the Form_Click event procedure.

1. Set the Scale Mode to pixels
2. Set the X co-ordinate position for the circle centre
3. Set the Y co-ordinate position for the circle centre
4. Set the radius of the circle
5. Draw the circle

Figure 8.9 The structured English representation of the Form_Click event.

1. Set the Scale Mode to pixels
2. Set the X co-ordinate position for the circle centre
3. Set the Y co-ordinate position for the circle centre
4. Set the radius of the circle
5. Draw the circle

The data table for the program is shown below:

Identifier	Type	Description
CentreX	INTEGER	Stores the X co-ordinate for the centre of the form.
CentreY	INTEGER	Stores the Y co-ordinate for the centre of the form.
Radius	INTEGER	Store the radius of the circle to be drawn.

The program for the event procedure is shown in Figure 8.10.

There is no user input for this program so there is no need for a test plan other than a statement that the output should be a circle drawn in the centre of the form.

Figure 8.10 The code for drawing a circle in the centre of a form.

```
Private Sub Form_Click()
Dim CentreX As Integer
Dim CentreY As Integer
Dim Radius As Integer ' Declare variables.

    ScaleMode = 3 ' Set scale to pixels.
    CentreX = Form1.ScaleWidth \ 2 ' Set X position.
    CentreY = Form1.ScaleHeight \ 2 ' Set Y position.
    Radius = 40
    Form1.Circle (CentreX, CentreY), Radius, RGB(0, 0, 0)

End Sub
```

Description trace for the 'circle' program

Statement	Description
ScaleMode = 3	There are several different scale modes and they are responsible for setting the units of measurement for the X and Y co-ordinates when drawing graphics. Setting the scale to 3 indicates that all measurements are in pixels. If the scale mode was set to 6, the units would be measured in millimetres. Refer to the VB online help for a list of all the other settings of unit measurements.
CentreX = Form1.ScaleWidth \ 2	ScaleWidth is a method that returns the interior width of an object in the units set by ScaleMode. In this case the method has been applied to a form. The division by 2 sets the X co-ordinate centre of the form.
CentreY = Form1.ScaleHeight \ 2	ScaleHeight is a method that returns the interior height of an object in the units set by ScaleMode. In this case the method has been applied to a form. The division by 2 sets the Y co-ordinate centre of the form.
Radius = 40	The Radius of the circle to be drawn has been set to 40 pixels.
Form1.Circle (CentreX, CentreY), Radius, RGB(0, 0, 0)	This is a method that draws a circle in the centre of the form as defined by the variables CentreX and CentreY. This circle has a radius equal to the contents of the variable Radius (i.e., 40 pixels) and is drawn in the colour generated by the RGB function (i.e., black).

PRACTICAL ACTIVITY 8.2

Enter and run the 'circle' program and perform the following experiments:

1. Drag the form to different sizes and click it – notice how the circle is always drawn in the centre of the form. This is because resizing the form alters its ScaleWidth and ScaleHeight properties.

2. Alter the value stored in the Radius variable and run the program again.

3. Change the colour of the circle being drawn.

9 Making decisions

Before selection and iteration constructs are considered it is necessary to look at how computer programs make decisions.

Conditional statements

A program is able to make decisions. These decisions may result in the actions of a program, or segment of a program, being repeated. A decision may also result in one segment of a program being chosen for execution over another segment.

Conditional statements make the decisions in a Visual Basic program. A conditional statement (or conditional test) can consist of comparisons between variables using relational operators. It can also consist of logical operators 'working on' variables. Also, a conditional statement can consist of a combination of both logical and relational operators. Table 9.1 shows relational operators and their meaning. Table 9.2 shows logical operators and their meaning.

Table 9.1 Relational operators and their meaning.

Relational Operator	Meaning
<	less than
<=	less than or equal to
>=	greater than or equal to
>	greater than
=	equal to
<>	not equal to
Like	Fuzzy string comparison

Table 9.2 Logical operators and their meaning.

Logical Operator	Meaning
AND	logical AND
OR	logical OR
NOT	logical NOT
XOR	exclusive OR
EQU	Equivalence
IMP	Implication

IMPORTANT: There is only one of two possible outcomes from a conditional statement (conditional test) **True** or **False**.

Examples of conditional statements using only relational operators

Example 9.1

FirstNumber > SecondNumber

This conditional test is asking whether the content of the variable FirstNumber is greater than the content of the variable SecondNumber.

If the FirstNumber content is greater than the SecondNumber content then the result is **True**.

If the FirstNumber content is less than the SecondNumber content then the result is **False**.

If the FirstNumber content is the *same* as the SecondNumber content then the result is **False** (FirstNumber has to be greater then SecondNumber to be true).

Example 9.2

FirstNumber >= SecondNumber

This conditional test is asking whether the content of the variable FirstNumber is greater than or equal to the content of the SecondNumber.

If the FirstNumber content is greater than the SecondNumber content then the result is **True**.

If the FirstNumber content is less than the SecondNumber content then the result is **False**.

If the FirstNumber content is the *same* as the SecondNumber content then the result is **True**.

QUESTION 9.1 (REVISION)

Decide whether each of the following conditional tests are true or false.

1. *FirstNumber <= SecondNumber*
2. *FirstNumber < SecondNumber*
3. *FirstNumber <> SecondNumber*
4. *FirstNumber > SecondNumber*
5. *FirstNumber >= SecondNumber*
6. *FirstNumber = SecondNumber*
7. *SecondNumber <> ThirdNumber*
8. *SecondNumber >= ThirdNumber*
9. *SecondNumber = ThirdNumber*
10. *SecondNumber > ThirdNumber*

The value of each variable in the examples is as defined by the following assignment statements:

FirstNumber = 5

SecondNumber= 6

ThirdNumber= 6

Like operator

It can be seen from Table 9.1 and Examples 9.1 and 9.2 that Visual Basic has the usual set of relational operators you would expect from a high-level language like Pascal. However, the Like operator is unique to Visual Basic.

The Like operator allows for the comparison to include wildcards. Consequently, it allows for **inexact** matches. Table 9.3 lists wildcards that can be used with the Like operator.

Table 9.3 Wildcards and their meaning.

Wildcards	Meaning
?	Any single character
#	Any single digit
*	Zero or more characters
[set]	Any character in the set
[!set]	Any character except those in the set

Examples of the use of the Like operator and wildcards

Example 9.3

If the variable Surname1 was assigned the string Smith (i.e., Surname1 = "Smith") and Surname2 was assigned Smyth (i.e., Surname2 = "Smyth") then both the following statements would be **True**.

Surname1 **Like** "Sm?th"

Surname2 **Like** "Sm?th"

The statements are true because the contents of each variable are exactly the same as the string Sm?th except for one character position. However, this position is represented by a wildcard which means that the variable being compared to Sm?th using the **Like** operator can have any value in this position.

Example 2

If the variable Digit was assigned the character 6 (i.e., Digit = "6") then the following statement would be **True**.

Digit **Like** "[0-9]"

This statement is **True** because the character 6 belongs to (is *in*) the set of characters from 0 to 9.

QUESTION 9.2 (REVISION)

Answer each of the following.

1. *A string variable is assigned the character a (i.e., Letter = "a") therefore is the following statement True of False?*
   Letter Like "[a-z]"

2. *A string variable is assigned the character R (i.e., Letter = "R") therefore is the following statement True of False*
   Letter Like "[a-z]"

Logical operators

Relational operators are fairly easy to understand in that they relate to everyday ideas, such as, is this value greater than that one etc.? To understand logical operators requires the learning of their definition. The following operators will be considered in turn:

1. Logical **Or**
2. Logical **And**
3. Logical **Imp**

4. Logical **Not**
5. Logical **XOR**
6. Logical **Eqv**

NOTE: Logical operators are defined by their truth tables.

Logical Or

Result = Expression1 **Or** Expression2

The truth table for logical Or is shown in Table 9.4. Table 9.5 shows the effect of the result when the **Null** value is present (Null indicates that a variable contains no valid data).

Table 9.4 The logical Or truth table.

Expression1	Expression2	Result
False	False	False
False	True	True
True	False	True
True	True	True

Table 9.5 When Null is included in a logical Or expression.

Expression1	Expression2	Result
Null	Null	Null
Null	False	Null
Null	True	True
False	Null	Null
True	Null	True

NOTE: For the **Or** operator the Result is true if **one or more** of the expressions are true. The Result is false if **all** the expressions are false.

Logical And

Result = Expression1 **And** Expression2

The truth table for logical And is shown in Table 9.6. Table. 9.7 shows the effect of the result when the **Null** value is present.

Table 9.6 A TWO input And truth table.

Expression1	Expression2	Result
False	False	False
False	True	False
True	False	False
True	True	True

Table 9.7 When Null is included in a Logical And expression.

Expression1	Expression2	Result
Null	Null	Null
Null	False	False
Null	True	Null
False	Null	False
True	Null	Null

NOTE: For the **And** operator the Result is true if **all** the expressions are true. The Result is false if one or more expressions are false.

Logical Imp

Result = Expression1 **Imp** Expression2

The truth table for logical **Imp** is shown in Table 9.8. Table 9.9 shows the effect of the result when the **Null** value is present.

Table 9.8 TWO input Imp truth table.

Expression1	Expression2	Result
False	False	True
False	True	True
True	False	False
True	True	True

Table 9.9 When Null is included in a Logical Imp expression.

Expression1	Expression2	Result
Null	Null	Null
Null	False	Null
Null	True	True
False	Null	True
True	Null	Null

Logical Not

Result = **Not** Expression

The truth table for logical Not is shown in Table 9.10. Table 9.11 shows the effect of the result when the **Null** value is present.

Table 9.10 NOT Truth table.

Expression	Result
False	True
True	False

Table 9.11 When Null is included in a Logical Not expression.

Expression	Result
Null	Null

NOTE: The Result is **Not** the expression. For the **Not** operator if the expression is false then the Result is true and if the expression is true the Result is false.

Logical Xor

Result = Expression1 **Xor** Expression2

The truth table for logical Xor is shown in Table 9.12.

Table 9.12 A TWO input Xor truth table.

Expression1	Expression2	Result
False	False	False
False	True	True
True	False	True
True	True	False

NOTE: For the **Xor** operator the Result is True if the expressions are different.

NOTE:

If either expression is a Null then the result is a Null.

If neither expression is a null then the result is determined according to Table 9.11.

Logical Eqv

Result = Expression1 **Eqv** Expression2

The truth table for logical Eqv is shown in Table 9.13.

Table 9.13 A TWO input Eqv truth table.

Expression1	Expression2	Result
False	False	True
False	True	False
True	False	False
True	True	True

NOTE: For the **Eqv** operator the Result is true when the expressions are the same, i.e., both true or both false.

NOTE:

If either expression is a Null then the result is a Null.

When neither expression is a Null the result is determined according to Table 9.13.

Demonstration of logical operators

The form click event procedure shown in Figure 9.1 is used to show the results from logical operations. Logical operators used in this program are taken out of context. However, the program represents a useful teaching aid and similar programs will be used to test your understanding in revision questions later in the chapter.

Figure 9.1 Demonstrating logical operators.

```
Private Sub Form_Click()
    Print False And False
    Print False And True
    Print True And False
    Print True And True
    Print
    Print False Or False
    Print False Or True
    Print True Or False
    Print True Or True
    Print
    Print Not (False Or False)
    Print Not (False Or True)
    Print Not (True And False)
    Print Not (True And True)
End Sub
```

Program trace

Statement	Description
Print False And False	The Print statement prints on the form, the result of '*Anding*' together False and False. Therefore it prints False.
Print False And True	The Print statement prints the result of '*Anding*' together False and True. Therefore it prints False.
Print True And False	The Print statement prints the result of '*Anding*' together True and False. Therefore it prints False.
Print True And True	The Print statement prints the result of '*Anding*' together True and True. Therefore it prints True.
Print	This prints an empty line.
Print False Or False	The Print statement prints the result of '*Or'ing*' together False and False. Therefore it prints False.
This program continues until the last statement which is described below:	
Print Not (True And True)	True And True is True. This value of True is then '*Not'ed*' to give false. Consequently, the Print statement prints False on the form.

The output for this program is shown in Figure 9.2.

QUESTION 9.3 (REVISION)

What is the output from the procedure shown in Figure 9.3?

Figure 9.2 Output from the *'logical operator'* program.

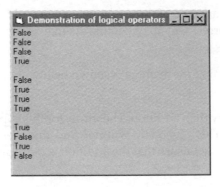

Figure 9.3 Form click event procedure.

```
Private Sub Form_Click()
    Print False Xor False
    Print False Imp True
    Print True Xor False
    Print True Imp True
    Print True Eqv True
    Print False Eqv False
    Print Not (False And False)
    Print Not (False Xor True)
    Print Not (True Imp False)
    Print Not (True And True)
    Print Not (True Eqv True)
    Print Not (True And False)
End Sub
```

Operator precedence

Logical operators

Consider the following logical operation

NOT TRUE AND FALSE

If the AND is performed first the result is as follows:

NOT TRUE AND FALSE = NOT FALSE = TRUE

However, if the NOT is performed first the result is as follows:

NOT TRUE AND FALSE = FALSE AND FALSE = FALSE

The results obtained differed. This must not be allowed to happen and a computer overcomes the problem by giving different priorities to operators and functions. The logical NOT function has a higher priority than the logical AND operator. This means that the computer will always 'calculate' the NOT **before** the AND. Consequently, the correct result to the above operation is:

NOT TRUE AND FALSE = FALSE AND FALSE = FALSE

All operators in the Visual Basic language have a priority.

117

Arithmetic operators

If you wished to obtain the average of three numbers you would add all three and divide by three. In Visual Basic the **correct** way to obtain the average is shown below:

Average = (x + y + z) / 3

The **incorrect** way for obtaining the average is shown below:

Average:= x + y +z / 3

Division has a higher priority than addition. Therefore, for this expression the division will be done **before** the addition. This obviously will not find the average. Whereas, for the first expression brackets are used to ensure that the addition is performed first. **Brackets have the highest priority.**

Operator categories

There are three main categories of operators:

1. Arithmetic operators (e.g. +, -, * and \)
2. Comparison operators (e.g. >, <> and >=)
3. Logical operators (e.g. And, Or and Xor)

When expressions contain operators from more than one category, arithmetic operators are evaluated first, comparison operators are evaluated next, and logical operators are evaluated last.

Comparison operators all have equal precedence and are evaluated in the left to right order in which they appear.

Arithmetic operators are evaluated in the order of precedence as shown in Table 9.14.

Logical operators are evaluated in the order of precedence as shown in Table 9.15.

Multiplication and division have the same priority and when they occur together in an expression, each operation is evaluated as it occurs from left to right. Likewise, when addition and subtraction occur together in an expression, each operation is evaluated in order of appearance from left to right.

NOTE: The string concatenation operator (&) is not an arithmetic operator, but in precedence it does fall after all arithmetic operators and before all comparison operators. Similarly, the Like operator, while equal in precedence to all comparison operators, is actually a pattern-matching operator. The Is operator is an object reference comparison operator. It does not compare objects or their values; it checks only to determine if two object references refer to the same object.

NOTE: The highest priority of all is the bracket. You are strongly advised to make frequent use of brackets to ensure the correct 'calculation' of logical, arithmetic and relational operations. Careful use of brackets will overcome all difficulties associated with priorities. *Indeed armed with the bracket you may never need to learn the order of priorities!*

Table 9.14 Precedence of arithmetic operators.

Operator	Priority number
Exponentiation (^)	1
Negation (-)	2
Multiplication and division (*,/)	3
Integer division (\)	4
Modulo arithmetic (Mod)	5
Addition and subtraction (+,-)	6

Table 9.15 Precedence of logical operators.

Operator	Priority number
Not	1
And	2
Or	3
Xor	4
Eqv	5
Imp	6

QUESTION 9.4 (REVISION)

What is the output from the program shown in Figure 9.4?

Figure 9.4 Program referred to in Question 9.4.

```
Private Sub Form_Click()
Dim A As Integer
Dim B As Integer
Dim C As Integer
Dim D As Integer
  A = 1
  B = 2
  C = 3
  D = 2
  Print A <> B And C = D
  Print A = B Or B = C
  Print B = C Xor D <> A
  Print A >= C Or D >= B
  Print A <= B And C <> D
  Print A <> B And B <> C
  Print B = C Xor D <> A
  Print A < C Or D > B
  Print Not (A < C) And Not (D > B)
  Print Not (A < C Or D > B)
End Sub
```

119

10 Selection

At the end of a calendar month the customers of a bank have their accounts inspected by a computer program. If an account is overdrawn then the program issues instructions to send a letter to the customer, asking them to bring their account into credit. However, if their account is in credit the program issues instructions to send a letter that asks the customer whether they would like a loan.

Depending on the balance of a customer's account the program will execute one of two sets of instructions. Either instructions to issue a 'warning letter', that is, you are overdrawn and do something about it or instructions to issue a 'friendly letter' to drum up business for the bank, that is, as a valued customer of the bank we would like to offer you a loan facility. The program will **select** which set of instructions to execute based upon a conditional test (i.e., if the balance is greater than or equal to zero, the customer is sent a friendly letter **else** the customer is sent a warning letter). Consequently, the program will choose one of two routes through the code, i.e., choose between two different actions.

Selection is the program construct that allows a program to choose between different actions. It allows for alternative paths to be taken through a program.

The selection constructs used in Visual Basic are:

- If..Then
- If..Then..Else
- If..Then..ElseIf..Else
- Select Case

Figure 10.1 shows the control flow for the IF..THEN selection construct and Figure 10.2 shows the control flow for the IF..THEN..ELSE selection construct.

For the IF…THEN, if the test is **True** then the flow of control follows the arrows to perform the actions represented by the rectangle. However, if the test is **False** the flow of control follows the other route represented by the other arrows and does not execute the actions represented by the rectangle.

Figure 10.1 Flow chart for the *If .. Then* Selection Construct.

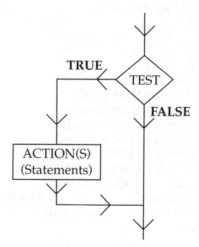

Figure 10.2 Flow chart for the *If..Then..Else* Selection Construct.
One of two routes is followed depending upon the outcome of the test.

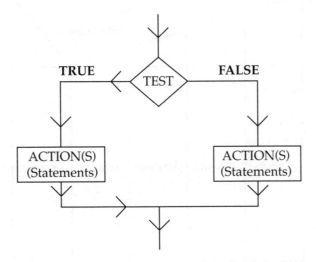

It has been previously stated that flow charts should never be used to express program design, but Figures 10.1 and 10.2 should remain with you as a 'mental picture' of the flow of control through selection constructs. Better methods, for use in program design, are N-S Charts and Structured English. Figures 10.3, 10.4 and 10.5 show the N-S chart representation for three selection constructs.

For the *If..Then* and the *If..Then..Else* constructs the state of their condition can be true or false. Figures 10.6 and 10.7 show the possible routes through the designs (and hence programs) represented by these constructs.

Figure 10.3 N-S Chart for the *If..Then* Construct.

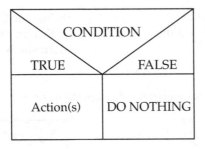

Figure 10.4 N-S Chart for the *If..Then..Else* Construct.

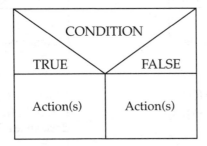

Figure 10.5 N-S Chart for the *Select Case* Construct.

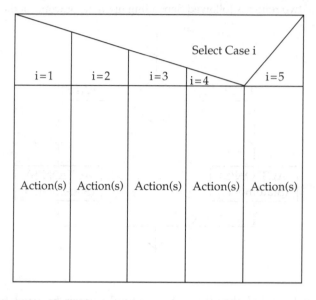

Figure 10.6 Possible routes through the *If..Then* construct.

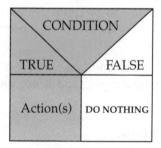

When the CONDITION
is TRUE the route is via the
dark shaded area

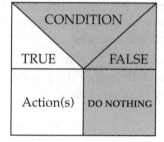

When the CONDITION
is FALSE the route is via the
dark shaded area

Figure 10.7 Possible routes through the *If..Then ..Else* construct.

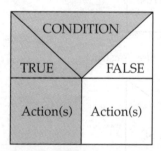

When the CONDITION
is TRUE the route is via the
dark shaded area

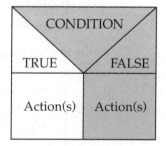

When the CONDITION
is FALSE the route is via the
dark shaded area

For the *Select Case* construct the number of possible routes can be greater than two and the route (and hence the actions executed) depend upon the value of the selector *i*. Possible routes are illustrated in Figure 10.8, again the dark shaded areas represent the route taken.

Figure 10.8 Examples of possible routes through the *Select Case* construct.

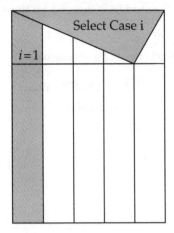 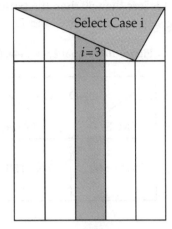

Route taken when *i*=1   Route taken when *i*=3

Format of the If..Then construct

Figure 10.9 shows the outline of an N-S Chart representing the *If..Then* construct and its relationship to a Visual Basic selection construct.

If the outcome of the condition is true then the actions represented by the shaded area are executed. For the VB construct if the outcome of the condition is true then the VB statements (represented by the shaded area) **between** the reserved words *If* and *End If* are executed. If the condition is false then the statements (represented by the shaded area) are **not** executed.

Example program using the If..Then construct

SPECIFICATION 10.1

Write a program that reads two numbers from the keyboard and multiplies them together (i.e., finds the product). If the product is less than 50 then the program reads another number from the keyboard and adds this to the product. However, if the product is greater than or equal to 50 then another number is not read from the keyboard (i.e., DO NOTHING).

The last line of the program displays the answer.

The answer may be the product of the first two numbers entered or the product with the addition of a third number.

The design for Specification 10.1 is shown in Figure 10.10.

Possible paths through this design

There are two possible paths through this program.

If the product is less than 50 then the path through the design is defined by the execution of the following steps: 1, 2, 3, 4, 5, 6, and 7.

Figure 10.9 Visual Basic Selection Construct (The *If..Then* construct).

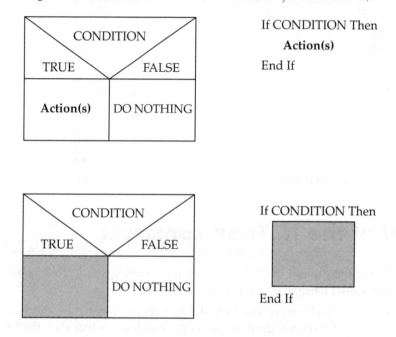

Figure 10.10 A design involving selection that implements Specification 10.1.

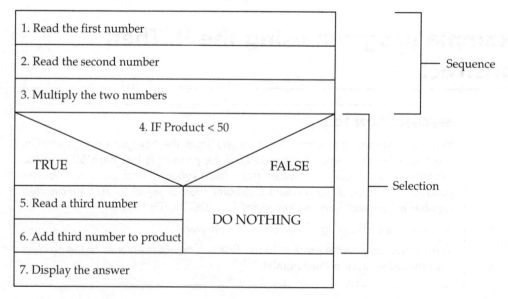

However, if the product is greater than or equal to 50 then the following steps are followed 1, 2, 3, 4, and 7, i.e., steps 5 and 6 are *not* executed.

In other words steps 5 and 6 *are* executed when the result of step 4 (the condition *If Product < 50*) is TRUE. When the condition of step 4 is FALSE then steps 5 and 6 are *not* executed.

The design of Figure 10.10 is represented in Figure 10.11 by Structured English.

Figure 10.11 Structured English design.

1. Read the first number
2. Read the second number
3. Multiply the two numbers
4. If Product < 50 Then
     5. Read a third number
     6. Add third number to the product
   End If
7. Display the Answer
END

The flow of control represented by the Structured English design, shown in Figure 10.11, is obviously the same as that for the Nassi-Schneiderman design shown in Figure 10.10. When the outcome of step 4 (IF Product < 50) is true then steps 5 and 6 are executed. The selection construct is represented by the words *If*, *Then* and *End If*. Whenever the outcome of the condition is true, then the steps embraced by the words *Then* and *End If* are executed and for the design shown in Figure 10.11 these are steps 5 and 6. The final *END* defines the end of the design and has nothing to do with the selection construct. *Notice how the steps within the selection construct are indented, this improves the visual appeal of the design.*

The design of Figure 10.10 will be coded and as in previous examples the following steps will be followed (step 1, the design, is already completed)

2. Produce a data table.
3. Derive a simple test plan.
4. Convert the design to code and run.
5. Test the run-time against the test plan.

Step 2: produce a data table

Identifier	Type	Description
FirstNumber	INTEGER	Stores the number entered at the keyboard
SecondNumber	INTEGER	Stores the number entered at the keyboard
ThirdNumber	INTEGER	Stores the number entered at the keyboard
Answer	INTEGER	Stores the answer and has its contents sent to the VDU. The answer stored in this variable may be the product or the product plus the third number. It all depends upon the path selected by the program and this selection depends upon the value of the product derived from the first two numbers.

Step 3: derive a test plan

The test plan must test the outcome of all the possible execution paths through the program. Consequently, the input numbers supplied must be chosen so that the product of the first two numbers is less than 50, for one test, and more than 50 (or equal to 50) for the second test.

Test 1

Supplied Input

User friendly message	Input data (user response)
Enter the first number	8
Enter the second number	9

Expected Output

User friendly message	Output data
The answer is	72

Test 2

Supplied Input

User friendly message	Input data (user response)
Enter the first number	8
Enter the second number	2
Enter the third number	5

Expected Output

User friendly message	Output data
The answer is	21

For Test 1 the product of the first two numbers is greater than 50 so the program will **not** ask for a third number and the answer is therefore the product of the supplied input (8 times 9). Whereas, for Test 2 the product of the first two numbers is less than 50, consequently, the program **does** ask for a third number. The output of Test 2 is therefore 8 times 2 plus 5, i.e., 21.

Step 4: convert the design to code and run

The code for the design is shown in Figure 10.12.

PRACTICAL ACTIVITY 10.1

Enter and run the program shown in Figure 10.12. Test it against test plans 1 and 2.

Figure 10.12 A Form_Click event procedure implementing the design of Figure 10.10.

```
Private Sub Form_Click ()

Dim FirstNumber As Integer
Dim SecondNumber As Integer
Dim ThirdNumber As Integer
Dim Answer As Integer
    FirstNumber = InputBox("Enter the first number")
    SecondNumber = InputBox("Enter the second number")
    Answer = FirstNumber * SecondNumber
    If Answer < 50 Then
        ThirdNumber = InputBox("Enter the third number")
        Answer = Answer + ThirdNumber
    End If
    MsgBox "The answer is "& Answer

End Sub
```

Routes through the program

There are two possible routes through the program of Figure 10.12. When run against test plan 1, the route through the program is represented by Figure 10.13. The statements that execute are highlighted in bold.

When run against test plan 2, the route through the program is represented by Figure 10.14, again the statements that execute are highlighted in bold.

Figure 10.13 One possible route through the 'selection' program when run against test plan 1.
The numbers input to the program are 8 and 9 and their product is 72.
The *If* constructs conditional test is therefore false, consequently,
the statements inside this construct are not executed, i.e., they are 'skipped over'.

```
Private Sub Form_Click ()

Dim FirstNumber As Integer
Dim SecondNumber As Integer
Dim ThirdNumber As Integer
Dim Answer As Integer

    FirstNumber = InputBox("Enter the first number")
    SecondNumber = InputBox("Enter the second number")
    Answer = FirstNumber * SecondNumber
    If Answer < 50 Then
        ThirdNumber = InputBox("Enter the third number")
        Answer = Answer + ThirdNumber
    End If
    MsgBox "The answer is "& Answer

End Sub
```

Figure 10.14 Another route through the program. This time the program is run against test plan 2. The first two numbers entered are 8 and 2; their product is 16, consequently, the conditional test of the *If* construct is true and the statements 'inside' this construct are executed. The third number entered is 5 and therefore the output from the program is 21 (16 + 5).

```
Private Sub Form_Click ()

Dim FirstNumber As Integer
Dim SecondNumber As Integer
Dim ThirdNumber As Integer
Dim Answer As Integer

    FirstNumber = InputBox("Enter the first number")
    SecondNumber = InputBox("Enter the second number")
    Answer = FirstNumber * SecondNumber
    If Answer < 50 Then
        ThirdNumber = InputBox("Enter the third number")
        Answer = Answer + ThirdNumber
    End If
    MsgBox "The answer is "& Answer

End Sub
```

Description trace when run against test plan 1

Statements	Description
FirstNumber = InputBox("Enter the first number")	The user enters the number 8 and this is stored in the variable *FirstNumber*.
SecondNumber = InputBox("Enter the second number")	The user enters the number 9 and this is stored in the variable *SecondNumber*.
Answer = FirstNumber * SecondNumber	The contents of *FirstNumber* and *SecondNumber* are multiplied together and the product (i.e., 72) is assigned to the variable *Answer* (stored in Answer).
If Answer < 50 Then	This conditional test asks if the content of the variable *Answer* is less than 50 (i.e., 72 < 50) and it is **not** so **False** is the outcome. Consequently, the statements 'inside' the *If..Then* construct are **not** executed, i.e., they are 'skipped over'.
MsgBox "The answer is "& Answer	The string *The answer is* and a copy of the content of the variable Answer are displayed in a message box. The ampersand sign (&) is always used to 'join together' strings with variables in this way.

Description trace when run against test plan 2

Statements	Description
FirstNumber = InputBox("Enter the first number")	The user enters the number 8 and this is stored in the variable *FirstNumber*.
SecondNumber = InputBox("Enter the second number")	The user enters the number 2 and this is stored in the variable *SecondNumber*.

Description trace when run against test plan 2 (cont.)

Statements	Description
Answer = FirstNumber * SecondNumber	The contents of *FirstNumber* and *SecondNumber* are multiplied together and the product (i.e., 16) is assigned to the variable *Answer*.
If Answer < 50 Then	The conditional test asks if the content of the variable *Answer* is less than 50 (i.e., 16 < 50) and it **is** so **True** is the outcome. Consequently, the statements 'inside' the *If.. Then* construct **are** executed.
ThirdNumber = InputBox("Enter the third number")	The user enters the number 5 which is assigned to the variable *ThirdNumber*.
Answer = Answer + ThirdNumber	The contents of the variable *Answer* and the variable *ThirdNumber* are added together; the result (16 + 5) is assigned to the variable *Answer*.
MsgBox "The answer is "& Answer	The string *The answer is* and a copy of the content of the variable *Answer* are displayed in a message box. Again the ampersand is used to join together the string and variable.

Another example of an If..Then construct

> **SPECIFICATION 10.2**
>
> *Write a program that asks the users to enter a positive number and have the program report the entry of a negative number. Attach the program to a form click event.*

Figure 10.15 illustrates the program that will implement this specification.

> **NOTE:** Figure 10.15 adopts the block structure for the *If.. Then* construct, which is good programming practice. Figure 10.16 illustrates another way to implement the program shown in Figure 10.15. I strongly recommend that you adopt the block structure approach to your code layout. It may, as in this case, result in more typing but it is a style that emphasises the language constructs used in the code, consequently, it is easier to read and debug.

Figure 10.15 A form click event procedure that implements Specification 10.2.

```
Private Sub Form_Click ()

Dim x As Integer

    x = InputBox("Please enter a positive number")
    If x < 0 Then
        MsgBox ("That was a negative number – please enter a positive number")
    End If

End Sub
```

Figure 10.16 An example of **poor** programming practice.

```
Private Sub Form_Click ()
Dim x As Integer

    x = InputBox("Please enter a positive number")
    If x < 0 Then MsgBox ("That was a negative number – please enter a positive number")

End Sub
```

Format of the If..Then..Else construct

Figure 10.17 shows the outline of an N-S Chart representing the *If..Then..Else* construct and its relationship to the Visual Basic selection construct.

For the N-S chart if the outcome of the condition is **True** then the actions represented by the light shaded area are executed. For the VB construct if the outcome of the condition is **True** then the VB statements (represented by the light shaded area) **after** the reserved word *Then* and **before** the reserved word *Else* are executed.

Figure 10.17 Visual Basic selection construct (The *If..Then..Else* construct).

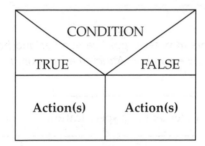

```
If CONDITION Then
        Action(s)A
Else
        Action(s)B
End If
```

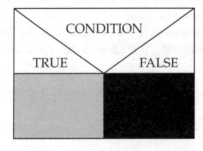

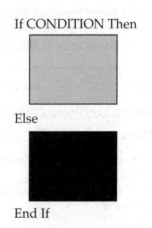

```
If CONDITION Then
```

Else

End If

For the N-S chart if the outcome of the condition is **False** then the actions represented by the dark shaded area are executed. For the VB construct if the outcome of the condition is **False** then the VB statements (represented by the dark shaded area) **after** the reserved word *Else* and **before** the reserved words *End If* are executed.

Example use of an If..Then..Else construct

SPECIFICATION 10.3

Write a program that asks users to enter their age. If they are old enough to vote the program reports back their age and asks them to collect their polling card, however, if they are not old enough to vote the program again reports back their age but this time tells them that they are too young to vote. Attach the program to a form click event.

Figure 10.18 illustrates the program that will implement specification 10.3.

Figure 10.18 An example use of the *If..Then..Else* construct that implements Specification 10.3.

```
Private Sub Form_Click()
Dim Age As Integer
Dim Message As String

    Age = InputBox("Please enter your age")
    If Age >= 18 Then
        Message = "collect your polling card"
    Else
        Message = "sorry you are too young to vote"
    End If
    MsgBox "You are "& Age & Message

End Sub
```

Routes through the program

Their are two possible routes through the program of Figure 10.18.

When the user enters their age as 18 or over, the route through the program is illustrated by Figure 10.19. If the user enters their age as 17 or under, the route through the program is illustrated by Figure 10.20. In both figures, the statements that execute are highlighted in bold.

Figure 10.19 The route through the program when the user enters their age as 18 or over.

```
Private Sub Form_Click()

Dim Age As Integer
Dim Message As String
```

Figure 10.19 (cont.)

Age = InputBox("Please enter your age")
If Age >= 18 Then
   Message = "collect your polling card"
Else
   Message = "sorry you are too young to vote"
End If
MsgBox "You are "& Age & Message

End Sub

Figure 10.20 The route through the program when the user enters their age as 17 or under.

Private Sub Form_Click()

Dim Age As Integer
Dim Message As String

Age = InputBox("Please enter your age")
If Age >= 18 Then
   Message = "collect your polling card"
Else
   Message = "sorry you are too young to vote"
End If
MsgBox "You are "& Age & Message

End Sub

Description trace when the user enters 18 or over

Statement	Description
Age = InputBox("Please enter your age")	The user enters 18 (or over) which is assigned to the variable *Age*.
If Age >= 18 Then	The content of *Age* is compared with 18 using the relational operator >= and **True** is the outcome. Consequently, the statement **after** the keyword *Then* and **before** the keyword *Else* is executed.
Message = "collect your polling card"	The string variable *Message* is assigned the string *collect your polling card*.
MsgBox "You are "& Age & Message	The string *You are*, the content of the integer variable *Age* and the content of the string variable *Message* are displayed in a message box.

Figure 10.21 illustrates the run-time when the user enters their age as 18.

Figure 10.21 Run-time when the user enters their age as 18.

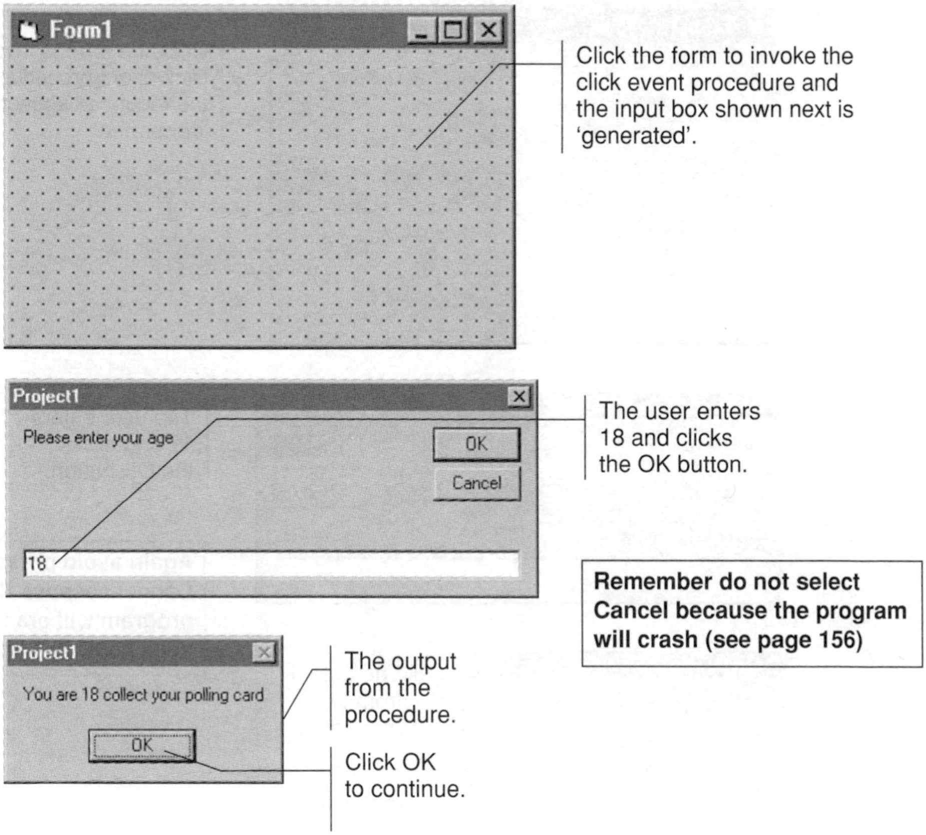
Form1
Click the form to invoke the click event procedure and the input box shown next is 'generated'.
Project1
Please enter your age
OK
Cancel
18
The user enters 18 and clicks the OK button.
Remember do not select Cancel because the program will crash (see page 156)
Project1
You are 18 collect your polling card
OK
The output from the procedure.
Click OK to continue.

Description trace when the user enters 17 or under

Statement	*Description*
Age = InputBox("Please enter your age")	The user enters 17 (or under) which is assigned to the variable Age.
If Age >= 18 Then	The content of *Age* is compared with 18 using the relational operator >= and **False** is the outcome. Consequently, the statement **after** the keyword *Else* and **before** the keywords *End If* is executed.
Message = "sorry you are too young to vote "	The string variable *Message* is assigned the string *'sorry you are too young to vote'*
MsgBox "You are "& Age & Message	The string *You are*, the content of the integer variable *Age* and the content of the string variable *Message* are displayed in a message box.

Figure 10.22 illustrates the run-time when the user enters their age as 17.

Figure 10.22 Run-time when the user enters their age as 17.

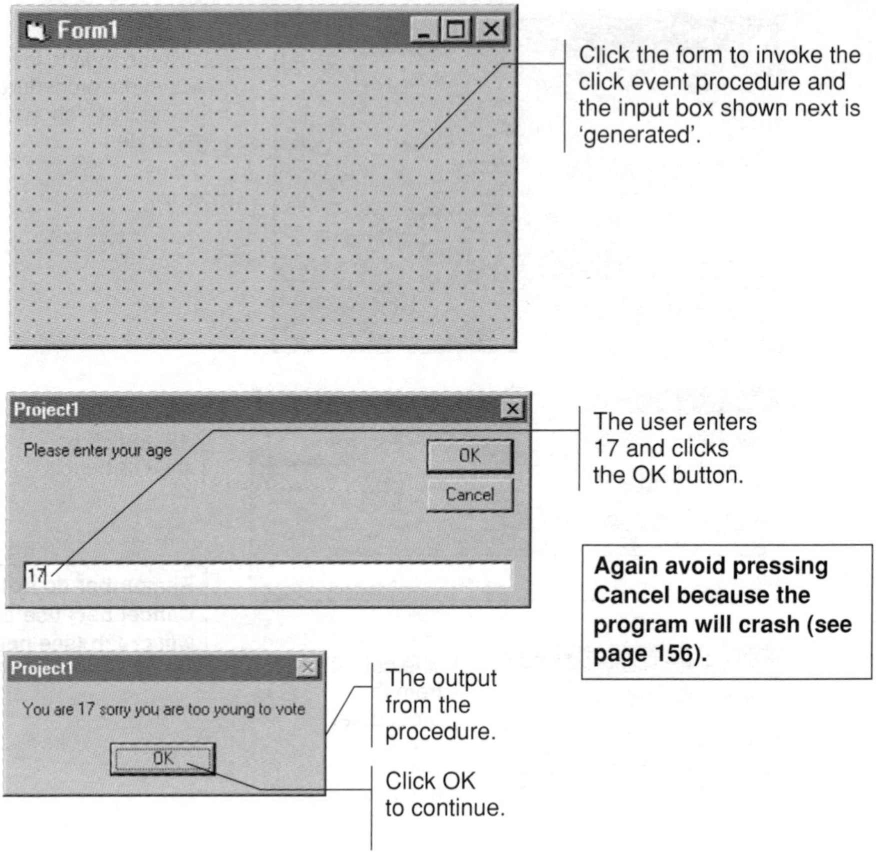
Form1
Click the form to invoke the click event procedure and the input box shown next is 'generated'.
Project1
Please enter your age
OK
Cancel
17
The user enters 17 and clicks the OK button.
Again avoid pressing Cancel because the program will crash (see page 156).
Project1
You are 17 sorry you are too young to vote
OK
The output from the procedure.
Click OK to continue.

ElseIf clause

The examples of selections just considered have offered two possible routes through a program. Using the *ElseIf* clause it is possible to arrange for more than two routes through a program. The program shown in Figure 10.23 implements Specification 10.4.

> **SPECIFICATION 10.4**
>
> *Amend the program that implemented specification 10.3 so that if the user enters their age as 17 they are told that they can vote next year.*

Figure 10.24 shows the route through the program if the user enters their age as 17.

Figure 10.25 shows the output from the procedure when the user enters their age as 17.

Figure 10.23 The Elself clause, implementing Specification 10.4.

```
Private Sub Form_Click()

Dim Age As Integer
Dim Message As String

    Age = InputBox("Please enter your age")
    If Age >= 18 Then
        Message = "collect your polling card"
    Elself Age = 17 Then
        Message = "you can vote next year"
    Else
        Message = "sorry you are too young to vote"
    End If
    MsgBox "You are "& Age & Message

End Sub
```

Figure 10.24 This shows the route through the program when the user enters their age as 17. Only one of the possible three routes is selected.

```
Private Sub Form_Click()
Dim Age As Integer
Dim Message As String

    Age = InputBox("Please enter your age")
    If Age >= 18 Then
        Message = "collect your polling card"
    Elself Age = 17 Then
        Message = "you can vote next year"
    Else
        Message = "sorry you are too young to vote"
    End If
    MsgBox "You are "& Age & Message

End Sub
```

Figure 10.25 The procedure output when the user enters 17.

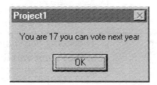

NOTE: The **Else** and **Elself** clauses are both optional. You can have as many **Elself** clauses as you want in an **If** construct, but none can appear after an **Else** clause. **If** selection constructs can be nested; that is, contained within one another to achieve multiple paths through a program.

135

Select Case construct

Another method for implementing selection is to use the Select Case construct. This can implement more than two routes through a program and is often preferred to using the *ElseIf* clause and **nested** *If.. Then.. Else* constructs. Figure 10.26 shows how Specification 10.4 can be implemented using a Select Case construct.

Figure 10.26 Implementing Specification 10.4 with a *Select Case* construct.

```
Private Sub Form_Click()
Dim Age As Integer
Dim Message As String

    Age = InputBox("Please enter your age")
    Select Case Age
    Case Is >= 18
        Message = "collect your polling card"
    Case Is = 17
        Message = "you can vote next year"
    Case Is < 17
        Message = "sorry you are too young to vote"
    End Select
    MsgBox "You are "& Age & Message

End Sub
```

Description trace when the user enters 17

Statement	Description
Age = InputBox("Please enter your age")	The user enters 17 which is assigned to the variable *Age*.
Case Is >= 18	The reserved word *Is* represents the Variable *Age* in the construct. In this case the comparison is asking whether 17 >= 18 which, of course, is **false**. Consequently, the statement *Message = 'collect your polling card'* is **not** executed.
Case Is = 17	In this case the comparison is asking whether 17 = 17 which, of course, is **true**. Consequently, the following statement is executed.
Message = "you can vote next year"	The string *you can vote next year* is assigned to the string variable *Message*.
Case Is < 17	This comparison is not made because only one path through a Select Case construct is ever executed and that has just happened.
MsgBox "You are "& Age & Message	The message box displays the output from the program.

The route through the program when the user enters their age as 17 is illustrated in Figure 10.27. Again the executed statements are shown in bold.

Figure 10.27 Route through the program when the user enters 17.

```
Private Sub Form_Click()
Dim Age As Integer
Dim Message As String
    Age = InputBox("Please enter your age")
    Select Case Age
    Case Is >= 18
        Message = "collect your polling card"
    Case Is = 17
        Message = "you can vote next year"
    Case Is < 17
        Message = "sorry you are too young to vote"
    End Select
    MsgBox "You are "& Age & Message
End Sub
```

PRACTICAL ACTIVITY 10.2

Enter and run the programs shown in Figures 10.15, 10.18, 10.24 and 10.26.

PRACTICAL ACTIVITY 10.3

Implement each of the N-S Chart designs shown in Figures 10.28, 10.29 and 10.30 as a Form_Click event procedure. Follow the recommended steps as below (*use MsgBox and InputBox as shown in the previous program listings*):

1. Produce a data table.
2. Derive a simple test plan.
3. Convert the design to code and compile.
4. Test the run-time against the test plan(s).

Figure 10.28 An N-S Chart design.

1.	DISPLAY 'Please enter a number'
2.	Obtain the number from the keyboard
3.	DISPLAY 'Please enter a number'
4.	Obtain the number from the keyboard

5. FirstNumber > SecondNumber	
TRUE	FALSE
6. Sum the two numbers	8. Find the product
7. Display the sum	9. Display the product
10. Display 'GOODBYE'	

Figure 10.29 An N-S Chart design.

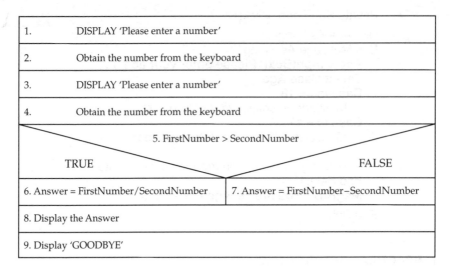

1.	DISPLAY 'Please enter a number'
2.	Obtain the number from the keyboard
3.	DISPLAY 'Please enter a number'
4.	Obtain the number from the keyboard

5. FirstNumber > SecondNumber

TRUE — FALSE

6. Answer = FirstNumber/SecondNumber	7. Answer = FirstNumber−SecondNumber

8. Display the Answer

9. Display 'GOODBYE'

Figure 10.30 An N-S Chart design.

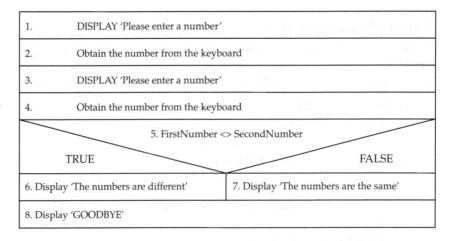

1.	DISPLAY 'Please enter a number'
2.	Obtain the number from the keyboard
3.	DISPLAY 'Please enter a number'
4.	Obtain the number from the keyboard

5. FirstNumber <> SecondNumber

TRUE — FALSE

6. Display 'The numbers are different'	7. Display 'The numbers are the same'

8. Display 'GOODBYE'

Validating user input and the tab order

All of the programs developed in this chapter are inherently 'unstable'. Consider the last program; if the user were to accidentally enter a non-numeric value (e.g., the letter q) instead of an integer then the program will exhibit a run-time error. This is because the input is assigned to the variable *Age* which is an integer type variable.

The following simple application will be used to demonstrate how to validate user input. It will also discuss tab order and the related properties TabIndex and TabStop.

SPECIFICATION 10.5

Develop an application that receives two integers from the user via text boxes. These numbers are either added, subtracted, divided or multiplied. The result is displayed in a text box. The arithmetic processing of the inputs is achieved using command buttons.

Figure 10.31 illustrates the GUI for this specification.

The properties for the GUI are set as represented by Table 10.1.

Table 10.1 The property settings for the GUI of Figure 10.31.

Control	Property	Setting
Form	Name	frmSimpleCalculator
	Caption	Simple Calculator
	Icon	c:\vb\icons\computer\Key04
Text Box	Name	txtInput1
	TabIndex	0
	Text	<empty>
Text Box	Name	txtInput2
	TabIndex	1
	Text	<empty>
Text Box	Name	txtOutput
	Locked	-1 'True
	TabStop	0 'False
Command Button	Name	cmdAddition
	Caption	+
	TabIndex	2
Command Button	Name	cmdSubtraction
	Caption	-
	TabIndex	3
Command Button	Name	cmdDivision
	Caption	/
	TabIndex	4
Command Button	Name	cmdMultiplication
	Caption	*
	TabIndex	5
Label	Name	lblInput1
	AutoSize	True
	Caption	INPUT 1
Label	Name	lblInput2
	AutoSize	True
	Caption	INPUT 2
Label	Name	lblOutput
	AutoSize	True
	Caption	OUTPUT

Figure 10.31 GUI for Specification 10.5 consists of three text boxes, three labels, four command buttons and one image box.

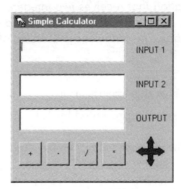

Tab order

Most controls have a TabIndex property which is a unique number that identifies each control on a form. At run-time a control TabIndex determines the order in which the control will receive the focus when the user presses the TAB key on the keyboard. Pressing the TAB key cycles through the controls on a form in a sequence defined by the TabIndex of each control. Pressing the SHIFT and TAB keys together cycles through the controls in the opposite direction.

When the 'Simple Calculator' application is run the text box used for INPUT 1 receives the focus because its TabIndex property is set to 0. When the user presses the TAB key, the focus moves to the Text Box used for INPUT 2 because its TabIndex is set at 1. Another press of the TAB key moves the focus to the command button responsible for adding the two input numbers because its TabIndex is set to 2. Figure 10.32 shows the GUI for the 'Simple

Figure 10.32 Effect of pressing the TAB key at runtime.

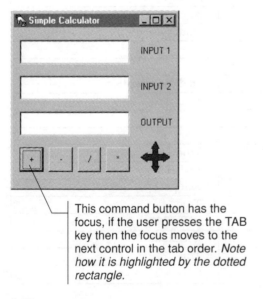

This command button has the focus, if the user presses the TAB key then the focus moves to the next control in the tab order. *Note how it is highlighted by the dotted rectangle.*

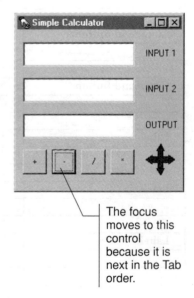

The focus moves to this control because it is next in the Tab order.

Calculator' with the add command button highlighted by a dotted rectangle (because it has the focus), it also shows the condition of the GUI when the user presses the TAB key again.

TabStop Property

This property enables you to add or remove a control from the tab order on a form. For example, there is no requirement for the calculator output text box to receive the focus. Consequently, it is removed from the tab order by setting its TabStop property to False. This property is True by default designating the control as a tab stop (i.e., by default it is part of the tab order).

When the TabStop is set to false the object is bypassed when the user is tabbing, although the object still holds its place in the actual tab order, as determined by the TabIndex property.

For the 'Simple Calculator' application the TabIndex property for two of the text boxes and the four command buttons were set at 0 through to 5 (refer to Table 10.1) and the TabStop property for the output text box was set to false, thus removing it from the tab order.

By default the TabIndex property for a control is set to a number that reflects the order in which it was drawn on to the form. If an empty form has three command buttons drawn, the TabIndex property for the first drawn will be 0 and for the third drawn it will be 2. If you carefully design the GUI then the tab order can be set to suit the application, however, if the controls are drawn in the wrong sequence it is easy to reset the TabIndex property to suit the application.

PRACTICAL ACTIVITY 10.4

Develop and run the GUI as represented by Figure 10.32 and Table 10.1. Experiment with the GUI to enable you to answer the following questions.

1. Immediately after launching the application which control has the focus?
2. Which control has the focus after the user presses the TAB key twice?
3. After one more TAB key press which control has the focus?
4. If the multiplication command button has the focus, which control will receive the focus after one TAB key press?

Validating user input

Both input text boxes are used for inputting whole numbers; however, as previously mentioned, the user could enter a non-numeric character which will cause the application to crash. User input to a text box can be validated by attaching code to its KeyPress event, which will only allow numeric characters entry (i.e., 0 through to 9), any accidental entry of non-numeric characters will be ignored and the user will be informed of their mistake by a beep.

KeyPress event

When a user presses a key on the keyboard (i.e., down and release) the KeyPress event is invoked. The event procedure, when invoked, is supplied with an integer parameter that stores the ANSI code for the key pressed. Consequently, if the user pressed capital A the KeyPress event is invoked and the ANSI value for capital A (i.e., 65, it is 66 for capital B) is passed to the event procedure. This relationship between the event, the event procedure and parameter is represented by Figure 10.33.

Figure 10.33 The KeyPress event procedure for the input text box (txtInput1).
The dotted arrow represents the event (key press) that invokes the KeyPress event procedure.
The circle and arrow (data couple) represents the ANSI value, for the key that was pressed, being 'passed to' the event procedure.

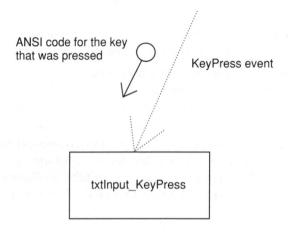

The heading to the KeyPress event procedure is slightly different to the examples used in previous chapters. It is still created from the name of the object and event but it has the addition of a parameter embraced by brackets. The heading for the KeyPress event procedure is illustrated and labelled in Figure 10.34.

The event procedure for validating the text entry to the txtInput1 text box is illustrated in Figure 10.36. The operation of this procedure is described by the two description traces that follow: one trace describes the operation of the procedure when the user enters 7 (a numeric character) and the other when the user enters A (a non-numeric character). However, before the description trace and procedure are considered the operation of system functions will be discussed because a system function is used in the event procedure (shown in Figure 10.36) about to be described.

Figure 10.34 The heading for the KeyPress event procedure.

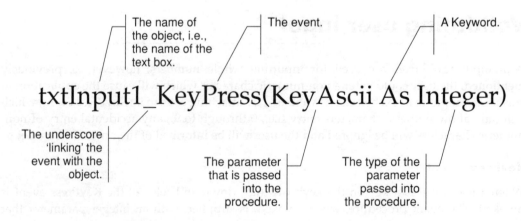

Functions

Figure 10.35 is a graphical representation of a Visual Basic function. The function receives an input and produces an appropriate output. Consideration has to be given to the data type for both input and output data. The input data type to a function could be integer with the output data type Boolean or the input data type could be integer with the output data type single.

Figure 10.35 A Visual Basic function.

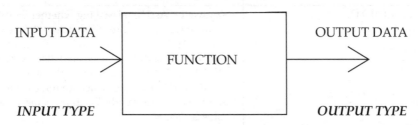

Within Visual Basic, standard and programmer defined functions can be used. Only standard functions are discussed here.

Consider a function to find the ANSI code for a character, i.e., *Asc*.

x = Asc(character)

The input to this function is the variable *character* and the output from the function is assigned to the variable x. A functions input is usually referred to as the **argument**. For this assignment statement to work the type of the argument and the type of the variable x have to be correctly chosen. In this example the argument has to be a string variable and the variable x must be chosen so that it can store the number returned by the function. Therefore x can be an integer.

In summary, the Asc function returns the character code (number) corresponding to the **first** letter in a string. The string argument is any valid string expression. Examples of assignment statements using the Asc function are listed below:

x = Asc("A")   ' Returns 65.

x = Asc("a")   ' Returns 97.

x = Asc("Apple") ' Returns 65.

Functions can also be used in conditional tests, for example, the following conditional test will produce TRUE.

Asc ("A") <= 65 '*Asc ("A") returns 65 and 65 equals 65, therefore, true.*

Figure 10.36 The KeyPress event procedure.

```
Private Sub txtInput1_KeyPress(KeyAscii As Integer)
If KeyAscii < Asc("0") Or KeyAscii > Asc("9") Then
        KeyAscii = 0
        Beep
    End If
End Sub
```

143

Description trace when the user enters the character 7

Statement	Description
Private Sub txtInput1_KeyPress(KeyAscii As Integer)	When the user presses the 7 key the KeyPress event procedure is invoked. The KeyPress procedure is supplied with the number 55 via the KeyAscii parameter (55 is the ANSI code for the numeric character 7).
If KeyAscii < Asc("0") Or KeyAscii > Asc("9") Then	KeyAscii < Asc("0") is asking whether 55 < 48 because KeyAscii stores 55 and Asc("0") returns 48. KeyAscii > Asc("9") is asking whether 55 > 57. Both of the conditional tests are **False**. Now False *Or* False is **False**, consequently, the statements 'inside' the *If..Then* construct are **not** executed and the procedure ends. *The entry of the numeric value is allowed.*

Description trace when the user enters the character A

Statement	Description
txtInput1_KeyPress(KeyAscii As Integer)	When the user accidentally presses the letter *A* the KeyPress event procedure is invoked. The KeyPress procedure is supplied with the number 65 via the KeyAscii parameter (65 is ANSI code for the character A).
If KeyAscii < Asc("0") Or KeyAscii > Asc("9") Then	KeyAscii < Asc("0") is 65 < 48 which produces False. KeyAscii > Asc("9") is 65 > 57 which is **true**. **False** *Or* **True** is **True**, consequently, the statements 'inside' the *If..Then* construct **are** executed.
KeyAscii = 0	This clears the parameter KeyAscii and therefore the keypress is ignored by the application, i.e., it is not allowed entry to the text box.
Beep	The user is informed that they have entered a non-numeric character by a Beep statement, which emits a sound through the PC speaker; then the procedure ends.

The code for the other input text box is shown in Figure 10.37.

Figure 10.37 The KeyPress event procedure for the second input text box.

```
Private Sub txtInput2_KeyPress(KeyAscii As Integer)
    If KeyAscii < Asc("0") Or KeyAscii > Asc("9") Then
        KeyAscii = 0
        Beep
    End If
End Sub
```

Code attached to the addition command button

The characters entered in the input text boxes are strings and before they can be manipulated by arithmetic operators they must be converted into numeric types. The *CInt* function is used twice to convert the string entered through the text box to an integer. Before the result of the arithmetic addition can be assigned to the Text property of the output text box it is converted to a string by the CStr function. Figure 10.38 shows the listing for the addition command button.

Figure 10.38 The click event procedure for the addition command button.

```
Private Sub cmdAddition_Click()
    txtOutput.Text = CStr(CInt(txtInput1.Text) + CInt(txtInput2.Text))
End Sub
```

NOTE: When writing code the type of variables and properties should always be considered. It is possible to allow Visual Basic to 'look after' the conversions that are required when manipulating variables and properties. However, this is not good programming practice and programmers that do not explicitly code for conversions between types risk the imposition of hard-to-find bugs (particularly if they continually use the variant data type).

Conversion functions can be used to document program code to show that the result of some operation should be expressed as a particular data type rather than the default data type. For example, use CInt to force integer arithmetic in cases where currency, single-precision, or double-precision arithmetic would normally occur.

The program listings for the rest of the command buttons are shown in Figure 10.39. The code for the division command button includes an *If..Then* construct that is used to avoid dividing by zero.

Figure 10.39 Code for the remaining three command buttons.

```
Private Sub cmdDivision_Click()
    If CInt(txtInput2.Text) = 0 Then
        MsgBox "You cannot divide by zero"
    Else
        txtOutput.Text = CStr(CInt(txtInput1.Text) / CInt(txtInput2.Text))
    End If
End Sub

Private Sub cmdMultiplication_Click()
    txtOutput.Text = CStr(CInt(txtInput1.Text) * CInt(txtInput2.Text))
End Sub

Private Sub cmdSubtraction_Click()
    txtOutput.Text = CStr(CInt(txtInput1.Text) – CInt(txtInput2.Text))
End Sub
```

When the user tabs to an input text box its previously entered text must be cleared; also the result of the previously calculated operation must be removed from the output text box. This can be achieved by the text boxes' GotFocus event. The code for the GotFocus event procedure for both input text boxes is shown in Figure 10.40.

Figure 10.40 Clearing the input and output text box.

```
Private Sub txtInput1_GotFocus()
    txtInput1.Text = ""
    txtOutput.Text = ""
End Sub

Private Sub txtInput2_GotFocus()
    txtInput2.Text = ""
    txtOutput.Text = ""
End Sub
```

NOTE: A GotFocus event is automatically generated whenever an object receives the focus.

PRACTICAL ACTIVITY 10.5

Finish the Simple Calculator application by attaching the code to the GUI developed during Practical activity 10.4. This will involve writing four command click event procedures, two GotFocus event procedures and two KeyPress event procedures.

Experiment with the application by commenting out the two GotFocus event procedures. Run a sequence of calculations and observe the difference when the GotFocus event procedures are not present.

To comment out the GotFocus event procedure merely involves entering the ' character on every line of the procedure. This is illustrated in Figure 10.41.

Figure 10.41 How to comment out a procedure. When you comment out the procedure its text will change colour usually to green (this depends upon how the colours have been set). During the execution (and compilation) of the application this procedure will be ignored.

```
Private Sub txtInput1_GotFocus()
'    txtInput1.Text = ""
'    txtOnput1.Text = ""
End Sub
```

The quotes comment out the statements.

PRACTICAL ACTIVITY 10.6

The Simple Calculator application will only arithmetically process integers. Amend the application so that it will process real numbers (i.e., numbers with fractional parts). Also add another command button that will find the square root of any number entered in the first input text box (i.e., txtInput1).

HINT 1: both KeyPress event procedures will have to be altered so that the decimal point is allowed entry.

HINT 2: use the **Sqr** function to find the square root.

HINT 3: use the **CDbl** function instead of the **CInt** function

11 Repetition (iteration)

To decide whether a customer has the appropriate funds to secure a loan a computer program asks a sequence of questions. Once these questions are answered the customer is given a rating that defines their suitability for the loan. These questions will be the same for all customers and a design for this program is represented by Figure 11.1.

Figure 11.1 Program design for calculating suitability rating.

1. Obtain customer's net monthly income.
2. Obtain customer's monthly outgoings.
3. Obtain the length of time the customer has been in their current employment.
4. Calculate the rating from the information supplied

The bank employee that uses this program, will, obviously, have more than one customer. Therefore, these program steps need to be repeated. Once step 4 has executed the program moves the flow of control back to step 1.

The program constructs in Visual Basic that allow a program segment to be repeated are listed below:

- Do..Loop Until
- Do..Loop While
- Do While..Loop
- Do Until..Loop
- For..Next
- While..Wend

Each construct will be dealt with in turn.

Do..Loop Until construct

The flow of control for this construct is illustrated by the flow chart of Figure 11.2. The actions within the loop are executed **at least once**. Further executions within the loop are dependent upon the outcome of the conditional test. If the test is false then the actions **are** repeated. However, if the conditional test is true then the actions are **not** repeated and the loop is exited.

N-S chart and VB representation

The N-S chart and program layout for the Do..Loop Until construct is illustrated in Figure 11.3.

The actions represented by the shaded area are repeated until the conditional test is true. In other words the actions are repeated when the conditional test is false.

The reserved words Do and Loop 'bracket' the actions to be performed. The VB statements perform the actions.

Figure 11.2 Do..Loop Until.

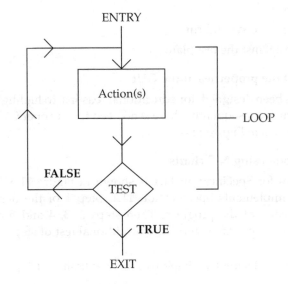

Figure 11.3 Do..Loop Until construct

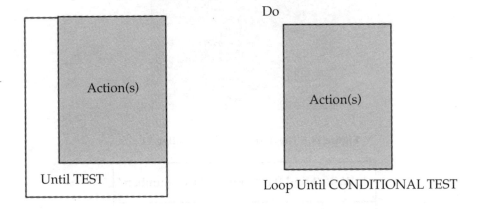

Example using the Do..Loop Until construct

SPECIFICATION 11.1

Write a command button click event procedure that upon execution states its purpose and upon completion indicates it is ending. In between its launch and completion it is to read two numbers from the keyboard, calculate and display their product. It continues to find the product of input numbers until their product is greater than 100.

This specification will be implemented as follows:

1. Build and set the properties of the GUI.
2. Design the code using N-S charts.

3. Produce a data table.

4. Derive a simple test plan.

5. Convert the design to code and run.

6. Test the run-time against the test plan.

Step 1: build and set the properties of the GUI

The specification has been designed, for educational reasons, to highlight the operation of the *Do..Loop Until* construct; consequently, there is no need for a proper GUI, it is just a command button on a form (shown in Figure 11.4).

Step 2: design the code using N-S charts

The design algorithm for Specification 11.1 is shown in Figure 11.5. The flow through the design successfully implements Specification 11.1. Step 1 of the design displays a string introducing the function of the program. Then steps 2, 3, 4 and 5 are executed (i.e., the instructions inside the loop). After step 5 the conditional test of step 6 is executed and if the

Figure 11.4 Simple GUI for Specification 11.1.

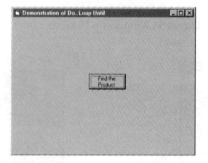

Figure 11.5 The design for Specification 11.1.

1. Write 'I find the product of two numbers'
2. Read the first number
3. Read the second number
4. Multiply both numbers
5. Display the Product
6. UNTIL Product > 100
7. Write 'Greater than 100 so I will finish'

Product (calculated in step 4) is greater than 100 (i.e., the conditional test is **True**) then step 7 is executed and a string is displayed to indicate the end of the program. However, if the conditional test is **False** then steps 2, 3, 4 and 5 are executed **again**, that is, they are repeated.

Step 3: produce a data table

Identifier	Type	Description
FirstNumber	String	Stores the number entered at the keyboard
SecondNumber	String	Stores the number entered at the keyboard
Product	INTEGER	Stores the product of FirstNumber and SecondNumber and has its contents sent to the VDU. Its value is also used in the conditional test to decide on whether the loop is repeated or not.

Step 4: derive a simple test plan

When developing a test plan for programs it is important that every conditional test is *fully* tested. For this design and program the conditional test asks whether the contents of a variable is greater than 100. Therefore, there is a need for three tests plans. These test plans must test the **boundary** around the conditional test. This means that the numbers input must produce a product that is **below**, **above** and **at the boundary** of the conditional test. The input numbers should therefore produce a product of 99, 100 and 101; which are a set of numbers that are below, above and at the boundary. The number 99 is just below the boundary of the conditional test, the number 100 is at the boundary and 101 is just above the boundary.

The three test plans used to test the boundary of the conditional test are shown below:

Test plan 1

Supplied Input

User friendly message	Input data (user response)
I find the product of two numbers	
Enter the first integer	33
Enter the second integer	3
Enter the first integer	i.e., the program repeats.

Expected output

User friendly message	Output data (user response)
The product is	99

Test plan 2

User friendly message	Input data (user response)
I find the product of two numbers	
Enter the first integer	50
Enter the second integer	2
Enter the first integer	i.e., the program repeats.

Expected output

User friendly message	Output data
The product is	100

Test plan 3

User friendly message	Input data (user response)
I find the product of two numbers	
Enter the first integer	101
Enter the second integer	1

Expected output

User friendly message	Output data
The product is	101
Greater than 100 so I will finish	i.e., the loop is exited.

Step 5: convert the design to code and compile

The program (illustrated in Figure 11.6) implements the design of Figure 11.5.

Figure 11.6 The code for the design illustrated in Figure 11.5

```
Private Sub cmdFindProduct_Click()
Dim FirstNumber As String
Dim SecondNumber As String
Dim Product As Integer
    MsgBox "I find the product of two numbers"
    Do
        FirstNumber = InputBox("Enter the first integer", "Read Number", 0)
        SecondNumber = InputBox("Enter the second integer", "Read Number", 0)
        Product = CInt(FirstNumber) * CInt(SecondNumber)
        MsgBox "The product is " & Product
    Loop Until Product > 100
    MsgBox "Greater than 100 so I will finish"
End Sub
```

PRACTICAL ACTIVITY 11.1

You complete step 6, that is, test the run-time against the test plans.

The output from the program when tested against test plan 1 is illustrated in Figure 11.7.

The output when tested against test plan 3 is almost the same as shown in Figure 11.7 until after the product is displayed. The difference is shown in Figure 11.8.

Figure 11.7 Output when tested against test plan 1.

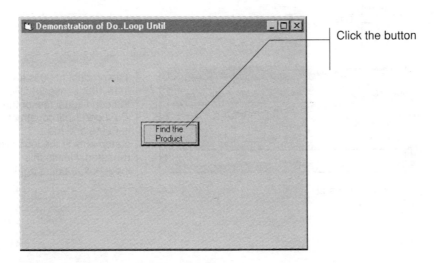

Click the button

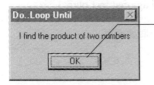

This was 'generated' by the following VB statement:
MsgBox "I find the product of two numbers"

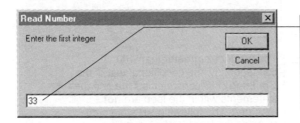

Enter 33 and click OK. This input box was 'generated' by the following VB statement:
FirstNumber = InputBox("Enter the first integer", "Read Number", 0)
33 is assigned to the variable FirstNumber.

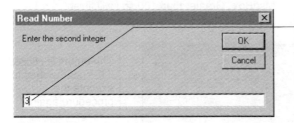

Enter 3 and click OK. This input box was 'generated' by the following VB statement:
SecondNumber = InputBox("Enter the second integer", "Read Number", 0)
3 is assigned to the variable SecondNumber.

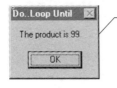

The procedure finds the product using the following VB statement:
Product = CInt(FirstNumber) * CInt(SecondNumber)
The contents of FirstNumber and SecondNumber are converted to integers by the CInt function.
The product is displayed using the following VB statement:
MsgBox "The product is" & Product

Figure 11.7 (cont.)

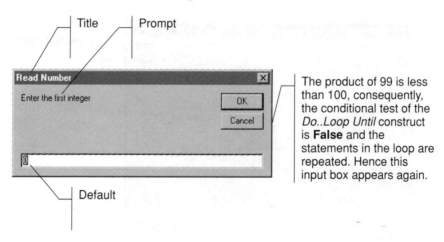

Title   Prompt

The product of 99 is less than 100, consequently, the conditional test of the *Do..Loop Until* construct is **False** and the statements in the loop are repeated. Hence this input box appears again.

Default

Figure 11.8 The output from the procedure when tested against test plan 3.

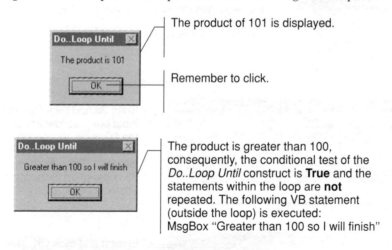

The product of 101 is displayed.

Remember to click.

The product is greater than 100, consequently, the conditional test of the *Do..Loop Until* construct is **True** and the statements within the loop are **not** repeated. The following VB statement (outside the loop) is executed: MsgBox "Greater than 100 so I will finish"

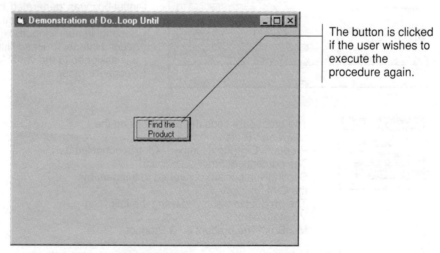

The button is clicked if the user wishes to execute the procedure again.

NOTE: The *Do..Loop Until* construct repeats its statements until its conditional test is **True**.

Trace table for program shown in Figure 11.6 (tested against test plans 1, 2 and 3)

Statement	Description
MsgBox "I find the product of two numbers"	I find the product of two numbers is displayed in a message box.
FirstNumber = InputBox("Enter the first integer", "Read Number", 0)	The user friendly message *Enter the first integer* is displayed in an input box and the number 33 is entered by the user – according to the test plan. Therefore, *FirstNumber* is assigned 33. The InputBox function has three string arguments, *Enter the first integer, Read Number* and *0*. The first arguments is the user friendly prompt the second is the title and the third is the default entry in the text box (see Figure 11.7).
SecondNumber = InputBox("Enter the second integer", "Read Number", 0)	The user friendly message *Enter the second integer* is displayed in an input box and the number 3 is entered by the user. Therefore, *SecondNumber* is assigned 3.
Product = FirstNumber * SecondNumber	*Product* is assigned 99 (i.e. 33 * 3)
MsgBox "The product is " & Product	The string and the contents of the variable Product are displayed in a message box.
Loop Until Product > 100	The variable **Product** is storing 99 therefore the test *Product > 100* is **False**, consequently, the loop **is** repeated.
FirstNumber = InputBox("Enter the first integer", "Read Number", 0)	The user friendly message is displayed in an input box and the number 50 is entered by the user.
SecondNumber = InputBox("Enter the second integer", "Read Number", 0)	The user friendly message is displayed in an input box and the number 2 is entered by the user.
Product = FirstNumber * SecondNumber	*Product* is assigned 100 (i.e., 50 * 2).
MsgBox "The product is " & Product	The string and the contents of the variable *Product* are displayed in a message box.
Loop Until Product > 100	This test is **False** therefore the loop is repeated.
FirstNumber = InputBox("Enter the first integer", "Read Number", 0)	The user friendly message is displayed in an input box and the number 101 is entered by the user.
SecondNumber = InputBox("Enter the second integer", "Read Number", 0)	The user friendly message is displayed in an input box and the number 1 is entered by the user.
Product = FirstNumber * SecondNumber	*Product* is assigned 101 (i.e., 101 * 1).
MsgBox "The product is " & Product	The string and the contents of the variable Product are displayed in a message box.
Loop Until Product > 100	This test is **True** therefore the loop is **not** repeated.
MsgBox "Greater than 100 so I will finish"	Displays the string *Greater than 100 so I will finish* in a message box

Nested structures

The procedure just developed will crash if the user clicks the cancel button on one or both of the input text boxes. This is illustrated in Figure 11.9.

Figure 11.9 Crashing the program.

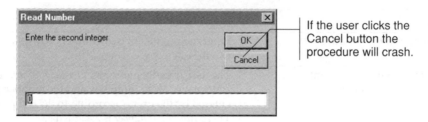

If the user clicks the Cancel button the procedure will crash.

If the user chooses OK the InputBox function returns whatever is in the text box, however, if the user chooses Cancel, the function returns a zero-length string (""). The product of the input numbers is calculated by the following VB statement:

Product = CInt(FirstNumber) * CInt(SecondNumber)

Pressing the Cancel button assigns a zero length string to the variable SecondNumber and the CInt function will not accept a zero length string. Thus the procedure will crash. A selection construct can be added to the procedure of Figure 11.5 to 'trap' the entry of a zero length string to stop the procedure crashing. The amended procedure is shown in Figure 11.10.

Figure 11.10 Amended procedure. The amendment is shown in bold.

```
Private Sub cmdFindProduct_Click()
Dim FirstNumber As String
Dim SecondNumber As String
Dim Product As Integer
    Product = 0
    MsgBox "I find the product of two numbers"
    Do
        FirstNumber = InputBox("Enter the first integer", "Read Number", 0)
        SecondNumber = InputBox("Enter the second integer", "Read Number", 0)
        If FirstNumber = "" Or SecondNumber = "" Then
            MsgBox "You cancelled at least one entry"
        Else
            Product = CInt(FirstNumber) * CInt(SecondNumber)
            MsgBox "The product is " & Product
        End If
    Loop Until Product > 100
    MsgBox "Greater than 100 so I will finish"
End Sub
```

If the user cancels the entry of the first or second number (or both) then the conditional test of the *If..Then..Else* construct is **True**, consequently, the *Then* part of the construct is executed and the procedure reports the cancelling to the user using a message box. The calculation of the product takes place in the *Else* part of the selection construct, and therefore, the CInt never 'sees' a zero length string and thus the program will not exhibit the same crash.

NOTE: The procedure shown in Figure 11.10 is an example of a nested structure. The *If..Then..Else* construct is nested inside the *Do..Loop Until* construct.

PRACTICAL ACTIVITY 11.2

Implement N-S Chart designs of Figure 11.11 and 11.12 as a Command_Click event procedure. Follow the recommended steps as below:

1. Produce a data table.
2. Derive a simple test plan.
3. Convert the design to code and run.
4. Test the run-time against the test plans.

Use MsgBox and InputBox to interact with the user for both designs.

Do..Loop While construct

The flow of control for this construct is illustrated by the flow chart of Figure 11.13. The actions within the loop are executed **at least once**. Further executions within the loop are dependent upon the outcome of the conditional test. If the test is true then the actions are repeated. However, if the conditional test is false then the actions are **not** repeated and the loop is exited.

Figure 11.11 Design for Practical activity 11.2

| 1. Read the first number |
| 2. Read a second number |
| 3. Read a third number |
| 4. Add all three numbers together |
| 5. Display the sum |

6. Loop Until Sum > 100

Figure 11.12 Design for Practical activity 11.2

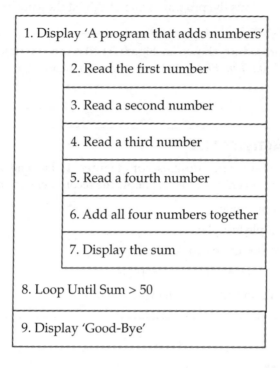

1. Display 'A program that adds numbers'
2. Read the first number
3. Read a second number
4. Read a third number
5. Read a fourth number
6. Add all four numbers together
7. Display the sum
8. Loop Until Sum > 50
9. Display 'Good-Bye'

Figure 11.13 Do..Loop While iteration.

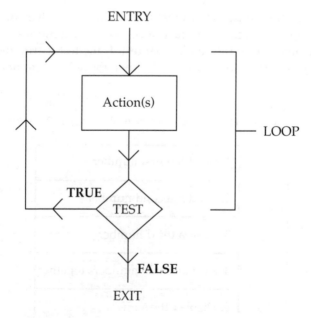

N-S Chart and VB representation

The N-S chart and program layout for the Do..While construct is illustrated in Figure 11.14.

Figure 11.14 Do..Loop While construct.

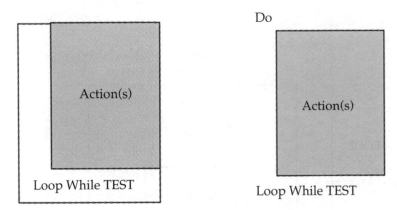

The actions represented by the shaded area are repeated while the condition test is **True**. The reserved words Do and Loop 'bracket' the actions to be repeated.

QUESTION 11.1 (REVISION)

Compare the Do..Loop Until and Do..Loop While constructs.

PRACTICAL ACTIVITY 11.3

Rewrite the event procedure shown in Figure 11.10 so that it performs in the same way except it uses the *Do..Loop While* construct **instead** of the *Do..Loop Until* construct.

Enter and run your solution.

HINT: While **Not** (*conditional test*)

Do While..Loop construct

The flow of control for this construct is illustrated by the flow chart of Figure 11.15. The actions of this loop are executed if the conditional test is **true** and are **not** executed if the conditional test is **false**. As the conditional test appears **before** the actions within the loop then it is possible that they may *never* be executed.

Upon the completion of the actions the flow of control returns to the conditional test, where an outcome of true results in the actions being repeated. However, if the outcome of the conditional test is false the loop is exited.

As the conditional test appears **before** the actions of the *Do While..Loop* the variables used within the conditional test must have valid values **before** the conditional test **as well as inside** the loop.

Figure 11.15 Do While..Loop iteration.

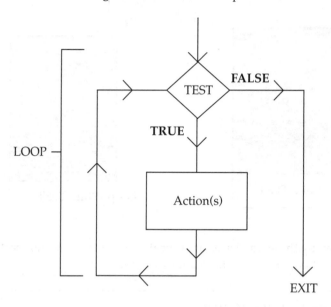

N-S Chart and VB representation

The N-S chart and program layout for the Do While..Loop construct is illustrated in Figure 11.16.

For the N-S chart, the actions represented by the shaded area are executed if the conditional test is true. When the conditional test is false the loop is exited.

For the VB construct the actions (statements) to be executed are 'bracketed' by the reserved words Do While and Loop.

Example using the Do While..Loop construct

> **SPECIFICATION 11.2**
>
> *Write a command button click event procedure that uses a Do..While loop to read in two numbers. It then divides the first number entered by the second number. However, if the second number entered is a zero, the procedure ends with a string message displaying Goodbye. Not allowing the second number to be a zero stops a division by zero run-time error!*

The specification is implemented as follows:

1. Build and set the properties of the GUI.
2. Design the code using N-S charts.
3. Produce a data table.
4. Derive a simple test plan.
5. Convert the design to code and run.
6. Test the run-time against the test plan.

Figure 11.16 The DoWhile.. Loop.

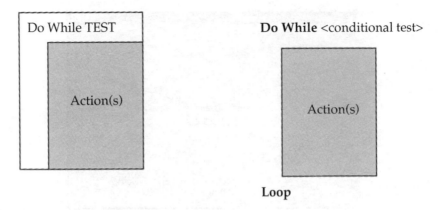

Step 1: build and set the properties of the GUI

The specification has been designed, for educational reasons, to highlight the operation of the *Do While..Loop* construct; consequently, there is no need for a proper GUI; it just is a command button on a form (shown in Figure 11.17).

Step 2: design the code using N-S charts

The N-S chart design of Figure 11.18 implements Specification 11.2; it includes a *Do While..Loop* construct, as requested by the specification.

For the design of Figure 11.18 actions 1 and 2 are executed in sequence. If the result of the conditional test is true then actions 4, 5, 6 and 7 are executed. Upon completion of action 7 the conditional test of action 3 is executed again. This is repeated until the conditional test is false. Upon false, action 8 is executed and the program ends.

Step 3: produce a data table

Identifier	Type	Description
FirstNumber	INTEGER	Stores the number entered at the keyboard. Used twice in the program *before* the loop and *within* the loop.
SecondNumber	INTEGER	Stores the number entered at the keyboard. Used three times in the program once before the loop, once within the loop and it is also used in the conditional test. If the SecondNumber is zero then the loop is not entered. This avoids the possibility of a division by zero – which would give a run-time error.
Result	INTEGER	Stores the result of the integer division of the FirstNumber by the SecondNumber and has its contents sent to the VDU.

Step 4: derive a simple test plan

There is a need for two test plans. The first test plan will check what happens when the loop is not entered. This happens when the value of the SecondNumber is zero. The second test plan will check what happens when the loop is entered. This occurs when the SecondNumber is not zero (non-zero).

Figure 11.17 GUI for Specification 11.2.

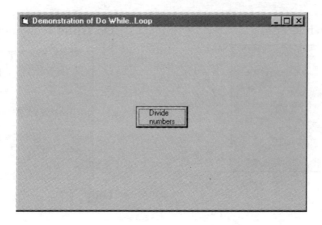

Figure 11.18 A design using a DoWhile.. loop

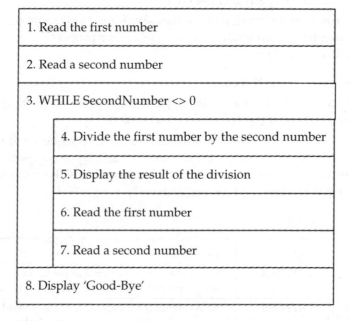

| 1. Read the first number |
| 2. Read a second number |
| 3. WHILE SecondNumber <> 0 |
| 4. Divide the first number by the second number |
| 5. Display the result of the division |
| 6. Read the first number |
| 7. Read a second number |
| 8. Display 'Good-Bye' |

Test plan 1

Supplied input

User friendly message	Input data (user response)
Enter the first number	4
Enter the second number	0

Expected output

User friendly message	Output data
Good-Bye	

Test plan 2

Supplied input

User friendly message	Input data (user response)
Enter the first number	4
Enter the second number	2
Enter the first number	19
Enter the second number	4
Enter the first number	0
Enter the second number	10
Enter the first number	98
Enter the second number	0

Expected output

User friendly message	Output data
The result of the integer division is	2
The result of the integer division is	4 (remember it is integer division)
The result of the integer division is	0
Good-Bye	

Step 5: convert the design to code and compile

Figure 11.19 illustrates the program for the design of Figure 11.18. The code is attached to a Command_Click event procedure.

Figure 11.19 Event procedure implementing the design of Figure 11.18.

```
Private Sub cmdDivide_Click()
Dim FirstNumber As Integer
Dim SecondNumber As Integer
Dim Result As Integer

    FirstNumber = InputBox("Enter the first number", "Read a number", 0)
    SecondNumber = InputBox("Enter the second number", "Read a number", 0)
    Do While SecondNumber <> 0
        Result = CInt(FirstNumber) \ CInt(SecondNumber)
        MsgBox "The result of the integer division is " & Result
        FirstNumber = InputBox("Enter the first number", "Read a number", 0)
        SecondNumber = InputBox("Enter the second number", "Read a number", 0)
    Loop
    MsgBox "GOODBYE"
End Sub
```

PRACTICAL ACTIVITY 11.4

You complete step 6, that is, test the run-time against the test plans.

Description trace when tested against test plan 1

Statement	Description
FirstNumber = InputBox("Enter the first number", "Read a number", 0)	The user friendly message *Enter the first number* is displayed on the VDU in an InputBox and the number 4 is entered by the user.
SecondNumber = InputBox("Enter the second number", "Read a number", 0)	A user friendly message is displayed on the VDU in an InputBox and the number 0 is entered by the user.
Do While SecondNumber <> 0	The outcome of the conditional test is **False** because the content of *SecondNumber* is equal to zero. Consequently, the *Do While loop* is **not** entered.
MsgBox "GOODBYE"	The string GOODBYE is sent to the VDU in a message box.

Description trace when tested against test plan 2

Statement	Description
FirstNumber = InputBox("Enter the first number", "Read a number", 0)	A user friendly message is displayed on the VDU in an InputBox and the number 4 is entered by the user.
SecondNumber = InputBox("Enter the second number", "Read a number", 0)	The user friendly message is displayed on the VDU in an InputBox and the number 2 is entered by the user.
Do While SecondNumber <> 0	The outcome of the conditional test is true because the content of *SecondNumber* does not equal zero. Consequently, Do While loop is entered.
Result = CInt(FirstNumber) \ CInt(SecondNumber)	*Result* is assigned 2 because 2 'goes into' 4 twice.
MsgBox "The result of the integer division is " & Result	The string, *The result of the integer division is,* and the content of the variable Result (i.e., 2) is displayed in a message box.
FirstNumber = InputBox("Enter the first number", "Read a number", 0)	A user friendly message is displayed in an InputBox and the number 19 is entered by the user.
SecondNumber = InputBox("Enter the second number", "Read a number", 0)	A user friendly message is displayed on the VDU in an InputBox and the number 4 is entered by the user.
Do While SecondNumber <> 0	The outcome of the conditional test is true because the content of *SecondNumber* does not equal zero. Consequently, the Do While loop is entered.
Result = CInt(FirstNumber) \ CInt(SecondNumber)	*Result* is assigned 4 because 4 'goes into' 19 four times (with a remainder of three).
MsgBox "The result of the integer division is " & Result	The string and the content of *Result* (i.e., 4) is displayed on the VDU in a message box.
FirstNumber = InputBox("Enter the first number", "Read a number", 0)	The user friendly message is displayed on the VDU in an InputBox and the number 0 is entered by the user.
SecondNumber = InputBox("Enter the second number", "Read a number", 0)	A user friendly message is displayed on the VDU in an InputBox and the number 10 is entered by the user.
Do While SecondNumber <> 0	The outcome of the conditional test is true because the content of *SecondNumber* does not equal zero. Consequently, the Do While loop is entered.

Description trace when tested against test plan 2 (cont.)

Statement	Description
Result = CInt(FirstNumber) \ CInt(SecondNumber)	*Result* is assigned 0 because 10 'goes into' 0 zero times (with a remainder of ten).
MsgBox "The result of the integer division is " & Result	The string and the content of *Result* (i.e., 0) is displayed on the VDU in a message box.
FirstNumber = InputBox("Enter the first number", "Read a number", 0)	The user friendly message is displayed on the VDU in an InputBox and the number 98 is entered by the user.
SecondNumber = InputBox("Enter the second number", "Read a number", 0)	A user friendly message is displayed in an InputBox and the number 0 is entered by the user.
Do While SecondNumber <> 0	The outcome of the conditional test is false because the content of *SecondNumber* equals zero. Consequently, the Do While loop is not entered.
MsgBox "GOODBYE"	The string GOODBYE is displayed on the VDU in a message box.

PRACTICAL ACTIVITY 11.5

If the user presses cancel then the procedure will crash. Amend the procedure so that is does not crash when the user presses the Cancel button on the InputBox.

HINT: Refer to the procedure of Figure 11.10.

QUESTION 11.2 (REVISION)

Compare the Do..Loop While construct with the Do While..Loop construct.

PRACTICAL ACTIVITY 11.6

Implement the N-S Chart design shown in Figure 11.20 as a Command_Click event procedure. Follow the recommended steps as below:

1. Produce a data table.
2. Derive a simple test plan.
3. Convert the design to code and compile.
4. Test the run-time against the test plans.

Use MsgBox and InputBox to interact with the user!

Figure 11.20 N-S chart design for Practical activity 11.6. This design represents a program that adds together two numbers and displays the sum. It will continue to add until the user enters a zero.

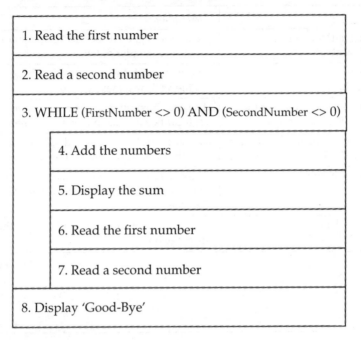

1. Read the first number
2. Read a second number
3. WHILE (FirstNumber <> 0) AND (SecondNumber <> 0)

Indented block inside the WHILE:

4. Add the numbers
5. Display the sum
6. Read the first number
7. Read a second number

8. Display 'Good-Bye'

Do Until..Loop construct

The flow of control for this construct is illustrated by the flow chart of Figure 11.21. The actions of this loop are executed if the conditional test is **False** and are **not** executed if the conditional test is **True**. As the conditional test appears **before** the actions then it is possible that the actions within the loop may *never* be executed.

Upon the completion of the actions the flow of control returns to the conditional test, where a further **False** outcome will result in the actions being repeated. However, if the outcome is **True** the loop is exited. As the conditional test appears **before** the actions of the loop the variables used within the conditional test must have valid values **before** the conditional test **as well as inside** the loop.

N-S chart and VB representation

The N-S chart and program layout for the *Do Until..Loop* construct is illustrated in Figure 11.22.

For the N-S chart the actions represented by the shaded area are executed if the conditional test is **False**. When the conditional test is **True** the loop is exited.

For the VB construct the actions (statements) to be executed are 'bracketed' by the reserved words Do Until and Loop.

Figure 11.21 The flow chart for a *Do Until..Loop*.

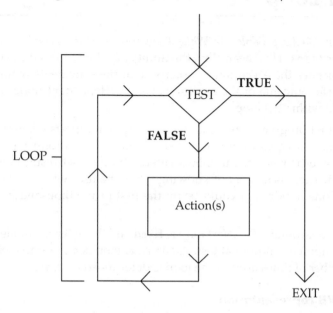

Figure 11.22 The *Do Until..Loop*.

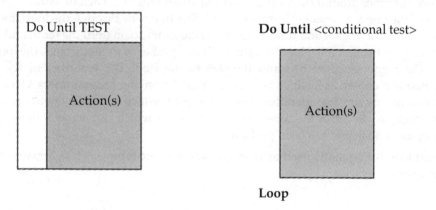

QUESTION 11.3 (REVISION)

Compare the Do Until..Loop with the Do While..Loop.

PRACTICAL ACTIVITY 11.7

Rewrite the event procedure shown in Figure 11.19 so that it performs in the same way but uses the *Do Until..Loop* construct **instead** of the *Do While..Loop* construct.

Enter and run your solution.

HINT: Use the Not function.

For..Next Loop

The *Do..Loop Until, Do..Loop While, Do While..Loop* and *Do Until..Loop* loops are examples of **non-deterministic loops**. This means that the number of times around the loop is **unknown** on entry. What dictates the execution or otherwise of the statements within the loop is the conditional test. The outcome of the conditional test is dependent upon data that is either input or processed within the loop.

For example, the first program in this chapter is a loop that repeats when the product of two numbers is less than or equal to one hundred. When will the product be greater than one hundred? The answer is when the numbers entered by the user result in a product greater than one hundred. There is no way of knowing when the user will enter numbers that take the product over one hundred, it could be on the first or the thousandth time through the loop.

The number of times around a *For..Next* loop is **fixed** and the entering and leaving of the loop is **not** dependent upon a conditional test. A *For..Next* loop is an example of a **deterministic loop**, i.e., the number of times around the loop is determined on entry.

N-S chart and VB representation

The N-S chart and program layout for the For..Next construct is illustrated in Figure 11.23.

The number of times around the loop is from 1 to 10 in steps of 1. Each time through the loop the value of the integer variable *i* is incremented. The first time through the loop the variable *i* has the value 1 and the second time it has the value 2 and so on until the tenth and last time through the loop the variable *i* has the value 10. The number of times through the loop can be fixed by the range assigned to *i* and the size of the step. The identifier of the variable incremented was chosen as *i*, which is common practice among programmers. Of course this variable can be any sensible identifier, such as, Count, which reflects a common use of the *For..Next* loop, i.e., to count the times through a loop – which can act as a measure of the number of times an action has been performed.

A *For..Next* loop is frequently used to access structured data types, such as arrays (covered in a later chapter).

Figure 11.23 The *For..Next* loop.

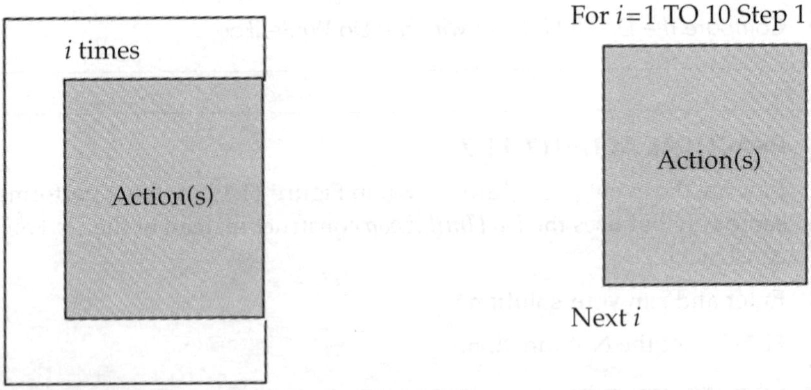

Example use of the For..Next construct

> ### SPECIFICATION 11.3
>
> *Write a Form_Click event procedure to output the ANSI character set (from A to Z) and their ordinal numbers to the form.*

The solution to this specification is shown in Figure 11.24.

Description trace of procedure in Figure 11.24

Statement	Description
Print "Number"; Tab; "Character"	This statement is outside the *For..Next* loop and is therefore only executed once. It puts the heading to two columns that are the Ordinal numbers and related ANSI characters. The Tab moves the cursor to the beginning of the next print zone (print zones begin every 14 columns).
For i = 65 To 90 Step 1	On the first pass through the loop the variable *i* is assigned the value 65.
Print i; Tab; Chr(i)	The Print statement prints the value of *i*, Tabs to the next print zone and prints the value returned by the Chr function (which is capital A).
Next i	This causes the flow of control to return into the loop again. However, this time the variable *i* has been incremented by 1 to the value of 2.
Print i; Tab; Chr(i)	The Print statement prints the value of *i*, Tabs to the next print zone and prints the value returned by the Chr function(which is capital B).
Next i	This causes the flow of control to return into the loop again. However, this time the variable *i* has been incremented by 1 to the value of 3. The loop is repeated until the value of *i* reaches 89 then the flow is as follows.
Print i; Tab; Chr(i)	The Print statement prints the value of *i*, Tabs to the next print zone and prints the value returned by the Chr function (which is capital Y).
Next i	This causes the flow of control to return into the loop again. However, this time the variable *i* has been incremented by 1 to the value of 90.
Print i; Tab; Chr(i)	The Print statement prints the value of *i*, Tabs to the next print zone and prints the value returned by the Chr function. The capital letter Z is returned by this function.
THE LOOPING ENDS	BECAUSE *i* IS AT 90 – the end of the range.

Figure 11.24 Solution to Specification 11.3

```
Private Sub Form_Click()
Dim i As Integer
    Print "Number"; Tab; "Character"
    For i = 65 To 90 Step 1
        Print i; Tab; Chr(i)
    Next i
End Sub
```

The output from this program is shown in Figure 11.25.

Figure 11.25 Output from *For..Next* loop.

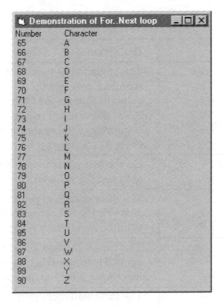

PRACTICAL ACTIVITY 11.8

Amend the last procedure so that it outputs the character set for the ordinal number range 33 to 126. Drag the form to a size that ensures the characters and their associated number do not scroll off the form. You may also need to display the numbers and characters in more than two columns

QUESTION 11.4 (DEVELOPMENT)

Use the VB online help to learn about the While ..Wend repetition construct.

12 Data arrays

All of the data types used in the book so far have been simple data types. You have been recommended to view these simple data types as different size 'boxes' as illustrated in Figure 12.1.

Figure 12.1 Simple data types.

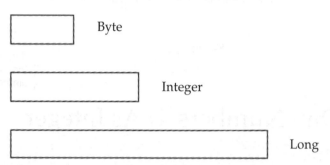

Byte

Integer

Long

Simple data types have an important role in programs but they are limited in the way they can represent data.

Data arrays provide a convenient means for storing data items of the same data type. Data stored in arrays are an example of a structured data type and the data stored in such structures are easy to access and process.

An array is an ordered collection of variables of the same type. Each member of the array is referred to as an element. Every element has the same data type and the same name with the addition of an identifying index number. An example of an array structure is shown in Figure 12.2.

The second element of the array is identified as Numbers(1) and the third element of the array as Numbers(2) and so on.

Figure 12.2 An array structure.

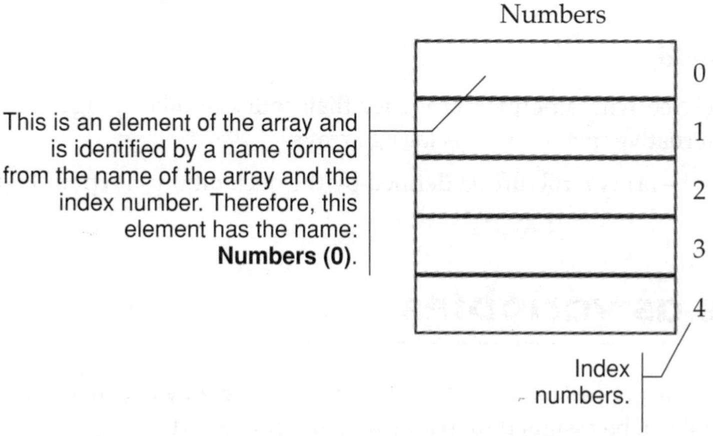

Numbers

This is an element of the array and is identified by a name formed from the name of the array and the index number. Therefore, this element has the name: **Numbers (0)**.

0

1

2

3

4

Index numbers.

Declaring arrays

The basic building blocks of an array are the thirteen 'simple' data types found in the Visual Basic language and it is possible to have an array of one of these data types (an array of integers, an array of longs and an array of singles, etc.). The declaration of a five-element array of integers, identified by the name Numbers is shown in Figure 12.3.

Figure 12.3 Declaring an integer array.

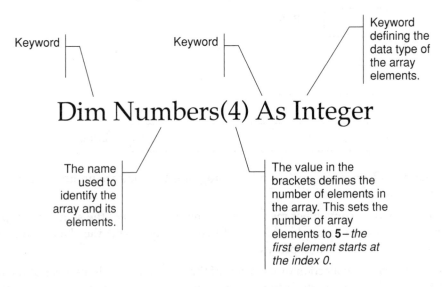

Keyword

Keyword

Keyword defining the data type of the array elements.

Dim Numbers(4) As Integer

The name used to identify the array and its elements.

The value in the brackets defines the number of elements in the array. This sets the number of array elements to **5** – *the first element starts at the index 0.*

QUESTION 12.1 (REVISION)

How would each of the following arrays be declared?

1. *An array of ten elements used to store whole numbers.*
2. *An array of twenty elements used to store the price of sports items.*
3. *An array of one hundred elements used to store numbers of the type single.*

Alternative method

Arrays can be declared with a defined range for their index numbers. Figure 12.4 shows an example of the alternative method for declaring arrays.

Figure 12.5 shows the array structure as defined by the declaration shown in Figure 12.4.

Elements as variables

Every element of an array can be treated in exactly the same way as any other variable. For example an element can be assigned to, read from, and processed.

Figure 12.4 An alternative method for declaring arrays.

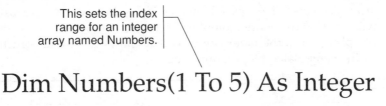

This sets the index range for an integer array named Numbers.

Dim Numbers(1 To 5) As Integer

Figure 12.5 An array with an index number range from 1 to 5.

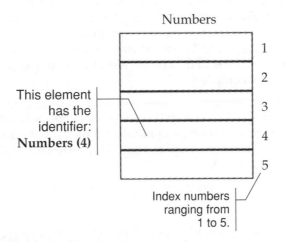

This element has the identifier: **Numbers (4)**

Numbers

Index numbers ranging from 1 to 5.

Assigning a value to an array element

The following sequence of VB assignment statements assigns integers to every element of the array declared in Figure 12.4.

```
Numbers(1) = 3
Numbers(2) = 32
Numbers(3) = 23
Numbers(4) = 300
Numbers(5) = 73
```

Assigning the contents of an array element to another variable

The contents of an array element can be assigned to a variable as shown below:

x = Numbers(4)

Here the integer variable x is assigned the contents of the fourth element of the integer array declared in Figure 12.4.

Displaying the contents of an array element in a text box

The contents of an array element can be displayed in a text box by the following statement.

```
txtOutput.Text = Str(Numbers(3))
```

A text box named txtOutput has its text property set to the string value of the integer contents of the third element of the integer array, declared in Figure 12.4.

NOTE: These three examples of accessing the elements of an array show that array elements behave exactly like variables. Indeed, they are just variables with a slightly more complex identifier. However, it is this added complexity (i.e., the index number) that allows these data structures to be easily manipulated by program code.

NOTE: An array is an example of a static data structure. The size of a static data structure is fixed. If the array declared in Figure 12.4 were used in a program it would be capable of storing 5 integers. Hopefully, this size would be suitable for the functioning of the program. However, if there proved a need for six integers to be stored then this array would not be suitable. Unfortunately, the size of the array is fixed so the source code would have to be altered and recompiled.

Static data structures are extremely useful for many applications but they do have their drawbacks, as described above. For applications that require data structures to 'grow' with their application dynamic data structures are used. To find out more about dynamic arrays look at **ReDim** and **Preserve** in the Visual Basic online help.

Operations on static data structures

The four basic operations that can be carried out on static data structures are listed below.

1. *Initialisation* loads the data structure with some appropriate starting data.
2. *Assignment* stores new information in the data structure replacing the data that was already there.
3. *Rearrangement* involves moving the information about in the data structure to, for example, put a list of names in alphabetical order.
4. *Retrieval* simply means reading the information in the data structure. It does not mean remove the data!

NOTE: Operations on dynamic data structures.

Six operations can be carried out on dynamic data structures. They are the four above on static data structures plus two others (insertion and deletion).

Dynamic data structures grow with the addition of information. Items of information that are added to the data structure are said to be **inserted**.

Dynamic data structures also shrink with the removal of information. Items of information that are removed from the data structure are said to be **deleted**. Deletion of information from a computer system usually removes all trace of the information. *Once the information is removed it cannot be retrieved.*

Using arrays

The following specification (and VB program that implements it) has been designed to illustrate all the four basic operations that can act on data arrays.

SPECIFICATION 12.1

Write a program that reads 5 integers from the keyboard, sorts them into numeric order and displays them.

IMPORTANT: The steps recommended for the implementation of the specification are:

1. Build and set the properties of the GUI.
2. Design the code using N-S charts.
3. Produce a data table.
4. Derive a simple test plan.
5. Convert the design to code and run.
6. Test the run-time against the test plan.

However, from this point onwards **only** the building of the GUI and the program listings will be covered. This is merely to save space in the book, the missing steps have been covered but are not reproduced. **They are still recommended steps that you should endeavour to follow.**

GUI for Specification 12.1

The graphical user interface suitable for Specification 12.1 is shown in Figure 12.6.

Figure 12.6 A suitable GUI for Specification 12.1.

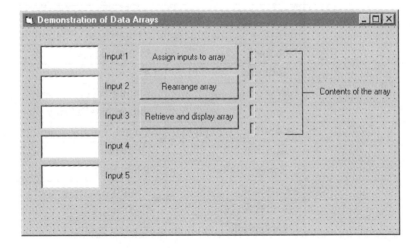

Table 12.1 shows the controls and their property settings that are not at their default value. Again all 'positional' property settings are **not** listed, set these by dragging the controls to the right size and position. Also note that the GUI has used four line controls to assist in labelling the contents of the array. The properties of these lines are also not listed; drag them to the right size and position (use VB help to learn about the line control).

Table 12.1 Property settings for the GUI.

Control	Property	Setting
Form	Name	frmDemoDataArrays
	Caption	Demonstration of Data Arrays
Command button	Name	cmdRetrieve
	Caption	Retrieve and display array
	TabIndex	7
Command button	Name	cmdRearrange
	Caption	Rearrange array
	TabIndex	6
Command button	Name	cmdAssign
	Caption	Assign inputs to array
	TabIndex	5
Text box	Name	txtInput1
	TabIndex	0
	Text	<empty>
Text box	Name	txtInput2
	TabIndex	1
	Text	<empty>
Text box	Name	txtInput3
	TabIndex	2
	Text	<empty>
Text box	Name	txtInput4
	TabIndex	3
	Text	<empty>
Text box	Name	txtInput5
	TabIndex	4
	Text	<empty>
Label	Name	lblContentsOfArray
	Caption	Contents of the array
	AutoSize	-1 'True
Label	Name	lblOutput1
	Caption	<empty>
	AutoSize	-1 'True
	BorderStyle	1 'Fixed Single

Table 12.1 (cont.)

Label	Name	lblOutput2
	Caption	<empty>
	AutoSize	-1 'True
	BorderStyle	1 'Fixed Single
Label	Name	lblOutput3
	Caption	<empty>
	AutoSize	-1 'True
	BorderStyle	1 'Fixed Single
Label	Name	lblOutput4
	Caption	<empty>
	AutoSize	-1 'True
	BorderStyle	1 'Fixed Single
Label	Name	lblOutput5
	Caption	<empty>
	AutoSize	-1 'True
	BorderStyle	1 'Fixed Single
Label	Name	lblInput1
	Caption	Input 1
	AutoSize	-1 'True
Label	Name	lblInput2
	Caption	Input 2
	AutoSize	-1 'True
Label	Name	lblInput3
	Caption	Input 3
	AutoSize	-1 'True
Label	Name	lblInput4
	Caption	Input 4
	AutoSize	-1 'True
Label	Name	lblInput5
	Caption	Input 5
	AutoSize	-1 'True

Code for the GUI

The application consists of:

- A declaration of a five-element array in the declarations section of the form.
- Three Command_Click event procedures.
- One Form_Load event procedure.
- Five Text_KeyPress event procedures.

Declaration of a five-element array

The declaration of the array is shown in Figure 12.7. It can be seen that the declaration of the array has been achieved through the use of constants.

> **NOTE**: A constant is a named item that **retains** a constant value throughout the execution of a program, as compared to a variable, whose value can change during execution. Constants can be used in code in place of actual values (literal values). An advantage of using constants is that they improve the readability of code, also just **one** change to the declaration of a constant will reflect throughout the program in **all** the places the constant is used.
>
> It is good programming practice to prefix every constant declared by a programmer with a lower-case **c**. Then when a constant is seen in program code it cannot be confused with a variable.

Figure 12.7 Where and how to declare the five-element array.

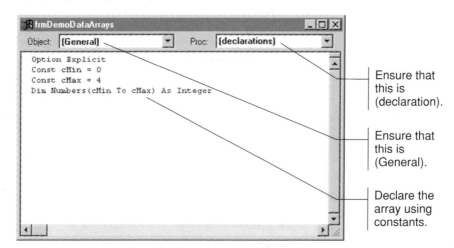

The three Command_Click event procedures

These event procedures are attached to the three command buttons on the GUI. All three are listed in Figure 12.8. These procedures show **three** of the four basic operations that can act upon static data structures (the fourth is shown in the Form_Load event procedure).

Figure 12.8 The three Command_Click event procedures.
NOTE that the conditional statement of the *If..Then..Else* construct is shown across two lines. When you enter this code make sure that it is on one line or it will not compile **or you can use the space and underscore symbol to split across lines.**

```
Private Sub cmdAssign_Click()
    If (txtInput1.Text = "") Or (txtInput2.Text = "") Or (txtInput3.Text = "") Or
(txtInput4.Text = "") Or (txtInput5.Text = "") Then
        Beep
        MsgBox "A zero length string is present in an input text box!"
    Else
        Numbers(0) = CInt(txtInput1.Text)
```

```
        Numbers(1) = CInt(txtInput2.Text)
        Numbers(2) = CInt(txtInput3.Text)
        Numbers(3) = CInt(txtInput4.Text)
        Numbers(4) = CInt(txtInput5.Text)
    End If
End Sub
Private Sub cmdRearrange_Click()
Dim i As Integer
Dim Pass As Integer
Dim Temp As Integer
Dim NoSwitches As Boolean
    Pass = 0
    Do
        Pass = Pass + 1
        NoSwitches = True
        For i = cMin To (cMax – Pass)
            If Numbers(i) > Numbers(i + 1) Then
                NoSwitches = False
                Temp = Numbers(i)
                Numbers(i) = Numbers(i + 1)
                Numbers(i + 1) = Temp
            End If
        Next i
    Loop Until NoSwitches
End Sub
Private Sub cmdRetrieve_Click()
    lblOutput1.Caption = Numbers(0)
    lblOutput2.Caption = Numbers(1)
    lblOutput3.Caption = Numbers(2)
    lblOutput4.Caption = Numbers(3)
    lblOutput5.Caption = Numbers(4)
End Sub
```

Form_Load event procedure

Whenever a form is loaded during the execution of an application, a Form_Load event occurs. An event procedure can be attached to this event. It is usual for all the initialisation code to be placed in this event procedure and this application is no different. The code to initialise the data array is placed in the Form_Load event procedure shown in Figure 12.9.

Figure 12.9 Initialising the data array.

```
Private Sub Form_Load()
Dim i As Integer
    For i = cMin To cMax
        Numbers(i) = 0
    Next i
    txtInput1.Text = Numbers(0)
    txtInput2.Text = Numbers(1)
    txtInput3.Text = Numbers(2)
    txtInput4.Text = Numbers(3)
    txtInput5.Text = Numbers(4)
End Sub
```

179

Text_KeyPress event procedures

Attached to each of the input text boxes is code to validate the entry of text. Only integers are allowed entry and any other key press is ignored and reported to the user with a beep. The code for this has been discussed in a previous chapter. One of these event procedures has been repeated in Figure 12.10 for your convenience.

Figure 12.10 Validating user input.

```
Private Sub txtInput1_KeyPress(KeyAscii As Integer)
    If (KeyAscii < Asc("0")) Or (KeyAscii > Asc("9")) Then
        KeyAscii = 0
        Beep
    End If
End Sub
```

Four of the event procedures are described in the following description trace tables.

Description trace for the Form_Load() event procedure

Statement	Description
For i = cMin To cMax	The range is from cMin To cMax which is 0 to 4. The first time through the loop the variable *i* is set at 0 (i.e. cMin).
Numbers(i) = 0	The first element of the array is assigned 0. It is the first element because the statement Numbers(*i*) is actually Numbers(0) because *i* is set to 0.
Next i	This increments the variable *i* by one. Thus *i* is now set at 1. The loop is entered again to execute the following statement.
Numbers(i) = 0	The second element of the array is assigned 0. It is the second element because the statement Numbers(i) is actually Numbers(1) because *i* is set to 1.
Next i	This increments the variable *i* by one. Thus *i* is now set at 2. The loop is entered again to execute the following statement.
Numbers(i) = 0	The third element of the array is assigned 0. It is the third element because the statement Numbers(i) is actually Numbers(2) because *i* is set to 2.
Next i	This increments the variable *i* by one. Thus *i* is now set at 3. The loop is entered again to execute the following statement.
Numbers(i) = 0	The fourth element of the array is assigned 0. It is the fourth element because the statement Numbers(i) is actually Numbers(3) because *i* is set to 3.
Next i	This increments the variable *i* by one. Thus *i* is now set at 4. The loop is entered for the **last** time to execute the following statement. It is the last time through the loop because the range defined is from 0 to 4.
Numbers(i) = 0	The fifth element of the array is assigned 0. It is the fifth element because the statement Numbers(i) is actually Numbers(4) because *i* is set to 4. Once this is executed the loop is exited and the entire array has been initialised with all its elements set to 0.

Description trace for the Form_Load() event procedure (cont.)

Statement	Description
txtInput1.Text = Numbers(0)	The content of the first element of the array is assigned **to** the text property of the txtInput1 text box.
txtInput2.Text = Numbers(1)	The content of the second element of the array is assigned **to** the text property of the txtInput2 text box.
txtInput3.Text = Numbers(2)	The content of the third element of the array is assigned **to** the text property of the txtInput3 text box.
txtInput4.Text = Numbers(3)	The content of the fourth element of the array is assigned **to** the text property of the txtInput4 text box.
txtInput5.Text = Numbers(4)	The content of the fifth element of the array is assigned **to** the text property of the txtInput5 text box.

Once this event procedure has been executed the five-element array is initialised with all zeros as shown in Figure 12.11

Figure 12.11 The five-element array after it has been initialised.

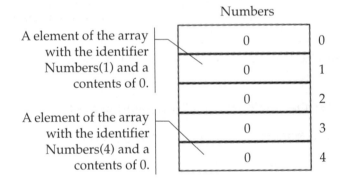

Numbers

A element of the array with the identifier Numbers(1) and a contents of 0.

A element of the array with the identifier Numbers(4) and a contents of 0.

0	0
0	1
0	2
0	3
0	4

Description trace for the cmdAssign_Click() event procedure

The following description trace describes the execution of the event procedure if one of the input text boxes contains a zero-length string, i.e., if the text box contains no text.

Statement	Description
If (txtInput1.Text = "") Or (txtInput2.Text = "") Or (txtInput3.Text = "") Or (txtInput4.Text = "") Or (txtInput5.Text = "") Then	If the text property of one or more input text box contains a zero-length string then this conditional test returns **True**. Consequently, the statements **between** the reserved words *Then* and *Else* are executed.
Beep	The computer beeps informing the user that a text box has an invalid entry, i.e., the text box, text property, contains a zero-length string.
MsgBox "A zero length string is present in an input text box!"	A message box also informs the user of an invalid input. Once this statement is executed the procedure ends.

The following description trace describes the execution of the event procedure if the text boxes contain the values as shown by Figure 12.12.

Statement	Description
If (txtInput1.Text = "") Or (txtInput2.Text = "") Or (txtInput3.Text = "") Or (txtInput4.Text = "") Or (txtInput5.Text = "") Then	There are no zero length strings and the outcome from this conditional test is **False**. Consequently, the statements **between** the reserved words *Else* and *End If* are executed.
Numbers(0) = CInt(txtInput1.Text)	The value of the Text property, of the text box (txtInput1), is converted to an integer and assigned to the first element of the Numbers array.
Numbers(1) = CInt(txtInput2.Text)	The value of the Text property, of the text box (txtInput2), is converted to an integer and assigned to the second element of the Numbers array.
Numbers(2) = CInt(txtInput3.Text)	The value of the Text property, of the text box (txtInput3), is converted to an integer and assigned to the third element of the Numbers array.
Numbers(3) = CInt(txtInput4.Text)	The value of the Text property, of the text box (txtInput4), is converted to an integer and assigned to the fourth element of the Numbers array.
Numbers(4) = CInt(txtInput5.Text)	The value of the Text property, of the text box (txtInput5), is converted to an integer and assigned to the fifth element of the Numbers array. **Once this statement executes the procedure ends**.

After the cmdAssign_Click event procedure has executed the Numbers array contains data as shown in Figure 12.13.

Description trace for the cmdRetrieve_Click() event procedure

If the user clicks the Retrieve and display array command button (Retrieve and display array) immediately after pressing the Assign inputs to array command button (Assign inputs to array) then the output appears as shown in Figure 12.14.

Statement	Description
lblOutput1.Caption = Numbers(0)	The content of the first element of the Numbers array, that is 200, is assigned the Caption property of the lblOutput1 label.
lblOutput2.Caption = Numbers(1)	The content of the second element of the Numbers array, that is 23, is assigned the Caption property of the lblOutput2 label.
lblOutput3.Caption = Numbers(2)	The content of the third element of the Numbers array, that is 10, is assigned the Caption property of the lblOutput3 label.
lblOutput4.Caption = Numbers(3)	The content of the fourth element of the Numbers array, that is 100, is assigned the Caption property of the lblOutput4 label.
lblOutput5.Caption = Numbers(4)	The content of the fifth element of the Numbers array, that is 1, is assigned the Caption property of the lblOutput5 label.

Figure 12.12 The data input by the user just **before** the user clicks the

Assign inputs to array command button (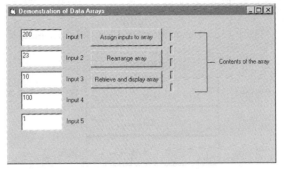)

Figure 12.13 The state of the array **after** the execution of the cmdAssign_Click event procedure.

Numbers

200	0
23	1
10	2
100	3
1	4

Figure 12.14 Output on the GUI **after** the command button ( ) is clicked.

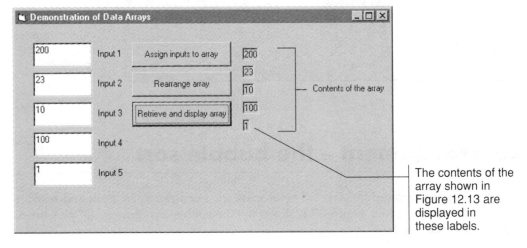

The contents of the array shown in Figure 12.13 are displayed in these labels.

Description of the cmdRearrange_Click() event procedure

Clicking the Rearrange array command button (Rearrange array) sorts the array of Figure 12.13 into the order shown in Figure 12.15.

Figure 12.15 The array **after** it has been rearranged.

Numbers

1	0
10	1
23	2
100	3
200	4

The output of the GUI after the user clicks (Rearrange array) followed by (Retrieve and display array) is shown in Figure 12.16.

The cmdRearrange_Click event procedure is based on a well-known bubble sort algorithm.

Figure 12.16 The output of the GUI.

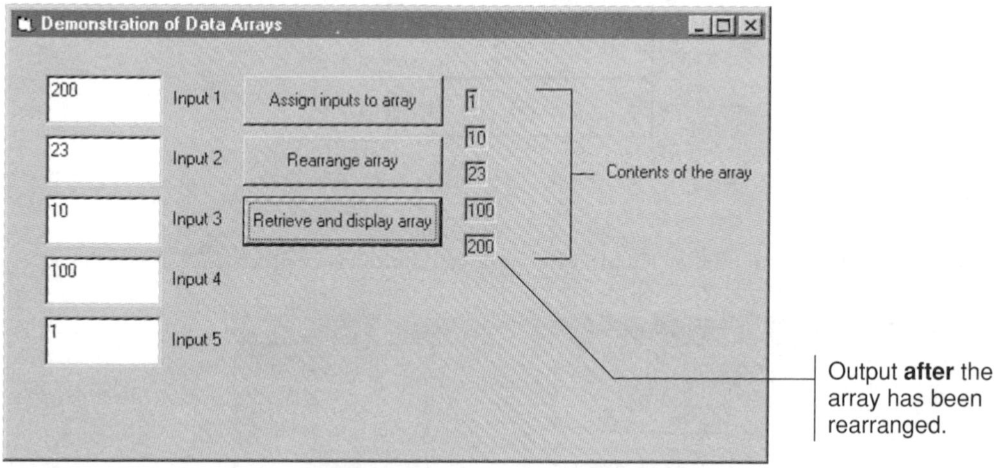

Rearrangement – the bubble sort

The rearrangement procedure takes a five-element integer array as its input and rearranges the data into numeric order. Figure 12.17 illustrates the bubble sort process, the data structure and the local data used.

The data structure (array) holds the data before and after the bubble sort. The local data are used for the reasons described in Table 12.2.

The bubble sort works in the following way:

On the first pass through the loop the content of the first element is compared to see if it is larger than the content of the second element and if it is then they are switched.

The content of the second element is then compared with the content of the third element and switched if the content of the second element is larger than the third.

This is repeated until the content of the fourth element is compared with the fifth element.

Figure 12.17 The bubble sort process.

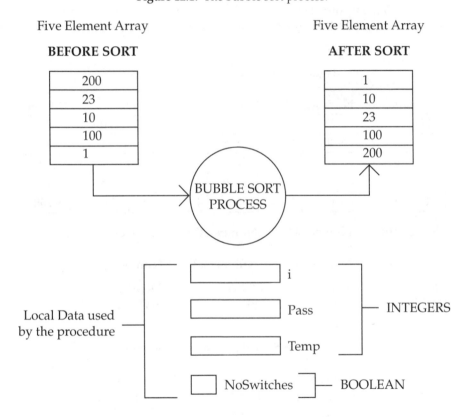

Table 12.2 Description of local data.

Local data	What it is used for
i	The index for the *For..Next* loop.
Pass	To count the number of passes through the *Do..Until* loop.
Temp	To assist in switching the variables in the array.
NoSwitches	If there are no switches on a pass through the *Do..Until* loop then NoSwitches is set to TRUE. If there is switching of elements then the NoSwitches is set to FALSE. Consequently, the *Do..Until* loop is executed until there are no more switches.

Upon completion of the first pass, the largest number in the array will be in the fifth element position.

The first pass through the loop is illustrated by Figure 12.18.

The second pass through the loop is illustrated by Figure 12.19.

The third pass through the loop is illustrated by Figure 12.20.

The fourth pass through the loop is illustrated by Figure 12.21.

At the end of the first pass the largest number in the array (i.e., 200) is at the bottom of the array. The rearrangement is referred to as the bubble sort because the smaller numbers in the array slowly 'bubble up' to the top of the array.

Further passes through the loop are necessary to continue to rearrange the array. However, on the next pass element four need not be compared with element five because the largest number is already in the fifth element position. After the next pass the next largest element

Figure 12.18 First pass through the loop.

Numbers		Numbers		Numbers		Numbers		Numbers	
200	0	➤ 23	0	23	0	23	0	23	0
23	1	➤ 200	1	➤ 10	1	10	1	10	1
10	2	10	2	➤ 200	2	➤ 100	2	100	2
100	3	100	3	100	3	➤ 200	3	➤ 1	3
1	4	1	4	1	4	1	4	➤ 200	4

Numbers(0)	Numbers(1)	Numbers(2)	Numbers(3)
>	>	>	>
Numbers(1)	Numbers(2)	Numbers(3)	Numbers(4)
TRUE SWITCH	TRUE SWITCH	TRUE SWITCH	TRUE SWITCH

Figure 12.19 Second pass through the loop.

Numbers		Numbers		Numbers		Numbers	
23	0	➤ 10	0	10	0	10	0
10	1	➤ 23	1	23	1	23	1
100	2	100	2	100	2	➤ 1	2
1	3	1	3	1	3	➤ 100	3
200	4	200	4	200	4	200	4

Numbers(0)	Numbers(1)	Numbers(2)
>	>	>
Numbers(1)	Numbers(2)	Numbers(3)
TRUE SWITCH	FALSE DO NOT SWITCH	TRUE SWITCH

Figure 12.20 The third pass through the loop.

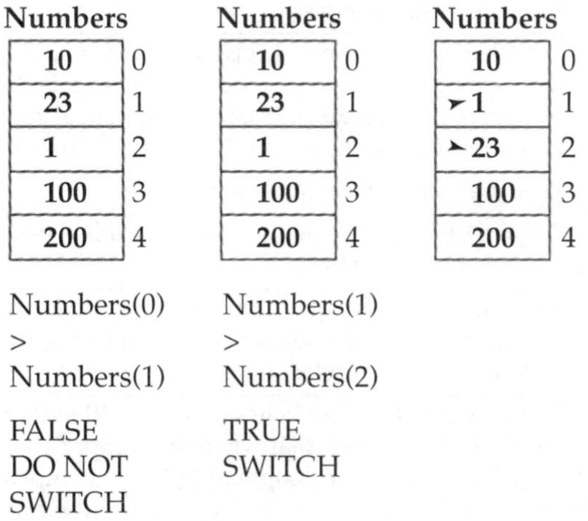

Numbers	
10	0
23	1
1	2
100	3
200	4

Numbers	
10	0
23	1
1	2
100	3
200	4

Numbers	
10	0
➤1	1
➤23	2
100	3
200	4

Numbers(0)
>
Numbers(1)

FALSE
DO NOT
SWITCH

Numbers(1)
>
Numbers(2)

TRUE
SWITCH

Figure 12.21 The fourth pass through the loop.

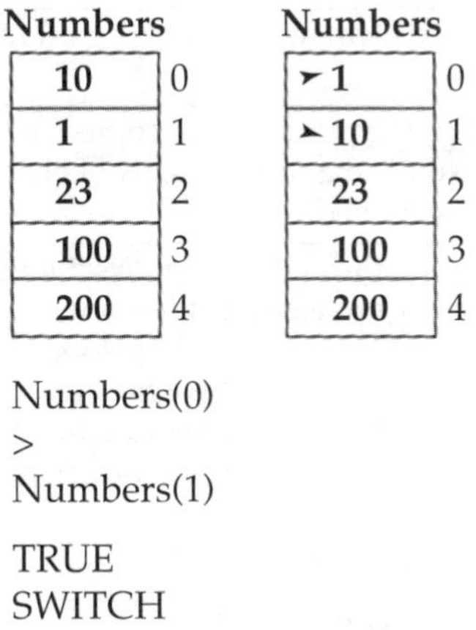

Numbers	
10	0
1	1
23	2
100	3
200	4

Numbers	
➤1	0
➤10	1
23	2
100	3
200	4

Numbers(0)
>
Numbers(1)

TRUE
SWITCH

will be in the fourth element position, consequently, the third pass will not need to compare the third element with the fourth element because the second largest element will be in the fourth position. Therefore the number of comparisons reduces for every pass through the loop.

The array is sorted when there are no more switches during a pass through the loop, i.e., when NoSwitches is True

Description trace for the cmdRearrange_Click() event procedure

The following description trace describes the execution of the rearrangement procedure when run against the input array shown in Figure 12.13.

Statement	Description
Pass = 0	Initialises the local data Pass to zero
Pass = Pass + 1	Increments the pass by one – keeps a running total of the number of passes through the loop. The Pass variable is used to ensure that the number of comparisons is reduced each time there is a pass through the *Do..Until* loop.
NoSwitches = True	Initialises the NoSwitches Boolean variable.
For i = cMin To (cMax – Pass)	Four comparisons will be made because (cMax – Pass) equals 3. The range is 0 to 3.
If Numbers(i) > Numbers(i + 1) Then	Compares the first element with the second element (i.e., is 200>23) and True is the outcome. Consequently; the *Then* part of the *If..Then* selection is selected.
NoSwitches = False	FALSE is assigned to NoSwitches to indicate that there has been a switch. This means that when the comparisons controlled by the *For..Next* loop have all been completed there will be a further pass necessary because the condition of the *Do..Until* loop (i.e., Until NoSwitches) is FALSE. Consequently; there will be a further pass through the loop.
Temp = Numbers(i)	The contents of the first element are 'saved' in a temporary variable.
Numbers(i) = Numbers(i + 1)	The contents of the second element (*i*+1) are copied to the first element (*i*).
Numbers(i + 1) = Temp	The contents of the temporary variable are copied to the second element. The result is that the contents of element one and two have been switched.
	There will be 3 more passes through the *For..Next* loop. With each pass switching (or otherwise) the content of the elements being compared. When the *For..Next* loop is complete the condition of the Until NoSwitches results in the *Do..Until* loop being re-entered and the statement Pass = Pass + 1 is executed. The description trace is picked up from this point.
Pass = Pass + 1	The running total is increased by one to the value 2.
NoSwitches = True	Initialised for the second pass through the loop.
For i = cMin To (cMax – Pass)	Only three comparisons will be made because cMax – Pass gives two. There is no need to make four comparisons this time because the largest number is already in the fifth element position. It can be seen that cMax – Pass will always be one less every time the loop is repeated; consequently, the number of comparisons reduces by one for each pass through the loop.
If Numbers(i) > Numbers(i + 1) Then	Compares the first element with the second element of the loop, etc.
	Eventually the passes through the loop will result in a completely sorted array. The final pass through the loop will not result in any switches in element content. On this pass NoSwitch will **not** be set to FALSE, inside the *If..Then* selection, because the Then part of the selection will not be executed. Consequently the condition of the *Do..Until* loop will be TRUE and the loop and hence the procedure will end.

NOTE: Every pass through the array is guaranteed to place the next largest number in its correct place. It should be noted that a pass can put more than one number in its correct place. The number of passes through the array is dependent upon the order of the original array. The bubble sort is an acceptable method for ordering an array. However, it is inefficient for arrays larger than one hundred elements.

QUESTION 12.2 (DEVELOPMENT)

The description trace for the cmdRearrange_Click() event procedure was not fully complete. You complete it!

PRACTICAL ACTIVITY 12.1

1. Implement Specification 12.1.

2. Amend the application developed so that it will work for a six-element integer array.

PRACTICAL ACTIVITY 12.2

This activity is to exercise your understanding of arrays. Implement each of the following specifications. Follow the recommended steps previously covered and use constants in your code.

SPECIFICATION 12.2

Write a program that fills a twelve-element integer array with multiples of two and then display the contents of each array element on the VDU.

SPECIFICATION 12.3

Write a program that fills a twelve-element integer array with multiples of five and then display the contents of each array element on the VDU.

SPECIFICATION 12.4

Write a program that fills a six-element integer array with multiples of three and fills another six-element array with multiples of six. Add the elements of each array to one another storing the result of the addition in a third array. Display each number of the third array on the VDU.

SPECIFICATION 12.5

Write a program that asks a user to enter ten whole numbers. The numbers are to be stored in a ten-element array. Once the numbers have been entered the program is to search the array for numbers greater than fifty. It is to display all the numbers greater than fifty and their position in the array (i.e., the index number).

SPECIFICATION 12.6

This exercise is a repeat of Specification 12.5 with the following additional requirements. As well as printing the numbers greater than fifty and their position it is to make a separate display of all numbers equal to or less than fifty and their position in the array.

SPECIFICATION 12.7

Write a program that asks a user to enter five whole numbers. The numbers are to be stored in a five-element array. Once the numbers have been entered the array is searched for the largest number. When the number is found it is displayed on the VDU.

SPECIFICATION 12.8

Write a program that asks a user to enter five whole numbers. The numbers are to be stored in a five-element array. Once the numbers have been entered the array is search for the smallest number. When the number is found it is displayed on the VDU.

SPECIFICATION 12.9

Write a program that asks a user to enter five whole numbers. The numbers are to be stored in a five-element array. The numbers are then to be displayed in the reverse order to which they were input.

A matrix array

The one-dimensional arrays considered so far have essentially been a sequence of elements, with each element being accessed by its index (subscript) number. However, it is possible to have a two-dimensional array (a matrix array). Such an array is not a sequence of elements, but is a matrix that requires more than one number to index each of its elements.

Consider the use of a matrix array data structure for the following specification.

SPECIFICATION 12.10

A small class of five students take four examinations. Write a program that will read the mark obtained by each student, in each of the examinations. The program should also display a matrix of the students' marks against the examination number. The data structure used for the implementation of the above specification is illustrated in Figure 12.22.

Figure 12.22 is a matrix array with 20 elements. Each element is capable of storing an integer. Every element is accessed by the name of the array (Marks) and two index numbers – one for the row and the other for the column.

The marks of student one for the first examination will be in array element Marks(0, 0) Similarly, the marks of student three for the fourth examination will be in element Marks(2, 3). The relationship between an element and its identifier is shown in Figure 12.23.

Declaring a matrix array

A matrix array is defined in a similar way to a one-dimensional array. Figure 12.24 illustrates how and where such an array is declared.

Figure 12.22 A matrix array suitable for Specification 12.10.

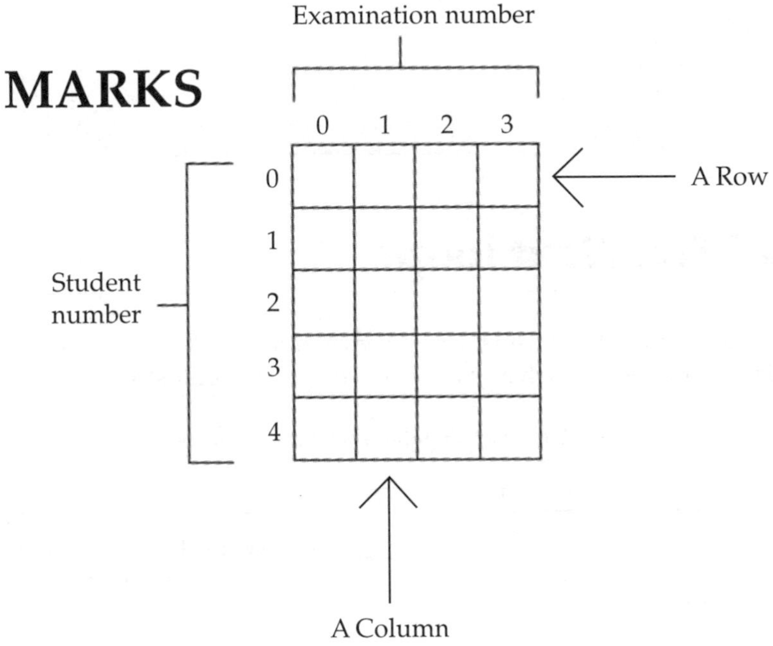

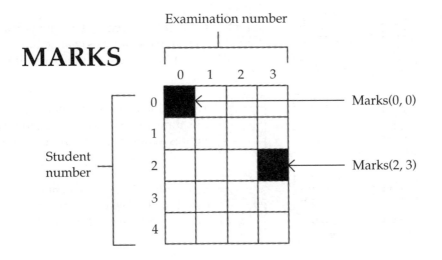

Figure 12.23 Identifying an element.

Figure 12.24 Declaring a matrix array.

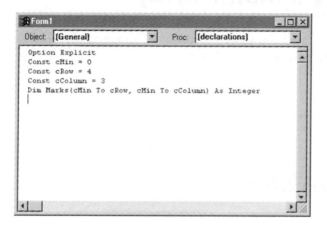

Nested *For..Next* loops

Matrix arrays are manipulated using nested *For..Next* loops. The elements of the matrix array can be **initialised** by setting each row to zero in turn. This is illustrated by Figure 12.25.

Figure 12.25 Initialising a matrix array.

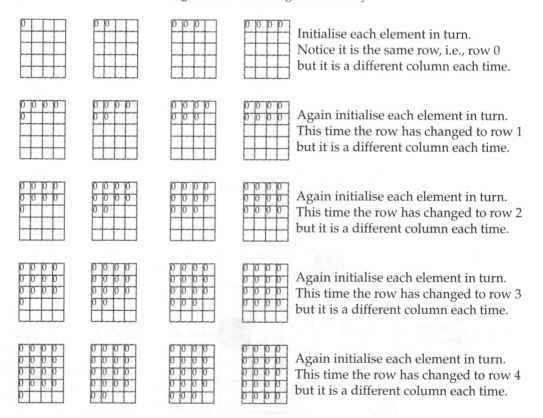

Initialise each element in turn.
Notice it is the same row, i.e., row 0
but it is a different column each time.

Again initialise each element in turn.
This time the row has changed to row 1
but it is a different column each time.

Again initialise each element in turn.
This time the row has changed to row 2
but it is a different column each time.

Again initialise each element in turn.
This time the row has changed to row 3
but it is a different column each time.

Again initialise each element in turn.
This time the row has changed to row 4
but it is a different column each time.

The initialising of the elements in the order shown in Figure 12.25 is achieved by nested *For..Next* loops as illustrated in Figure 12.26.

Figure 12.26 Nested *For..Next* loops.

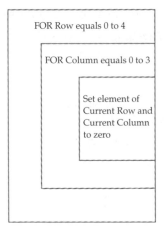

The outer loop sets the row to 0 and the inner loop selects the columns in turn. Consequently, all the first row is set to zero. On exit from the inner loop control is passed back to the outer loop where the row is changed to 1. The inner loop is then entered and each of the columns is then selected in turn. This is repeated until the matrix is full of zeros.

Implementing Specification 12.10

Figure 12.27 shows the GUI for the specification. It consists of a form, two command buttons, a picture box, two labels and eight lines.

The procedures and declarations for the GUI are listed in Figure 12.28.

Figure 12.27 The GUI for Specification 12.10.

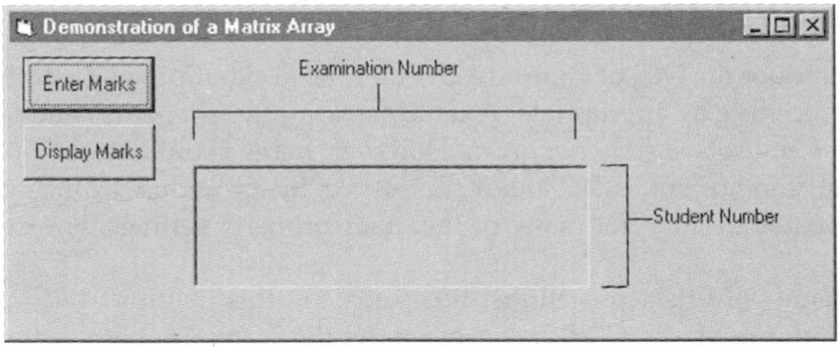

Figure 12.28 Declarations and procedure listings for Specification 12.10.

```
Option Explicit
Const cMin = 0
Const cRow = 4
Const cColumn = 3
Dim Marks(cMin To cRow, cMin To cColumn) As Integer

Private Sub cmdDisplayMarks_Click()
Dim Row As Integer
Dim Column As Integer

    For Row = cMin To cRow
        For Column = cMin To cColumn
            picDisplayMarks.Print Marks(Row, Column); Tab;
        Next Column
        picDisplayMarks.Print
    Next Row
End Sub

Private Sub cmdEnterMarks_Click()
Dim Row As Integer
Dim Column As Integer

    For Row = cMin To cRow
        For Column = cMin To cColumn
            Marks(Row, Column) = InputBox("Please enter the marks for
            student number " & Row, "Examination number " & Column, 0)
        Next Column
    Next Row
End Sub

Private Sub Form_Load()
Dim Row As Integer
Dim Column As Integer

    For Row = cMin To cRow
        For Column = cMin To cColumn
            Marks(Row, Column) = 0
        Next Column
    Next Row
End Sub
```

> Enter as **one** line or use space and the underscore character.

PRACTICAL ACTIVITY 12.3

Produce the GUI of Figure 12.27, enter the declarations and attach the event procedure as appropriate. A table showing the properties and settings for the controls used is **not** given. However, many should be obvious from the appearance of the GUI and if you inspect the procedure listings you should be able to interpret many of the other property settings. For example the

name of the procedure attached to this button (Enter Marks)is cmdEnterMarks_Click(), consequently, the Name property setting for this command button must be cmdEnterMarks.

NOTE: Make sure you build the GUI and set its properties **before** you attach the code.

PRACTICAL ACTIVITY 12.4

Amend the last program so that a small class of **six** students take **five** examinations. Attach two more command buttons to the GUI. One command button will be used to process the data to find and display the average mark obtained in each examination. The other command button will find and display the overall average mark obtained by each student.

FINAL COMMENT ON ARRAYS: Arrays are a useful method for structuring data to be manipulated by a program. However, an array has two main drawbacks. Firstly, it is an example of a static data structure and once an array has been declared its size is fixed (however, **ReDim** and **Preserve** can be used to resize arrays at run-time). Secondly, the elements of an array are all of the same type. A later chapter, on records, will show a data structure that is capable of storing different data types. A record is also an example of a static data structure.

13 Control arrays

Just as a data array 'groups' together variables under the same name a control array 'groups' together controls under the same name.

A control array is a group of controls that share the same **Name**, **type**, and **event procedures**. A control array can have from one to as many elements as your system resources and memory permit. Control arrays are useful if you want several controls to share code and if you wish to create a control at run-time.

During the last chapter a program was developed to implement Specification 12.1. The GUI for this program is repeated, for your convenience, in Figure 13.1. This program will be redeveloped, in this chapter, to highlight the features of control arrays.

Figure 13.1 The GUI for Specification 12.1

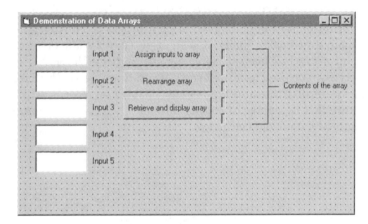

The five input text boxes will be implemented as a control array. Also, the five output labels will be implemented as another control array.

Creating a control array

Visual Basic asks if you wish to implement a control array when you attempt to give the same identifier to the name property of a common control. Figure 13.2 shows the sequence of steps involved in creating a control array.

To add other elements to this control array draw another text box on the form and set its Name property to txtInput.

Properties of control arrays

The elements of the same control array can have their properties set to different values. For example, Figure 13.3 shows two elements of a control array (both are text boxes) one text box has its BorderStyle set to *0-None* and the other has its BorderStyle set to *1-Fixed Single*. Consequently, their appearance is different but they are still elements of the same control array.

Control array code

All elements of a control array share the same code. This is a very useful feature of control arrays. Consider the program developed to implement specification 12.1. The validation of user input was achieved with the code shown in Figure 13.4.

Figure 13.2 The sequence of steps involved in creating a control array.

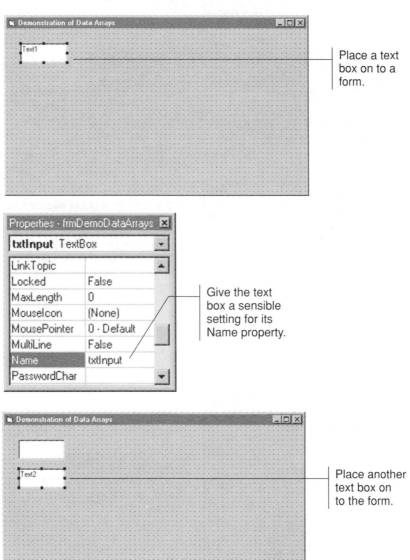

Place a text box on to a form.

Give the text box a sensible setting for its Name property.

Place another text box on to the form.

Figure 13.2 (cont.)

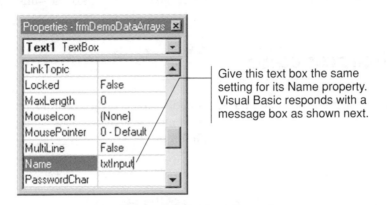

Give this text box the same setting for its Name property. Visual Basic responds with a message box as shown next.

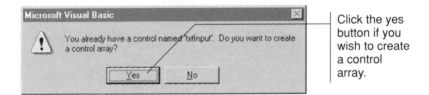

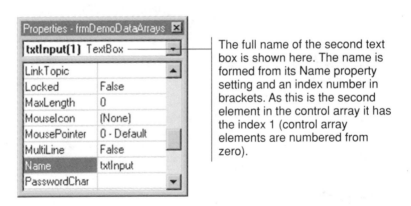

Click the yes button if you wish to create a control array.

The full name of the second text box is shown here. The name is formed from its Name property setting and an index number in brackets. As this is the second element in the control array it has the index 1 (control array elements are numbered from zero).

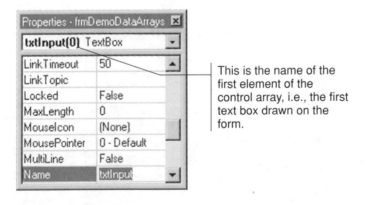

This is the name of the first element of the control array, i.e., the first text box drawn on the form.

Figure 13.3 Control array elements with different property settings.

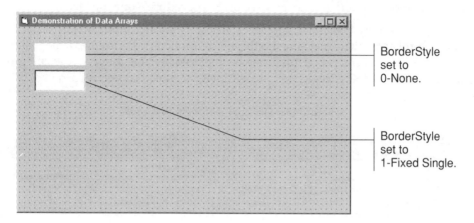

BorderStyle
set to
0-None.

BorderStyle
set to
1-Fixed Single.

Figure 13.4 Code for validating data entry.

```
Private Sub txtInput1_KeyPress(KeyAscii As Integer)
    If (KeyAscii < Asc("0")) Or (KeyAscii > Asc("9")) Then
        KeyAscii = 0
        Beep
    End If
End Sub

Private Sub txtInput2_KeyPress(KeyAscii As Integer)
    If (KeyAscii < Asc("0")) Or (KeyAscii > Asc("9")) Then
        KeyAscii = 0
        Beep
        End If
End Sub

Private Sub txtInput3_KeyPress(KeyAscii As Integer)
    If (KeyAscii < Asc("0")) Or (KeyAscii > Asc("9")) Then
        KeyAscii = 0
        Beep
    End If
End Sub

Private Sub txtInput4_KeyPress(KeyAscii As Integer)
    If (KeyAscii < Asc("0")) Or (KeyAscii > Asc("9")) Then
        KeyAscii = 0
        Beep
    End If
End Sub

Private Sub txtInput5_KeyPress(KeyAscii As Integer)
    If (KeyAscii < Asc("0")) Or (KeyAscii > Asc("9")) Then
        KeyAscii = 0
        Beep
    End If
End Sub
```

It is not important to describe again how these event procedures validate input, however, it is important to point out that there are **five** event procedure – one for each text box!

If the program was redeveloped, replacing all the 'separate' input text boxes with a five-element control array that was named txtInput (as implied by Figure 13.2), then all these five separate KeyPress event procedures can be replaced by one KeyPress event procedure. Figure 13.5 shows the KeyPress event procedure for the text box control array.

Figure 13.5 The KeyPress event procedure.

```
frmDemoControlsArrays                                            _ □ ×
Object: txtInput              ▼     Proc: KeyPress              ▼
   Private Sub txtInput_KeyPress(Index As Integer, KeyAscii As Integer)
   If (KeyAscii < Asc("0")) Or (KeyAscii > Asc("9")) Then
           KeyAscii = 0
           Beep
       End If
   End Sub
```

Attaching code to a control array

Double click on **any** element of the control array and a code window, common to all the elements, will appear. Once the window is in focus enter the code. This code is now shared by all the elements of the control array.

NOTE: A text box, for example, can have many types of event procedures attached. For instance, a Click event procedure or a GotFocus event procedure, etc. The GotFocus event procedure will be shared by all the elements of a text box control array, likewise the Click event procedure, etc.

Improving the structure of code using control arrays

The use of control arrays does not just reduce the number of procedures used in a program, it also allows for improvement in the structure of the code by allowing easier processing using, for example, the *For..Next* loop construct.

Implementing Specification 12.1 using control arrays

The following description of the program code, for implementing Specification 12.1, assumes that the GUI has been developed using a five-element text box control array called, txtInput (used to enter numbers) and a five-element label control array, called lblOutput (used to display the contents of the **data** array).

Figure 13.6 shows the event procedure for assigning the input data to the data array when a control array is used to implement Specification 12.1. It also shows the event procedure, developed to implement Specification 12.1, when a control array is not used (i.e., as it was developed in Chapter 12).

Assigning the values to the data array from the control array of text boxes is achieved using the following segment of code.

```
For i = cMin To cMax
        Numbers(i) = CInt(txtInput(i).Text)
Next i
```

The text boxes are elements of a control array, consequently, they can be accessed through their index number, using a *For..Next* loop as shown above. The first time through the loop the value of the variable *i* is 0 (cMin = 0), therefore, the statement in the loop is effectively as follows:

```
Numbers(0) = CInt(txtInput(0).Text)
```

Figure 13.6 Comparison of two event procedures that perform the same function.

```
Private Sub cmdAssign_Click()
Dim i As Integer
    If (txtInput(0).Text = "") Or (txtInput(1).Text = "") Or (txtInput(2).Text = "")
    Or (txtInput(3).Text = "") Or (txtInput(4).Text = "") Then
        Beep
        MsgBox "A zero length string is present in an input text box!"
    Else
        For i = cMin To cMax
            Numbers(i) = CInt(txtInput(i).Text)
        Next i
    End If
End Sub
```

Enter as **one** line.

```
Private Sub cmdAssign_Click()
    If (txtInput1.Text = "") Or (txtInput2.Text = "") Or (txtInput3.Text = "")
    Or (txtInput4.Text = "") Or (txtInput5.Text = "") Then
        Beep
        MsgBox "A zero length string is present in an input text box!"
    Else
        Numbers(0) = CInt(txtInput1.Text)
        Numbers(1) = CInt(txtInput2.Text)
        Numbers(2) = CInt(txtInput3.Text)
        Numbers(3) = CInt(txtInput4.Text)
        Numbers(4) = CInt(txtInput5.Text)
    End If
End Sub
```

Enter as **one** line.

Thus the first element of the data array is assigned the text setting of the first element of the control array, **after** it has been converted to an integer by CInt function.

The second time through the loop the variable *i* is incremented and the statement effectively becomes:

Numbers(1) = CInt(txtInput(1).Text)

and so on for each pass through the loop.

The segment of code used in the original program, to perform this task, is shown below:

Numbers(0) = CInt(txtInput1.Text)

Numbers(1) = CInt(txtInput2.Text)

Numbers(2) = CInt(txtInput3.Text)

Numbers(3) = CInt(txtInput4.Text)

Numbers(4) = CInt(txtInput5.Text)

The code developed using the control array offers a better structure and if the size of the data array was increased then the saving in typing alone would justify the use of control arrays.

Figure 13.7 shows the two event procedures for displaying the data arrays. Observe the difference in the segment of code responsible for copying the data array elements to the output labels – the segments have been highlighted in bold.

Figure 13.7 Comparison of event procedures.

```
Private Sub cmdRetrieve_Click()
Dim i As Integer

    For i = cMin To cMax
        lblOutput(i).Caption = Numbers(i)
    Next i
End Sub
Private Sub cmdRetrieve_Click()
    lblOutput1.Caption = Numbers(0)
    lblOutput2.Caption = Numbers(1)
    lblOutput3.Caption = Numbers(2)
    lblOutput4.Caption = Numbers(3)
    lblOutput5.Caption = Numbers(4)
End Sub
```

Figure 13.8 shows the two Form_Load event procedures initialising the data array. Again observe the difference in the segments of code that have been highlighted in bold.

Figure 13.8 Comparison of the Form_Load event procedures.

```
Private Sub Form_Load()
Dim i As Integer
    For i = cMin To cMax
        Numbers(i) = 0
    Next i
```

Figure 13.8 (cont.)

```
        For i = cMin To cMax
            txtInput(i).Text = Numbers(0)
        Next i
    End Sub

    Private Sub Form_Load()
    Dim i As Integer
        For i = cMin To cMax
            Numbers(i) = 0
        Next i
        txtInput1.Text = Numbers(0)
        txtInput2.Text = Numbers(1)
        txtInput3.Text = Numbers(2)
        txtInput4.Text = Numbers(3)
        txtInput5.Text = Numbers(4)
    End Sub
```

PRACTICAL ACTIVITY 13.1

Write a program to implement Specification 12.1 using a control array for the input text boxes and another control array for the output labels.

Identifying an element of a control array

The heading for the KeyPress event, attached to the first text box of the program developed in Chapter 12 (to implement Specification 12.1), is shown below:

Private Sub txtInput1_KeyPress(KeyAscii As Integer)

It has one input parameter and that is KeyAscii. Whereas, the heading for the KeyPress event attached to the text box control array has two input parameters and is shown next:

Private Sub txtInput_KeyPress(Index As Integer, KeyAscii As Integer)

The relationship between the event procedure and its input parameters is illustrated in Figure 13.9.

Both event procedures receive the *KeyAscii* parameter as input, this contains the ANSI value of the key pressed by the user. However, the txtInput_KeyPress event procedure receives another parameter; *Index*. This parameter passes in the element number of the control that had the focus when the user pressed the key on the keyboard. Consequently, the code has a means of identifying which element of the control array received the event and, therefore, which invoked the event procedure. In the case of the txtInput_KeyPress event procedure the value of Index was ignored. The following example shows how the Index value can be used.

Figure 13.9 Relationship between event procedures and their input parameters.

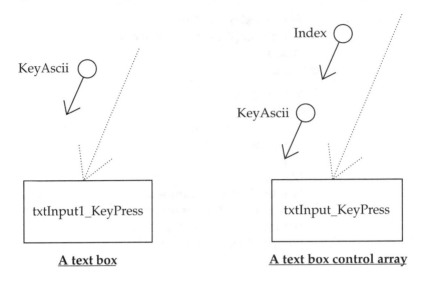

A text box

A text box control array

SPECIFICATION 13.1

Write a program that displays four 'source' pictures in a four-element picture box array. Whenever a source picture is clicked a copy of its picture is displayed in a 'destination' picture box.

Again only two of the recommended six steps will be covered in the development of the program that implements Specification 13.1, i.e., a description of the GUI and the program listings. A suitable GUI for this program is shown in Figure 13.10.

This GUI consists of four line controls, two labels, a four-element Picture Box control array (for the source pictures) and one separate Picture Box used for the destination of the picture.

The pictures loaded into the picture property of the source Picture Boxes are all found in c:\metafile\business (this assumes that Visual Basic has been installed on drive c).

The code for this program is shown in Figure 13.11.

The code consists of a simple assignment statement attached to the click event. At run-time, if the user clicks the satellite picture then the picSource_Click event procedure is supplied with its input parameter *Index* set to the value 0. Consequently, the assignment statement is, effectively, as shown in Figure 13.12.

The picture property of the destination Picture Box is assigned a copy of the picture property setting of the first element of the control array.

If the user clicks the bag of money then the value of the *Index* input parameter is set at 1 and the bag of money is copied to the destination picture box, as shown in Figure 13.13.

Figure 13.10 The GUI for Specification 13.1.

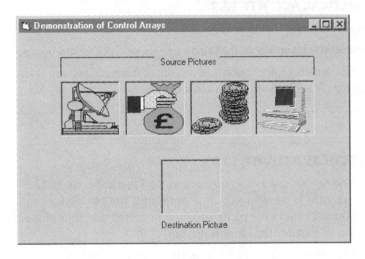

Figure 13.11 Code for Specification 13.1.

```
Private Sub picSource_Click(Index As Integer)
    picDestination.Picture = picSource(Index).Picture
End Sub
```

Figure 13.12 How the value of Index is supplied as an input parameter.

Supplied by the setting of the input parameter *Index*.

picDestination.Picture = picSource(0).Picture

Figure 13.13 Effect of clicking a source picture.

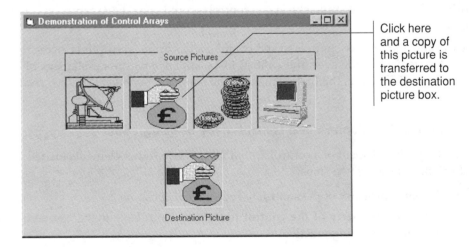

Click here and a copy of this picture is transferred to the destination picture box.

PRACTICAL ACTIVITY 13.2

Implement Specification 13.1

Amend the program so that there are six source picture boxes.

Further amend the program so a copy of a source picture is transferred on a double click event and not a click event.

PRACTICAL ACTIVITY 13.3

Amend the program you developed for Practical activity 13.2 so that a copy of a picture is transferred on a **command button** click event. This implies that the user clicks the picture to be transferred and then clicks the command button to transfer the chosen picture.

HINT: The setting of the *Index* input parameter will need to be assigned to a variable that the command button event procedure has access to.

Creating controls at run-time

A form that contains five picture boxes takes up more memory than a form that contains three picture boxes. When developing large applications the usage of memory is an important factor in its efficiency. One way of saving memory space is to load controls when they are required and to unload them when they are not required. Also, unloading and then loading a control is a useful technique for setting the properties of the control to their original value.

To create a new control at run-time requires that it is a new member of an existing control array. Each new element of a control array inherits the common event procedures of the array. *Without* the control array mechanism, creating new controls at run-time, is *not* possible, because a completely new control would **not** have any predefined event procedures.

You can add and remove controls to and from a control array, at run-time, using the Load and Unload statements. However, the control to be added must be an element of an existing control array. Therefore, the first element of the control array *must have been created at design time*.

Creating the first element of a control array at design time

To create the first element of a control array that will have other elements loaded at run-time, perform the following two steps:

1. Set the name property of the control to reflect its purpose
2. **Set the Index property of the control to 0** (it does not have to start at zero, but this is common programming practice).

Creating another element of a control array at run-time

Assume the first element of the array was created at design time with its name property set to picSource and its Index property set to 0. This first element has the 'full name' of picSource(0). To create the second element at run-time the following VisualBasic statement is required:

Load picSource(1)

This new element will acquire **most** of the property settings from the first element of the array. However, the following properties are **not** automatically copied to the new element of the array.

- Visible.
- Index.
- TabIndex.

The purposes of both Index and TabIndex have been previously discussed. The Visible property has two settings True and False. If this property is set to False then the control is *not* visible at run-time. Obviously, if it is set to True, then it is visible at run-time. Therefore to create a new visible element of a control array at run-time requires the following statements:

Load picSource(1)
picSource(1).Visible = True

> **NOTE**: Visual Basic generates an error if you attempt to use the Load statement with an index number already in use in the array.

Removing an element of a control array at run-time

You can use the Unload statement to remove any control created with Load. However, you cannot use Unload to remove controls created at design time. Therefore, to remove the control picSource(1) use the following Visual Basic statement:

Unload picSource(1)

The implementation of Specification 13.2 will demonstrate how to add and remove controls at run-time.

SPECIFICATION 13.2

Allow a user to add up to four picture boxes on a form. Also allow the user to remove picture boxes from the form. Clicking a picture box will enter a metafile (picture) into the clicked box. The path to the metafile is entered in a text box.

A Boolean data array is to be used to 'keep track' of whether an element is present or otherwise. The GUI is to display the content of the Boolean data array.

Suitable GUI for Specification 13.2

A GUI suitable for implementing Specification 13.2 is shown in Figure 13.14. It consists of three command buttons, a five-element label control array, two independent labels and a picture box that is the first element of a control array that is to be added to (and reduced) at run-time.

Figure 13.14 GUI for Specification 13.2.

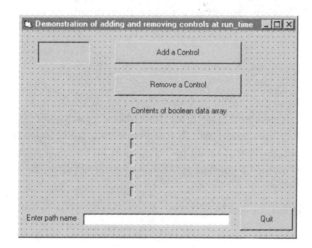

Program listing for Specification 13.2

The full program listing that implements Specification 13.2 is shown in Figure 13.15. It lists; the **non**-default properties for all the controls used, one general procedure, four event procedures, a Boolean data array declaration, general declarations of two constants and a variable declaration.

Figure 13.15 The full program listing.

```
VERSION 4.00
Begin VB.Form frmRunTimeControls
    Caption = "Demonstration of adding and removing controls at run_time"
    ClientHeight = 4575
    ClientLeft = 1710
    ClientTop = 1725
    ClientWidth = 6285
    Height = 4980              Properties
    Left = 1650               of the form
    LinkTopic = "Form1"
    ScaleHeight = 4575
    ScaleWidth = 6285
    Top = 1380
    Width = 6405
    Begin VB.TextBox txtPath
        Height = 285
        Left = 1440           Properties of
        TabIndex = 10         the text box
        Top = 4080
        Width = 3375
End
```

Figure 13.15 (cont.)

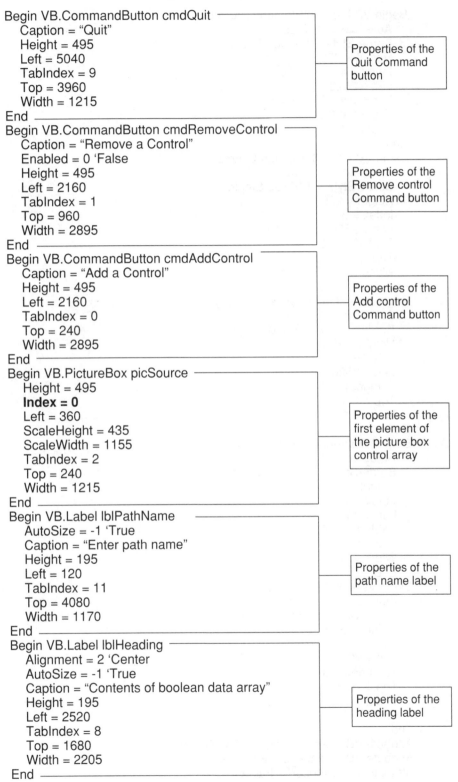

```
Begin VB.CommandButton cmdQuit
    Caption = "Quit"
    Height = 495
    Left = 5040
    TabIndex = 9
    Top = 3960
    Width = 1215
End
```
Properties of the Quit Command button

```
Begin VB.CommandButton cmdRemoveControl
    Caption = "Remove a Control"
    Enabled = 0 'False
    Height = 495
    Left = 2160
    TabIndex = 1
    Top = 960
    Width = 2895
End
```
Properties of the Remove control Command button

```
Begin VB.CommandButton cmdAddControl
    Caption = "Add a Control"
    Height = 495
    Left = 2160
    TabIndex = 0
    Top = 240
    Width = 2895
End
```
Properties of the Add control Command button

```
Begin VB.PictureBox picSource
    Height = 495
    Index = 0
    Left = 360
    ScaleHeight = 435
    ScaleWidth = 1155
    TabIndex = 2
    Top = 240
    Width = 1215
End
```
Properties of the first element of the picture box control array

```
Begin VB.Label lblPathName
    AutoSize = -1 'True
    Caption = "Enter path name"
    Height = 195
    Left = 120
    TabIndex = 11
    Top = 4080
    Width = 1170
End
```
Properties of the path name label

```
Begin VB.Label lblHeading
    Alignment = 2 'Center
    AutoSize = -1 'True
    Caption = "Contents of boolean data array"
    Height = 195
    Left = 2520
    TabIndex = 8
    Top = 1680
    Width = 2205
End
```
Properties of the heading label

Figure 13.15 (cont.)

```
        Begin VB.Label lblElementOfArray
            AutoSize = -1 'True
            BorderStyle = 1 'Fixed Single
            Height = 255
            Index = 4
            Left = 2520
            TabIndex = 7
            Top = 3480
            Width = 105
        End
        Begin VB.Label lblElementOfArray
            AutoSize = -1 'True
            BorderStyle = 1 'Fixed Single
            Height = 255
            Index = 3
            Left = 2520
            TabIndex = 6
            Top = 3120
            Width = 105
        End
        Begin VB.Label lblElementOfArray
            AutoSize = -1 'True
            BorderStyle = 1 'Fixed Single
            Height = 255
            Index = 2
            Left = 2520
            TabIndex = 5
            Top = 2760
            Width = 105
        End
        Begin VB.Label lblElementOfArray
            AutoSize = -1 'True
            BorderStyle = 1 'Fixed Single
            Height = 255
            Index = 1
            Left = 2520
            TabIndex = 4
            Top = 2400
            Width = 105
            End
        Begin VB.Label lblElementOfArray
            AutoSize = -1 'True
            BorderStyle = 1 'Fixed Single
            Height = 255
            Index = 0
            Left = 2520
            TabIndex = 3
            Top = 2040
            Width = 105
            End
        End
        Attribute VB_Name = "frmRunTimeControls"
        Attribute VB_Creatable = False
        Attribute VB_Exposed = False
```

Figure 13.15 (cont.)

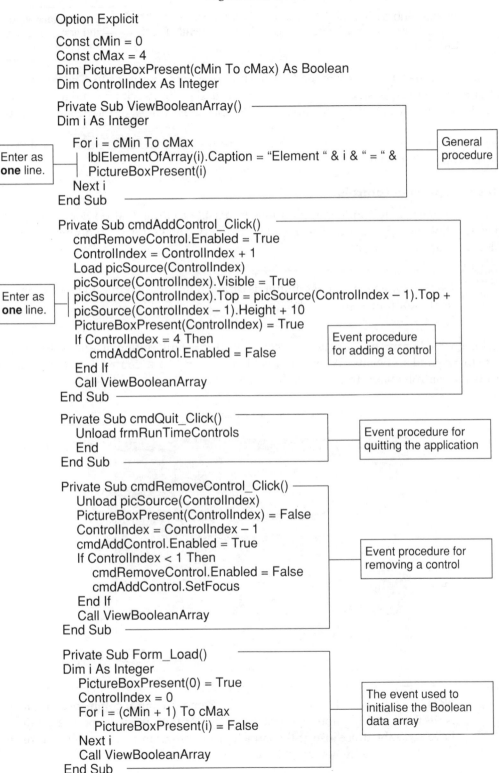

```
Option Explicit

Const cMin = 0
Const cMax = 4
Dim PictureBoxPresent(cMin To cMax) As Boolean
Dim ControlIndex As Integer

Private Sub ViewBooleanArray()
Dim i As Integer

    For i = cMin To cMax
        lblElementOfArray(i).Caption = "Element " & i & " = " &
        PictureBoxPresent(i)
    Next i
End Sub
```

General procedure

Enter as **one** line.

```
Private Sub cmdAddControl_Click()
    cmdRemoveControl.Enabled = True
    ControlIndex = ControlIndex + 1
    Load picSource(ControlIndex)
    picSource(ControlIndex).Visible = True
    picSource(ControlIndex).Top = picSource(ControlIndex – 1).Top +
    picSource(ControlIndex – 1).Height + 10
    PictureBoxPresent(ControlIndex) = True
    If ControlIndex = 4 Then
        cmdAddControl.Enabled = False
    End If
    Call ViewBooleanArray
End Sub
```

Enter as **one** line.

Event procedure for adding a control

```
Private Sub cmdQuit_Click()
    Unload frmRunTimeControls
    End
End Sub
```

Event procedure for quitting the application

```
Private Sub cmdRemoveControl_Click()
    Unload picSource(ControlIndex)
    PictureBoxPresent(ControlIndex) = False
    ControlIndex = ControlIndex – 1
    cmdAddControl.Enabled = True
    If ControlIndex < 1 Then
        cmdRemoveControl.Enabled = False
        cmdAddControl.SetFocus
    End If
    Call ViewBooleanArray
End Sub
```

Event procedure for removing a control

```
Private Sub Form_Load()
Dim i As Integer
    PictureBoxPresent(0) = True
    ControlIndex = 0
    For i = (cMin + 1) To cMax
        PictureBoxPresent(i) = False
    Next i
    Call ViewBooleanArray
End Sub
```

The event used to initialise the Boolean data array

Figure 13.15 (cont.)

Private Sub picSource_Click(Index As Integer)
    picSource(Index).Picture = LoadPicture(txtPath.Text)
End Sub

Event attached to
the first element of
the control array

When launched the GUI looks like the 'screen shot' shown in Figure 13.16. The Form_Load event procedure is responsible for loading the Boolean data array with its initial values and calling the ViewBooleanArray procedure which displays the values of the data array in the five-element label control array. The command button (Remove a Control)has its **Enabled** property set to false.

Enabled property of controls

It is common practice in Window applications to disable controls that do not apply to the current state of the application. The Enabled property allows forms and controls to be enabled or disabled at run-time.

NOTE: When a command button is disabled its caption appears in a lighter font indicating its disabled state.

When the Enabled property of a control is set to True (the default setting) it **allows** the control (object) to respond to events. When the Enabled property of a control is set to False it **prevents** the control (object) from responding to events.

Figure 13.16 The GUI at launch.

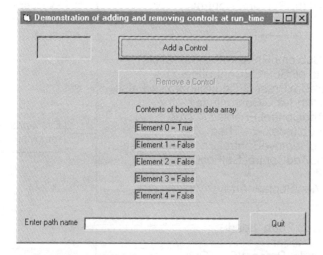

NOTE: At the launch of the program the Remove control command button is disabled and its caption appears in a lighter font. It is common sense to have it disabled because at the launch of the program there are no picture boxes to remove (remember it is **not** possible to remove the first element).

Declaration of two constants, a data array and a variable

Figure 13.17 shows the constants, data array and variable used throughout the program.

> **NOTE**: The data array does not have a purpose for the implementation of Specification 13.2. It is, to some extent, included to give you more practice at using data arrays and will allow for a direct comparison with control arrays. However, programs manipulate data and data structures and the advantage of using a data array to reflect the presence or otherwise of a control (picture box) offers a structure that is easy to process. For instance, it would be easy to count the number of picture boxes present by accessing the Boolean data array with an appropriate *For..Next* loop and a nested selection construct.

Description of the ViewBooleanArray() general procedure

Statements	Description
For i = cMin To cMax lblElementOfArray(i).Caption = "Element " & i & " = " & PictureBoxPresent(i) Next i	The *For..Next* loop executes its statement five times (i.e., cMin to cMax is 0 to 4). The Caption property of each element, of the label **control** array, is assigned a string, the index number of the data array (i.e., *i*) and the content of the Boolean **data** array. The data array was initialised during the Form_Load event procedure.

Description trace of the Form_Load event procedure

This event procedure initialises the Boolean data array and calls the general procedure responsible for displaying the contents of the data array.

Statement	Description
PictureBoxPresent(0) = True	Sets the first element of the Boolean data array to True, which indicates the presence of one element of the control array.
ControlIndex = 0	This variable is used to represent the index number of the highest control element **currently** present on the form. At the launch of the program there is one control present and its index is 0. Therefore this variable is assigned zero.
For i = (cMin + 1) To cMax PictureBoxPresent(i) = False Next i	This *For..Next* loop sets the remainder of the data array elements to False, indicating that no more picture boxes are present at the launch of the program.
Call ViewBooleanArray	This calls the general procedure, which displays the contents of the data array on the GUI.

Description of the cmdAddControl_Click event procedure (shown after Figure 13.7)

This procedure adds a picture box to the form. It only allows the addition of up to four picture boxes. The following description trace reports on what happens when the user clicks the Add control command button for the *first time*.

Figure 13.17 Declaration of constants, Boolean data array and a variable used throughout the program.

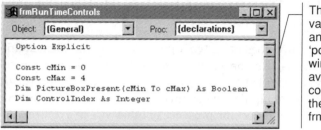

The declaration of the variable, data array and constants in this 'position' of the code window makes them available to all the code associated with the form, frmRunTimeControls.

Statement	Description
cmdRemoveControl.Enabled = True	Invoking this procedure adds a picture box to the form. Consequently, it is common sense to enable the Remove control command button because there is now a control present that can be removed. Therefore, its Enabled property is set to True.
ControlIndex = ControlIndex + 1	A picture box will be added so the variable ControlIndex is incremented to 1 which represents the index of the highest element of the control array present.
Load picSource(ControlIndex)	This statement is effectively:Load picSource(1) because the ControlIndex variable is set at 1. The effect of this statement is to load another element of the control array.
picSource(ControlIndex).Visible = True	This statement makes the new control Visible.
picSource(ControlIndex).Top = picSource(ControlIndex – 1).Top + picSource(ControlIndex – 1).Height + 10	This positions the new control on the form. A later chapter on **graphics** deals with how controls are positioned. For the time being accept that this works.
PictureBoxPresent(ControlIndex) = True	The second element of the Boolean **data** array is assigned True to indicate the presence of a second element of the **control** array.
If ControlIndex = 4 Then cmdAddControl.Enabled = False End If	*The variable ControlIndex is assigned 1, consequently, the conditional test is false and the statement inside the *If..Then* construct is **not** executed.
Call ViewBooleanArray	The general procedure is called to display the up-to-date contents of the data array.

*When this event procedure is invoked for the fourth time (assuming that the remove control button has not been invoked) the statement inside the *If..Then* construct **is** executed and the Add control command button is disabled, thus, no more than four picture boxes can be added.

Description of the cmdRemoveControl_Click event procedure

The following trace table describes what happens **after** one control has been added at run-time.

Statement	Description
Unload picSource(ControlIndex)	The value of ControlIndex is currently set at 1, consequently, the second element of the control array is Unloaded from the form.
PictureBoxPresent(ControlIndex) = False	The second element of the **data** array is set to false to reflect the removal of the second element of the **control** array.
ControlIndex = ControlIndex – 1	The variable ControlIndex is decremented by 1 so that it represents the index number of the highest element of the array element present, i.e., it is set back to zero indicating that there is only one control present.
cmdAddControl.Enabled = True	Ensures that the Add control command button is enabled because one has just been removed. Therefore it is valid to be able to add another (remember what happens when all four controls are added?)

If ControlIndex < 1 Then
    cmdRemoveControl.Enabled = False
    cmdAddControl.SetFocus
End If
	Zero is less than one so the statements inside the *If..Then* construct **are** executed and the Remove control command button is disabled. This makes sense because there are no more controls to remove. The second statement sets the focus back to the Add control command button.

Call ViewBooleanArray	This general procedure is called to display the current contents of the data array.

Description trace of the picSource_Click event procedure

The user enters the path name to a graphics file in the text box of the GUI, the user then clicks the picture box that will act as the destination for the picture. This event procedure is attached to the first element of the picture box control array.

Every new element of the control array created at run-time will invoke this event procedure, if it is clicked (i.e., if the new picture box control is clicked).

Statement	Description
picSource(Index).Picture = LoadPicture(txtPath.Text)	LoadPicture is a function that loads a graphic into a Form object, Picture Box control, or Image control. It takes as its argument the path to the file to be loaded. The user enters the path name of the graphic file in the text box (txtPath)of the GUI which acts as the argument for this function.

PRACTICAL ACTIVITY 13.4

Implement Specification 13.2.

QUESTION 13.1 (DEVELOPMENT)

For the program you developed in Practical activity 13.4 comment out the line of code as shown in bold in Figure 13.18 and run the application.

*Click the Add control command button **five** times.*

The program crashes why?

Figure 13.18 Comment out the code – associated with Question 13.1.

```
Private Sub cmdAddControl_Click()
    cmdRemoveControl.Enabled = True
    ControlIndex = ControlIndex + 1
    Load picSource(ControlIndex)
    picSource(ControlIndex).Visible = True
    picSource(ControlIndex).Top = picSource(ControlIndex – 1).Top +
picSource(ControlIndex – 1).Height + 10
    PictureBoxPresent(ControlIndex) = True
    If ControlIndex = 4 Then
        'cmdAddControl.Enabled = False
    End If
    Call ViewBooleanArray
End Sub
```

QUESTION 13.2 (DEVELOPMENT)

For the program you developed in Practical activity 13.4 comment out the line of code as shown in bold in Figure 13.19 and run the application.

*Click the Add control command button **four** times and then click the Remove control button **five** times.*

The program crashes why?

Figure 13.19 Comment out the code – associated with Question 13.2.

```
Private Sub cmdRemoveControl_Click()
    Unload picSource(ControlIndex)
    PictureBoxPresent(ControlIndex) = False
    ControlIndex = ControlIndex – 1
    cmdAddControl.Enabled = True
    If ControlIndex < 1 Then
        'cmdRemoveControl.Enabled = False
        cmdAddControl.SetFocus
    End If
    Call ViewBooleanArray
End Sub
```

PRACTICAL ACTIVITY 13.5

Amend the program developed during Practical activity 13.4 so that it has the following additional features.

A command button, that when clicked, will report, in a label, the number of controls currently loaded.

HINT: Use a loop to read the contents of the Boolean **data** array.

14 Procedures

Procedures are small programs that perform a specific task. There are two major benefits of programming with procedures.

1. Procedures allow a program to be split up in to small logical units, where each unit performs a simple task. Consequently, a program developed with procedures is much easier to debug than a large 'monolithic' program developed without procedures.

2. Procedures are portable sections of code that can be used in other programs with little or no modification. They can act as building blocks for other programs.

Types of procedures

There are three types of Visual Basic procedures:

1. **Sub** procedures that can return and receive values via parameters.
2. **Function** procedures that return a value.
3. **Property** procedures that can return and assign values, and set references to objects.

General procedures

A general procedure, like an event procedure, contains program code. However, unlike an event procedure, a general procedure cannot be directly executed in response to an event. A general procedure must, in the first instance, be called by an event procedure. Code must exist inside an event procedure to call a general procedure. The relationship between an event and general procedure is shown in Figure 14.1.

 NOTE: A general procedure can call another general procedure. However, the invoking general procedure must have first been invoked by an event procedure.

Why have general procedures?

Several different event procedures might need the same actions performed. Consequently; rather than duplicate the code to perform the actions within these event procedures, the code can be put into a general procedure. This general procedure can then be called from the event procedures requiring the actions it performs.

Figure 14.1 The relationship between an event and general procedure.
The dotted arrow represents an event, invoking an event procedure, and the arrow
represents the event procedure calling the general procedure.

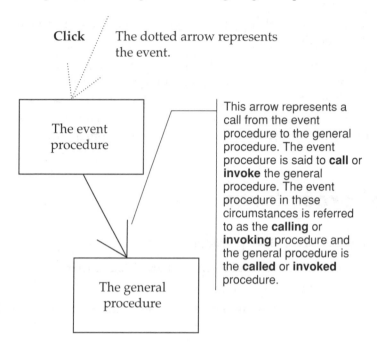

Methodologies

There are numerous methodologies that assist programmers when writing code. All of these methodologies have uses specific to various stages of the software life cycle. Each methodology has a group of advocates that claim they greatly improve software production. Whereas these claims are often overstated there is no doubt that it is *better to use a methodology than not.*

NOTE: Visual Basic is an evolving product, it differs from traditional procedural programming because of the way it uses events. However, it has many of the features of traditional procedural programming, for instance, it has procedures that work in exactly the same way as procedures in procedural languages. These procedures are declared and called and parameters are passed between the calling and called procedures (modules). Consequently, it is valid to use methodologies with Visual Basic that are derived from traditional procedural programming because Visual Basic can and does implement code in a very similar way. However, Visual Basic is evolving towards object oriented programming and this is also different to traditional procedural programming. Consequently, some of the methodologies discussed in this chapter are **not** suitable for all the programming facilities and techniques offered by Visual Basic. Nevertheless, they are valid for the way a significant part of Visual Basic is still 'based' in the 'procedural-like' implementation of code. The development of Visual Basic code through objects as defined in class modules will require different supporting methodologies.

To summarise, Visual Basic (in my opinion) needs design methodologies to support three strands of its code development. One for events, one for implementation through procedures and one for its implementation through objects. This chapter introduces two of these three strands and *suggests* suitable methodologies.

Structure charts and process activation diagrams

Consider the following specification.

SPECIFICATION 14.1

Write a program that calculates the weekly salary of company employees. The program must have a GUI that will allow for the entry of the weekly hours worked, the pay rate per hour, the employees works number and name. When details on one employee are entered these are logged to a file. It must also allow for the details on an employee to be printed and have a search facility to locate details on one employee. At the end of every week the wage slip of every employee is printed and this is achieved by the user clicking an appropriate command button.

A suitable GUI for Specification 14.1 is shown in Figure 14.2.

Figure 14.2 A suitable GUI for Specification 14.1.

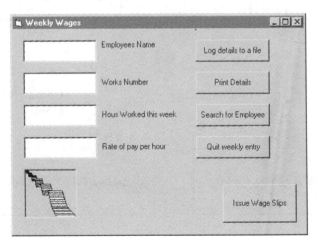

By inspection, it can be seen that this GUI will respond to five user-invoked events (one for each of the command buttons). A suitable diagram to represent the events attached to this GUI is shown in Figure 14.3.

Figure 14.4 shows an alternative method for representing the events to which the form responds.

The thick vertical bar (line) represents the form and is labelled with the name of the form (frmWeeklyWages). The dotted lines to the left of the bar represent events that invoke event procedures that are attached to the controls on the form (or the form itself). Each event is labelled with the type of event it is. In this case, all the events are command button event procedures and therefore are all labelled the same. To the right of the bar are rectangles that represent the event procedures that are invoked by the dotted lines. The names of the event procedures appear in the rectangles.

Visual Basic programs can consists of many forms, in which case each form will have its own process activation diagram.

The code attached to each event (i.e., each event procedure) will need designing and this can be achieved through **stepwise refinement**. As a useful guide, procedure code should cover no more than one side of A4 paper. Code of this size is easy to read and debug. Of course, an individual procedure can consist of many more lines, and they often do, but they are unpleasant to work with. Procedures that are 'too big' are often the result of a solution that has not been effectively partitioned – which is the result of poor design. The partitioning of a solution into code modules that perform smaller tasks, that work together to produce a solution, to implement a specification, is a very important aspect of program design. The

Figure 14.3 Event procedures attached to GUI.

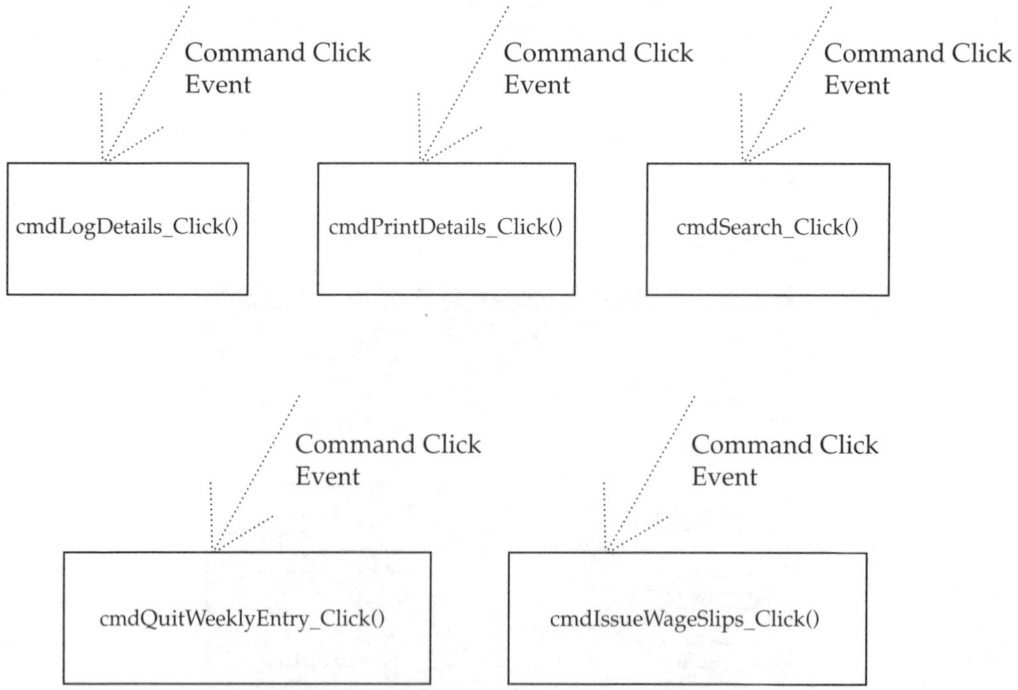

Command Click
Event

Command Click
Event

Command Click
Event

cmdLogDetails_Click()

cmdPrintDetails_Click()

cmdSearch_Click()

Command Click
Event

Command Click
Event

cmdQuitWeeklyEntry_Click()

cmdIssueWageSlips_Click()

Figure 14.4 Events and the procedures they invoke. This is an example of a 'process activation diagram'.

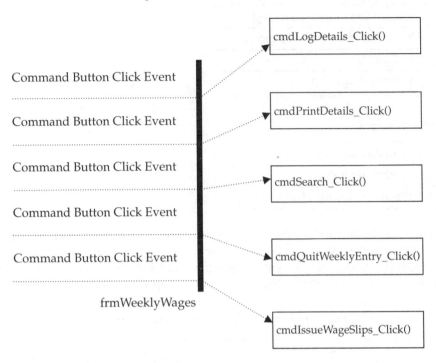

decomposition of a design (solution) in smaller tasks (i.e., program modules, which are procedures) can be represented by a **structure chart**.

QUESTION 14.1 (REVISION)

Produce a process activation diagram for the form described below.

A form with its name property set to frmDemo, responds to a double click event that activates an event procedure that changes the background colour of the form. Drawn on the form are two picture boxes and a command button. These controls, their name property and attached events are as follows:

- *Picture box 1. The name property is set to picCircle, and when it is double clicked, its attached event procedure draws a circle in the picture box.*

- *Picture box 2. The name property is set to picSquare, and when it is double clicked, its attached event procedure draws a Square in the picture box.*

- *Command button 1. The name property is set to cmdQuit, and when it is clicked, its attached event procedure ends the application.*

Stepwise refinement

Stepwise refinement involves designing a program in gradual stages, beginning with the overall structure and omitting the detail. Future steps in the design process involve the designing of the details. The best way to illustrate the stepwise process is by example. The design for the event procedure responsible for issuing wage slips will act as the example.

Top Level design

1. While not last employee record
2. Obtain the employee record
3. Calculate net pay
4. Print Wage slip

Refinement of step 3

3.1 Calculate Gross Pay
3.2 Calculate deductions
3.3 Subtract deductions from gross pay

These designs can be further represented by a structure chart which can act as a 'picture' of all the 'software parts' used during the development of a program. The structure chart shows all the procedures used to implement the program and how they communicate with each other. Figure 14.5 shows a simple structure chart that represents the design of the 'software

Figure 14.5 Structure chart for issuing wage slips.

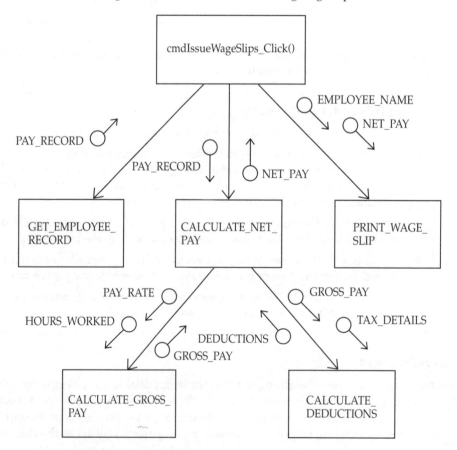

parts' (i.e., procedures) for the design of the event procedure that issues wage slips. *Using a structure chart increases the* **probability** *that any one procedure will be no greater than one side of A4 paper. This assists in making code easier to read and debug.*

The structure chart shows a design (software system) partitioned into the following communicating modules (the boxes):

- ISSUE_WAGE_SLIPS (cmdIssueWageSlips_Click)
- GET_EMPLOYEE_RECORD
- CALCULATE_NET_PAY
- PRINT_WAGE_SLIP
- CALCULATE_GROSS_PAY
- CALCULATE_DEDUCTIONS

Communication between all of the modules is shown by the following data couples (the circle and arrow) – which are procedure parameters.

- PAY_RECORD (a compound data couple)
- NET_PAY
- EMPLOYEE_NAME (obtained from the PAY_RECORD)
- PAY_RATE (obtained from the PAY_RECORD)
- HOURS_WORKED (obtained from the PAY_RECORD)
- GROSS_PAY
- TAX_DETAILS (obtained from the PAY_RECORD)
- DEDUCTIONS

Advantages of structure charts

1. A structure chart is able to convey an overview of the software system it represents. For instance, the structure chart shown in Figure 14.5, obviously, represents the design of a software system that calculates employee wages and prints their pay slip – it would be difficult to interpret it as the design for anything else. This overview is achieved without the need to see any program listing for the software system. Indeed it is difficult to obtain an overview from a program listing.

2. Shows the system as partitioned communicating modules, that can be separately developed and tested. A team of programmers can all be given a separate module to develop and test. All of the complete and tested modules can then be linked together to produce the final program, which after integration testing can be released as the final product. Consequently, the development of the code is more efficient and reliable. The structure chart of Figure 14.5 can be quickly developed by a team of six programmers each responsible for developing and testing one module. This obviously improves productivity because it allows for the parallel development of all six modules. Although an oversimplification, it is fair to say that if only one programmer were to develop the software system it would take six times as long.

3. Managers are able to monitor the development of the software because they can keep a close check on the progress of each module. If there were no design then managers could only 'weigh' the code and assume from its 'weight' that progress is or is not being made. By using the overview gained from the structure chart they are able to check the functionality of the code for each module and actually check that all are working.

4. It is easier to maintain code. For example, suppose the customer requires an upgrade to the printer that prints the wage slip. One look at the structure chart shows that the PRINT_WAGE_SLIP module is responsible for the printing of the wage slips. The maintenance programmer merely locates the code that implements this module (the module name within the code should be the same) and makes the appropriate changes. If a structure chart design for the code were not available the maintenance programmer *may* only have access to the program listing. The task of finding the appropriate code for alteration is now a difficult and frustrating task.

5. However, possibly the most important advantage to be gained from using structure charts is that they can be measured for quality. The structure chart 'guides' the development of the code. Consequently, improving the quality of the structure chart will result in better quality code. In other words the *probability* of achieving quality code is improved if the structure chart is improved. Thus there is no need to wait for the code to be produced before an attempt is made to improve the quality. There are a number of ways that the quality of a structure chart can be measured and subsequently improved. Two of the most important are coupling and cohesion (many texts are available on the techniques of coupling and cohesion).

Structure chart modules

Each module in the structure chart can be implemented by a Visual Basic procedure. The data to be processed by each module is the data supplied by the data couples. For instance, consider the module CALCULATE_GROSS_PAY and the data couples associated with it, as shown in Figure 14.6

The module of Figure 14.6 is one of six from the original design shown in Figure 14.5. Associated with each module is a module specification (MSPEC). Every module has up to four basic attributes that are defined in their MSPECS. These basic attributes are:

- Input and output parameters
- Function
- Mechanics
- Local Data

Figure 14.6 An isolated CALLED module.

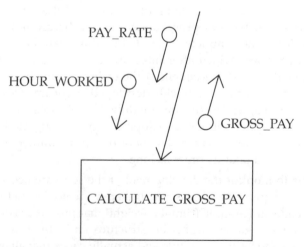

Input and output parameters

Every module is usually called by another module. For example, the module CALCULATE_GROSS_PAY is called by CALCULATE_NET_PAY. CALCULATE_NET_PAY is referred to as the calling module or invoking module and CALCULATE_GROSS_PAY is referred to as the called or invoked module. The communication between called and calling modules is through parameters (data couples). The called module views these parameters as either input or output parameters. Figure 14.6 shows a called module together with three parameters (data couples). PAY_RATE and HOURS_WORKED are the input parameters, and GROSS_PAY the output parameter.

Function

The function of the module is (usually) what it does to the input parameter(s) to produce the output parameter(s). A module name indicates its functionality. Consequently, the module of Figure 14.6 has a function that is to obtain the gross pay from the input parameters.

Mechanics

This is the code or logic (defined by an N-S Chart or Structured English design) by which a module carries out its function (i.e., it is the program statements).

Local data

This is an area of memory to which only the module can gain access. The module uses this area for the storage of information only it requires.

MSPEC for CALCULATE_GROSS_PAY

Input Parameter(s)	HOURS_WORKED PAY_RATE
Output Parameter(s)	GROSS_PAY
Function	CALCULATE_GROSS_PAY
Local Data	There are none for this module
Mechanics	GROSS_PAY equals PAY_RATE times HOURS_WORKED

A programmer will use the details supplied by the MSPEC to develop and test a program module. This module will be a procedure in Visual Basic.

Declaring and calling a procedure

Making your own procedure in Visual Basic involves two steps:

1. The procedure declaration.

2. One or more procedure calls.

The *procedure declaration* defines the input and output parameters, local data and the function as defined by the program statements (mechanics). *A procedure call causes the procedure to execute.*

225

The procedure call and return

Figure 14.7 illustrates a generalised diagram of a called procedure, a calling procedure and data couples.

Figure 14.7 Calling procedures.

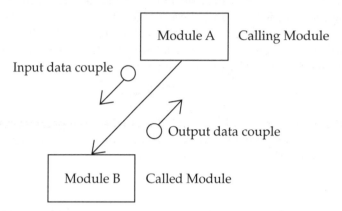

The statements (mechanics) of Module A are executed, as illustrated in Figure 14.8 (shown in bold) before the call to Module B.

Figure 14.8 Executing statements in the calling module. Module A executes its statements **BEFORE** the call.

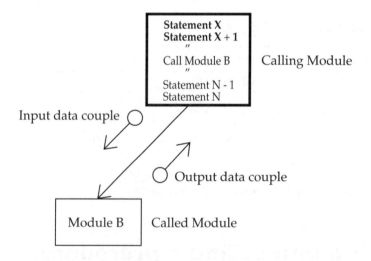

Module A calls Module B passing the input data couple at the same time (Figure 14.9).

Module B executes its mechanics. It processes the input data couple to produce the output data couple (Figure 14.10).

Upon completion of the Module B mechanics, control is returned to Module A, with the output data couple being passed back (Figure 14.11).

Module A then completes its mechanics (Figure 14.12).

Figure 14.9 Calling Module B.

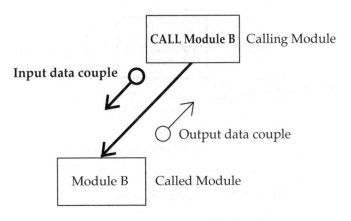

Figure 14.10 Module B executes its statements.

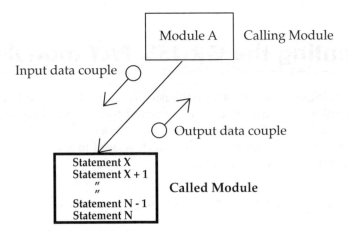

Figure 14.11 The return to Module A.

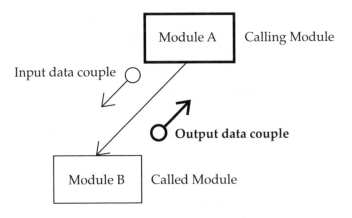

Figure 14.12 Module A completing its mechanics.

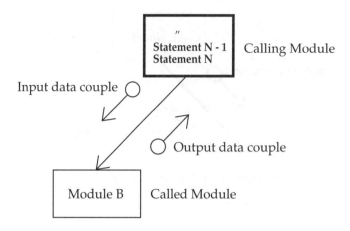

Input data couple

Statement N - 1
Statement N — Calling Module

Output data couple

Module B — Called Module

Implementing the **GROSS_PAY** module

The module will be implemented by a Visual Basic procedure that needs to be declared and called. The declaration is used to define the action(s) (i.e., the mechanics), the input and output parameters and the local data (none in this case) specified in the MSPEC. The call will be from a command button event procedure, which is used to test the functionality of the procedure. This relationship is shown in Figure 14.13.

Figure 14.13 Calling CALCULTE_GROSS_PAY from a Command click event.

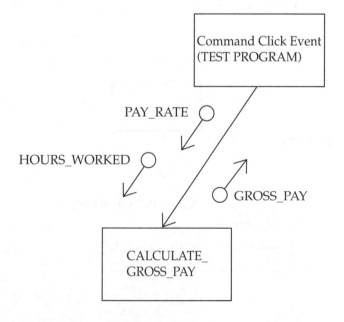

Command Click Event
(TEST PROGRAM)

PAY_RATE

HOURS_WORKED

GROSS_PAY

CALCULATE_
GROSS_PAY

Flow of control for modules

The Command Click event procedure executes its own instructions then calls the module CALCULATE_GROSS_PAY this module completes its instructions and then control is passed back to the Command Click event procedure.

Parameter passing mechanism

The Command Click event procedure will ask for the PAY_RATE and HOURS_WORKED from the keyboard. It then calls the CALCULATE_GROSS_PAY module sending it the values of PAY_RATE and HOURS_WORKED. The CALCULATE_GROSS_PAY module uses these *input parameters* to calculate the gross pay. The GROSS_PAY (*output parameter*) is returned to the Command Click event procedure and is displayed on the VDU by the code in the Command Click event procedure.

The GUI and Visual Basic procedures used to implement this test are shown in Figure 14.14 and 14.15 respectively.

Relating a procedure to its MSPEC

- The **function** of the procedure is suggested by the procedure name, in this case, CalculateGrossPay.
- pHoursWorked and pPayRate are the **input** parameters to the procedure.
- pGrossPay is the **output** parameter from the procedure.
- pGrossPay = pHoursWorked * pPayRate form the **mechanics** of the procedure.
- There are no **local data** for this procedure.

> **NOTE**: The lower-case p is placed in front of the parameters used in the procedure so they can easily be identified as parameters. This is an adopted style that is an example of good programming practice.

Figure 14.14 The test GUI.

Test Program

Hours worked TEST DATA

Rate of pay per hour TEST DATA

TEST Calculate Gross Pay

Gross Pay TEST DATA

Figure 14.15 Test program and procedure under test.

```
Private Sub cmdTESTCalculateGrossPay_Click()
Dim HoursWorked As Single
Dim PayRate As Single
Dim GrossPay As Single
    HoursWorked = CSng(txtInputTestData(0).Text)
    PayRate = CSng(txtInputTestData(1).Text)
    Call CalculateGrossPay(HoursWorked, PayRate, GrossPay)
    txtOutputFromProcedure.Text = Str(GrossPay)
End Sub

Private Sub CalculateGrossPay(ByVal pHoursWorked As Single, ByVal
pPayRate As Single, pGrossPay As Single)

    pGrossPay = pHoursWorked * pPayRate
End Sub
```

Enter as
one line or
use space
and the
underscore
character.

Declaring the procedure

The procedure for calculating the gross pay can be declared as a form level procedure. The steps for declaring such a procedure are shown in Figure 14.16.

> **QUESTION 14.2 (DEVELOPMENT)**
>
> *Use the Visual Basic online help to discover another way of declaring procedures.*
>
> ***HINT***: *It involves selecting* Procedure ... *from the* Insert Menu.

A procedure call and its parameters

A procedure is called using the keyword *Call* and the procedure name. In this case the name is CalculateGrossPay. Following the identifier are brackets that contain the parameters to be passed. The number of parameters in brackets must match the number of parameters in the procedure declaration – three in this case. The call to the procedure is shown below:

Call CalculateGrossPay(HoursWorked, PayRate, GrossPay)

> **NOTE**: For the declaration of the procedure and the call, the parameters, shown in the brackets, are referred to as the argument list.

Relating parameters (arguments) in the call and declaration

The parameters are related by the **order** they appear in their respective lists. Consequently, the relationship between the arguments is as shown below:

HoursWorked	⟶	pHoursWorked(Both first in their respective lists)
PayRate	⟶	pPayRate(Both second in their respective lists)
GrossPay	⟶	pGrossPay(Both third in their respective lists)

When the procedure is called the value stored in PayRate is passed to pPayRate and the value stored in HoursWorked is passed to pHoursWorked. On returning from the procedure the value calculated in the procedure is passed out to GrossPay.

For a correct relationship, arguments in the declaration and the call have to be the same type. For example PayRate and pPayRate have both been declared as single and this is correct. If one was declared as single and the other string the program would not compile.

How arguments (parameters) are passed between a procedure and its call

The sequence of figures, from Figure 14.17 to Figure 14.21, illustrate how arguments (parameters) are passed between a procedure call and the procedure (its declaration). The arguments (parameters) in the Visual Basic declaration are referred to as the formal arguments. The arguments in the procedure call are referred to as the actual arguments. Formal arguments pHoursWorked and pRatePay are examples of **pass-by-value** arguments and are used to receive input values from the calling module. The formal argument

Figure 14.16 Declaring a form level procedure.

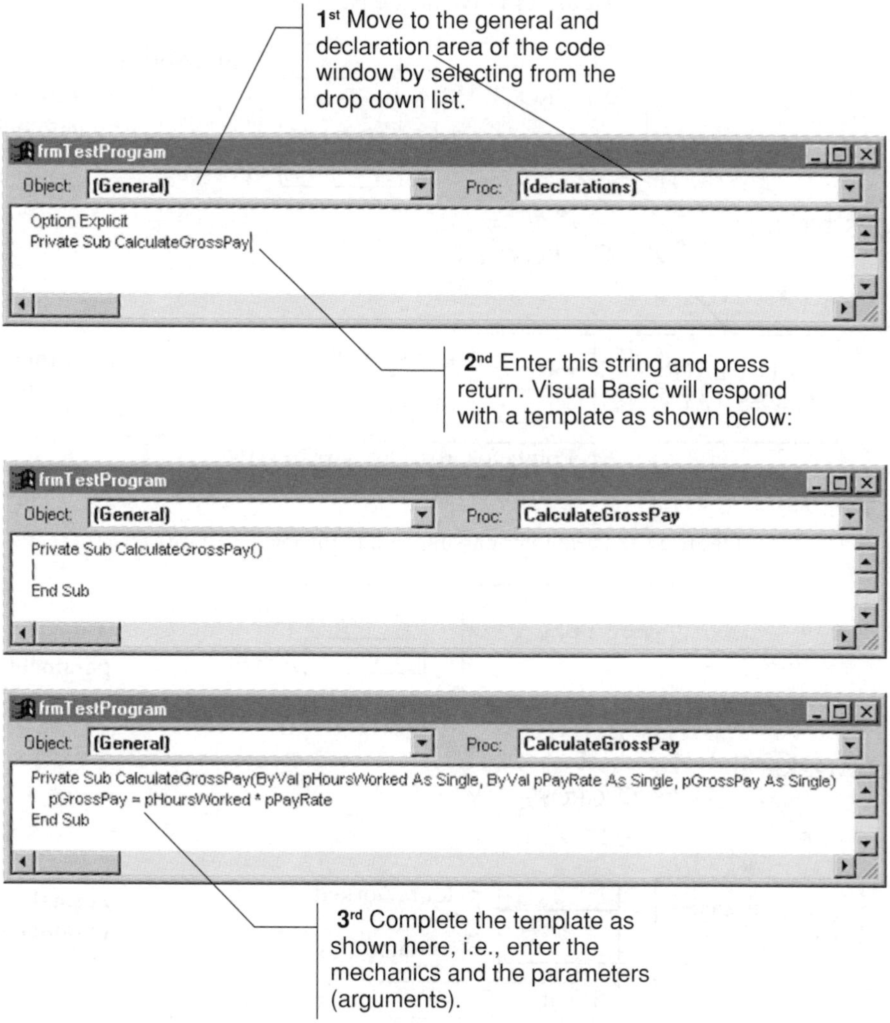

1st Move to the general and declaration area of the code window by selecting from the drop down list.

2nd Enter this string and press return. Visual Basic will respond with a template as shown below:

3rd Complete the template as shown here, i.e., enter the mechanics and the parameters (arguments).

pGrossPay is an example of a **pass-by-reference** argument and it is used here to direct the output back to the actual argument GrossPay.

 NOTE: A pass-by-reference parameter can act as an input and output parameter – more on this later.

A pass-by-value argument (parameter) is identified by the **presence** of the reserved word *ByVal* in front of its identifier.

A pass-by-reference argument (parameter) is identified by the **absence** of the reserved word *ByVal*.

Still in the test program

Figure 14.18 shows the condition of the variables (actual parameters) immediately after the user of the program enters 35 and 5 for the hours worked and rate of pay per hour respectively.

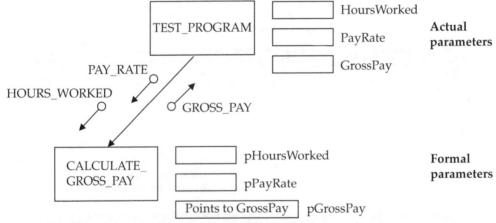

Figure 14.17 Parameter passing.

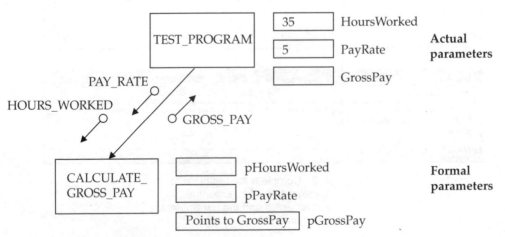

Figure 14.18 Parameter passing (still in the test program).

The call

Figure 14.19 shows the parameter values being passed from the TEST_PROGRAM module to CALCULATE_GROSS_PAY module. The value in the actual parameter HoursWorked is passed to the formal parameter pHoursWorked. Both these parameters are related because they are first in their respective lists. The value in PayRate is passed to pPayRate because they are listed second in their respective lists.

Figure 14.19 Parameter passing (the call).

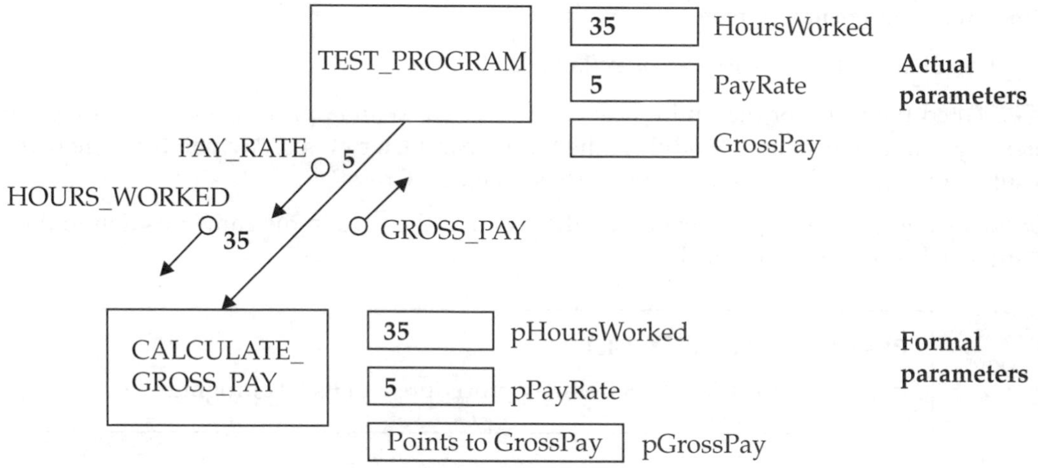

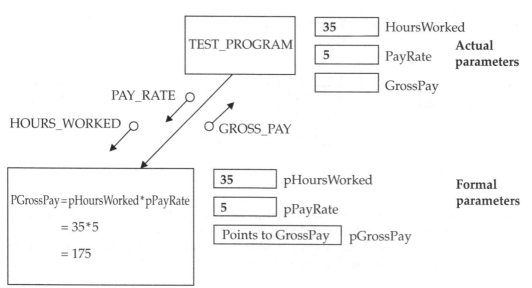

Execution of the module

The module now processes its data by executing its mechanics (Figure 14.20).

Figure 14.20 Parameter passing (execution of the mechanics).

The return

Once the called module (procedure) has finished its processing, control is returned to the calling module. The result of the module mechanics (i.e., 175) is passed back to the actual parameter GrossPay. The test program then displays the gross pay (£175) on the VDU (refer to Figure 14.21).

The 175 is passed back to the actual parameter GrossPay. The formal parameter pGrossPay contains the address of the actual parameter GrossPay. Consequently, a pass-by-reference formal parameter points to the actual parameter GrossPay because it 'knows' its address.

When the assignment statement

pGrossPay = pHoursWorked * pPayRate;

is executed the result of the multiplication is directed to an appropriate area of computer memory. Upon returning to Module A the formal parameter pGrossPay points to where the result of the multiplication should be returned, namely, GrossPay.

GrossPay and pGrossPay are related by the fact that they are in the same position in their respective list (i.e., both are third).

PRACTICAL ACTIVITY 14.1

Implement the CalculateGrossPay procedure and its test program.

Figure 14.21 Parameter passing (the return).

	35	HoursWorked	
TEST_PROGRAM			**Actual**
	5	PayRate	**parameters**
	175	GrossPay	

PAY_RATE

HOURS_WORKED

GROSS_PAY
175

CALCULATE_ GROSS_PAY		pHoursWorked	**Formal**
		pPayRate	**parameters**
	Points to GrossPay	pGrossPay	

Extra information

All program variables are stored in the computer's memory. A computer memory is a sequence of storage locations that hold binary patterns. Each storage location has a unique address. A typical (simplified) computer memory is illustrated in Figure 14.22.

The memory has 65 536 locations and each location is 16 bits wide. The binary address of the first location is 0000 0000 0000 0000 and the binary address of the last location is 1111 1111 1111 1111.

The binary content of the first location is 0000 0001 0000 1111. This is 271 in decimal.

A significant advantage of using a high-level language over a low-level language is that details of the machine level, such as memory space, are unnecessary. A high-level programmer is not concerned with which address is used to store data. The compiler is responsible for deciding where a variable is to be stored in memory. For instance, an integer variable with the identifier FirstNumber may be given the storage location with the binary address 0000 0000 0000 0000. A user of the program may, in response to a request for input, enter 271. Consequently, the storage location with the address 0000 0000 0000 0000 will have the binary contents 0000 0001 0000 1111. This level of detail is not the concern of the high-level language programmer. They use the identifier FirstNumber whenever its content requires access.

However, to fully understand the difference between pass-by-value and pass-by-reference parameters an understanding of computer memory is necessary.

When a pass-by-value parameter is used the content of the memory location is passed between modules, that is, the content of the variable.

When a pass-by-reference parameter is used the address of the parameter is passed, that is, the address of the storage location used to store the parameter. Therefore, a pass-by-reference formal parameter is able to point to the address of the actual parameter. This knowledge of the address allows for access to the content of the actual parameter and the content can be written to and read. Consequently, declaring parameters as pass-by-reference allows for data to pass in either direction between the calling and called module. Therefore, a pass-by-reference parameter can be an input and/or output parameter.

Pass-by-value and pass-by-reference

When relating pass-by-value and pass-by-reference parameters to a structure chart, as a first approximation, the pass-by-value parameter can be regarded as an input parameter to the procedure, and pass-by-reference parameter as an output from the procedure.

Pass-by-value arguments, pass the contents of a variable from the calling procedure to the called procedure. Consequently, the called procedure works with a *copy* of the variable and the content of the variable in the calling procedure **cannot** be altered by the called procedure.

Pass-by-reference arguments pass in the address of the calling procedures variable. Consequently, the called procedure works with the variable of the calling procedure and **not** a copy. Therefore, the called procedure **can** alter the contents of the calling procedures variable. The called procedure has access to the variable in the calling procedure because it is

Figure 14.22 A typical computer memory.

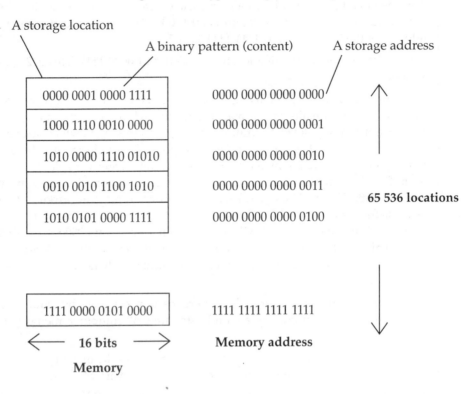

able to 'point to it' using its address. Consequently, a pass-by-reference argument can act as an input and an output parameter. Therefore, the procedure shown in Figure 14.15 can be implemented using pass-by-reference arguments as shown in Figure 14.23. *However, whenever possible use pass-by-value because only a copy of the originating data is used and the called procedure will not be able to alter this data, which may be required in its original form by another procedure.*

NOTE: The relationship between the test program and the CalculateGrossPay procedure requires that the called procedure returns the GrossPay argument. The position of the CALCULATE_GROSS_PAY module in the original structure chart (Figure 14.5) also requires that it return the GrossPay parameter (data couple) to its calling module, CALCULATE_NET_PAY. The relationship between the calling and called module shows that the data couples PayRate and HoursWorked are input parameters to the CALCULATE_GROSS_PAY module. So although it is possible to code the CALCULATE_GROSS_PAY module with PayRate and HoursWorked as pass-by-reference arguments, it is not logical to do so. Make them pass-by-value parameters; this way the called procedure will deal with a copy of the calling procedures variable, and it will not have the type of access that is able to change this variable, i.e., it can only act as an input which is in 'sympathy' with its place in the logic of the structure chart.

Figure 14.23 A procedure using just pass-by-reference arguments.

```
Private Sub CalculateGrossPay(pHoursWorked As Single, pPayRate As
Single, pGrossPay As Single)
    pGrossPay = pHoursWorked * pPayRate
End Sub
```

Pass-by-value and pass-by-reference arguments (parameters) summary

A pass-by-value argument passes *content* between modules. Whereas, a pass-by-reference passes an *address* between modules and the address allows for direct access to the calling procedures variable, it does not just deal with a copy of the contents, it deals with the variable itself.

Procedures and libraries

Structure charts are an excellent way to develop the design for large software systems. As previously discussed, procedures are an essential mechanism for implementing structure charts. However, procedures are not just used to implement the modules for large software systems. Developing code in procedures makes sense regardless of the size and complexity of the software being developed. A well designed procedure can be added to a collection of other procedures to form a library. The contents of the library can then be 'tapped' during the development of other software systems.

The procedure used to calculate the gross pay is declared as a form level procedure. This is a valid technique for procedure declarations in Visual Basic and it allows for a form to be developed as a 'tight and complete entity'. Although it is possible to call this procedure from other forms throughout a project, it is far better to **declare all useful and general purpose procedure in a standard module (.BAS module).**

Standard modules (.BAS)

Standard modules are containers for procedures **and declarations** used by other parts of an application. They are ideal for creating a library of useful procedures.

Standard modules can contain:

- Public declarations of types, constants, variables and public procedures.
- Module-level declarations of types, constants and variables.

Standard modules have a .BAS file name extension.

Adding a standard module to a project

A module can be added to a project by selecting *Module* from the *Insert* menu or by clicking the module icon ()on the tool bar. Once added to a project its presence is reflected in the project window as shown in Figure 14.24.

The code window for a standard module is shown in Figure 14.25.

Figure 14.26 shows how to add the CalculateGrossPay procedure to the standard module code window.

PRACTICAL ACTIVITY 14.2

Implement the CalculateGrossPay module and test program but this time declare the CalculateGrossPay procedure in a standard (.BAS) module (remember to use the keyword **Public** instead of the keyword **Private**).

Figure 14.24 The project window showing the presence of a standard module.

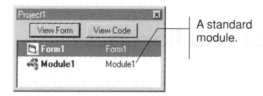

Figure 14.25 Code window for a standard module.

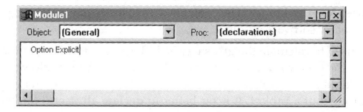

Figure 14.26 Adding a procedure to the code window of a standard module.

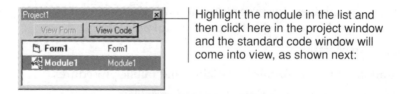

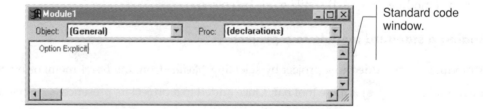

Figure 14.26 (cont.)

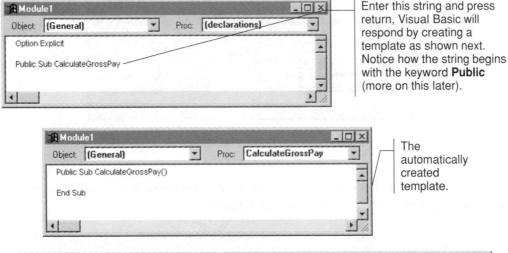

Enter this string and press return, Visual Basic will respond by creating a template as shown next. Notice how the string begins with the keyword **Public** (more on this later).

The automatically created template.

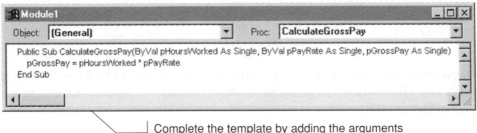

Complete the template by adding the arguments (parameters) and VB statement (mechanics).

Use of the keywords Public and Private

The keyword Private is used when the procedure declared is only to be used within the module, where the declaration is made.

The keyword Public is used when the procedure declared is to be made available to all other procedures, in all modules. The keyword Public 'offers up' the procedure to be used throughout the application.

The code used to implement the simple Specification 14.2 will illustrate the difference between Public and Private declared procedures. *Note: the naming conventions for the command buttons and forms have not been applied; they remain at their default settings.*

SPECIFICATION 14.2

Develop an application that consists of two forms each containing one command button. A general procedure called DisplayHello is declared within the code window of Form1 (i.e., it is a form level procedure) the function of this procedure simply displays Hello on Form1. The command button on Form1 calls this procedure when clicked. The command button on Form2 also calls this procedure. The GUI for this application is shown in Figure 14.27.

Figure 14.27 The GUI for Specification 14.2.

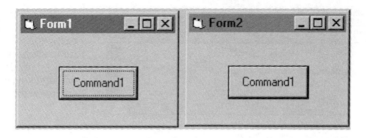

At start up Form1 is loaded and its Form_Load event is responsible for loading Form2. This Form_Load event procedure is shown in Figure 14.28.

Figure 14.28 The Form_Load event procedure.

```
Private Sub Form_Load()
    Form2.Show
End Sub
```

The DisplayHello procedure is declared within the code window of form1 and hence, when saved, is a procedure within the Form1.frm module. The code for the DisplayHello procedure is shown in Figure 14.29.

Figure 14.29 The DisplayHello procedure.

```
Public Sub DisplayHello()
    Form1.Print "hello"
End Sub
```

This procedure is declared using the keyword Public, consequently, it is not only available to all the code within the Form1.frm module it is also available throughout the application and can be called from the code associated with the other form, Form2 (i.e., the Form2.frm module). The mechanics of the procedure applies the Print method to Form1 resulting in the displaying of hello every time the procedure is invoked.

The code attached to the event procedure of the Command button drawn on Form1 is shown in Figure 14.30.

Figure 14.30 The code attached to the command button of form1.

```
Private Sub Command1_Click()
    Call DisplayHello
End Sub
```

The mechanics of this procedure calls the procedure DisplayHello. This event procedure and general procedure belong to the same code module, that is, Form1.frm.

The code attached to the event procedure of the Command button of Form2 is shown in Figure 14.31.

Figure 14.31 The code attached to the command button of form2.

```
Private Sub Command1_Click()
    Call Form1.DisplayHello
End Sub
```

The mechanics of this event procedure calls the DisplayHello procedure that was declared within Form1 (Form1.frm). To achieve this it had to use the name of the procedure (DisplayHello) and the name of the form (Form1), where the procedure was declared, 'joined' with a period. It is allowed to invoke this general procedure (DisplayHello) because the general procedure is declared with the keyword Public.

PRACTICAL ACTIVITY 14.3

Implement Specification 14.2. Ensure that the DisplayHello procedure is declared with the keyword Public.

Once the application is working, amend the DisplayHello procedure so that it is declared with the reserved word Private as shown in Figure 14.32. Click the command button on Form1 first, what happens? Then click the command button on Form2, what happens?

Figure 14.32 The procedure declared using the keyword Private.

```
Private Sub DisplayHello()
    Form1.Print "hello"
End Sub
```

When the command button on Form1 is clicked the procedure DisplayHello is correctly invoked because the event procedure and general procedure both 'belong' to the Form1.frm module. DisplayHello is only available throughout the module, where it is declared, because the keyword Private is used.

When the command button on Form2 is clicked Visual Basic responds by displaying the message box shown in Figure 14.33.

The code within Form2.frm **cannot** call procedures from other modules, when their procedures are declared with the keyword Private.

Figure 14.33 The message box that appears when a procedure is incorrectly called.

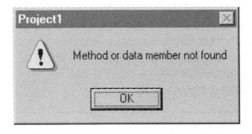

PRACTICAL ACTIVITY 14.4

Implement Specification 14.2 again. However, this time declare the DisplayHello procedure in a standard (Module1.bas) module with the word Public and run the application. What happens?

PRACTICAL ACTIVITY 14.5

Implement Specification 14.2 once more. Again declare the DisplayHello procedure in a standard (Module1.bas) module but this time use the keyword Private. What happens?

NOTE: When calling a procedure that has been declared within a standard code module (e.g., Module1.bas) it is sufficient to use just the name of the procedure. However, it is good programming practice to use the name of the module and the procedure 'joined' by a period as shown below:

Call Module1.DisplayHello

Here the name of the standard code module is set at its default value. However, it is usual to collect similar functioning procedures together in one standard code module and give this module a user friendly name. For example, all graphical manipulating procedures developed by a programmer would typically be grouped together in a standard code module called Graphics. If a procedure called ConcentricCircles drew two concentric circles around a point x and y with a radius of a and b then the 'full' call to this procedure would be:

Call Graphics.ConcentricCircles (x, y, a, b)

Visual Basic is able to build a library of useful procedures using standard code modules.

Although using the 'full' call to a procedure involves more typing, the assistance it offers when debugging code is worth the small amount of extra typing.

A general procedure can be called without using the keyword *Call*. However, I recommend that you stick to one way of calling a procedure and that is, use the keyword Call together with the name of the procedure and the module in which it resides. Of course it is important that you learn the other ways of calling procedures because they will be used in other texts and programming magazines. Use the VB online help to discover the other methods for calling a procedure.

Passing an expression to a procedure

The following procedure calculates the amount of VAT (at 17.5%) on the cost of goods.

```
Private Sub CalculateVAT(ByVal pCost As Currency, pVAT As Currency)
Const cCurrentVATRate = 0.175 ' the VAT rate is set to 17.5%
  pVAT = pCost * cCurrentVATRate
End Sub
```

A typical call to this procedure is shown below:

```
Call CalculateVAT(CostOfElectricalGoods, VATOnElectricalGoods)
```

The procedure is sent the cost of electrical goods (via the argument CostOfElectricalGoods) and the rate of VAT is returned (via the argument VATOnElectricalGoods). This procedure could be used in a program that calculates the amount of VAT charged every week on a shopkeeper's takings. It could be used numerous times to calculate the amount of VAT on a variety of goods as shown below:

```
Call CalculateVAT(CostOfVegetableGoods, VATOnVegetableGoods)
```

```
Call CalculateVAT(CostOfMeatGoods, VATOnMeatGoods)
```

However, it is possible to send an expression to the procedure as shown in the example below:

```
Call CalculateVAT(CostOfElectricalGoods + CostOfMeatGoods, VATOnElectrical&MeatGoods)
```

Here the expression CostOfElectricalGoods + CostOfMeatGoods acts as **one** argument to the procedure and the value of CostOfElectricalGoods + CostOfMeatGoods is passed to the formal parameter pCost in the procedure.

PRACTICAL ACTIVITY 14.6

(a) Write a test program to test the functioning of the procedure (declared at form level) that calculates the amount of VAT paid. Make sure that you test it with and without an expression argument.

(b) Amend and test the procedure to reflect a change in the rate of VAT from 17.5% to 22%. **HINT**: use the Visual Basic online help to read about the keyword *Const*.

(c) Redo the test program and procedure but this time have the VAT rate set to 25% and have the procedure declared in a standard module (i.e., module1.bas).

QUESTION 14.3 (DEVELOPMENT)

Can an expression argument be sent as pass-by-reference?

Functions

A function Procedures is similar to a Sub Procedure in that it is a small segment of code that performs a particular task. However, it is not usual to call a function using the keyword *Call*, instead they are usually invoked from within an expression. They are declared in almost the same way as a Sub Procedure except they are declared with the keyword *Function* instead of *Sub*. Like the Sub Procedure they can be declared as Private and Public and can also be declared in a form or standard module.

Function to calculate simple interest

Interest is the sum of money gained by an investment. Simple interest can be found by using the following formula:

$$I = \frac{PRT}{100}$$

where P is the principal (£) amount invested; R is the rate of interest per annum (%p.a.); T is the length of time the money is invested, in years, and I is the amount of simple interest gained.

The function responsible for implementing this formula is shown in Figure 14.34.

Figure 14.34 A function for calculating simple interest.

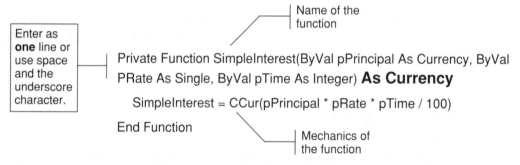

This function has as its input arguments pPrincipal, pRate and pTime. Unlike the Sub Procedure it does not have an output argument. Instead the name of the function is used to return the output from the function. The mechanics of the functions merely implement the formula by multiplying together all the input argument and then dividing the result by 100. This result is converted to the Currency type using the CCur function and assigned to SimpleInterest – which is the name of the function. A function must always have at least one line of its mechanics assign a value to the name of the function.

At the end of argument list, outside the closing bracket, are the keywords **As Currency** (shown in bold), the type of the value returned from the function is defined by these keywords. Of course, this type can be any of the types available within Visual Basic.

A function, its name and argument list, is usually part of an expression or it is 'imbedded' somewhere in a line of code. The following figures (Figure 14.35 to Figure 14.38) show various ways of invoking the SimpleInterest function from a variety of simple test programs that are attached to the click event of a command button.

Figure 14.35 A test program that displays (prints) the interest gained onto a form. Here the function is invoked from an assignment statement.

```
Private Sub Command1_Click()
Dim Principal As Currency
Dim Rate As Single
Dim Time As Integer
Dim InterestGained As Currency
    Rate = 10
    Principal = 1000
    Time = 2
    InterestGained = SimpleInterest(Principal, Rate, Time)
    Form1.Print InterestGained
End Sub
```

Figure 14.36 Again, the interest gained is printed on a form. This time the function is invoked from its 'imbedded' position in a line of Visual Basic code.

```
Private Sub Command1_Click()
Dim Principal As Currency
Dim Rate As Single
Dim Time As Integer
    Rate = 10
    Principal = 1000
    Time = 2
    Form1.Print SimpleInterest(Principal, Rate, Time)
End Sub
```

Figure 14.37 This test program prints the amount of money saved after two years, that is, the addition of the original principal (£1000) and the simple interest calculated. Here the SimpleInterest Function is invoked from an expression that adds the interest calculated to the original principal amount.

```
Private Sub Command1_Click()
Dim Principal As Currency
Dim Rate As Single
Dim Time As Integer
Dim SumAfterTwoYears As Currency
    Rate = 10
    Principal = 1000
    Time = 2
    SumAfterTwoYears = Principal + SimpleInterest(Principal, Rate, Time)
    Form1.Print MoneyAfterTwoYears
End Sub
```

Figure 14.38 Here the function is invoked from an expression that is 'imbedded' in a line of VB code.

```
Private Sub Command1_Click()
Dim Principal As Currency
Dim Rate As Single
Dim Time As Integer
    Rate = 10
    Principal = 1000
    Time = 2
    Form1.Print Principal + SimpleInterest(Principal, Rate, Time)
End Sub
```

PRACTICAL ACTIVITY 14.7

(a) Implement each of the test programs shown in Figures 14.35 to 14.38. Declare the functions within a form module.

(b) Repeat the implementation of the test programs but this time declare the function in a standard module.

(c) Experiment with the use of the keywords Private and Public when declaring the function and observe the effects. Do the same rules apply to Function Procedures as do to Sub Procedures? **HINT**: Have two forms both with one command button and see if you can call the Form1 level declared function from the command click event of Form2.

System provided functions

As just seen, Visual Basic provides the means to allow programmers to devise their own functions. Visual Basic also provides system or intrinsic functions like **Sqr** (finds the square root of a number) and **Time** (returns the current system time).

Visual Basic has a vast range of system functions that can be used throughout an application. System functions are invoked, like programmer declared functions, from expressions or from within lines of Visual Basic code.

To improve as a Visual Basic programmer you need an extensive **knowledge** of the available system functions and the task they all perform. These functions can only truly be understood in context. However, you should use the Visual Basic online help to read about as many system functions as time permits and write a simple test program to confirm your understanding of a system function.

Figure 14.39 shows how to use the online help to read about system functions.

Input and output types of a function

When dealing with functions it is important to find out what data type it will return and what data type it will receive via its argument. For example, the **Abs** function will receive any numeric type and it will return a numeric type (or a null). If you use the Abs function with a non-numeric argument (e.g., a string argument) a compilation error will occur. You must also ensure that the returned value is returned to the correctly typed variable when the function is invoked from an assignment statement.

Testing a function

As previously mentioned it is useful to improve your knowledge of functions by incorporating them in a simple test program. The following describes one way of testing the **Abs** function.

Step 1 Develop a suitable GUI (shown in Figure 14.40).

Step 2 Attach code to test the function as shown in Figure 14.41.

Step 3 Devise a test plan to fully test the function (refer to table 14.1).

Figure 14.39 Using the Visual Basic help to find information on system functions.

Step 1 Select *Search For Help On...* from the *Help* menu.

Step 2 Select the *Index* tab.

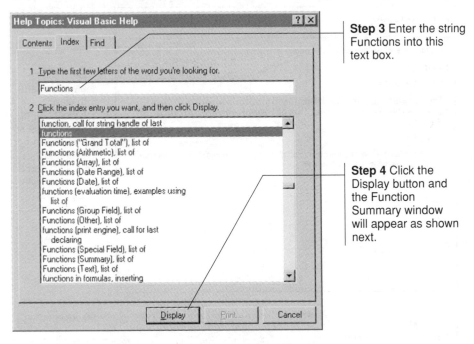

Step 3 Enter the string Functions into this text box.

Step 4 Click the Display button and the Function Summary window will appear as shown next.

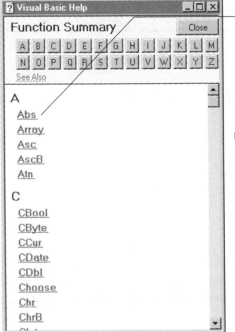

Step 5 Click on one of the functions you wish to read about. As an example the Abs function has been chosen. Details on the selected function appear as shown next.

▸ To scan the available system function use the vertical scroll bar associated with the Function Summary window. To list the function you wish to view quickly, select a letter at the top of the Function Summary window and all functions beginning with the selected letter are listed.

Figure 14.39 (cont.)

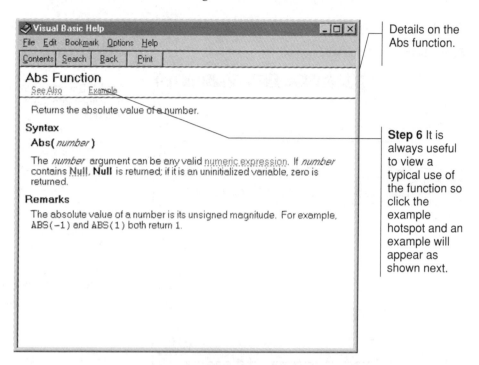

Details on the Abs function.

Step 6 It is always useful to view a typical use of the function so click the example hotspot and an example will appear as shown next.

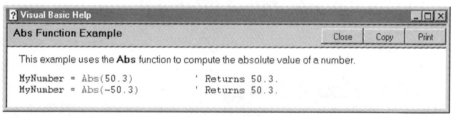

Figure 14.40 A suitable GUI for testing the Abs function.

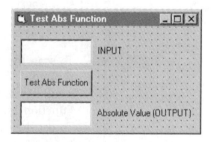

NOTE: When testing a function there is little point in validating input because the code is not going to be released as part of an application. You are testing the function as a programmer so just be careful not to enter data that will crash the test program. If it does crash just end the test and run it again with more care.

Figure 14.41 A suitable test program for obtaining an understanding of the Abs system function.

```
Private Sub Command1_Click()
Dim InputNumber As Single
Dim OutputNumber As Single
    InputNumber = CSng(txtInput.Text)
    OutputNumber = Abs(InputNumber)
    txtOutput.Text = CStr(OutputNumber)
End Sub
```

Table 14.1 A suitable test plan.

INPUT *(via input text box)*	EXPECTED OUTPUT *(shown in output text box)*
21	21
-31	31
45.23	45.23
-35.88	35.88
45.9	45.9

PRACTICAL ACTIVITY 14.8

The code of Figure 14.41 does not fully test the Abs function. Amend it so that it does fully test the function.

HINT: If the input argument contains Null, Null is returned; if it is an uninitialised variable, zero is returned.

PRACTICAL ACTIVITY 14.9

Improve you knowledge of the functions listed in Table 14.2 by devising suitable test programs or by using the examples supplied by the Visual Basic online help. I suggest that you do not complete all of this activity now but rather 'dip into it' as time permits. However, you should do about half a dozen before you move on.

NOTE: The important technique of passing an object as an argument to a procedure is covered in Chapter 16 (Graphics)

Table 14.2 List of system functions.

Function	Description
Asc	Returns the character code corresponding to the first letter in a string.
CCur	Converts an expression to a Currency type.
Day	Returns a whole number between 1 and 31 inclusive, representing the day of the month.
Fix	Returns the integer portion of a number.
Hour	Returns a whole number between 0 and 23 inclusive, representing the hour of the day.
Int	Returns the integer portion of a number.
IsNumeric	Returns a Boolean value indicating whether an expression can be evaluated as a number.
Left	Returns a specified number of characters from the left side of a string.
LoadPicture	Loads a graphic into a Form object, PictureBox control, or Image control.
LTrim	Returns a copy of a string without leading spaces.
Mid	Returns a specified number of characters from a string.
Minute	Returns a whole number between 0 and 59 inclusive, representing the minute of the hour.
MsgBox	Displays a message in a dialogue box, waits for the user to choose a button, and returns a value indicating which button the user has chosen.
Now	Returns the current date and time according to the setting of your computer's system date and time.
Oct	Returns a string representing the octal value of a number.
PPmt	Returns the principal payment for a given period of an annuity based on periodic, constant payments and a constant interest rate.
QBColor	Returns the RGB colour code corresponding to a colour number.
Rnd	Returns a random number.
RGB	Returns a whole number representing an RGB colour value.
RTrim	Returns a copy of a string without trailing spaces.
Right	Returns a specified number of characters from the right side of a string.
Second	Returns a whole number between 0 and 59 inclusive, representing the second of the minute.
Sgn	Returns an integer indicating the sign of a number.
Space	Returns a string consisting of the specified number of spaces.
StrComp	Returns a value indicating the result of a string comparison.
Spc	Used with the Print # statement or the Print method to position output.
Shell	Runs an executable program.
Tab	Used with the Print # statement or the Print method to position output.
Timer	Returns the number of seconds elapsed since midnight.
Trim	Returns a copy of a string without leading and trailing spaces.
UBound	Returns the largest available subscript for the indicated dimension of an array.
UCase	Returns a string that has been converted to upper-case.
Val	Returns the numbers contained in a string.
Weekday	Returns a whole number representing the day of the week.
Year	Returns a whole number representing the year.

15 Managing projects

To build an application in Visual Basic, you work with a project – **which is a collection of files**. This chapter describes projects and how you build and manage them.

The development of an application is managed by a project, which controls all the different files that are created and used by the programmer. A project can consists of

- One file for each form (.FRM).
- One file for each code module (.BAS).
- One, two or three files, for each custom control (.VBX and .OCX).
- One project file that keeps track of all the components (.VBP).
- One file for each class module (.CLS).
- One resource file (.RES).
- One binary file for each form that contains controls with properties that have binary settings (.FRX).

> **NOTE**: When controls are drawn onto a form and their properties are set, Visual Basic updates a file ready for saving. This file contains all the code necessary for the implementation of the GUI being built and it is saved with a .frm extension. If you build an application that uses more than one form, then more than one file will be saved when the project is saved. There is one file for each form. So when a GUI is built on a form, the programmer literally sees the form, and Visual Basic automatically generates a file that contains information necessary to create the form.

Project file

The project file is fundamental to the management of Visual Basic projects and it basically consists of a list of all the files and objects associated with a project. It also maintains information on the environment options set by the programmer. This information is updated every time you save the project. Visual Basic saves a project file in text format. Consequently, the file can be loaded into any text editor to be inspected. Figure 15.1 shows the listing of the project file associated with the program developed to implement Specification 10.5 (from Chapter 10).

Format

At the top of the listing are the filenames for the forms, class modules and standard modules included in the project. The listing of Figure 15.1 only has one filename listed because the project only has one form file, called frmSimpleCalculator.frm. Whereas Figure 15.2 shows a project that includes two forms, an MDIform, one code module (.BAS) and one class module (.CLS). They are, for your convenience, highlighted in bold.

Figure 15.1 A project file listing.

```
Form=frmSimpleCalculator.frm
Object={F9043C88-F6F2-101A-A3C9-08002B2F49FB}#1.0#0;
COMDLG32.OCX
Object={BDC217C8-ED16-11CD-956C-0000C04E4C0A}#1.0#0;
TABCTL32.OCX
Object={3B7C8863-D78F-101B-B9B5-04021C009402}#1.0#0;
RICHTX32.OCX
Object={6B7E6392-850A-101B-AFC0-4210102A8DA7}#1.0#0;
COMCTL32.OCX
Object={FAEEE763-117E-101B-8933-08002B2F4F5A}#1.0#0;
DBLIST32.OCX
Object={00028C01-0000-0000-0000-000000000046}#1.0#0;
DBGRID32.OCX
Reference=*\G{BEF6E001-A874-101A-8BBA-
00AA00300CAB}#2.0#0#C:\WINDOWS\SYSTEM\OLEPRO32.DLL#
Standard OLE Types
Reference=*\G{00025E01-0000-0000-C000-
000000000046}#3.0#0#C:\PROGRAM FILES\COMMON
FILES\MICROSOFT SHARED\DC:\PROGRAM FIL#Microsoft
DAO 3.0 Object Library
ProjWinSize=73,399,251,121
ProjWinShow=2
IconForm="frmSimpleCalculator"
Name="Project1"
HelpContextID="0"
StartMode=0
VersionCompatible32="0"
MajorVer=1
MinorVer=0
RevisionVer=0
AutoIncrementVer=0
ServerSupportFiles=0
VersionCompanyName="Shedware Inc"
```

The rest of the file lists a variety of information that relates to the project. For example, a separate entry exists for each control or object included in the project. This is of the format:

Object = "object path"

The project name is listed in the following format:

Name = "string expression" (i.e. project name).

A comprehensive description of the project file is outside the scope of this book. However, the most important information offered by the project file is the list of files included in the project (as shown by the bold text in Figure 15.2). If you wish to move the development of an application to a different computer then the project file will list all the files you need to move. A common mistake is to move just the project file believing this to be the project. However, all the form files (.FRM) and class files (.CLS), etc. must also be moved.

Figure 15.2 Another project listing.

Form=Form1.frm
Form=Form2.frm
Form=MDIForm1.frm
Module=Module1; Module1.bas
Class=Class1; Class1.cls
Object={F9043C88-F6F2-101A-A3C9-08002B2F49FB}#1.0#0;
COMDLG32.OCX
Object={BDC217C8-ED16-11CD-956C-0000C04E4C0A}#1.0#0;
TABCTL32.OCX
Object={3B7C8863-D78F-101B-B9B5-04021C009402}#1.0#0;
RICHTX32.OCX
Object={6B7E6392-850A-101B-AFC0-4210102A8DA7}#1.0#0;
COMCTL32.OCX
Object={FAEEE763-117E-101B-8933-08002B2F4F5A}#1.0#0;
DBLIST32.OCX
Object={00028C01-0000-0000-0000-000000000046}#1.0#0;
DBGRID32.OCX
Reference=*\G{BEF6E001-A874-101A-8BBA-
00AA00300CAB}#2.0#0#C:\WINDOWS\SYSTEM\OLEPRO32.DLL#
Standard OLE Types
Reference=*\G{00025E01-0000-0000-C000-
000000000046}#3.0#0#C:\PROGRAM FILES\COMMON
FILES\MICROSOFT SHARED\DC:\PROGRAM FIL#Microsoft
DAO 3.0 Object Library
ProjWinSize=99,314,237,160
ProjWinShow=2
Name="Project1"
HelpContextID="0"
StartMode=0
VersionCompatible32="0"
MajorVer=1
MinorVer=0
RevisionVer=0
AutoIncrementVer=0
ServerSupportFiles=0
VersionCompanyName="Shedware Inc"

Project window

Throughout the development of a project as you create, add, or remove files, Visual Basic will reflect your changes in the Project window. The project window contains a current list of the files in the project. A typical project window was illustrated in Figure 2.10 (Chapter 2). When you start Visual Basic a default project is automatically loaded. It is possible to edit a file called autoload, to alter the default setting of the project window when a new project is started.

Main elements of a project

As already stated a project consists of forms, standard modules, class modules, controls and a resource file. Facts about each one are given below.

Forms

Forms contain textual descriptions of

- The form's property settings.
- Controls and their property settings.
- Form-level declarations of types, constants and variables.
- Form level declarations of subroutines that handle event and general procedures.

Forms have a .FRM file name extension.

Standard modules

Standard modules can contain

- Public declarations of types, constants, variables and procedures.
- Module-level declarations (Private).

Standard modules have a .BAS file name extension.

Class modules

Class modules can be used to create programmer defined objects, that include properties and code for methods associated with the defined object. Although objects created in class modules can have their own properties and methods they *cannot* have their own events. Class modules are similar to form modules except they do not have a visible interface (GUI).

Class modules have a .CLS file name extension.

VBX custom controls

The setting for the Visual Basic toolbox usually displays all the standard controls for developing the GUI. These standard controls when used in the GUI are included in the Visual Basic .EXE file. Custom controls are **not** included in the .EXE file, they are separate files that can be added to a project. These files offer additional controls over and above the standard controls. If you were developing an application that required the use of a spell checker, then it is possible to purchase a .VBX custom control that will perform this function. This spell checking custom control is then added to the toolbox and used like all other controls. When the application is released the EXE file would need to be accompanied by the spell checking VBX file for the application to work.

One of the reasons for the success of Visual Basic is its ability to use 'component technology' in building applications. If a spell checking VBX exists, then buy it, and use it, rather than reinvent the wheel and attempt to write software to perform spell checking.

VBX controls are used with earlier versions of Visual Basic and they will still work with the 16-bit version of Visual Basic.

VBX custom controls have a .VBX file name extension.

OLE custom controls

OLE custom controls have the filename extension OCX and are the modern version of VBX custom controls. They are to be used in place of the older VBX controls. When you install Visual Basic the OCX files that are supplied with Visual Basic are copied to the \windows\system subdirectory (folder). Several OCX files are supplied with Visual Basic, however, many more can be purchased from third-party suppliers (e.g., spell checking custom controls). OCX custom controls are used by simply adding them to the toolbox and using them like any other control.

There are usually two versions of OCX custom controls one for 16-bit operating systems and one for 32-bit operating systems.

Insertable controls (objects)

Other applications, such as Microsoft Excel, are being developed as a set of objects. These objects can be used as controls within the Visual Basic toolbox. Again they are just added to the toolbox and used like any other control. As all applications move towards being developed as a set of objects there will be a rich set of 'custom controls' that will allow for the development of integrated applications that include objects from data bases, spreadsheets and word processors (e.g., spell checkers).

Resource file

There can only be one resource file per project and it is used to store text strings and bitmaps that are to be used in the project. The contents of the resource file can be edited and the changes will reflect in the developed program without having to edit the program. A common use of a resource file is to tailor the application to the language of the country in which it will be used.

Adding custom controls to a project

Figure 15.3 shows the Visual Basic toolbox when it contains all of the standard controls that are supplied with VB and the toolbox *after* **custom** controls have been added.

To add custom controls to the toolbox perform the sequence of actions shown in Figure 15.4.

If you wish to view only the custom controls then just select the Controls check box. This is illustrated in Figure 15.5.

To view only the insertable objects then just select the insertable object check box.

The Browse button is used to search the system directory to add custom controls to the Custom Control dialogue box. So if you purchased a third-party custom control you can add it to this dialogue box. It is usual practice to locate all OCX and VBX files in the windows\system directory

> **NOTE**: Every OCX file has an associated OCA file that stores cache type library information and other data specific to the custom control.

Figure 15.3 VB standard controls.

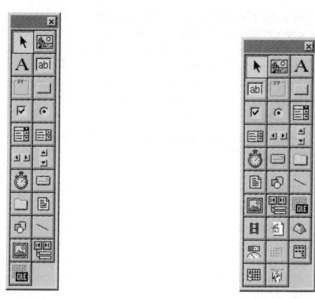

Standard controls   **After custom controls are added**

Figure 15.4 Adding custom controls.

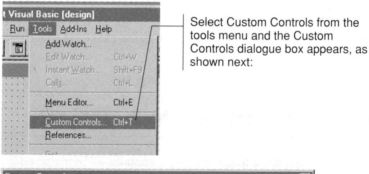

Select Custom Controls from the tools menu and the Custom Controls dialogue box appears, as shown next:

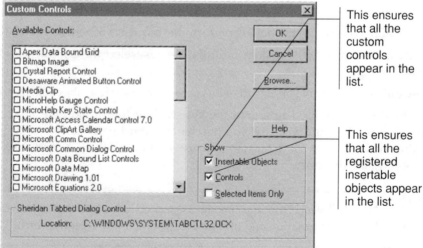

This ensures that all the custom controls appear in the list.

This ensures that all the registered insertable objects appear in the list.

Figure 15.4 (cont.)

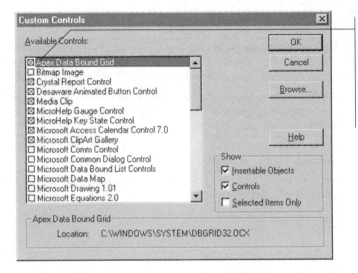

To add a
control or
insertable
object to the
toolbox,
select the
checkbox and
click OK.

Figure 15.5.Viewing the custom controls.

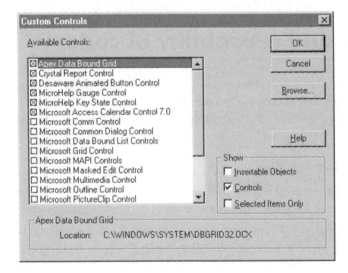

Removing custom controls from a project

To remove a custom control from a toolbox, and hence the project, choose Custom Controls from the Tools menu, clear the check box next to the control to be removed and then click the OK button. The control **cannot** be removed if it is being used somewhere in the project.

Creating, opening and saving projects

Four commands on the File menu allow you to create, open, and save projects. Each of the

Table 15.1 Creating, opening and saving projects.

Menu command	Description
New Project	Closes the current project and prompts you to save any files that have changed. It then creates a new project, adding a new form plus any forms, modules, and custom controls listed in the AUTOLOAD.VBP file.
Open Project	Closes the current project and prompts you to save any changes. An existing project is selected by the programmer (you) and it then loads the forms, modules, and custom controls listed in its project (.VBP) file.
Save Project	Updates the project file of the current project and all of the other files associated with the project.
Save Project As	Updates the project file of the current project, saving it under a file name you specify, also prompts you to save any forms or modules that have changed.

commands are described in Table 15.1.

Visual Basic and reusability of code

Only one project can be open at a time. However, it is possible to share files between projects. A single file, such as a form, can also be part of more than one project. The way that a file can be **easily** added to other projects is another important factor in the commercial success of Visual Basic.

Adding, removing and saving files

Allied to adding a file is its removal from a project. Four commands on the File menu allow you to add, remove, and save files. Each of the commands are described in Table 15.2.

Removal of a file from a project updates the project file when the project is saved. However, the project file is NOT updated if a file is deleted outside of Visual Basic (e.g., in DOS, in Windows explorer or with file manager). When opening a project VB always gives an error message informing you of any missing files.

Table 15.2 Adding, Removing, and Saving files.

Menu command	Description
Add File	Adds an existing form module, standard module, class module or resource file to a project.
Remove File	Removes a form module, standard module, class module or resource file from a project.
Save File	Saves form module, standard module or class module.
Save File As	Saves a form module, standard module, class module or resource file under a file name that you specify.

projects, first choose Save File As from the File menu, and save the file under a **new** file name. **YOU ARE STRONGLY ADVISED TO DEVELOP EVERY PROJECT IN ITS OWN SUB DIRECTORY.**

> **NOTE**: It is possible to add files to a project window by dragging and dropping files from Windows Explorer, File Manager or Network Neighborhood. It is also possible to add new custom controls by dragging and dropping .OCX files onto the Toolbox.

Creating new forms and code modules

Four commands on the Insert menu allow you to create new forms and modules. Each command is described in Table 15.3

Inserting a text file into program code

You may have a useful piece of code on a disc and require it for your current project. To add this code perform the following steps.

1. From the Project window select the form or module into which you wish to insert code.
2. Choose view code (or double click the form or module) and move the cursor to the position where you want to insert the code.
3. Choose *File* from the *Insert* menu.
4. Select the name of the text file you wish to insert and click OK.

> **PRACTICAL ACTIVITY 15.1**
>
> The following describes how to build a simple application by loading text files into a new project. Follow this method and run the application.
>
> 1. Create the following code in a suitable editor and save it.
>     ```
>     Private Sub Command1_Click ()
>        Print "Fred"
>     End Sub
>     ```
> 2. Start a new project and draw a command button on the form
> 3. Activate the code window for the command button
> 4. With the code window highlighted select *Load Text* from the *File* menu
> 5. Select the text file and then click new.
>
> The command button should now have an event procedure. Run the application.

Table 15.3 Creating new forms and code modules.

Menu command	Description
New Form	Creates a new form and adds it to the project.
New MDI Form	Creates a new MDI form and adds it to the project.
New Module	Creates a new standard module (.BAS) and adds it to the project.
New Class Module	Creates a new class module (.CLS) and adds it to the project.

Making and running an executable file (.EXE)

Perform the following steps:

1. Choose *Make EXE file* from the *file* menu.
2. Type a filename and click OK.

When software is under development it is continually updated and refined. The first copy of software released for sale is often referred to as version 1. It is highly likely that bugs will be found by customers and these are reported back to the software developers. Amendments are then made to the code to remove the bugs and fixes are sent to the customers. However, the next release of the software will include the fixes and is referred to as version 1.1. The lifetime of a software product will go through many version numbers.

Whenever a software product undergoes major changes in its operation, and the features it offers, it is usual to release a major revision. The software will then be referred to as version 2.

All versions of software have to maintained by the software developers so that they are able to maintain their support for all their products regardless of the version.

When creating an executable file it is possible to include a version number and version specific details in the EXE file. This can be achieved by altering the contents of the EXE Options dialogue box. This dialogue box is shown in Figure 15.6 (select *Make EXE File...* from the *File* menu).

Refer to the Visual Basic online help to learn how to use this dialogue box.

Setting Visual Basic options

From Visual Basic, you can set

- Environment options.
- Project options.

The settings of Environment options are saved to the VB.INI file and the settings of project options are saved to the Project.VBP file.

Figure 15.6 The Options dialogue box.

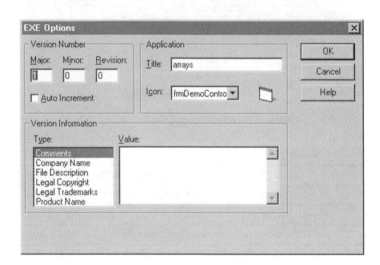

Click here to
bring the
EXE options
dialogue box
into view.

Environment options

Choose *Options* from the *Tools* menu and click the Environment tab on the Options dialogue box. This dialogue box is shown in Figure 15.7.

Table 15.4 lists the available options and briefly describes them.

> *NOTE*: A twip is a graphical unit and it is 1/20 of a printer's point. There are 1,440 twips to one inch and 567 to one centimetre.

Project options

To modify any of the settings in the Project Options dialogue box choose *Options* from the *Tools* menu and click the project tab. Figure 15.8 shows the Project options Tab. Table 15.5 lists the options and briefly describes them.

Figure 15.7 The Environment tab on the Options dialogue box.

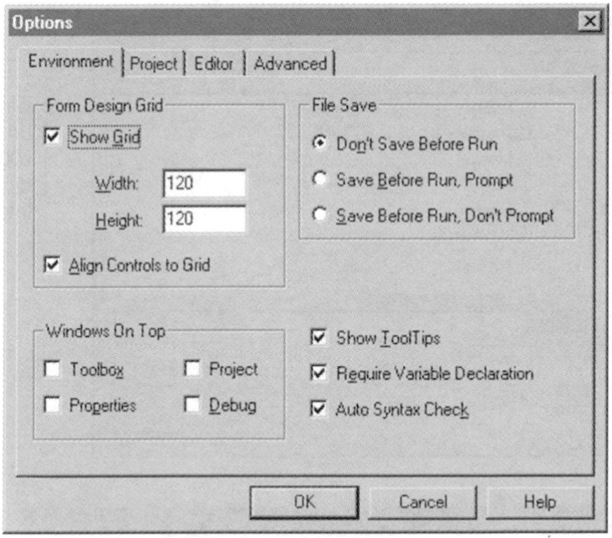

Table 15.4 Environment Options.

Options	Description
Show Grid	If this is checked then a grid appears on the form during design time.
Grid Width	Sets the width of the grid cells; can be in the range 45 to 1,485 *twips
Grid Height	Sets the height of the grid cells; can be in the range 45 to 1,485 twips
Align Controls to Grid	Automatically positions the outer edge of controls to the grid lines.
Windows On Top	If any of the listed windows are checked they will be displayed at the front of the VB desktop.
File Save	Determines whether to automatically save all files before running the application from design mode or whether it should prompt the user to save before running. When developing an application you may have spent a considerable time coding it, only for it to crash your system when you run it. All the work you have just completed will not be saved. This option allows you to decide whether you should save before you run. If you are using API calls I recommend that you save your work or at least prompt for saving your work.
Show ToolTips	If checked it shows ToolTips for the toolbar and Toolbox buttons (i.e., a label appears informing you of the function of the buttons).
Require Variable Declaration	If checked then **Options Explicit** is added to the general declarations in modules. This forces the declaration of variables. **I strongly recommend that you check this box.**
Auto Syntax Check	If checked, error messages are displayed when syntax errors occur when writing code.

Figure 15.8 The Project Options Tab.

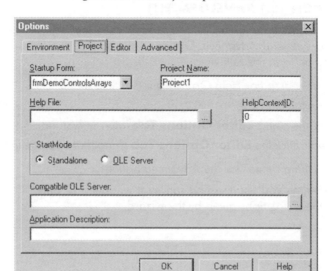

Table 15.5 The Project Options dialogue box.

Options	Descriptions
Command Line Argument	The command-line argument that Visual Basic sends to an application (sent only when you choose start from the Run menu).
Start Up Form	The first form that Visual Basic displays at run-time. Visual Basic may not actually start a form it can also start from a special procedure called Sub Main ( ). This is useful if the forms to be loaded are very large, because, for instance, they contain many bitmaps. The Sub Main () procedure can immediately reassure the user that the application is loading.
Help File	The name of a Help file you want to link to the application.
HelpContextID	Used in conjunction with the object browser. It 'links' the "?" button to a specific Help topic.
Start Mode	This is not available in the standard version of Visual Basic and it is only valid whilst in the development environment. It indicates how the application is started and it does not affect the start mode of any EXE file. For the projects developed in this book it should be set to Standalone.
Compatible OLE server	The name given to the .EXE file for a programmer derived OLE server.
Application Description	A user friendly name for the project which is displayed in the Object Browser dialogue box.

QUESTION 15.1 (DEVELOPMENT)

Use the Visual Basic online help to discover the facilities offered by the Editor Options Tab and Advanced Options Tab. To find the details on the Editor Options perform the following:

1. *Select* $\underline{S}$*earch For Help On … from the Help Menu.*
2. *Select the Find Tab.*
3. *Enter the string* **Editor Options Tab** *into the first 'box'.*
4. *Double click the* **Editor Options Tab** *string that appears in the third 'box'.*

Do something similar for the Advanced options.

The first time you use the find facility it will need to build its word list – just follow the instructions given by the wizard.

Referencing other applications' objects

Other applications, such as, Microsoft Excel are being developed as a set of objects. These objects can be used as controls within the Visual Basic toolbox and they are just added to the toolbox and used like any other control.

These objects can also be set as programmable objects (and not controls) and accessed from code. To make another application's object available in code, but not as a control, a reference to the object in the objects library is made. To add a reference to another application's object library perform the sequence of actions shown in Figure 15.9.

NOTE: When a reference to an object is set as shown in Figure 15.9 then it can be viewed by the Object Browser. Clearing references to objects not required speeds up the compilation of Visual Basic code.

Editing the AUTO32LD.VBP file

When a new project is created Visual Basic automatically adds the files listed in the AUTO32LD.VBP file. It also specifies how the Visual Basic environment appears when you open new projects.

The AUTO32LD.VBP file can be edited as you would edit any project file.

Adding files

1. From the *File* menu, choose *Open Project*.
2. Select AUTO32LD.VBP.
3. Choose the OK button.

Figure 15.9 Referencing another objects library.

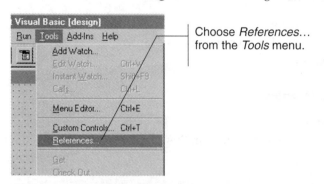

Choose *References...*
from the *Tools* menu.

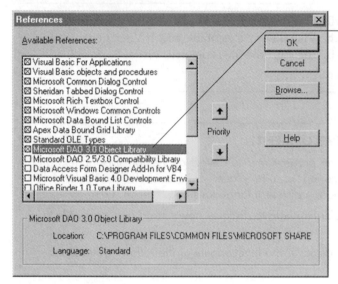

Select the check box next to each reference to be added to the project and then click OK. If the reference is not listed use the browse button to search for it.

4. Chose *Add file* from the *file* menu.

5. For each file you want to add, select it in the file list box window and then click OK.

6. From the *File* menu, choose *Save Project*.

Removing files

1. From the *File* menu, choose *Open Project*.

2. Select AUTO32LD.VBP.

3. Choose the OK button.

4. For each file you want to remove, select it in the Project window and then choose *Remove File* from the *File menu*.

5. From the *File* menu, choose *Save Project*.

Changing options

1. Select *Options* from the *Tools* menu.

2. Change the options as required.

3. From the *File* menu, choose *Save Project*.

Adding and removing custom controls

1. Select *Custom Controls* from the *Tools* menu.
2. Select or clear the check boxes as previously described in this chapter.
3. From the *File* Menu choose *Save Project*.

Adding and removing references to objects

1. Select *References* from the *Tools* menu.
2. Select or clear the check boxes as previously described in this chapter.
3. From the *File* Menu choose *Save Project*

NOTE: Visual Basic will read the AUTO32LD.VBP file only if it appears in the same directory as the Visual Basic executable file. If Visual Basic cannot find the AUTO32LD.VBP file, or if the file is deleted, Visual Basic will add a single form to new projects.

QUESTION 15.2 (DEVELOPMENT)

A resource file allows the programmer to collect all version-specific text and bitmaps for an application in one place. This is useful particularly for developing an application in different languages (e.g. French, German, etc.).

1. *Use the Visual Basic online help to discover how to add a resource file to a project.*
2. *Also use the help to discover the functionality of the following functions.*
   - *LoadResString*
   - *LoadResPicture*
   - *LoadResData*

Conditional compilation

Conditional compilation allows for the selective compilation of parts of a program. It is used to create code that is common across different platforms. Although the 16-bit and 32-bit systems are very similar they, nevertheless, have differences that have to be considered by the programmer. For example, it is possible for Visual Basic to call the operating system's functions directly. These functions differ for the 16-bit and 32-bit operating systems. Consequently, there is a need for conditional compilation.

Code for conditional compilation is placed between the keywords *#If..Then..#Else* and *#End If*. Figure 15.10 shows a template suitable for conditional compilation needed for an application that will compile to both 16-bit and 32-bit systems.

Figure 15.10 Conditional compilation.

```
#If Win32 Then
    'Code for 32 bit systems is placed here
#Else
    'Code for 16 bit systems is placed here
#End If
```

Win32 is a Visual Basic constant and it is used in the test as shown. If the program is compiled to a 32-bit system then the code after the *Then* is compiled. However, if it is not a 32-bit system then the code after the *Else* is compiled.

Extensions to Visual Basic

Microsoft and third-party developers have created many extensions to Visual Basic that add special capabilities. These are added to Visual Basic from the *Add- Ins* menu.

16 Graphics

Visual Basic enables a programmer to easily create applications that include graphics. Fundamental to programming with graphics are the graphical co-ordinate system, graphical units (twips), and colour.

Graphical co-ordinate system

The co-ordinate system is a two-dimensional grid (rather like graph paper) that is used to define locations on a form or other controls, such as picture boxes and printer objects.

The co-ordinate system is based on an x- and y-axis with a pair of x and y co-ordinates defining one point on the grid. Figure 16.1 illustrates the x- and y-axis of a form and two co-ordinate positions.

The upper left corner of the form is defined by the co-ordinate position (0, 0), that is x = 0 and y = 0.

Figure 16.1 The x- and y-axis of a form.

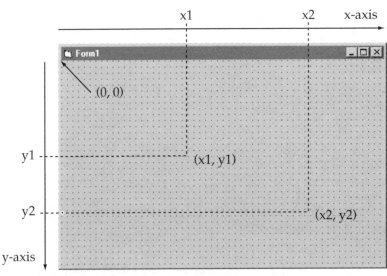

Graphical units

The co-ordinate system is, by default, based on the twips graphical unit. There are 1,440 twips per inch and it is 1/20 of a printer's point. Each increase and decrease along the x-axis and the y-axis is one twip at a time.

ScaleMode property

The graphical unit can be changed by setting the ScaleMode property of the form (or control) used as the container for the graphics. Setting the ScaleMode to 5 sets the graphical unit to inches, setting it to 6 sets the graphical unit to millimetres and setting it to 3 sets the graphical unit to a pixel (smallest unit of monitor resolution).

> **NOTE**: These measurements designate the co-ordinate scale size when a graphic object is printed. Actual physical distances on the screen vary according to the monitor size.

ScaleHeight property

This property can be set to define the number of graphical units (set by the ScaleMode property) for the vertical measurement of the **interior** of a Form, Picture Box, Printer object or MDIForm.

This property also returns the number of graphical units for the vertical measurement of the interior of an object. It is good programming practice to apply graphics methods with reference to the ScaleHeight property to ensure their correct positioning and scaleability. For example, to define the vertical centre of the interior of an object use ScaleHeight/2.

ScaleWidth property

This property can be set to define the number of graphical units, for the horizontal measurement, of the **interior** of a Form, Picture Box, Printer object or MDIForm.

This property also returns the number of graphical units for the horizontal measurement of the interior of an object. Again it is good programming practice to apply graphics methods with reference to the ScaleWidth property, to ensure their correct positioning and scaleability. To define the horizontal centre of the interior of an object use ScaleWidth /2.

> **NOTE**: You can use the ScaleWidth and ScaleHeight properties to create a custom co-ordinate scale for drawing or printing. For example, the statement ScaleHeight = 100 defines the interior height as 100 units or one vertical unit as 1/100 of the height of the object.

ScaleLeft and ScaleTop properties

The co-ordinates for the upper-left corner of a 'graphics container' object (i.e., a Form, PictureBox and Printer object) is set by default to (0, 0), that is x = 0 and y = 0. This default setting can be altered by using the ScaleLeft and ScaleTop properties. Using these properties and the related ScaleHeight and ScaleWidth properties, you can set up a full co-ordinate system with both positive and negative co-ordinates.

Scale method

This method is used to define the co-ordinate system for a Form, PictureBox, or Printer. It enables resetting of the co-ordinate system to any scale and affects the co-ordinate system for both run-time graphics statements and the placement of controls.

Height and Width properties

Returns or sets the **external** height and width of a form including the borders and title bar. For a control, the height and width is measured from the centre of the control's border, so that controls with different border widths align correctly.

Left and Top properties

The Left property returns or sets the distance between the **internal** left edge of an object and the left edge of its container. The Top property returns or sets the distance between the **internal** top edge of an object and the top edge of its container.

For a form, the Left and Top properties are always expressed in twips, whereas, for a control, they are measured in units depending on the co-ordinate system of its container. For example, if a command button is contained by a form, that has its ScaleMode set to pixels, then the Left and Top properties of the command button will be measured in pixels.

> **NOTE**: Use the Left, Top, Height, and Width properties for operations based on an object's external dimensions, such as moving or re-sizing the object.
>
> Use the ScaleLeft, ScaleTop, ScaleHeight, and ScaleWidth properties for operations based on an object's internal dimensions, such as drawing or moving objects that are contained within the object.

Colours

A colour is represented by a long integer and this value has the same meaning in all contexts that specify a colour. There are four ways to specify a colour and they are:

- The RGB function.
- The QBColor function.
- A colour constant listed in the Object Browser.
- A colour value is directly entered.

There are two fundamental ways of creating graphics for applications developed using Visual Basic.

1. Using Graphical Methods.
2. Using Graphical Controls.

Graphical methods

Visual Basic provides several methods designed to create graphics in an application. These methods apply to forms and picture boxes and are listed in Table 16.1.

Table 16.1 Graphical methods.

Method	Description
Cls	Clears graphics and text generated at run-time from a Form or PictureBox.
Pset	Sets a point on an object to a specified colour.
Point	Returns, as a long integer, the red-green-blue (RGB) colour of the specified point on a Form or PictureBox.
Line	Draws lines and rectangles on an object.
Circle	Draws a circle, ellipse, or arc on an object.
PaintPicture	Draws the contents of a graphics file (.BMP, .WMF, .EMF, .ICO, or .DIB) on a Form, PictureBox, or Printer.

Line method

The line method is capable of drawing lines, Boxes and Filled boxes. A line is drawn – in the foreground colour (set by the forecolor property) of the object on which the line is drawn – between two co-ordinate locations as shown below:

Line (StartX, StartY) – (EndX, EndY)

To draw a specified coloured line (red) use the statement below:

Line (StartX, StartY) – (EndX, EndY), RGB(255, 0, 0)

To draw a box (in the foreground colour) use the statement below:

Line (StartX, StartY) – (EndX, EndY),, B

The co-ordinate locations defined by StartX, StartY and EndX, EndY define the upper left and the lower left corners of a box. If the colour of the box to be drawn is not specified (i.e., it is drawn in the foreground colour of the object) then the two commas before the capital B are required.

To draw a specified coloured box (blue) use the statement below:

Line (StartX, StartY) – (EndX, EndY), RGB (0, 0 255), B

To draw a filled box use the statement below:

Line (StartX, StartY) – (EndX, EndY),, BF

The F causes the box to be filled with whatever colour was used to draw the box outline.

The following statement draws a green box:

Line (StartX, StartY) – (EndX, EndY), RGB(0, 255, 0), BF

The values of StartX, StartY and EndX, EndY can be any literal value, for example, the following statement will draw a line between the co-ordinate locations (0, 0) and (100, 100).

Line (0, 0) – (100, 100)

It is not advisable to use literal values; it is far better to draw all graphics with reference to the container in which they are drawn. Consequently, StartX, StartY and EndX, EndY should be set to an appropriate ratio of one of the following: ScaleHeight, ScaleWidth, ScaleLeft and ScaleTop.

SPECIFICATION 16.1

(a) *Write a form_click event procedure that draws a line through the horizontal centre of a form.*

(b) *Amend the form_click event procedure so that it draws the line through horizontal centres of a picture box.*

The code for implementing part (a) of this Specification 16.1 is shown in Figure 16.2 (note how the 'scaling' properties are used to set the location co-ordinates). The output is shown in Figure 16.3.

NOTE: All of the programs in this chapter are designed to show the use of graphics in Visual Basic. The programming practice of renaming the controls and forms, by setting the name property, has **not** been adopted. This is simply to allow for speed of creating the code, for the demonstration of graphics, and is consistent with the approach used for the examples shown in the VB online help – which you should get used to. **When you are using the graphics code within an application you should use sensible names for the controls and forms to reflect their function**.

Figure 16.2 The program code for Specification 16.1 (a).
NOTE: It has been assumed that ScaleLeft is set to its default value of zero.

```
Private Sub Form_Click()
Dim x1, x2, y1, y2 As Single
    x1 = Form1.ScaleLeft
    y1 = Form1.ScaleHeight / 2
    x2 = Form1.ScaleWidth
    y2 = Form1.ScaleHeight / 2
    Form1.Line (x1, y1)-(x2, y2)
End Sub
```

Figure 16.3 The output from the program of Figure 16.2.

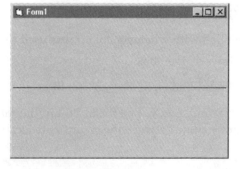

The code for implementing part (b) of Specification 16.1 is shown in Figure 16.4 (again note how the 'scaling' properties are used to set the location co-ordinates) and the output is shown in Figure 16.5.

Figure 16.4 The program code for Specification 16.1 (b).
NOTE: It has been assumed that ScaleLeft is set to its default value of zero.

```
Private Sub Form_Click()
Dim x1, x2, y1, y2 As Single
    x1 = Picture1.ScaleLeft
    y1 = Picture1.ScaleHeight / 2
    x2 = Picture1.ScaleWidth
    y2 = Picture1.ScaleHeight / 2
    Picture1.Line (x1, y1)-(x2, y2)
End Sub
```

Figure 16.5 The output from the program code of Figure 16.4.

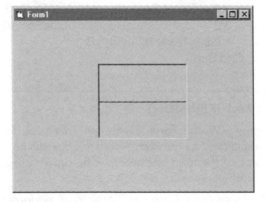

PRACTICAL ACTIVITY 16.1

For each of the following use the 'Scaling' properties of the objects to draw the graphics and not literal values.

(a) Write a Form_Click event procedure to draw a line through the vertical centre of the form.

(b) Amend the Form_Click event of part (a) so that it draws a line through the vertical centre of a picture box.

(c) Write a Form_Click event procedure to draw a line from the top left corner of a form to the bottom right corner of the form.

(d) Amend the Form_Click event procedure of part (c) so that it draws a line from the top left corner of a PictureBox to the bottom right corner of the PictureBox.

SPECIFICATION 16.2

Have a Form_Click event procedure draw a box, one half of the dimensions of its container form, around the centre of the same container form.

The code to implement Specification 16.2 is shown in Figure 16.6 and the program output is shown in Figure 16.7.

Figure 16.6 The program code to implement Specification 16.2.

```
Private Sub Form_Click()
Dim x1 As Single
Dim x2 As Single
Dim y1 As Single
Dim y2 As Single
Const ScaleFactor1 = 0.25
Const ScaleFactor2 = 0.75
    Form1.Cls
    x1 = Form1.ScaleWidth * ScaleFactor1
    y1 = Form1.ScaleHeight * ScaleFactor1
    x2 = Form1.ScaleWidth * ScaleFactor2
    y2 = Form1.ScaleHeight * ScaleFactor2
    Line (x1, y1)-(x2, y2), , B
End Sub
```

QUESTION 16.1 (REVISION)

(a) If the form – with the Form_Click event of Figure 16.6 attached – were resized and clicked by the user, would the box still be drawn to dimensions half the size of the form and would it be drawn around the centre of the form?

(b) Would the same Form_Click event procedure perform the same function if the following statement was added as its first line of code?

ScaleMode = 3

(c) Amend the Form_Click event so that the box is one quarter of the dimensions of the Form.

PRACTICAL ACTIVITY 16.2

Amend the Event procedure of Figure 16.6 so that it draws the box in a PictureBox control.

PRACTICAL ACTIVITY 16.3

The output shown in Figure 16.8 was produced by a Form_Click event procedure that drew four lines and one box. Reproduce this event procedure using the 'scaling' properties (i.e., ScaleLeft, ScaleTop, ScaleWidth and ScaleHeight) and the Line Method.

Figure 16.7 The output from the code of Figure 16.6.

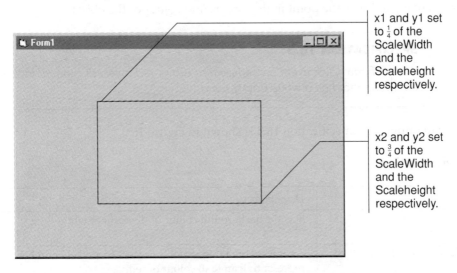

x1 and y1 set to $\frac{1}{4}$ of the ScaleWidth and the Scaleheight respectively.

x2 and y2 set to $\frac{3}{4}$ of the ScaleWidth and the Scaleheight respectively.

Figure 16.8 The output referred to by Practical activity 16.3.

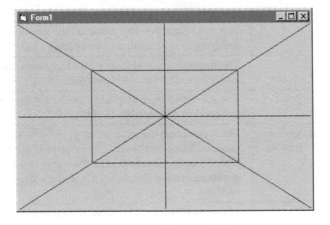

QUESTION 16.2 (DEVELOPMENT)

The full syntax for the line method is:

object.Line Step (x1, y1) – Step (x2, y2), color, BF

Use the Visual Basic online help to find out the purpose of the Step part of the method.

Also what effect do the following properties have when using the line method?

FillColor; FillStyle; DrawMode; DrawStyle and DrawWidth.

PSet method

This method sets a point on an object to a specified colour and has the syntax:

object.PSet (x, y), colour

It draws a point at co-ordinate location (x, y), on the object, in the specified colour. If the colour is missing it draws the point in the foreground colour of the object.

> **SPECIFICATION 16.3**
>
> *Write a Form_Click event procedure that draws red pixels at random locations on a form that has a white background.*

The code to implement Specification 16.3 is shown in Figure 16.9.

Trace description

Statement	Description
Form1.BackColor = RGB(255, 255, 255)	Sets the background colour of the form to white.
ColourRed = RGB(255, 0, 0)	Assigns to the Long variable *ColourRed* a whole number representing an RGB colour of red.
LowerBoundX = Form1.ScaleLeft	The minimum possible value on the *x*-axis, for the form, is assigned to the variable *LowerBoundX*
UpperBoundX = Form1.ScaleWidth	The maximum possible value on the *x*-axis, for the form, is assigned to the variable *UpperBoundX*
LowerBoundY = Form1.ScaleTop	The minimum possible value on the *y*-axis, for the form, is assigned to the variable *LowerBoundY*
UpperBoundY = Form1.ScaleHeight	The maximum possible value on the *y*-axis, for the form, is assigned to the variable *UpperBoundY*
x = Int((UpperBoundX – LowerBoundX + 1) * Rnd + LowerBoundX)	The formula on the right of the equal sign will generate a random number between the value of *UpperBoundX* and *LowerBoundX*. Consequently, the value of *x* will be a random number between the minimum and maximum value on the *x*-axis.
y = Int((UpperBoundY – LowerBoundY + 1) * Rnd + LowerBoundY)	The same formula is used but this time the random number generated will be between the maximum and minimum values on the *y*-axis and the number generated is assigned to *y*.
Form1.PSet (x, y), ColourRed	A red point is placed at the location specified by the values of *x* and *y* just generated.
DoEvents	The statements within the *Do Loop* will continually execute because there is no conditional test to allow for an exit from the loop. Under these conditions it is important that the user is able to stop the execution of the loop by performing some other action, for example, closing the form. Consequently, the placing of the *DoEvents* function **inside** an infinite loop (i.e., a never-ending loop) allows its execution to be interrupted. The loop is said to **yield** execution so that the operating system can process other events. If you forget to include this function you will not be able to gracefully quit or stop the execution of the program.
x = Int((UpperBoundX – LowerBoundX + 1) * Rnd + LowerBoundX)	The next random value of *x* is generated, i.e., the loop is continually executed until the program is stopped. The result is that red dots will be continually drawn on the form.

Figure 16.9 The code to implement Specification 16.3.

```
Private Sub Form_Click()
Dim x As Single
Dim y As Single
Dim ColourRed As Long
Dim UpperBoundX As Integer
Dim LowerBoundX As Integer
Dim UpperBoundY As Integer
Dim LowerBoundY As Integer
    Form1.BackColor = RGB(255, 255, 255)
    ColourRed = RGB(255, 0, 0)
    LowerBoundX = Form1.ScaleLeft
    UpperBoundX = Form1.ScaleWidth
    LowerBoundY = Form1.ScaleTop
    UpperBoundY = Form1.ScaleHeight
    Do
        x = Int((UpperBoundX − LowerBoundX + 1) * Rnd + LowerBoundX)
        y = Int((UpperBoundY − LowerBoundY + 1) * Rnd + LowerBoundY)
        Form1.PSet (x, y), ColourRed 'draw a red point at the location (x,y)
        DoEvents
    Loop
End Sub
```

PRACTICAL ACTIVITY 16.4

(a) Implement Specification 16.3

(b) Amend the program so that blue dots are drawn on the form.

(c) Further amend the program so that the dots are drawn in the top left quarter of the form only.

(d) Amend the program again so that the dots are drawn at random positions in a picture box.

QUESTION 16.3 (DEVELOPMENT)

The full syntax for the Pset method is:

    object.PSet Step (x, y), colour

Use the Visual Basic online help to find out the purpose of the Step part of the method.

Also what effect does the DrawWidth property have on the size of the point drawn?

Circle method

This method draws a circle, ellipse, or arc on a Form, PictureBox Control or Printer Object and has the syntax:

    object.Circle (x, y), radius, colour

This draws a circle of the specified radius at co-ordinate location (x, y), on the object, in the specified colour. If the colour is missing it draws the circle in the foreground colour of the container object.

SPECIFICATION 16.4

Write a Form_Click event procedure that draws a green circle in the centre of a form, with a radius equal to 90% of the smaller dimension of either ScaleWidth or ScaleHeight (i.e., if the ScaleHeight is smaller than the ScaleWidth then the radius is 90% of the ScaleHeight value).

Code that implements Specification 16.4

```
Private Sub Form_Click()
Dim x As Single
Dim y As Single
Dim Radius As Single
Dim GreenColour As Single
    Form1.Cls
    x = Form1.ScaleWidth / 2
    y = Form1.ScaleHeight / 2
    If x > y Then
        Radius = y * 0.9
    Else
        Radius = x * 0.9
    End If
    GreenColour = RGB(0, 255, 0)
    Form1.Circle (x, y), Radius, GreenColour
End Sub
```

Trace description (assumes that the form width is greater than its height)

Statement	Description
Form1.Cls	The Cls method is applied to the object Form1 therefore Form1 is cleared of any drawn graphic.
x = Form1.ScaleWidth / 2	*x* is assigned the centre of the *x*-axis.
y = Form1.ScaleHeight / 2	*y* is assigned the centre of the *y*-axis.
If x > y Then	*x* is greater than *y* therefore the statement after the *Then* is executed.
Radius = y * 0.9	The variable *Radius* is assigned a value slightly smaller than half the length of the *y*-axis. This ensures that the circle will fit inside the form.
GreenColour = RGB(0, 255, 0)	The RGB function returns a whole number representing green.
Form1.Circle (x, y), Radius, GreenColour	The Circle method draws a green circle.

QUESTION 16.4 (DEVELOPMENT)

The full syntax for the Circle method is:

> *object.Circle Step (x, y), radius, colour, start, end, aspect*

Use the Visual Basic online help to find out the purpose of the following parts of the method: Step; start; end and aspect.

PRACTICAL ACTIVITY 16.5

Write a Form_Click event procedure to produce a graphic on the form that consists of a concentric circle of randomly generated colours. The output is illustrated in Figure 16.10 (obviously shown here in black and white).

Amend the program you develop so that the circles are drawn in a picture box.

HINT: Use a For..Next loop.

Figure 16.10 Output from the program developed in Practical activity 16.5.

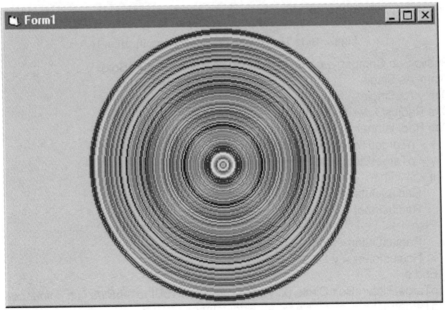

Paint event

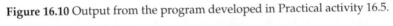

The paint event occurs when part or all of a form, or PictureBox control, is exposed after it has been moved or enlarged or after a window that was covering the object has been moved.

If you wish a graphic to be drawn by graphic methods when a form is loaded then attach the code to the form's paint event. Forms are not visible during the load event and graphic methods will not function on forms that are not visible. However, setting the AutoRedraw property of the form to True will allow the graphic method to work when attached to the load event.

An object as an argument to a procedure

It is advisable to create code that produces graphics in a standard module (possibly called graphics.bas) so that they can easily be called throughout the project (or easily ported to other projects) when required.

Furthermore, it would be useful if the target object on which the graphic is to be drawn, can be specified in the argument list of the procedure. The technique for achieving this result is shown during the implementation of Specification 16.5.

SPECIFICATION 16.5

The logo of a company is a red circle drawn inside a blue circle. Write a procedure that will draw this logo in any PictureBox control that appears in a project. The logo is to be drawn relative to the size of the PictureBox.

The code to implement this specification is shown in Figure 16.11.

Figure 16.11 The code to implement Specification 16.5.

```
Public Sub CompanyLogo(pTargetPictureBox As PictureBox)
Dim x As Single
Dim y As Single
Dim RadiusOuter As Single
Dim RadiusInner As Single
    x = pTargetPictureBox.ScaleWidth / 2
    y = pTargetPictureBox.ScaleHeight / 2
    If x > y Then
       RadiusOuter = y * 0.9
       RadiusInner = y * 0.5
    Else
       RadiusOuter = x * 0.9
       RadiusInner = y * 0.5
    End If
    pTargetPictureBox.Circle (x, y), RadiusOuter, vbBlue 'vbBlue is a colour constant
    pTargetPictureBox.Circle (x, y), RadiusInner, vbRed
End Sub
```

The call to this procedure would be as follows:

    Call Module1.CompanyLogo(Picture1)

The keyword *Call* is used to invoke the procedure. *Module1* is used to specify the standard module in which the procedure is declared. *CompanyLogo* is the name of the procedure. Note how the module and procedure name are linked by a period. *Picture1* is the name of the target control for the graphic.

The heading of the declared procedure is shown below:

Public Sub CompanyLogo(pTargetPictureBox As PictureBox)

The procedure is declared with public scope and the argument (parameter) pTargetPictureBox is declared as an object (PictureBox control). This argument is then used in the mechanics of the procedure to refer to the target for the drawing of the logo.

If the call included the argument Picture1 then the logo will be drawn in the picture box whose name property is set to Picture1.

If the call included the argument Picture2 then the logo will be drawn in the picture box whose name property is set to Picture2.

In an actual project it would be usual for the standard module to be given a name that reflected the function of the code it contained; likewise the PictureBox. A sensible name for *Module1* would be *Graphics* and for the PictureBox a typical name could be LogoDestination. Then the call to the CompanyLogo procedure would be more meaningfully stated as follows:

Call Graphics.CompanyLogo(LogoDestination)

PRACTICAL ACTIVITY 16.6

Position a PictureBox in the top left corner of a form and another in the top right corner of the same form. Attach code to the form's Paint event that will draw the logo in both picture boxes using the CompanyLogo procedure.

Declare the CompanyLogo procedure in a standard module.

PRACTICAL ACTIVITY 16.7

(a) The code of Figure 16.12 will draw the logo on any **form,** a typical call to this procedure is shown Figure 16.13. Add the procedure to a standard module and add the call to the paint event of a form and run the project.

(b) Add another form (Form2) to the project and attach the following code to the load event of Form1. Position both forms so that they can be observed at run-time.

Form2.Show

Add the following call to the paint event of Form2

Call Module1.logo(Form2)

Run the project.

Figure 16.12 This code will draw the company logo on any form.
Note how the argument (parameter) has been declared as a form object!

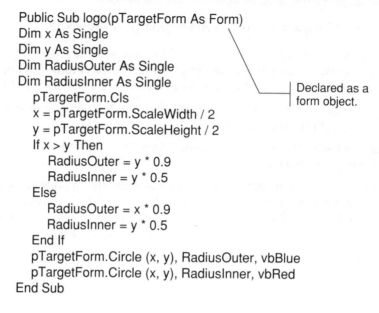

```
Public Sub logo(pTargetForm As Form)
Dim x As Single
Dim y As Single
Dim RadiusOuter As Single
Dim RadiusInner As Single
    pTargetForm.Cls
    x = pTargetForm.ScaleWidth / 2
    y = pTargetForm.ScaleHeight / 2
    If x > y Then
        RadiusOuter = y * 0.9
        RadiusInner = y * 0.5
    Else
        RadiusOuter = x * 0.9
        RadiusInner = y * 0.5
    End If
    pTargetForm.Circle (x, y), RadiusOuter, vbBlue
    pTargetForm.Circle (x, y), RadiusInner, vbRed
End Sub
```

Declared as a form object.

Figure 16.13 The call to the Logo procedure.

```
Call Module1.logo(Form1)
```

A form object passed to the procedure.

PRACTICAL ACTIVITY 16.8

Write a procedure that will draw the Olympic games logo on any picture box. The logo is to be drawn relative to the size of the picture box.

Test the procedure by Calling it to draw the logo in three different size picture boxes. Attach the calls to the Paint event procedure of a form.

Persistent graphics

If the graphics (drawn by graphic methods) on a form are covered by the user moving another form over them; then once the covering form is moved away the graphics have to be redrawn (persistent graphics). To ensure persistent graphics always set the AutoRedraw property of the form to True.

To ensure persistent graphics for a PictureBox set its AutoRedraw property to true.

If the AutoRedraw property is set to false then the covered graphics are lost, when the covering form is moved.

It takes more memory to ensure that graphics are persistent on a form than a PictureBox. Saving memory improves the efficiency of executing code, consequently, it is advisable to always use PictureBoxes for drawing graphics.

> **PRACTICAL ACTIVITY 16.9**
>
> Experiment with the AutoRedraw property. Create a project with two forms, on Form1 draw a circle. Set the AutoRedraw property of Form1 to **false**, run the project and move Form2 so that it partly covers the circle and then move it away. Observe the effect on the circle. Alter the AutoRedraw property as appropriate to create persistent graphics; run the project and move Form2 in the same way.
>
> **Remember** to *Show* Form2 in the load event of Form1.

Graphical controls

The Visual Basic toolbox provides three graphic controls that can create graphics at *design time*. These controls produce graphics with less coding than graphical methods. The buttons for these controls are shown in Figure 16.14.

Figure 16.14 Graphic controls.

Shape control.

Line control.

Image control.

Line control

A Line control is a straight horizontal, vertical, or diagonal line that can be drawn at design time, on a form, picture box or frame. A line can be placed and moved on a form (also picture box and frame – when they have the focus) by double clicking the control in the toolbox. The line can be moved and resized like any other control, that is dragged and dropped, etc.

During run-time a line control can be used instead of a Line method and lines drawn with a line control remain on the form even if the AutoRedraw property setting is False. A line control can be moved and altered at run-time by altering its X1, X2, Y1, and Y2 properties. The code of Figure 16.15 will randomly draw a line all over a form by the random setting of the lines X1, X2, Y1, and Y2 properties.

Figure 16.15 Code to randomly draw a line control.

```
Private Sub Form_Click()
Dim UpperBoundX As Single
Dim UpperBoundY As Single
Dim LowerBoundX As Single
Dim LowerBoundY As Single
Dim i As Integer
    UpperBoundX = ScaleWidth
    UpperBoundY = ScaleHeight
    LowerBoundX = ScaleLeft
    LowerBoundY = ScaleTop
    Do
        Line1.X1 = Int((UpperBoundX – LowerBoundX + 1) * Rnd + LowerBoundX)
        Line1.Y1 = Int((UpperBoundY – LowerBoundY + 1) * Rnd + LowerBoundY)
        Line1.X2 = Int((UpperBoundX – LowerBoundX + 1) * Rnd + LowerBoundX)
        Line1.Y2 = Int((UpperBoundY – LowerBoundY + 1) * Rnd + LowerBoundY)
        For i = 1 To 1000
            DoEvents
        Next i
        DoEvents
    Loop
End Sub
```

PRACTICAL ACTIVITY 16.10

(a) Enter and run the program listing shown in Figure 16.15. Explain the resulting output. The *For Next* loop is used to slow down the execution of the program. Depending upon the speed of your computer you may need to increase or decrease the range for the *For Next* loop.

(b) Amend the program so that the ForeColor property is set to draw a blue line at random.

(c) Set the BorderWidth of the line to 6 and observe the effect. What does the BorderWidth property control?

QUESTION 16.5 (DEVELOPMENT)

Use the Visual Basic online help to discover the effect of changing the DrawMode Property.

Shape control

This control is used to display a rectangle, square, oval, circle, rounded rectangle, or rounded square.

PRACTICAL ACTIVITY 16.11

Use the shape control to draw a rectangle, square, oval, circle, rounded rectangle, and a rounded square on a form and a picture box.

QUESTION 16.6 (DEVELOPMENT)

Use the Visual Basic online help to discover the effect of changing the settings for each of the following properties of the Shape control:

BackStyle; BorderColor; BorderStyle; BorderWidth; FillStyle and FillColor.

Draw some Shapes onto a form and experiment with the property settings and observe the effect when they are changed.

Image control

The Image control is used to display a graphic, it is very similar to a picture box and supports the same picture formats. The Image control uses less system resources and repaints faster than a PictureBox control. However, it supports only a subset of the PictureBox properties, events, and methods. An Image control **cannot** act as a container although an image control has the advantage that pictures can be stretched to fit the control's size, which is not possible with the picture box.

A picture can be loaded into a picture box at

- Design time.
- Run-time.

Loading a picture at design time

From the properties window select *Picture* from the *properties list* and click the *Properties* button. Visual Basic will respond by displaying a dialogue box from which a picture file can be selected.

Loading a picture at run-time

There are four ways to load a picture at run-time (two are discussed in this chapter – use the online help to learn about the other two) and they are:

- Using the LoadPicture function
- Copying from one object to another.
- Using the LoadResPicture function.
- Copying from the clipboard – which is a special case of copying from another object.

Using the LoadPicture function

The following statement will load a bitmap file in to an image box named imgDisplayFish.

imgDisplayFish.Picture = LoadPicture ("c:\vb\bitmaps\assorted\fish.bmp")

The string in the brackets represent the absolute path name to the bitmap file. Loading a picture into an image box completely replaces the existing picture.

Graphics can be cleared from an image control by assigning LoadPicture with no argument. The statement below will clear the picture from the image box.

imgDisplayFish.Picture = LoadPicture

Copying from one object to another

This is achieved with an assignment statement that assigned the picture property of one object to the picture property of another object. The statement below copies the picture from an image box (named Image1) to another image box (named Image2).

Image2.Picture = Image1.Picture

PRACTICAL ACTIVITY 16.12

Implement Specification 16.6.

SPECIFICATION 16.6

Draw two image boxes onto a form and set their BorderStyle property to fixed single (so that they can be seen at run-time). Have the Image1_Click event of the first image box (Image1) load a suitable bitmap into Image1. Have the double click event of the same image box clear this bitmap. Have the click event of the second image box (Image2) copy the picture from the image box, Image1, to the image box, Image2.

Moving and resizing controls at run-time

The Top and Left properties of an object are used to position an object within its container. Whereas the Width and Height properties are used to resize an object. All four properties are measured in units that depend on the co-ordinate system of the object's container.

Controls (e.g., Image and Picture boxes) are usually contained by forms and consequently have their Top, Left, Height and Width properties measured in the units of the form – which is usually twips.

Forms can be contained by an MDIForm or the screen. If contained by the screen then the forms Top, Left, Height and Width properties are measured in the units of the screen. Forms are positioned relative to the screen's dimensions. These dimensions are obtained from the screen properties which are *available only at run-time*. The screen properties that are frequently used for positioning forms are its Width and Height properties.

The implementation of the following specification will demonstrate how to move and resize forms and controls.

> ### SPECIFICATION 16.7
>
> *A form contains four command buttons. Regardless of the size of the form every corner of the form must contain one button. In other words the command buttons must move with the form as it is resized by the user (the code is attached to the resize event of the form, obviously, this event is activated every time the form is resized).*

Figure 16.16 shows the code that implements Specification 16.7.

Figure 16.16 The code that implements Specification 16.7.

```
Private Sub Form_Resize()
    Command1.Top = Form1.ScaleTop
    Command1.Left = Form1.ScaleLeft
    Command2.Top = Form1.ScaleTop
    Command2.Left = Form1.ScaleWidth – Command2.Width
    Command3.Top = Form1.ScaleHeight – Command3.Height
    Command3.Left = Form1.ScaleLeft
    Command4.Top = Form1.ScaleHeight – Command4.Height
    Command4.Left = Form1.ScaleWidth – Command4.Width
End Sub
```

Trace description

Statement	Description
Command1.Top = Form1.ScaleTop	The top edge of the Command1 button is placed at the top of the inner dimension of its container, Form1 (i.e., y-axis co-ordinate = 0)
Command1.Left = Form1.ScaleLeft	The left edge of the command button is placed at the left of the inner dimension of its container, Form1 (i.e., x-axis co-ordinate = 0). Consequently, this statement and the last statement place the Command1 button at the top left corner of its container.
Command2.Top = Form1.ScaleTop	The top edge of the Command2 button is placed at the top of the inner dimension of its container, Form1 (i.e., y-axis co-ordinate = 0)
Command2.Left = Form1.ScaleWidth – Command2.Width	The left edge of the Command2 button is placed its own width dimension away from the right of the inner dimension of its container, Form1. Consequently, the Command2 button is placed in the top right corner of its container.
Command3.Top = Form1.ScaleHeight – Command3.Height	The top edge of the Command3 button is placed its own width dimension away from the bottom of the inner dimension of its container, Form1.
Command3.Left = Form1.ScaleLeft	The left edge of the Command3 button is placed at the left of the inner dimension of its container, Form1 (i.e., x-axis co-ordinate = 0). Consequently, the Command3 button is placed in the bottom left corner of its container.
Command4.Top = Form1.ScaleHeight – Command4.Height	The top edge of the Command4 button is placed its own height dimension away from the bottom of its container.
Command4.Left = Form1.ScaleWidth – Command4.Width	The left edge of the Command4 button is placed its own width dimension away from the right of the inner dimension of its container, Form1. Consequently, the Command4 button is placed in the bottom right corner of its container.

PRACTICAL ACTIVITY 16.13

(a) Implement Specification 16.7 then resize the form by dragging it and observe the movement of the command buttons.

(b) Amend the code by removing all the four subtractions that take place in the code e.g. let

Command2.Left = Form1.ScaleWidth – Command2.Width

become Command2.Left = Form1.ScaleWidth

Run the project and observe the results.

SPECIFICATION 16.8

Write a command button click event procedure that toggles the size of a button between its original size and double its original size.

Figure 16.17 shows the code that implements Specification 16.8.

Figure 16.17 The code that implements Specification 16.8.

```
Private Sub Command1_Click()
Static Toggle As Integer
    If Toggle = 0 Then
        Command1.Height = Command1.Height * 2
        Command1.Width = Command1.Width * 2
        Toggle = 1
    Else
        Command1.Height = Command1.Height / 2
        Command1.Width = Command1.Width / 2
        Toggle = 0
    End If
End Sub
```

PRACTICAL ACTIVITY 16.14

(a) Implement Specification 16.8 using the code shown in Figure 16.17 and run the program.

(b) Amend the program code so the command button is always positioned **exactly** in the centre of the form when it is both its original size and double its original size.

SPECIFICATION 16.9

Position a form, that has exactly one-quarter the area of the screen, in the centre of the screen. The form is resized and moved when it is clicked.

Figure 16.18 shows the code that implements Specification 16.9.

Figure 16.18 The code that implements Specification 16.9.

```
Private Sub Form_Click()
    Form1.Width = Screen.Width * 0.5 ' Set width of form.
    Form1.Height = Screen.Height * 0.5 ' Set height of form.
    Form1.Left = (Screen.Width – Form1.Width) / 2 ' Centre form horizontally.
    Form1.Top = (Screen.Height – Form1.Height) / 2 ' Centre form vertically.
End Sub
```

PRACTICAL ACTIVITY 16.15

(a) Implement Specification 16.9 using the code of Figure 16.18.

(b) Amend the project so that the form is positioned as soon as it is run (i.e., it does not need to be clicked)

(c) Amend the code so that the form appears in the top left corner of the screen.

Move method

This method will **move** and **resize** a control or form and has the following syntax:

object.Move left, top, width, height

The object will be moved to the position as defined by the arguments left and top and the object will be resized according to arguments width and height. The code of Figure 16.19 illustrates a use of the move method (it implements Specification 16.9).

Figure 16.19 Using the Move method to implement Specification 16.9.

```
Private Sub Form_Click()
Dim WidthOfForm As Single
Dim HeightOfForm As Single
Dim XLocation As Single
Dim YLocation As Single
    WidthOfForm = Screen.Width * 0.5 '
    HeightOfForm = Screen.Height * 0.5
    XLocation = (Screen.Width – WidthOfForm) / 2
    YLocation = (Screen.Height – HeightOfForm) / 2
    Form1.Move XLocation, YLocation, WidthOfForm, HeightOfForm
End Sub
```

QUESTION 16.7 (DEVELOPMENT)

Properties used in the dynamic re-sizing of controls are listed below:

Align, Height, Width, AutoSize and Stretch.

The Height and Width properties have been described in this chapter. Use the Visual Basic online help to learn about the other three properties in the list.

Comparison of graphic control and graphic methods

Graphic controls are useful for creating graphics at design time and they require less code than graphic methods.

The effect of graphic control is easier to see than graphics generated by methods, because the code has to be run to see the effect of graphic methods. Changing the appearance of graphic controls at design time is easier than modifying and testing code.

Graphic methods should be used when the work associated with graphic controls will take too much effort. For example, the drawing of a grid is easily achieved by calling the line method from within a loop. Whereas, it would require the drawing and positioning of every line at design time if the line control was used to draw the grid.

Graphic methods offer effects that cannot be created by graphic controls, for example, graphic methods can control the appearance of a single pixel, consequently, any shape can be generated by a graphic method (random shapes, sine waves, etc.).

Simple animation

Simple animation can be achieved, for example, by changing the picture property of an image (or picture) box at run-time. Follow the following steps to perform an animation that makes a book look as if it is opening and closing.

1. Draw three image boxes on a form and set their name properties to imgClosedBook, imgOpenBook and imgAnimation.

2. Draw a command button and set its name property to cmdAnimation and its caption property to Animate.

3. Set the picture property of the imgClosedBook to the Book01a icon ( )found in c:\vb\icons\writing.

4. Set the picture property imgOpenBook to the Book02a icon ( ) found in c:\vb\icons\writing.

5. Set the visible property of imgClosedBook and imgOpenBook to false.

6. Set the BorderStyle of imgAnimate to 1-Fixed Single.

7. Attach the code shown in Figure 16.21 to the command button click event.

Figure 16.20 shows the form at **design** time.

Figure 16.20 The form at design time.

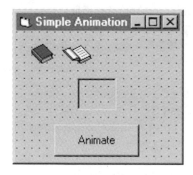

Trace description

Statement	Description
Toggle = 0	The integer variable Toggle is initialised with the value of one.
Do	The loop is entered.
Select Case Toggle	Toggle is 0 therefore the statements after **Case 0** are executed.
imgAnimate.Picture = imgClosedBook.Picture	The image control, that exhibits the animation, is assigned a copy of the picture that resides in the image control, imgClosedBook.
Toggle = 1	The Toggle variable is set at one so that the next time around the loop the statements after **Case 1** will be executed.
DoEvents	The code for the animation resides in an infinite loop, the presence of the DoEvents function allows other processes (such as close the window) to occur, i.e., it yields to other processes.
For i = 1 To 1000 DoEvents Next i	This is an 'idling loop' that slows down the animation. That is, this loop executes (which takes a certain length of time) before the next picture is copied into the image control imgAnimate.
Loop	The loop repeats.
Select Case Toggle	Toggle is 1 therefore the statements after **Case 1** are executed
imgAnimate.Picture = imgOpenBook.Picture	The image control, that exhibits the animation, is assigned a copy of the picture that resides in the image control, imgOpenBook – animation occurs.
Toggle = 0	The Toggle variable is set at zero so that the next time around the loop the statements after **Case 0** will be executed.
DoEvents	Yields to other processes.
For i = 1 To 1000 DoEvents Next i	Delays
Loop	Repeats again and again. The result is that the image box, imgAnimate, displays the closed book followed by the open book followed by the closed book followed by the open book followed by ... and so on – simple animation.

Figure 16.21 The animation code.

```
Private Sub cmdAnimate_Click()
Dim Toggle As Integer
Dim i As Integer
    Toggle = 0
    Do
        Select Case Toggle
            Case 0
                imgAnimate.Picture = imgClosedBook.Picture
                Toggle = 1
            Case 1
                imgAnimate.Picture = imgOpenBook.Picture
                Toggle = 0
        End Select
        DoEvents
        For i = 1 To 1000
            DoEvents
        Next i
    Loop
End Sub
```

PRACTICAL ACTIVITY 16.16

(a) Implement the example of simple animation just discussed.

(b) Amend the project so that it loads the pictures into the image control imgAnimate using the LoadPicture function instead of copying the pictures from other image controls.

(c) Repeat (a) and (b) but this time use a Picture box instead of an image control.

(d) Develop a simple animation that uses three pictures instead of two. Use the three icons of faces found in c:\vb\icons\misc.

17 Records

A record is another example of a data structure. The difference between an array and a record, is that the record is able to store **different types** of related data.

Consider a suitable data structure to store information on a bank customer. The bank would, for example, need to know the customer's name, balance, age and whether the customer is overdrawn. A record is an ideal data structure for holding the details on the customer. The customer's name would need to be stored in a string. The balance would be stored in a Currency variable, age in an integer variable and overdrawn in a Boolean variable.

Figure 17.1 illustrates the record for a bank customer. The record has the identifier Customer and has four fields. The fields are Name, Balance, Age and OverDrawn. An individual field is identified by the record identifier and the field identifier separated by a full stop. For example, the age field is identified by **Customer.Age** and the Balance field by **Customer.Balance**.

A record could also be used to store the co-ordinates, radius and colour of a circle to be used in an animation sequence, as illustrated in Figure 17.2.

> **QUESTION 17.1 (REVISION)**
> *Figure 17.3 illustrates a record for an account holder of a bank, it has six fields. How is each field identified?*

Defining (declaring) a record type

As with the definition of all *user defined types* a record is defined under the keyword *Type*. The definition of the record illustrated in Figure 17.1 is shown in Figure 17.4.

Figure 17.1 An example of a record.

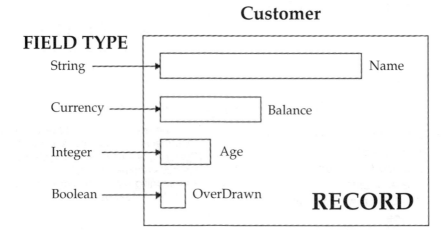

Figure 17.2 A record suitable for storing data on the drawing of a circle.

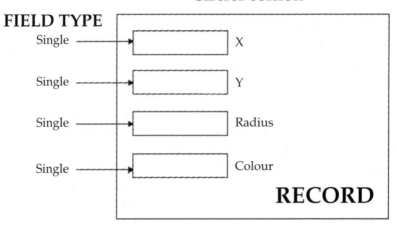

Figure 17.3 The record referred to in Question 17.1.

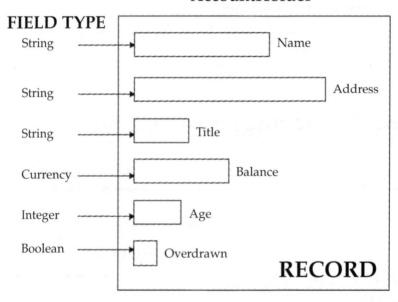

Figure 17.4 Declaring a user defined type.

```
Private Type tCustomer
    Name As String
    Balance As Currency
    Age As Integer
    OverDrawn As Boolean
End Type
```

The lower-case t in front of the identifier *Customer* is used to emphasise that *tCustomer* is a user-defined type. It illustrates another example of programming style and is **not** actually part of the Visual Basic syntax.

A user-defined type must be placed in the declaration section of a module and can be declared as Private or Public. This definition is a template, and variables of this new type can be declared in exactly the same way as simple data types, that is, after the keyword Dim.

> **NOTE**: Visual Basic supports a number of data types (e.g. integer, single, etc.) all of these types are extensively used in program code to store data to be manipulated. However, they are limited in the way they can represent data. These simple data types can be 'gathered together' to build more complex data structures. They are the building blocks for forming more useful data structures to represent data. These structures are referred to as user-defined types because the programmer has 'built' the structures and is responsible for declaring (defining) them.

Declaring an instance of the record type (i.e., variable)

The declaration of an instance of the type is declared, as usual, after the keyword Dim. The declaration of a variable, of the type shown in Figure 17.4, is shown in Figure 17.5.

A record (like an array) is an example of a static data structure, and, consequently, the four basic operations that can be carried out on a record structure are:

1. Initialisation

2. Assignment

3. Rearrangement

4. Retrieval

The implementation of Specification 17.1 illustrates three of the operations from this list, namely, initialisation, assignment and retrieval.

Figure 17.5 Declaring an instance (variable) of a user-defined type.

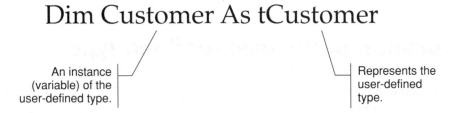

SPECIFICATION 17.1

Write a program that reads the following information on one customer of a bank.

Name, balance and age.

The program must also output a string that summarises details on this one customer. For example if the following details were entered:

- Name entered as Fred Smith.
- Balance entered as 100 pounds.
- Age entered as 42.

the string summary would be:

Customer Fred Smith is aged 42 has a balance of 100 pounds and is therefore in credit.

If the input details were: Name is John Hartly. Balance is −67 (i.e., nagative value) pounds. Age is 39.

Then the output string would be:

Customer John Hartly is aged 39 has a balance of −67 pounds and is therefore over drawn.

The program must use the user-defined type shown in Figure 17.4.

Suitable GUI for implementing Specification 17.1

The GUI shown below consists of four text boxes (three for input and one for output), four labels and two command buttons.

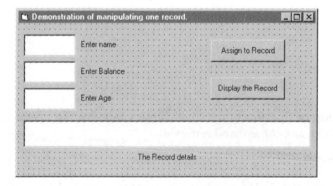

The properties for all the controls should be obvious from the GUI and the program code.

Declaration of the user-defined type

The Private declaration of the user-defined type and a variable of this type is declared in the declaration section of the form. This is shown below:

```
Option Explicit

Private Type tCustomer
    Name As String
    Balance As Currency
    Age As Integer
    OverDrawn As Boolean
End Type

Dim Customer As tCustomer
```

Initialisation code

The code to initialise the user defined variable *Customer* is attached to the form load event and is shown below:

```
Private Sub Form_Load()
    Customer.Name = ""
    Customer.Balance = 0
    Customer.Age = 0
    Customer.OverDrawn = False
End Sub
```

The *Name* field is assigned a zero length string, the *Balance* and *Age* fields are assigned 0 and the *OverDrawn* field is assigned false.

Assignment code

The assignment code is attached to a command button and is shown below:

```
Private Sub cmdAssignToRecord_Click()
    Customer.Name = CStr(txtName.Text)
    Customer.Balance = CCur(txtBalance.Text)
    Customer.Age = CInt(txtAge.Text)
    If Customer.Balance < 0 Then
        Customer.OverDrawn = True
    Else
        Customer.OverDrawn = False
    End If
End Sub
```

The first three fields of the record are assigned values from those entered via the input text boxes. The OverDrawn field is assigned True or False depending upon the route taken through the selection construct.

Retrieval code

This code reads the fields of the array, forms a suitable string, and displays it in the output text box. The code is attached to a command button and is shown below:

```
Private Sub cmdDisplayRecord_Click()
Dim OutputString As String
Dim BalanceComment As String
    If Customer.Balance < 0 Then
        BalanceComment = "and is therefore over drawn."
    Else
        BalanceComment = "and is therefore in credit."
```

End If

OutputString = "Customer " & Customer.Name & " is aged " &
CStr(Customer.Age) & " has a balance of " & CStr(Customer.Balance)
& " pounds " & BalanceComment

> Enter as **one** line.

txtOutput.Text = OutputString
End Sub

This event procedure uses a selection construct to comment on the balance of the account. The variable *Customer.Balance* (i.e., the *Balance* field of the record) is compared to zero using the less than relational operator; the local String variable *BalanceComment* is assigned one of two strings depending upon the outcome of the conditional test.

An output string is formed from all of the fields of the record, literal strings and the contents of the BalanceComment variable. The & operator is used to force string concatenation (i.e., join strings together) of expressions.

NOTE: There are two types of strings; *fixed-length strings* and *variable length strings*. By default a string variable is a variable length string that grows or shrinks as new data is assigned to it. A variable length string is declared as shown below:

Dim Address As String

A fixed length string is declared as shown below:

Dim Address As String * 40

This is an example of a string that has room to store 40 characters.

A fixed length string can be declared as Private or Public in a standard module, however, in forms and class modules it must be declared as Private.

PRACTICAL ACTIVITY 17.1

(a) Implement Specification 17.1.

(b) Consider the record shown in Figure 17.3. It has six fields and holds information on a bank customer.

Write a program, with a suitable GUI, consisting of three procedures that will:

1. Initialise each field.

2. Assign, from the keyboard via text boxes, to five of the fields. The last field will be assigned TRUE or FALSE depending upon the balance entered.

3   Display a string that summarises the details of the account.

Note: The program required is very similar to the program that implemented Specification 17.1 except the data structure is a record with six not four fields.

A record is a useful data structure for storing data, however, as the examples have shown, it is limited to storing data on one thing, i.e., it will store the details on *one* customer or the position and size of *one* circle. Records are more useful when they are 'grouped together' so that they are capable, for example, of storing data on **more** than one customer. This can be achieved in two ways:

1. Storing records one after each other in a file on disc and reading one record when required.
2. Forming a table; which is an array whose elements are a record structure.

Table structures are covered in this chapter and files of records (binary files) are covered in a later chapter.

Tables

If the elements of an array are records then this data structure is referred to as a table. The record shown in Figure 17.2 is used as the element for an array to form a table and this is shown in Figure 17.6.

This table consists of a five-element array, with each element being the same data type, i.e., a record. The name of the table is Customers and a specific field of one record is identified by the table name, an index number and the field name separated by a full stop.

The identifier for the first field in the first record (element) is as follows:

Customers(1).Name

The identifier for the second field in the first record (element) is as follows:

Customers(1).Balance

The identifier for the first field in the third record (element) is as follows:

Customers(3).Name

The identifier for the fourth field in the fifth record (element) is as follows:

Customers(5).OverDrawn

QUESTION 17.2 (REVISION)

The table shown in Figure 17.7 is an array consisting of three records. For this table identify the following:

1. *The sixth field in the second element.*
2. *The first field in the third record.*
3. *The third field in the first element.*
4. *The fourth field in the second record.*

Figure 17.6 An example of a table.

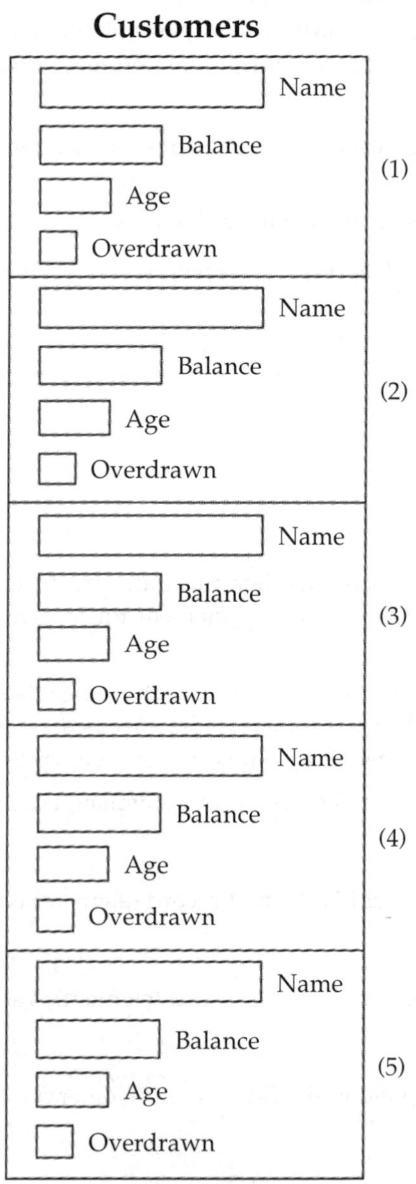

Customers

Defining (declaring) a table type and variable of a table type

A table type is another example of a *user-defined* type. It is an array of records where the record is a user-defined type. Therefore to define a table the record must be defined first, this is shown below:

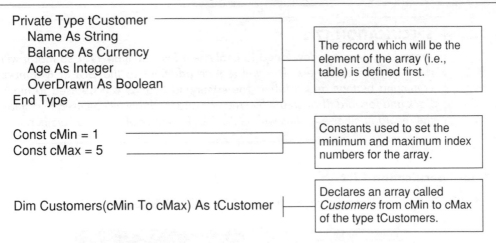

```
Private Type tCustomer
    Name As String
    Balance As Currency
    Age As Integer
    OverDrawn As Boolean
End Type
```
The record which will be the element of the array (i.e., table) is defined first.

```
Const cMin = 1
Const cMax = 5
```
Constants used to set the minimum and maximum index numbers for the array.

```
Dim Customers(cMin To cMax) As tCustomer
```
Declares an array called *Customers* from cMin to cMax of the type tCustomers.

Here the variable Customers is used to hold information on up to five bank customers and it implements the table shown in Figure 17.6. The implementation of the Specification 17.2 shows a program using a table.

Figure 17.7 Another example of a table.

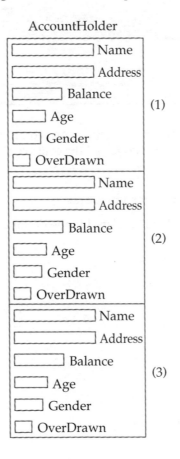

SPECIFICATION 17.2

Amend the program developed to implement Specification 17.1 so that it will deal with five customers. This will require additions to the GUI of two more command buttons and a label. The command buttons will be used to move back and forward through the five records and the label will be used to display the record number (i.e., this will be the index number of the array element).

GUI for Specification 17.2

A suitable GUI for implementing Specification 17.2 is shown below:

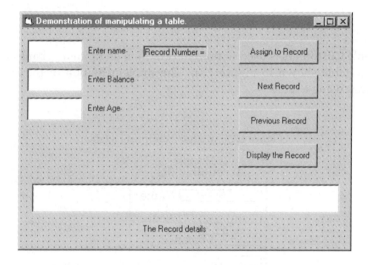

The implementation of Specification 17.2 will again require three procedures and they are dealt with in turn. Again, the properties for all the controls should be obvious from the GUI and the program code.

Declaration of the table and other variables

The Private declaration of the table is declared in the declaration section of the form. This is shown below:

```
Option Explicit
Private Type tCustomer
    Name As String
    Balance As Currency
    Age As Integer
    OverDrawn As Boolean
End Type

Const cMin = 1
Const cMax = 5

Dim Customers(cMin To cMax) As tCustomer
Dim SelectElement As Integer
```

The integer variable SelectElement is used to navigate through the five records of the table. It holds the index number of the current record being dealt with.

Initialisation code

The code to initialise the table variable *Customers* is attached to the form load event and is shown below:

```
Private Sub Form_Load()
Dim i As Integer
    For i = cMin To cMax
        Customers(i).Name = ""
        Customers(i).Balance = 10
        Customers(i).Age = 0
        Customers(i).OverDrawn = False
    Next i
    SelectElement = 1
    lblRecordNumber.Caption = lblRecordNumber.Caption & CStr(SelectElement)
End Sub
```

Each element (record) of the array is accessed in turn by the code in the *For Next* loop. The *Name* field is assigned a zero length string, the *Balance* and *Age* fields are assigned 0 and the *OverDrawn* field is assigned false. On the first pass through the loop all of the fields of the first element are initialised and on the fifth pass all of the fields of the fifth element (record) are initialised. The integer variable *SelectElement* is assigned one, which sets the code to 'point to' the first element of the array. The label caption property is set to the string *Record Number = 1*.

Assignment code

The assignment code is attached to a command button and is shown below:

```
Private Sub cmdAssignToRecord_Click()
    Customers(SelectElement).Name = CStr(txtName.Text)
    Customers(SelectElement).Balance = CCur(txtBalance.Text)
    Customers(SelectElement).Age = CInt(txtAge.Text)
    If Customers(SelectElement).Balance < 0 Then
        Customers(SelectElement).OverDrawn = True
    Else
        Customers(SelectElement).OverDrawn = False
    End If
End Sub
```

This code deals with the **current** record 'pointed to' by the contents of the variable SelectElement. The first three fields of the **current** record are assigned values from those entered via the input text boxes. The OverDrawn field is assigned True or False depending upon the route taken through the selection construct.

Retrieval code

This code reads the fields of the **current** record and forms a suitable string and displays it in the output text box. The code is attached to a command button and is shown below:

```
Private Sub cmdDisplayRecord_Click()
Dim OutputString As String
Dim BalanceComment As String
    If Customers(SelectElement).Balance < 0 Then
        BalanceComment = "and is therefore over drawn."
    Else
        BalanceComment = "and is therefore in credit."
    End If

    OutputString = "Customer " & Customers(SelectElement).Name &
    " is aged " & CStr(Customers(SelectElement).Age) & " has a balance of
    " & CStr(Customers(SelectElement).Balance) & " pounds " &
    BalanceComment

    txtOutput.Text = OutputString
End Sub
```

Enter as **one** line.

This event procedure uses a selection construct to comment on the balance of the account for the **current** record. The variable Customers(SelectElement).Balance (i.e., the Balance field of the **current** record) is compared to zero, using the less than relational operator, the local String variable BalanceComment is assigned one of two strings depending upon the outcome of this conditional test.

An output string is formed from all of the fields of the **current** record, literal strings and the contents of the *BalanceComment* variable. The & operator is used to force string concatenation (i.e., join strings together) of expressions.

Next record code

This code is attached to a command button and when the button is clicked the code increments the integer variable SelectElement, consequently, the next record in the array is pointed to. It also updates the label that specified the current record. The code is shown below:

```
Private Sub cmdNextRecord_Click()
    SelectElement = SelectElement + 1
    lblRecordNumber.Caption = "Record Number = " & CStr(SelectElement)
End Sub
```

Previous record code

This code is attached to a command button and when the button is clicked the code decrements the integer variable SelectElement, consequently, the previous record in the array is pointed to. It also updates the label that specified the current record. The code is shown below:

```
Private Sub cmdPreviousRecord_Click()
    SelectElement = SelectElement - 1
    lblRecordNumber.Caption = "Record Number = " & CStr(SelectElement)
End Sub
```

PRACTICAL ACTIVITY 17.2

Implement Specification 17.2 using the code and GUI just described.

NOTE: The application developed during Practical activity 17.2 (using the code recommended) does **not** function properly for a Windows environment. For example, there are only five records yet clicking the *Next Record* command button can increment SelectElement past five and point to the 'sixth element' which of course does not exist. If you click on the sixth record and then click the **Display Record** command button then an error occurs (Subscript out of range). Similarly the **Previous Record** command button can take the SelectElement variable into negative numbers and attempting to display the '-1 record' will result in the same error.

The solution to these problems is not to allow the variable SelectElement to go above five and below one. This can be achieved by disabling (set the Enabled property to false) the *Next Record* command button when the variable SelectElement reaches five and disabling the *Previous Record* command button when SelectElement reaches one.

Also, when the Next and Previous command buttons are clicked the input text boxes remain set to the values entered by the user and the output text box remains set to a summary string. This should not be allowed to happen and code should be added to these buttons to clear the output and input text boxes.

Alternatively, the text boxes could also be used to display the field of each record and clicking the Next and Previous command buttons could update the input text boxes with the current record and the output text box with the summary string (i.e., display the fields of the current record).

PRACTICAL ACTIVITY 17.3

Amend the program that implements Specification 17.2 so that it does **not** cause a Subscript out of range error when the Next and Previous command buttons are clicked. Also write a form level general procedure for clearing the one output and three input text boxes. Call this procedure from the click event procedure attached to the Next and Previous Record command buttons.

HINT: The code in Figure 17.8 shows how to correctly amend the code attached to the Next Record command button and Figure 17.9 shows the code for the Previous Record command button.

Figure 17.8 Code to stop the Subscript out of range error occurring.

```
Private Sub cmdNextRecord_Click()
    If SelectElement < 5 Then
        SelectElement = SelectElement + 1
        lblRecordNumber.Caption = "Record Number = " & CStr(SelectElement)
        cmdPreviousRecord.Enabled = True
    Else
        cmdNextRecord.Enabled = False
    End If
End Sub
```

When the variable SelectElement is less than five the code after the *Then* part of the selection construct is executed. SelectElement is incremented and the label is updated to indicate the current record number. As Clicking the *Next Record* command button moves to the next record, there must now be a previous record, so the Enabled property of the *Previous Record* command button is set to True (it may have been set to false by the cmdPreviousRecord_Click() event procedure).

When the variable SelectElement is not less than five the *Else* part of the selection construct is executed and the Enabled property of the Next Record command button is set to false. This disables the command button and stops the possibility of the variable SelectElement going beyond five and causing a *Subscript out of range* error.

Figure 17.9 Code to stop the Subscript out of range error occurring.

```
Private Sub cmdPreviousRecord_Click()
    If SelectElement > 1 Then
        SelectElement = SelectElement – 1
        lblRecordNumber.Caption = "Record Number = " & CStr(SelectElement)
        cmdNextRecord.Enabled = True
    Else
        cmdPreviousRecord.Enabled = False
    End If
End Sub
```

When the variable SelectElement is greater than one the code after the *Then* part of the selection construct is executed. SelectElement is decremented and the label is updated to indicate the current record number. As clicking the *Previous Record* command button moves to the previous record, there must now be a next record, so the Enabled property of the *Next Record* command button is set to True (it may have been set to false by the cmdNextRecord_Click() event procedure).

When the variable SelectElement is not greater than one the *Else* part of the selection construct is executed and the Enabled property of the Previous Record command button is set to false. This disables the command button and stops the possibility of the variable SelectElement going below one and causing a *Subscript out of range* error.

18 Files

This chapter discusses files in general and covers sequential text files in particular. Binary files, random and binary access, are covered in the next chapter.

All of the programs to date have been examples of interactive programs. That is, all of the input data has been received from the user via the keyboard and all the output displayed on the VDU for the user to read. Whereas this has been a useful mechanism for learning the Visual Basic language very few commercial software systems are totally interactive.

Consider the issuing of payslips to employees of a company. Part of the program will involve reading each employee record (e.g., hours worked, rate of pay per hour, etc.) and then calculating the gross pay, etc. If the company has two hundred employees then implementing the solution as an interactive program, taking its data from the keyboard, would be very inefficient. The computer would remain idle most of the time, waiting for the user to enter the details at the keyboard. The more employees there are in the company the greater the idle time.

A much more sensible arrangement is for the details on all the employees to be entered into a file using an appropriate editor. Consequently, the details on all of the employees can be in place **before** the program that issues wage slips is run. The computer would then not suffer from the idle time associated with an interactive process. Instead the program would read the employee details from the text file – this is a much faster process.

The outputs from programs are also sent to files where they are stored for future reference.

Input and output files are stored on magnetic media (or other storage media) and their contents are brought into silicon memory (RAM) from where they are processed by the CPU. Once the data is processed it is returned to magnetic media (files) from the RAM. This is illustrated in Figure 18.1.

The transfer of data between files and RAM is between files and program variables (variables are data allocated regions of RAM). Variables that deal with data supplied to and from files are often referred to as buffer variables. The relationship between program variables and a file is shown in Figure 18.2.

Figure 18.1 The relationship between files and memory.

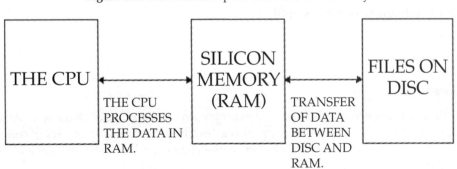

Figure 18.2 The relationship between program variables and a file.

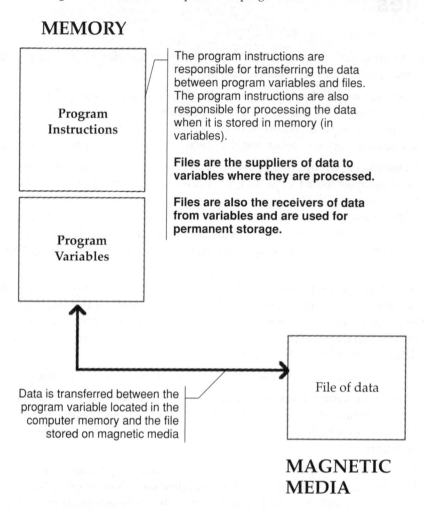

Types of file

There are two fundamental types of files:

1. Text files.
2. Binary files.

Text files

A text file is a sequence of ANSI codes that represent alphanumeric characters. An editor (e.g., notepad found in accessories) produces text files that consist of ANSI codes. For example, the capital letter A is represented by the code 65, B by 66, lower-case a by 97 and b by 98. Table 18.1 shows the ANSI character set for codes from 0 to 127.

Table 18.1 The ANSI character set from 0 to 127.

Code	Character	Code	Character	Code	Character	Code	Character
0	N/A	32	[space]	64	@	96	`
1	N/A	33	!	65	A	97	a
2	N/A	34	"	66	B	98	b
3	N/A	35	#	67	C	99	c
4	N/A	36	$	68	D	100	d
5	N/A	37	%	69	E	101	e
6	N/A	38	&	70	F	102	f
7	N/A	39	'	71	G	103	g
8	*Note 1*	40	(	72	H	104	h
9	*Note 2*	41	)	73	I	105	i
10	*Note 3*	42	*	74	J	106	j
11	N/A	43	+	75	K	107	k
12	N/A	44	,	76	L	108	l
13	*Note 4*	45	-	77	M	109	m
14	N/A	46	.	78	N	110	n
15	N/A	47	/	79	O	111	o
16	N/A	48	0	80	P	112	p
17	N/A	49	1	81	Q	113	q
18	N/A	50	2	82	R	114	r
19	N/A	51	3	83	S	115	s
20	N/A	52	4	84	T	116	t
21	N/A	53	5	85	U	117	u
22	N/A	54	6	86	V	118	v
23	N/A	55	7	87	W	119	w
24	N/A	56	8	88	X	120	x
25	N/A	57	9	89	Y	121	y
26	N/A	58	:	90	Z	122	z
27	N/A	59	;	91	[	123	{
28	N/A	60	<	92	\	124		
29	N/A	61	=	93	]	125	}
30	N/A	62	>	94	^	126	~
31	N/A	63	?	95	_	127	N/A

Note 1 The value 8 has no graphical representation but depending on the application may affect the display of text by causing a **backspace**

Note 2. The value 9 has no graphical representation but depending on the application may affect the display of text by causing a **Tab**.

Note 3. The value 10 has no graphical representation but depending on the application may affect the display of text by causing a **Line feed**.

Note 4 The value 13 has no graphical representation but depending on the application may affect the display of text by causing a **Carriage return.**

All of the codes marked with N/A are not supported by Microsoft Windows.

> **NOTE**: Use the online help to view the ANSI character set for the codes between 128 and 255.

Text files are a sequence of ANSI characters. Figure 18.3 shows text as it would appear on the VDU in a text editor (e.g., notepad). It also shows the sequence of ANSI characters that represent this text.

Figure 18.3 Text and its ANSI representation.

ABC abc

XYZ xyx

65 66 67 <u>32</u> 97 98 99 **13 10** 88 89 90 <u>32</u> 120 121 122 **13 10**

Six of the ANSI codes shown may not at first be apparent, they have been highlighted by underlining or by being bold. The ANSI code 32 represents the space that occurred in the text. The ANSI codes 13 and 10 (carriage return and line feed) mark the end of a line of text. Line feed moves on to the next line and carriage return moves to the beginning of the line. Historically, the terms line feed and carriage return come from the old line printers that were similar to typewriters.

End-of-file markers

The operating system, and Visual Basic, is able to identify the end of a text file (and other types of file). This is a useful mechanism that allows code to identify when it is at the end of the text so it can, for example, count characters in a file and stop reading the file when it reaches the end. If the end of the file can be located then it is possible to append (add) another file to the end of the current file. The *concept* of an end of file marker is illustrated in Figure 18.4.

Figure 18.4 A file and its end-of-file marker (concept).

ABC abc

XYZ xyx

End of file marker.

65 66 67 <u>32</u> 97 98 99 **13 10** 88 89 90 <u>32</u> 120 121 122 **13 10**

How the end of the file is marked is not that important, what is important is that Visual Basic code is able to use a function (called EOF) that will indicate when the end of a file is reached – more on this later.

Binary files

Programs write data to binary files and programs read data from binary files. In this respect they are no different from a text file. However, whereas the information stored in a text file is in the form of ANSI codes, in a binary file the information is stored in the internal format of the computer system. For example, a file that stores integer type variables stores the data in the same format as it is stored in the computers memory (i.e., in '16-bit chunks' – the length of an integer variable).

Access times to binary files are quicker because there is no need to convert between ANSI codes and the internal representation of the computer system, also, text representations can be larger.

An integer storing three thousand five hundred and twenty-one (3521) is stored in two bytes of memory and will only take up two bytes of storage in a binary file. Whereas, if the same number was stored in a text file it would require four bytes of storage space – one ANSI code for each figure in the number (an ANSI code is one byte long).

The disadvantage of binary files is that their content cannot be viewed in an editor. If the content of a binary file is sent to the VDU all you will see is gobble-de-gook. The operating system interprets the binary information as though it were ANSI codes – which it is not.

> **NOTE**: Information cannot be entered in a binary file by a text editor, it is put there by a running program.

File systems

Files (text or binary) are stored on disk in a file system. A file system is a logical representation of a physical disk or disks. For Visual Basic to read and write to and from a file it has to interface with the file system.

Consider a computer that has three disk drives a, c and d. This computer stores files on each disk and each file is identified by an absolute path name, which is a combination of the drive letter, the file name and path to it through all the sub directories from the root directory. An example of a file system that applies to drive *C* is shown in Figure 18.5.

Figure 18.5 A file system for drive C.

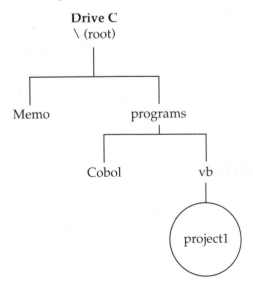

The circle represents a file (named project1) stored in the VB directory. This file is identified and located by its path name. The absolute path to this file is shown below:

   c:\ programs\vb\ project1

Visual Basic code needs to know where a file is located in the file system and this is achieved by referencing its path name using the **Open** statement covered later.

QUESTION 18.1 (REVISION)

For the file system shown in Figure 18.6 what are the absolute path names to file1, file2 and file3? (Do not forget the root.)

Figure 18.6 A file system.

DRIVE A

programs

cobol   pascal

documents   code

file1

DRIVE B

memos

internal   external

software   hardware

file2

DRIVE C

letters

accounts   orders

file3

File access modes

In Visual Basic there are three general modes of file access:

1. Sequential.
2. Random.
3. Binary.

Sequential access

This type of access is designed for use with text files. When a file is opened for sequential access it is opened in one of the following modes:

- Input
- Output
- Append

Input

A file opened in this mode can have its contents read by a Visual Basic program, i.e., data can be transferred from the file to the program variables. When Visual Basic tries to open a sequential file for Input the file must already exist in the file system otherwise an error will occur.

Output

A file opened in this mode can be written to by a Visual Basic program, i.e., data can be transferred from the program variables to the file. The file does not need to exist to be opened for Output, it will be created by the Visual Basic Open statement.

Append

A file opened in this mode can be written to by a Visual Basic program, i.e., data can be transferred from the program variables to the file. The output is added (appended) to the end of the file.

> **NOTE**: All opened files, regardless of the mode, must always be closed when finished with and this is achieved using the Visual Basic **Close** statement (covered later).

Random access

This type of access is designed for use with binary files and it stores data in the format of standard types (e.g., integer, single, etc.) or in the form of user-defined types which are usually Records.

A random binary file storing ten integers stores twenty bytes, that is, ten lots of two bytes (two bytes is the storage taken by an integer type). A binary file storing ten single data types takes up forty bytes (4 times 10). Figure 18.7 illustrates a random access file storing five integers.

QUESTION 18.2 (REVISION)

Ignoring line return and other non-graphical characters how many bytes does it take to store the integer, thirty-one thousand four hundred and fifty-six, in

(a) A text file?

(b) A random access binary file?

Figure 18.7 A random access binary file storing five integers.

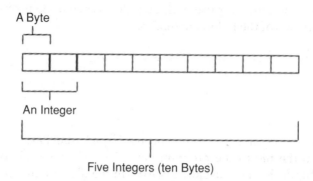

The following user-defined type (record) consists of four fields and takes 24 bytes of storage.

```
Private Type tCustomer
        Name As String * 12          (12 bytes of storage)
        Balance As Currency          (8 bytes of storage)
        Age As Integer               (2 bytes of storage)
        OverDrawn As Boolean         (2 bytes of storage)
End Type
```

Figure 18.8 shows a random access binary file storing two *tCustomer* type records.

Figure 18.8 Storing two *tCustomer* type records in a file.

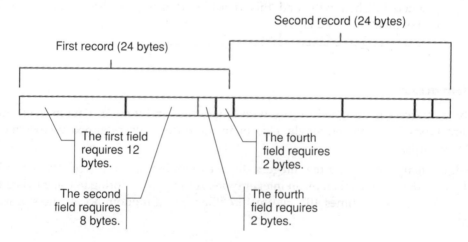

To enable proper access to random access files Visual Basic needs to know the length of the variables stored (standard or user defined). This can be obtained using the **Len** function.

The Len Function

This function returns the number of characters in a string or the number of bytes required to store a variable.

QUESTION 18.3 (REVISION)

The following code is entered in the declaration section of a form.

```
Private Type tAccountHolder
    Name As String * 12
    Address as String * 24
    Title as String * 4
    Balance As Currency
    Age As Integer
    OverDrawn As Boolean
End Type
Dim AccountHolder As tAccountHolder
```

and the following code is attached to the click event of the same form.

```
Private Sub Form_Click()                    The Len function
    Form1.Print Len(AccountHolder)
End Sub
```

What will be printed on the form, when it is clicked, during run-time?

Each 'entry' (usually a record) in a random access file has a predefined size which imposes a structure on the file. The structure is a collection of identical records with an associated index number that can be used to locate an individual record in the file. Consequently, a file can be accessed in any order as defined by its index number, i.e., the records can be randomly accessed. The file structure and its associated index numbers are illustrated in Figure 18.9.

Figure 18.9 Random access file structure.

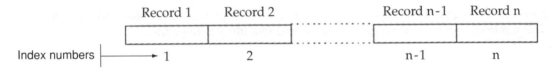

Records are read from and written to a random access file one at a time.

Binary access files

This type of access is designed for use with text, binary files and specialised files. Both sequential and random access files have an imposed structure. Sequential files are structured in 'lines of text' and random access files are structured with identical length records.

Binary access 'overrides' the structure imposed on sequential and random files and accesses their content **one byte** at a time. Data is transferred between the file and **Byte** data type variables.

Binary access is used in some specialised cases where you need to read or write to any byte position in a file, for example, when storing or displaying a bitmap image, or placing the serial number of an applications EXE file at a specific location to avoid the illegal copying of applications.

Editing files

To edit a file, read its contents to a program variable, then change the content of the variable, and then copy the altered variable back to the same place in the file.

Operations permitted on open files

There are three types of operation permitted:

1. Read access.
2. Write access.
3. Read/Write access.

Read access

When a file is opened for read access it can only be read, i.e., it is not possible to write to the file. This mode should be used when the content of the file supplies information or fixed data to a program.

Write access

When a file is opened for write access it can only be written to, i.e., it is not possible to read the file. Use this mode when a program is generating data for storage. The file can be opened for read access at a later time.

Read/write access

As the name suggests this type of access allows a file to be opened for read and write access. This mode should be used when the data stored in a file is being edited.

Locking a file

Files within the file system can be accessed by any running process. It is possible that several processes may require access to the same file at the same time. This may or may not be allowed to happen depending on the type of operations allowed by each process. An individual process may open a file and then lock it, not allowing another process access, until it has finished; at which time it will unlock the file.

Opening files with the open statement

The **Open** statement enables input/output from/to a file and is used for both types of files, all three general modes of access and all three permitted operations.

The **Open** statement informs the Visual Basic code of:

1. The location of the file in the file system (i.e., its path name).
2. The mode of file access (Sequential, Random or Binary).
3. The type of permission allowed (Read, Write, Read Write).
4. For Random access files it informs the code of the size of the records stored in the file.

All of the information derived by the **Open** statement is given to a *file number*. Visual Basic refers to the file in the file system using this file number. A function called **FreeFile** is used to supply the open statement with a file number it can use.

The syntax for the open statement is shown in below:

Open *pathname* [**For** *mode*] [**Access** *access*] [*lock*] **As** [#] *filenumber* [**Len**=*reclength*]

The words Open, For, Access, As and Len are reserved words. The other parts of the statement (shown in italics) are described in Table 18.2.

Table 18.2 Parts of the open statement.

Part	Description
Pathname	This is a string expression that specifies the path to a file in the file system.
Mode	This is a KeyWord that specifies one of the following modes of access; Append, Binary, Input, Output or Random.
Access	Keyword specifying the operations permitted on the open file: Read, Write, or Read Write.
Lock	This is a keyword that specifies operations allowed on the file by other processes. The keyword can be one of the following; Shared, Lock Read, Lock Write, Lock Read Write
Filenumber	This is the number used in the Visual Basic code to reference the open file. It is a number in the range 1 to 511 and it is good programming practice to use the **FreeFile** function to obtain the next available file number.
reclength	For files opened, for random access, this value is the length of the record in bytes. For files opened, for sequential access, this is the number of characters buffered. It has a value less than or equal to 32,767 bytes.

NOTE: You must open a file before any I/O operation can be performed on it. Open allocates a buffer for I/O to the file and determines the mode of access to use with the buffer.

If the file specified by path name does not exist, it is created when a file is opened for Append, Binary, Output, or Random modes.

If the file is already opened by another process and the specified type of access is not allowed, the Open operation fails and an error occurs.

The Len part is ignored if the mode is Binary.

In Binary, Input, and Random modes, you can open a file using a different file number without first closing the file. However, in Append and Output modes, you must close a file before opening it with a different file number.

Opening a file for sequential read access

The following statement opens a file located at c:\Info.txt for read access.

Open " c:\Info.txt " For Input Access Read As #1

The Visual Basic code will reference the file using the file number #1, for example, to close the file the following statement would be used:

Close #1

The above method of opening a file can be improved by using the FreeFile function as shown below:

FileNumber = FreeFile
Open " c:\Info.txt " For Input Access Read As #FileNumber

To close the file the following statement would be used:

Close (#FileNumber)

It is common practice to assign a path name to a string variable and use this in the open statement, this is shown below:

Open PathName For Input Access Read As #FileNumber

where PathName is a string variable that had previously been assigned the path name to a file. A file system control would normally be used to supply a path name to the string variable – see later.

The implementation of Specification 18.1 illustrates the reading of a text file.

SPECIFICATION 18.1

Write a program that reads the contents of a file called sample.txt located at c:\sample.txt and display its content on a form.

Suitable GUI for Specification 18.1

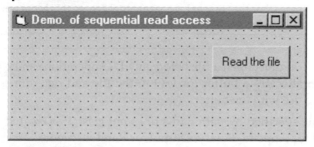

Code attached to the command button

```
Private Sub cmdReadTheFile_Click()
Dim FileNumber As Integer
Dim PathName As String
Dim StoreLine As String
    PathName = "c:\sample.txt"
    FileNumber = FreeFile
    Open PathName For Input Access Read As FileNumber
```

```
        Do While Not EOF(FileNumber)
            Line Input #FileNumber, StoreLine
            frmDemoRead.Print StoreLine
        Loop
        Close FileNumber
    End Sub
```

Content of the sample.txt file

The content of the file is shown below:

> This is sample of text
> across two lines.

Description trace

Statement	Description
PathName = "c:\sample.txt"	This assigns the absolute path name of the text file to the string variable *PathName*.
FileNumber = FreeFile	The integer variable FileNumber is assigned the next free file number.
Open PathName For Input Access Read As FileNumber	This opens the specified file (c:\sample.txt) for Input with Read only access.
Do While Not EOF(FileNumber)	The file has just been opened, consequently, the buffer as represented by *FileNumber* is pointing to the beginning of the file, i.e., the first line of the file. The EOF function takes as its argument *FileNumber* and because the end of file has **not** been reached it returns false. This false value is then inverted by the Not operator to true. Therefore, the loop is entered so that the contents of the file can be read.
Line Input #FileNumber, StoreLine	The **Line Input** statement reads a line from the text file referenced by *FileNumber* (the first line) and assigns it to the string variable *StoreLine*. It does **not** read the non_graphic **line feed** and **carriage return** characters at the end of the line. However, once a line is read the next line is pointed to by the referencing *FileNumber* variable. Consequently, the second line of text in the file is now pointed to.
frmDemoRead.Print StoreLine	The contents of the variable *StoreLine* (obtained from the file) are printed onto the form using the Print method.
Loop	The end of the loop is encountered and the conditional test is again repeated.
Do While Not EOF(FileNumber)	Not at the end of the file yet so the loop is entered.
Line Input #FileNumber, StoreLine	This time the second line of text is assigned to the string variable *StoreLine*. The variable *FileNumber* now references the end of the file because there are no more lines of text.
frmDemoRead.Print StoreLine	The second line of text is sent to the form.
Loop	End of loop repeat test again.
Do While Not EOF(FileNumber)	This time the EOF function returns true because the *FileNumber* variable is referencing the end of the file. This true is inverted to false by the Not operator, therefore, the loop is not entered again.
Close #FileNumber	The opened file referenced by *FileNumber* is closed.

NOTE: The EOF function, and the *filenumber* part of the Open statement, are able, with the co-operation of the operating system that controls the file system, to detect the end of any file. The operating system keeps information on every file in its file system, including its size in bytes. Obviously, if the size of a file is known then the end of the file is easily detected.

PRACTICAL ACTIVITY 18.1

Implement Specification 18.1. This will require that you produce the sample text file using an appropriate editor (Notepad, found in accessories, will do).

The code used to implement Specification 18.1 uses the **Line Input** statement, it is also possible to use **Input #** and **Input()** to copy file contents to program variable.

Input # statement

This statement reads data from an open sequential file and assigns the data to variables. It is used to read a list of values from files to a list of program variables. Each entry in the list must be delimited by a comma. The implementation of Specification 18.2 shows how to use this statement.

SPECIFICATION 18.2

A text file stores a list of integers that represent the percentage marks awarded to three students in an examination. Read this list and display each in a text box.

Suitable GUI for Specification 18.2

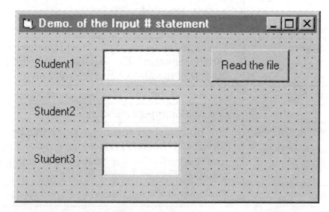

Code attached to the command button

```
Private Sub cmdReadFileFindAverage_Click()
Dim Mark1 As Integer
Dim Mark2 As Integer
Dim Mark3 As Integer
Dim PathName As String
Dim FileNumber As Integer
    PathName = "c:\marks.txt"
    FileNumber = FreeFile

    Open PathName For Input Access Read As #FileNumber
    Input #FileNumber, Mark1, Mark2, Mark3
    Close #FileNumber

    txtStudent(0).Text = CStr(Mark1)
    txtStudent(1).Text = CStr(Mark2)
    txtStudent(2).Text = CStr(Mark3)
End Sub
```

Content of the marks.txt file

123,456,789

This is a list of three values delimited by commas. When they are stored in the file they are a sequence of ANSI codes. They are supplied to integer variables in the code. However, they could have been supplied to other data type variables.

Description trace

Most of the code is left for you to study, however, the three lines used to access the file are described in the following table.

Statement	Description
Open PathName For Input Access Read As #FileNumber	The file located by the content of the string variable PathName is opened for input with read access permission.
Input #FileNumber, Mark1, Mark2, Mark3	The content of the file referenced by #FileNumber is copied to each of the variables Mark1, Mark2 and Mark3. The first entry of the file is copied to Mark1, the second entry in the file (after the comma) is copied to the variable Mark2 and the last entry in the file is copied to the last variable in the list (Mark3).
Close #FileNumber	Closes the file.

PRACTICAL ACTIVITY 18.2

Implement Specification 18.2. Use NotePad to create the text file.

NOTE: The list of variables in the Input # statement must have corresponding entries in the text file and these entries must be delimited by a comma. Data items in the file must appear in the same order as the variables in variable list and match variables of the same data type. If a variable is numeric and the data is not, a value of zero is assigned to the variable. *If the end of the file is reached while a data item is being input the input is terminated and an error occurs.*

The comma-delimited list of variables cannot be an array or object variable. However, they can be variables that describe an element of an array or user-defined type fields.

The Input # statement is usually used to read files that have been created by the Write # statement; because the Write # statement ensures that each separate data field in the file is properly delimited by a comma.

The implementation of Specification 18.3 illustrates the use of an Input # statement that transfers a copy of a text file contents to a matrix array.

SPECIFICATION 18.3

A small class of five students takes four examinations. Write a program that will read the mark obtained by each student in each of the examinations from a text file using the Input # statement. An editor is used to enter the data into the text file (e.g., NotePad) and the program stores the data read from the file into a matrix array. Once the data is read from the file it displays a matrix of the students' marks against the examination number.

The data structure used for the implementation of Specification 18.3 is illustrated in Figure 18.10.

Suitable GUI for Specification 18.3

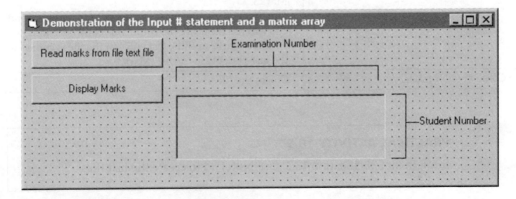

Figure 18.10 A matrix array suitable for Specification 18.3.

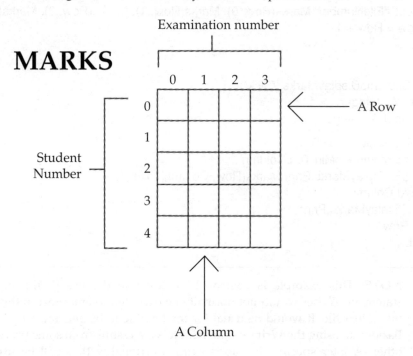

Content of the marks.txt file

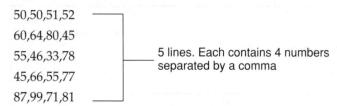

```
50,50,51,52
60,64,80,45
55,46,33,78      5 lines. Each contains 4 numbers
45,66,55,77      separated by a comma
87,99,71,81
```

Code attached to the declaration section of the form

```
Option Explicit
Const cMin = 0
Const cRow = 4
Const cColumn = 3
Dim Marks(cMin To cRow, cMin To cColumn) As Integer
```

Code attached to the command button

```
Private Sub cmdReadMarksFromFile_Click()
Dim PathName As String
Dim FileNumber As Integer
Dim Row As Integer
    FileNumber = FreeFile
    PathName = "c:\marks.txt"
    Open PathName For Input Access Read As FileNumber
    Row = 0
```

```
      Do While Not EOF(FileNumber)
        Input #FileNumber, Marks(Row, 0), Marks(Row, 1), Marks(Row, 2), Marks(Row, 3)
        Row = Row + 1
      Loop
End Sub

Private Sub cmdDisplayMarks_Click()
Dim Row As Integer
Dim Column As Integer

    For Row = cMin To cRow
      For Column = cMin To cColumn
          picDisplayMarks.Print Marks(Row, Column); Tab;
      Next Column
      picDisplayMarks.Print
    Next Row
End Sub
```

NOTE: This example is contrived to illustrate the use of the Input # statement. A user would not normally be expected to enter text in this way into a text file. It would be usual for the text file to be generated by Visual Basic code using the **Write #** statement to save results from some process or other. A later specification adds extra functionality that will be used to illustrate the **Write #** statement.

PRACTICAL ACTIVITY 18.3

Implement Specification 18.3.

QUESTION 18.4 (DEVELOPMENT)

Make sure that the text file only has five lines, that is, avoid empty lines after the values listed. If empty lines are included the program will crash. Why?

Input() function

The **Input()** function returns characters from an open sequential (or binary file). Unlike the **Input #** and **Line Input** statement the **Input()** function returns **all** of the characters it reads, including commas, carriage returns, linefeeds, quotation marks, and leading spaces.

This function can be used to copy any number of characters from a file to a program variable **providing the variable is big enough**. The syntax for the function is shown below:

Input(*number*, [#]*filenumber*)

The parts of the function (shown in italics) are described in Table 18.3.

The implementation of Specification 18.4 will be used to illustrate the use of the Input() function.

Table 18.3 Parts of the Input() function.

Part	Description
number	Any valid numeric expression specifying the *number of characters to return*.
filenumber	Any valid file number.

SPECIFICATION 18.4

Transfer the entire contents of a text file to a program variable and display the variable contents on a maximised form. The display on the form should adopt the same layout as the text in the text file. Attach the code to a form click event.

Code attached to the Form_Click event

```
Private Sub Form_Click()
Dim FileNumber As Integer
Dim PathName As String
Dim ContentsOfFile As String
Dim SizeOfFile As Integer

    PathName = "c:\sample2.txt"
    FileNumber = FreeFile
    Open PathName For Input Access Read As FileNumber
    SizeOfFile = LOF(FileNumber)
    ContentsOfFile = Input(SizeOfFile, FileNumber)
    frmDemoOfInputFunction.Print ContentsOfFile
End Sub
```

Description trace

Statement	Description
PathName = "c:\sample2.txt"	Assigns the path name of the file to the string variable, *PathName*.
FileNumber = FreeFile	Finds the next free file number.
Open PathName For Input Access Read As FileNumber	Opens the file for input with read only access.
SizeOfFile = LOF(FileNumber)	Finds the size of the **opened** file in bytes using the LOF (**l**ength **o**f **f**ile) function.
ContentsOfFile = Input(SizeOfFile, FileNumber)	Reads the number of bytes specified by the contents of the *SizeOfFile* variable from the file referenced by *FileNumber* and assigns **all** the bytes read to the string variable *ContentsOfFile*.
frmDemoOfInputFunction.Print ContentsOfFile	Uses the Print method to display the contents of the string variable onto the form.

PRACTICAL ACTIVITY 18.4

Implement Specification 18.4.

Opening a file for sequential write access

The following statement opens a file for output and has write only access:

Open PathName For Output Access Write As #FileNumber

There are two statements that will output data to a sequential file:

- The **Print #** statement.
- The **Write #** Statement

Print # statement

The implementation of Specification 18.5 will demonstrate the process of writing to a file using the Print # statement.

SPECIFICATION 18.5

Write a program that will save the contents of a text box, entered by a user, in a file called sample1.txt

Suitable GUI for Specification 18.5

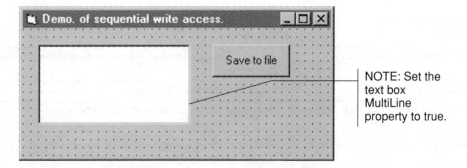

Code attached to the command button

```
Private Sub cmdSaveToFile_Click()
Dim PathName As String
Dim FileNumber As Integer
Dim TextToSave As String
    PathName = "c:\sample1.txt"
```

```
        FileNumber = FreeFile
        TextToSave = txtUserInput.Text
        Open PathName For Output Access Write As #FileNumber
        Print #FileNumber, TextToSave
        Close #FileNumber
    End Sub
```

Description trace

Statement	Description
PathName = "c:\sample1.txt"	Sets the path to the file that will be used for the output.
FileNumber = FreeFile	Finds the next free file number.
TextToSave = txtUserInput.Text	Assigns the contents of the text box, text property, to the string variable *TextToSave*.
Open PathName For Output Access Write As #FileNumber	Opens the file defined by the content of the variable *PathName*, for output, with write only access. **If the file does not exist then the open statement creates it. However, if the file does exist its contents will be destroyed.** *It is usual to have Visual Basic code check for the presence of a file in the file system before it is opened, so that the contents of the file are not accidentally erased by the open statement.*
Print #FileNumber, TextToSave	The Print # statement writes display-formatted data to a sequential file. The variable, *FileNumber*, references the file that is to receive a copy of the content of the program variable *TextToSave*.
Close #FileNumber	The file is closed.

PRACTICAL ACTIVITY 18.5

Implement Specification 18.5. When it is run open the sample1.txt file from a suitable editor and compare the text to that entered in the text box.

Make sure that the path name you choose for the file does not reference an important file in your file system because its contents will be lost when you run this program.

QUESTION 18.5 (DEVELOPMENT)

The program shown in Figure 18.11 shows the **Print** *# statement being used in numerous ways. Study this program, the output it produces, and together with the VB online help discover the reasons for the output.*

Figure 18.11 Program listing associated with Question 18.5.

```
Private Sub Form_Click()
Dim MyBool As Boolean
Dim MyError As Variant
Dim PathName As String
Dim FileNumber As Integer
Dim MyNull As Variant
    PathName = "c:\sample3.txt"
    FileNumber = FreeFile
    Open PathName For Output Access Write As #FileNumber ' Open file for output.
    Print #FileNumber, "This is the first line of text" ' Print text to file.
    Print #FileNumber, ' Print blank line to file.
    Print #FileNumber, "Zone 1"; Tab; "Zone 2" ' Print in two print zones.
    Print #FileNumber, "Hello"; " "; "World" ' Separate strings with space.
    Print #FileNumber, Spc(5); "5 leading spaces " ' Print five leading spaces.
    Print #FileNumber, Tab(10); "Hello" ' Print word at column 10.
    MyBool = False ' Assign Boolean, Null and Error values.
    MyNull = Null ' True, False, Null, and Error are translated using locale settings of
'your system.
    MyError = CVErr(32767)
    Print #FileNumber, MyBool; " is a Boolean value"
    Print #FileNumber, MyNull; " is a null value"
    Print #FileNumber, MyError; " is an error value"
    Close #FileNumber ' Close file.
End Sub
```

QUESTION 18.6 (DEVELOPMENT)

Use the VB online help to find out how Visual Basic code can check for the presence of a file in a file system.

HINT: *A good place to start, is to read about the **Dir** function.*

PRACTICAL ACTIVITY 18.6

Write a project that will save the contents of an input text box in a file whose path is entered by the user in another text box. The code must check for the presence of the file in the file system **before** any attempt is made to save the contents of the text box. If the file exists then the path name to the file is cleared from the text box and the user is asked to enter a different file name.

The same project must also be capable of displaying the contents of any file in an output text box. The path name to the file is entered by the user in another input text box and if the file does not exist then the path name is cleared and the user is informed that the file does not exist.

NOTE: In a later chapter you will see how file controls offer a much better way of obtaining path names to files in the file system. However, in the meantime the implementation of this project will give you valuable practice in applying the techniques just covered.

Write # statement

The Write # statement writes data to a sequential file and is usually used in conjunction with the Input # statement. The Write # statement will store program variables in a file separated by commas and the Input # statement will read back from the file to program variables. The syntax of the write statement is shown below:

Write #*filenumber*, [*outputlist*]

The parts of the statement (shown in italics) are described in Table 18.4.

The Windows environment is able to tailor its settings to different regions (locale) of the world. For example, the way it represents dates can be in a number of formats, two such formats are listed below:

- dd MMMM, yyyy This format displays the day of the week followed by the number of the month followed by the month followed by the year, for example; **Sunday, 15 December, 1996**
- MMMM dd, yyyy For example; **December 15, 1996**

When the Write # statement is used to write data to a file it makes several universal assumptions so the data can always be read and correctly interpreted using Input #, regardless of locale. Date data, for example, is written to the file using the universal date format. When either the date or the time component is missing, or zero, only the part provided gets written to the file.

Further assumptions are listed below:

- Numeric data is always written using the period (.) as the decimal separator.
- For Boolean data, either #TRUE# or #FALSE# is printed. The True and False keywords are not translated, regardless of locale.
- Nothing is written to the file if outputlist data is Empty. However, for Null data, #NULL# is written.
- For Error data, the output appears as #ERROR errorcode#. The Error keyword is not translated, regardless of locale.

Unlike the Print # statement, the Write # statement inserts commas between items and quotation marks around strings as they are written to the file. Write # also inserts a newline character, that is, a carriage return (Chr(13)) or carriage return-linefeed (Chr(13) + Chr (10)), after it has written the final character, in the outputlist, to the file.

Table 18.4 Parts of the Write # statement.

Part	Description
outputlist	One or more comma-delimited numeric or string expressions that are to be written to a file.
filenumber	Any valid file number.

Example of using the Write # statement

Consider a matrix (2d array) as defined by the following declaration:

```
Option Explicit
Const cMin = 0
Const cRow = 4
Const cColumn = 3
Dim Marks(cMin To cRow, cMin To cColumn) As Integer
```

The following procedure will copy the contents of this matrix to a file one row at a time.

```
Private Sub CopyMatrixToFile()
Dim PathName As String
Dim FileNumber As Integer
Dim Row As Integer
    PathName = "c:\Marks.txt"
    FileNumber = FreeFile
    Open PathName For Output Access Write As #FileNumber
    For Row = cMin To cRow
        Write #FileNumber, Marks(Row, 0), Marks(Row, 1), Marks(Row, 2), Marks(Row, 3)
    Next Row
    Close #FileNumber
End Sub
```

If the matrix was full of zeros then the output from the file, i.e., the contents of the c:\marks.txt would be:

```
0,0,0,0
0,0,0,0
0,0,0,0
0,0,0,0
0,0,0,0
```

The following procedure copies from the file c:\marks.txt to the matrix:

```
Private Sub CopyFromFileToMatrix()
Dim PathName As String
Dim FileNumber As Integer
Dim Row As Integer
    PathName = "c:\Marks.txt"
    FileNumber = FreeFile
    Open PathName For Input Access Read As #FileNumber
    For Row = cMin To cRow
        Input #FileNumber, Marks(Row, 0), Marks(Row, 1), Marks(Row, 2), Marks(Row, 3)
    Next Row
    Close #FileNumber
End Sub
```

PRACTICAL ACTIVITY 18.7

Build the application described by the GUI and general and event procedures shown in Figures 18.12 to 18.15. The application is incomplete; it only allows the entry, saving and recalling of student examination marks. A later activity will suggest additions to the application, such as calculating the average mark obtained by a student, etc.

The property setting for the controls should be obvious from the GUI and the event procedures' names. For example, the caption property for one of the labels is Examination Number. The name property for the control array of text boxes is txtMatrix because the name of the LostFocus event procedure (shown in Figure 18.15) is txtMatrix_LostFocus. As the event procedure name is constructed from the name of the object and the event the object name property must be txtMatrix.

Following the same reasoning the name property for one of the command buttons must be cmdAssignToMatrix because its click event procedure is named cmdAssignToMatrix_Click().

Remember to set the properties of the controls *before* you attach the code. This way the code always refers to the correctly named controls.

Figure 18.12 The GUI consists of five command buttons, a **control array** of 20 text boxes, 11 labels and 8 line controls.

Demo. of Output # and Input # statements

Examination Number

0   1   2   3

Student Number

0
1
2
3
4

Assign from text boxes to Matrix   Read from file to Matrix

Save Matrix contents to file   Display Matrix in text boxes

Set Matrix entries to zero

Figure 18.13 The form level declarations.

```
Option Explicit
Const cMin = 0
Const cRow = 4
Const cColumn = 3
Dim Marks(cMin To cRow, cMin To cColumn) As Integer
```

Figure 18.14 The form level general procedures.

```
Private Sub CopyFileToMatrix()
Dim PathName As String
Dim FileNumber As Integer
Dim Row As Integer
    PathName = "c:\Marks.txt"
    FileNumber = FreeFile
    Open PathName For Input Access Read As #FileNumber
    For Row = cMin To cRow
        Input #FileNumber, Marks(Row, 0), Marks(Row, 1), Marks(Row, 2), Marks(Row, 3)
    Next Row
    Close #FileNumber
End Sub

Private Sub CopyMatrixToFile()
Dim PathName As String
Dim FileNumber As Integer
Dim Row As Integer
    PathName = "c:\Marks.txt"
    FileNumber = FreeFile
    Open PathName For Output Access Write As #FileNumber
    For Row = cMin To cRow
        Write #FileNumber, Marks(Row, 0), Marks(Row, 1), Marks(Row, 2), Marks(Row, 3)
    Next Row
    Close #FileNumber
End Sub

Private Sub CopyMatrixToTextBoxes()
Dim Row As Integer
Dim Column As Integer
Dim ControlSelector As Integer
ControlSelector = 0
    For Row = cMin To cRow
        For Column = cMin To cColumn
            txtMatrix(ControlSelector).Text = CStr(Marks(Row, Column))
            ControlSelector = ControlSelector + 1
        Next Column
    Next Row
End Sub
```

Figure 18.14 (cont.)

```
Private Sub CopyTextBoxesToMatrix()
Dim Row As Integer
Dim Column As Integer
Dim ControlSelector As Integer
ControlSelector = 0
    For Row = cMin To cRow
        For Column = cMin To cColumn
            Marks(Row, Column) = CInt(txtMatrix(ControlSelector).Text)
            ControlSelector = ControlSelector + 1
        Next Column
    Next Row
End Sub

Private Sub InitialiseMatrix()
Dim Row As Integer
Dim Column As Integer
    For Row = cMin To cRow
        For Column = cMin To cColumn
            Marks(Row, Column) = 0
        Next Column
    Next Row
End Sub
```

Figure 18.15 The event procedures.

```
Private Sub Form_Load()
    Call InitialiseMatrix
    Call CopyMatrixToTextBoxes
End Sub

Private Sub txtMatrix_GotFocus(Index As Integer)
    txtMatrix(Index).Text = ""
End Sub

Private Sub txtMatrix_LostFocus(Index As Integer)
    If txtMatrix(Index).Text = "" Then
        txtMatrix(Index).Text = CStr(0)
    End If
End Sub

Private Sub cmdAssignToMatrix_Click()
    Call CopyTextBoxesToMatrix
End Sub

Private Sub cmdSave_Click()
    Call CopyMatrixToFile
End Sub

Private Sub cmdReadFile_Click()
    Call CopyFileToMatrix
End Sub
```

Figure 18.15 (cont.)

```
Private Sub cmdDisplayMatrix_Click()
    Call CopyMatrixToTextBoxes
End Sub

Private Sub cmdClearMatrix_Click()
    Call InitialiseMatrix
End Sub
```

PRACTICAL ACTIVITY 18.8

Amend the application developed during Practical activity 18.7 in the ways described below:

(a) The average mark of each student is calculated, displayed and saved in a text file.

(b) The average mark obtained in each examination is calculated, displayed and saved in a text file.

NOTE The next two practical activities are difficult and you may want to leave them for the time being. However, they do represent important dynamic programming techniques.

PRACTICAL ACTIVITY 18.9 (this is difficult!)

The application developed during Practical activity 18.7 (and amended in Practical activity 18.8) is limited in its use. It can only deal with five students and four examinations. It uses a static data structure. Amend the application so that it allows the user to specify the number of students and the number of examinations. From this information a suitable control array of text boxes is correctly positioned on the form and a correctly dimensioned Matrix is used to store the data.

The solution will involve the loading of text boxes, and the generation of a 2d array, at *run-time*.

HINT 1: You will have to use the Load statement covered in an earlier chapter. When the controls are loaded they will have to be correctly positioned. The positioning of controls was covered in the chapter on graphics.

HINT 2: You will have to use the ReDim statement; this has not been covered but information and examples of its use can be found in the VB online help.

PRACTICAL ACTIVITY 18.10 (this is difficult!)

Further amend the application so that all of the controls resize with reference to the size of the form. Therefore as the form is increased/decreased in size the controls are increased/decreased in size. Do not let the form decrease below one half of the area of the screen.

PRACTICAL ACTIVITY 18.11

Using an appropriate editor create two text files so that both contain a small section of different text. Open one file for **Append** and add the contents of the other file. Use an editor to confirm that the program has worked (i.e., load the file into the editor and see if text has been appended).

19 Random and binary access

Random access

The bytes stored in a random access file form identical records, with each record containing one or more fields. A record with one field corresponds to any Visual Basic standard type, such as an integer or fixed-length string. A record with more than one field corresponds to a user-defined type.

Variables required when performing random access

There are at least four variables required. they are

1. A user-defined type variable.
2. A variable to store the current record number.
3. A variable to store the length of the record.
4. A variable to store the number of the last record in the file.

User-defined type variable

This requires the declaration of a user-defined type as shown below:

```
Private Type tCustomer
        Name As String * 12      (12 bytes of storage)
        Balance As Currency      (8 bytes of storage)
        Age As Integer           (2 bytes of storage)
        OverDrawn As Boolean     (2 bytes of storage)
End Type
```

After the declaration of the type the variable is declared as shown below:

```
Dim Customer as tCustomer
```

The file will be used to store a number of records of the type tCustomer and each record will be transferred between the file and a program variable of the same type (i.e., Customer).

Variable to store the current record

It is important to track the number of the record currently being accessed; a suitable variable is used to hold the *number* of the current record being accessed and processed. An appropriate declaration is shown below:

```
Dim CurrentRecord as Long
```

Variable to store the length of the record

The **Len** function is used to find the length of the record used in the file and this is assigned to a variable. This variable is used in the open statement to 'inform' the *filenumber* of the length of the record, so that it can be correctly accessed. It can also be used in conjunction with another variable (that holds the size of the file in bytes) to calculate the number of identical length records there are in any one file.

The length of a record is found using the Len function as shown below:

RecordLength = Len(Customer)

Variable to store the number of the last record in the file

The first record in a file is at position 1, and the second at position 2 and so on. It is useful to know the number of the last record in the file and this can be found by dividing the length of the file (in bytes) by the length of the record (in bytes).

The length of an *open* file can be found using the LOF function as shown below:

FileLength = LOF(FileNumber)

The length of an *unopened* file can be found using the FileLen function as shown below:

FileLength = FileLen(pathname)

where pathname is the location of the file in the file system.

The number of the last record can be found as shown below:

LastRecord = FileLength/RecordLength

Writing a record to a file

To write a record to a file involves the following steps:

1. Set a string variable to the path of the file to be opened.
2. Find a suitable free file number using the **FreeFile** function.
3. Obtain the length of the Record to be written to the file.
4. Open the file for Random access.
5. Set the position at which the record is to be written to the file.
6. Transfer the record to the file using the **Put** statement.
7. Close the file.

The following code opens a file, that has the path **c:\customers**, and stores a record variable **Customer** at the **first** position in the file.

```
PathToFile = "c:\customers"
FileNumber = FreeFile
RecordLength = Len(Customer)
Open PathToFile For Random As FileNumber Len = RecordLength
CurrentRecord = 1
Put #FileNumber, CurrentRecord, Customer
Close (FileNumber)
```

Trace description

Statement	Description
PathToFile = "c:\customers"	This sets a string variable to the path of the file that is to be accessed.
FileNumber = FreeFile	This assigns the next available free file number to the integer variable *FileNumber*.
RecordLength = Len(Customer)	The **Len** function returns the length of the record variable *Customer* in bytes.
Open PathToFile For Random As FileNumber Len = RecordLength	The open statement opens the file defined by the path stored in the *PathToFile* variable. It opens the file for Random access. The variable *FileNumber* will be used to reference the file from Visual Basic code. *Len = RecordLength* 'informs' the open statement as to the size of the record it will be storing – this is needed to ensure that records are always written to the correct position in a file.
CurrentRecord = 1	The variable *CurrentRecord* is assigned one and this is used in the **Put** statement to define the position at which the record will be placed in the file.
Put #FileNumber, CurrentRecord, Customer	The file referenced by *FileNumber* has a copy of the program variable *Customer* transferred to the file at the position defined by *CurrentRecord*. In this case the record is stored at position one in the file c:\customers.
Close (FileNumber)	The file is closed.

QUESTION 19.1 (REVISION)

How would a Customer record variable be stored at the second position in a file?

Reading a record from a file

To read a record from a file involves the following steps:

1. Set a string variable to the path of the file to be opened.
2. Find a suitable free file number using the **FreeFile** function.
3. Obtain the length of the Record to be read from the file.
4. Open the file for Random access.
5. Set the position at which the record is to be read from the file.
6. Transfer the record from the file using the **Get** statement.
7. Close the file.

The following code opens a file and reads the record variable **Customer** from the **first** position in a file that has the path **c:\customers**.

```
PathToFile = "c:\customers"
FileNumber = FreeFile
RecordLength = Len(Customer)
Open PathToFile For Random As FileNumber Len = RecordLength
CurrentRecord = 1
Get #FileNumber, CurrentRecord, Customer
Close (FileNumber)
```

Trace description

Statement	Description
PathToFile = "c:\customers"	This sets a string variable to the path of the file that is to be accessed.
FileNumber = FreeFile	This assigns the next available free file number to the integer variable FileNumber.
RecordLength = Len(Customer)	The **Len** function returns the length of the record variable *Customer* in bytes.
Open PathToFile For Random As FileNumber Len = RecordLength	The open statement opens the file defined by the path stored in the *PathToFile* variable. It opens the file for Random access. The variable *FileNumber* will be used to reference the file from Visual Basic code. *Len = RecordLength* 'informs' the open statement as to the size of the record it will be storing – this is needed to ensure that a record is always read from the correct position in a file.
CurrentRecord = 1	The variable *CurrentRecord* is assigned one and this is used in the **Get** statement to define the position at which the record will be read from the file.
Get #FileNumber, CurrentRecord, Customer	The file referenced by *FileNumber* has the record, stored at the position defined by *CurrentRecord*, transferred from the file to the program variable Customer.
Close (FileNumber)	The file is closed.

QUESTION 19.2 (REVISION)

How would a record variable be read from the second position in a file?

IMPORTANT: The *Name* field of the user-defined type *tCustomer* is a string of 12 characters (i.e., Name As String * **12**). If you intend to save user-defined types to a file then the length of any string field must be defined. The random accessing of records using the Put and Get assumes that all the stored records are the same size in bytes. String sizes that are not defined can grow and shrink in size.

PRACTICAL ACTIVITY 19.1

(a) Specification 17.2, from Chapter 17, dealt with five bank customers and used a table to store the details on the customers. Amend the code and GUI so that a file is used to store the Customer details instead of a table.

HINTS: The Next Record and Previous Record command buttons will need to increment and decrement the value of the *CurrentRecord* respectively.

For the code to write and read to and from the c:\customers file remove the line **CurrentRecord = 1**. Declare *CurrentRecord* with a suitable scope that allows access by all the code attached to the command buttons on the GUI access i.e., declare it with form level scope.

Attach the statement CurrentRecord = CurrentRecord + 1 to the Next Record command button.

The *Assign to Record* command button will have to assign the contents of the text boxes to a variable of type tCustomer and then store it in a file. The next entries in the text boxes will be assigned to the **same** variable and it will be stored to the file again, however, this time it will be stored in the next position in the file. The next position in the file is 'pointed to' by the variable CurrentRecord and it will have been incremented by clicking the Next Record command button. There is only a need for one *program* variable to store details on one customer and this variable is used as a 'buffer' to all of the customer records held on file.

(b) Implement the following change to the original specification:

- It will deal with any number of customers (not just five customers).
- Clicking a command button will display, in a message box, the number of records stored in the file.

How to edit a record stored on file

To edit a record stored on file perform the following steps:

1. Transfer the record to be edited from the file to a program variable (of the same type).
2. Edit the program variable.
3. Transfer the program variable back to the same position in the file.

Adding records to the end of a file opened for random access

Increment the variable LastRecord (so that it points beyond the last record) and use the following statement:

    Put #FileNumber, LastRecord, Customer

How to delete records from a file

The fields of a record can be cleared but this would not remove the record from a file. When a record is not required it is best removed from the file because they waste space and slow down sequential access to the file. To delete a record from a file perform the following tasks.

1. Create a new file.
2. Copy all the *valid* records from the original file to the new file.
3. Save the path to the original file.
4. Close the original file and use the **Kill** statement to delete it.
5. Use the **Name** statement to rename the new file with the name of the original file.

PRACTICAL ACTIVITY 19.2

(a) Amend the project developed during Practical activity 19.1 so that it will allow the editing of any record held on file.

(b) Further amend the project so that it allows the deletion of any record from the file.

QUESTION 19.1 (DEVELOPMENT)

Use the Visual Basic online help to learn about the Seek function and Seek statement.

Searching a file

It would be useful if the user of the project developed during Practical activity 19.1 could find and display the details on an individual customer. This would involve the user entering a string and comparing this to the name field of every record until a match was found. Alternatively, the records on file could be ordered alphabetically and a 'split by two search' could be performed. Both of these methods will be discussed in due course, but in the meantime, string comparison within Visual Basic will be discussed because it is fundamental to performing the search for an individual customer.

String comparison function

This function returns a value indicating the result of a string comparison. Its syntax is shown below:

StrComp(*string1*, *string2*[, *compare*])

The three parts of the function are described in Table 19.1.

Table 19.1 Parts of the StrComp function.

Part	Description
string1	Any valid string expression, i.e., one of the strings to be compared.
string2	Any valid string expression, i.e., one of the strings to be compared.
compare	Specifies the type of string comparison. The compare argument can be 0 or 1. Specify 0 (default) to perform a binary comparison which is case sensitive. Specify 1 to perform a textual comparison which is not case sensitive.

Table 19.2 describes the values returned from the StrComp function.

Table 19.2 Return values from the StrComp function.

If	Strcomp returns
string1 is less than string2	-1
string1 is equal to string2	0
string1 is greater than string2	1
string1 or string2 is Null	Null

The code shown in Figure 19.1 illustrates the use of the StrComp function and Figure 19.2 shows the output from the code when the Form_Click event is invoked.

Figure 19.1 Code showing the return values of the StrComp function.

```
Private Sub Form_Click()
Dim String1 As String
Dim String2 As String
Dim String3 As String

    String1 = "XYZ"
    String2 = "xyz"
    String3 = "XYZ"
    Form1.Print StrComp(String1, String2, 1) ' Returns 0.
    Form1.Print StrComp(String1, String2, 0) ' Returns -1.
    Form1.Print StrComp(String1, String3, 0) ' Returns 0.
    Form1.Print StrComp(String1, String3, 1) ' Returns 0.
End Sub
```

Figure 19.2 Output from the Form_Click event procedure.

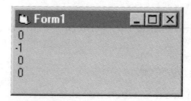

Trace description

Statement	Description
String1 = "XYZ"	Assigns a value to a string variable to be used in the StrComp function in later program statements.
String2 = "xyz"	Assigns a value to a string variable to be used in the StrComp function in later program statements.
String3 = "XYZ"	Assigns a value to a string variable to be used in the StrComp function in later program statements.
Form1.Print StrComp(String1, String2, 1)	The string *XYZ* is compared with *xyz* using textual comparison (because the third argument in the list is 1), consequently, the StrComp function returns 0 and this is printed on the form using the Print method. The setting of the third argument to one results in the StrComp function ignoring the case of the string. Therefore, this arrangement of the StrComp function would indicate that the string JONES is the same as jones.
Form1.Print StrComp(String1, String2, 0)	The string *XYZ* is compared with *xyz* using binary comparison (because the third argument in the list is 0), consequently, the StrComp function returns -1 and this is printed on the form using the Print method. The setting of the third argument to zero results in the StrComp function taking notice of the string case. Therefore, this arrangement of the StrComp function would indicate that the string JONES is different to jones.
Form1.Print StrComp(String1, String3, 0)	The string *XYZ* is compared with *XYX* using binary comparison (because the third argument in the list is 0), consequently, the StrComp function returns 0 and this is printed on the form using the Print method. The setting of the third argument to zero results in the StrComp function taking notice of the string case. Therefore, this arrangement of the StrComp function would indicate that the string JONES is the same as JONES.
Form1.Print StrComp(String1, String3, 1)	The string *XYZ* is compared with *XYZ* using textural comparison (because the third argument in the list is 1), consequently, the StrComp function returns 0 and this is printed on the form using the Print method. The setting of the third argument to one results in the StrComp function ignoring the case of the string. Therefore, this arrangement of the StrComp function would indicate that the string JONES is the same as JONES.

PRACTICAL ACTIVITY 19.3

Amend the project developed during Practical activities 19.1 and 19.2 so that the user can enter a string (in a text box) that represents the name of a customer held on file. This string is then compared to the name field of each record held on file until a match is found. The matching record is then displayed.

For the purpose of this activity create a file of bank customers that have only their surname stored in the Name field of the record.

HINT: In an appropriate loop (repetition construct) compare the user entered string to the Name field of each record until the end of the file. Stop searching the file when a match is found. Use the StrComp function for the comparisons, make sure the comparison is **not** case sensitive.

Split by two search

If strings held on file are in alphabetic order it is **not** necessary to search all the file from beginning to end. Consider the list of strings shown in Figure 19.3.

If the string e was to be located in this list, using a sequential search, would involve five comparisons before it was found, i.e., it would be compared to a, then b, then c, then d, and finally e. However, the 'split by two search' would locate e after three comparisons.

Searching for e in this list using the 'split by two' method is described below:

1. Find the number of strings (records) in the list, in this case there are six.
2. Using integer division, divide the number of strings by two (i.e., 6/2) and in this case it will give three.
3. Compare the string e with the third string in the list (i.e., the 6/2 string). The string e is greater than c (the third string in the list). Consequently, it must be further on in the list.
4. Divide the remaining strings beyond the third string by two and add this number to the 'position number' of the last comparison. The integer division of three (the remaining records) by two added to three (the number representing the last comparison position) results in four.
5. The string e is compared to the fourth string in the list and found to be greater. Divide the remaining strings beyond the fourth string by two and add this number to the 'position number' of the last comparison. The integer division of two (the remaining records) by two added to four (the number representing the last comparison position) results in five.
6. The string e is compared to the fifth string in the list and found to be the same.

Only three comparisons were needed to locate the string e, this represents a saving of two comparisons. If the list was much longer then the saving in the number of comparisons can be much greater.

Figure 19.3 A list of ordered strings.

a	b	c	d	e	f

QUESTION 19.1 (DEVELOPMENT)

From the description of the 'split by two search' derive an algorithm, represented by an N-S Chart, to perform this type of search on a file of records, where one field is a string representing the surname of a bank customer, i.e., search for a customer's surname.

PRACTICAL ACTIVITY 19.4

Amend the searching function of Practical activity 19.3 by adapting the bubble sort algorithm covered in Chapter 12. Have the code, derived from the algorithm, order the bank customers on file by their surnames. Then use the 'split by two search' to locate and display the details on one customer.

Binary access

Random files are accessed record by record and sequential files are accessed line by line. Binary files are accessed byte by byte. Once a file is opened for binary access you can read and write to any byte location in the file. The ability to access any byte makes binary access the most flexible

Opening a file for binary access

The open statement is used to open a file for binary access as shown below:

    Open PathToFile For Binary As #FileNumber

where PathToFile is a string variable that has been assigned the path of the file to be opened and FileNumber is an integer variable that has been assigned the next free file number using the FreeFile function.

Writing bytes to a binary file

Once a file has been opened for binary access the **Put #** statement can be used to write a **byte or bytes** to any byte location in the file.

The following **Put #** statement will write the contents of the integer variable FirstNumber to the tenth location of a binary file.

    BytePosition = 10
    Put #FileNumber, BytePosition, FirstNumber

The **Put #** statement has three arguments; the first is the FileNumber used to reference the file, the second is the position at which the writing starts and the third argument is the name of the variable whose contents is written to the file.

345

After the execution of a **Put #** statement the position 'pointed to' within the file is automatically adjusted so that it points to the next byte after the position of the last byte written to the file. Consequently, after the last Put # statement the twelfth position will be 'pointed to' because the variable FirstNumber is of the type integer and an integer is two bytes long. The integer is stored in the tenth and eleventh position in the file.

? QUESTION 19.2 (REVISION)

What position will be pointed to after each of the following writes to a file opened for binary access (FirstName is of integer type; Surname is a 20 character string and IncreasedMoney is of type currency).

BytePosition = 20
Put #FileNumber, BytePosition, FirstNumber

BytePosition = 200
Put #FileNumber, BytePosition, FirstNumber

BytePosition = 10
Put #FileNumber, BytePosition, Surname

BytePosition = 10
Put #FileNumber, BytePosition, IncreasedMoney

NOTE: The **Put #** statement can be used without specifying a byte position. In which case the variable or literal value is omitted, but the commas must be included as shown below:

put #FileNumber, , FirstNumber

The content of the variable FirstNumber will be written to the file at a position defined by the *last* **Put** statement, i.e., if the last Put # statement finished writing at location 19 then the above Put will store the contents of FirstNumber (integer type) at location 20 and 21.

Readings bytes from a binary file

Once a file has been opened for binary access the **Get #** statement can be used to read a **byte or bytes** from any byte location in the file.

The following **Get #** statement will read the contents of the integer variable FirstNumber from the tenth location (actually, it will be 10 and 11 because an integer type is two bytes long) of a binary file.

BytePosition = 10

Get #FileNumber, BytePosition, FirstNumber

PRACTICAL ACTIVITY 19.5

Use binary access to encrypt and decrypt the contents of a text file. This will involve the following steps:

TO ENCRYPT

1. Read a byte from the file and alter it in some way (e.g., add one to it).
2. Write the altered byte back to the same position.
3. Repeat this for all the bytes in the file (i.e., until the end of the file).

TO DECRYPT

1. Read a byte from the file and alter it back to its original value (i.e., subtract one from it).
2. Write the altered byte back to the same position.
3. Repeat this for all the bytes in the file (i.e., until the end of the file).

NOTE: When dealing with byte type variables adding one to 255 will cause an overflow. Give careful consideration to how this could be avoided. **HINT**: You might find the data conversion functions useful.

20 List boxes

Visual Basic offers five types of list boxes that allow a user to select from a list of items. Three of the list boxes are used to interface with the operating system file structure. Each box is briefly described and the implementation of specifications is used to illustrate a use of each box.

The five list boxes are:

1. List box (ListBox).
2. Combo box (ComboBox).
3. Drive list box (DriveListBox).
4. Directory list box (DirListBox).
5. File list box (FileListBox).

List box (ListBox) control ( )

A ListBox control displays a list of items from which the user can select one or more. If the number of items exceeds the number that can be displayed, a scroll bar is automatically added to the ListBox control. An example of a list box is shown in Figure 20.1.

Four of the properties frequently used with the list box control are ListIndex; ListCount, List and Sorted. Two methods frequently used with the list box control are AddItem and RemoveItem.

ListIndex property

This property determines the index of the currently selected item in the list. It is **not** available at design time but can be accessed at run-time. The ListIndex property settings are shown in Table 20.1.

ListCount property

This property specifies the number of items in the list. It is **not** available at design time and is read-only at run-time. ListCount is always one more than the largest ListIndex value.

List property

This property determines the items contained in the list and is a string array in which each element is a list item. This property is used to access list items. The index of the first item in the list is 0 and the last item has the index (ListCount -1).

> **NOTE**: The List property works in conjunction with the ListCount and ListIndex properties.

Table 20.1 The ListIndex property and its setting.

Setting	Description
-1	Indicates no item is currently selected.
n	A number indicating the index of the currently selected item.

Sorted property

This property specifies whether the elements of a list box are automatically sorted alphabetically. The Sorted property settings are shown in Table 20.2

Figure 20.1 illustrates a list box containing five names (i.e., five items). For this list box, the ListCount property has the value of 5 (i.e., the number of items in the list); ListIndex can be in the range 0 to 4, and List is a string array as illustrated in Figure 20.2.

Table 20.2 The Sorted property and its settings.

Setting	Description
True	List items are sorted alphabetically (case-insensitive).
False	(Default) List items are not sorted alphabetically.

Figure 20.1 An example of a list box.

Figure 20.2 The List string array.

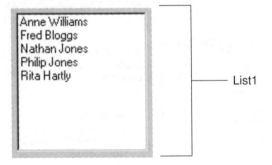

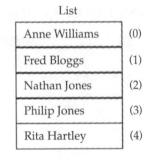

> **NOTE**: For this list box a string variable X would store Fred Bloggs *after* the execution of the following assignment statement:
>
> X = List1.List(1)
>
> The expression List(List1.ListIndex) returns the string for the *currently* selected item.

AddItem method

This method, when applied to a list box, adds a new item at run-time. For example, the following statement adds to a list box (List1) the value of the text property of a text box (Text1).

List1.AddItem Text1.Text

The full syntax for the AddItem method is shown below:

object.AddItem item, index

The three parts of the method are described in Table 20.3.

RemoveItem method

This method removes an item from a list box at run-time. For example, the following statement removes from a list box (List1) the item at the position indicated by the Index.

List1.RemoveItem Index

The full syntax for the RemoveItem method is shown below:

object. RemoveItem, index

The three parts of the method are described in Table 20.4.

The implementation of Specification 20.1 will demonstrate the use of a list box.

SPECIFICATION 20.1

Write a program that will allow a user to enter, in a text box, the surname of customers. These surnames are to be added to a list box in alphabetical order. Surnames can also be removed from the list and the entire list can also be cleared.

Suitable GUI for Specification 20.1

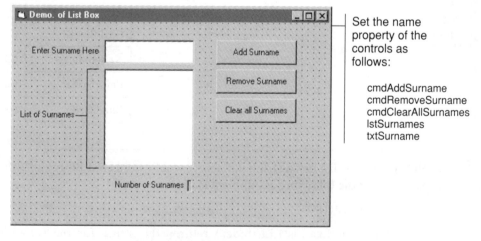

Table 20.3 Parts of the AddItem method.

Part	Description
object	The object to which the method applies (can be a list box, Combo box or grid control).
item	String expression specifying the item to add to the object.
index	Integer specifying the position within the object where the new item is placed. For the first item in a ListBox the index is 0. This part is optional.

Table 20.4 Parts of the RemoveItem method.

Part	Description
object	The object to which the method applies.
index	Integer specifying the position within the object from where the item is removed.

Code attached to the GUI

```
Private Sub cmdAddSurname_Click()
    lstSurnames.AddItem txtSurname.Text
    txtSurname.Text = ""
    txtSurname.SetFocus
    lblNumberOfSurnames.Caption = lstSurnames.ListCount
End Sub

Private Sub cmdRemoveSurname_Click()
Dim Index As Integer
    Index = lstSurnames.ListIndex
    If Index >= 0 Then
        lstSurnames.RemoveItem Index
        lblNumberOfSurnames.Caption = lstSurnames.ListCount
    End If
    If lstSurnames.ListIndex <> -1 Then
        cmdRemoveSurname.Enabled = True
    Else
        cmdRemoveSurname.Enabled = False
    End If
End Sub

Private Sub cmdClearAllSurnames_Click()
    lstSurnames.Clear
    lblNumberOfSurnames.Caption = lstSurnames.ListCount
    cmdRemoveSurname.Enabled = False
End Sub

Private Sub Form_Load()
    cmdRemoveSurname.Enabled = False
End Sub

Private Sub lstSurnames_Click()
    If lstSurnames.ListIndex <> -1 Then
        cmdRemoveSurname.Enabled = True
    Else
        cmdRemoveSurname.Enabled = False
    End If
End Sub
```

PRACTICAL ACTIVITY 20.1

Implement Specification 20.1 Remember to set the sort property of the list box to true.

QUESTION 20.1 (DEVELOPMENT)

A description of the code is not given. Produce your own Description Trace Table for each of the event procedures. Use the VB online help to discover the operation of any methods not covered (e.g., Clear).

Combo box (ComboBox) control ( )

A ComboBox control combines the features of a TextBox and a ListBox control. Users can enter information in the text box or select an item from the list box of the control.

The implementation of Specification 20.2 will be used to demonstrate the use of a ComboBox.

SPECIFICATION 20.2

A control array of four picture boxes is drawn onto one form. Each box contains a logo that can be transferred to a picture box on the same form. The picture to be transferred is selected from a ComboBox.

Suitable GUI for Specification 20.2

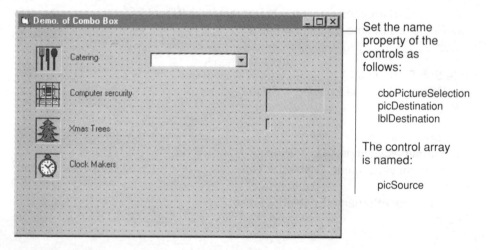

Set the name property of the controls as follows:

    cboPictureSelection
    picDestination
    lblDestination

The control array is named:

    picSource

Code attached to the GUI

```
Private Sub Form_Load()
    cboPictureSelection.AddItem "Catering"
    cboPictureSelection.AddItem "Computer sercurity"
    cboPictureSelection.AddItem "Xmas Trees"
    cboPictureSelection.AddItem "Clock Makers"
End Sub

Private Sub cboPictureSelection_Click()
Select Case cboPictureSelection.Text
    Case "Catering"
        picDestination.Picture = picSource(0).Picture
        lblDestination.Caption = cboPictureSelection.Text
    Case "Computer sercurity"
        picDestination.Picture = picSource(1).Picture
        lblDestination.Caption = cboPictureSelection.Text
    Case "Xmas Trees"
        picDestination.Picture = picSource(2).Picture
        lblDestination.Caption = cboPictureSelection.Text
    Case "Clock Makers"
        picDestination.Picture = picSource(3).Picture
        lblDestination.Caption = cboPictureSelection.Text
End Select
End Sub
```

PRACTICAL ACTIVITY 20.2

Implement Specification 20.2

QUESTION 20.2 (DEVELOPMENT)

A description of the code is not given. Produce your own Description Trace Table for each of the event procedures.

File list box (FileListBox) control( )

A FileListBox control, locates and lists files at run-time from a directory, specified by its Path property. This control is used to display a list of files selected by file type. A user is able to select items in the list by using the List, ListCount, and ListIndex properties (which behave almost in exactly the same way as the same properties of the list box).

The implementation of Specification 20.3 will demonstrate the use of a file list box.

SPECIFICATION 20.3

Select from a file list box, metafiles to be displayed in a picture box.

Suitable GUI for Specification 20.3

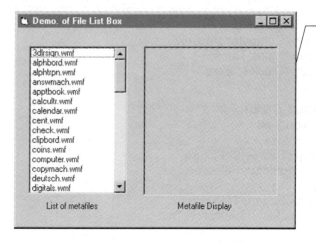

NOTE:
Set the file list box name property to filSelectFiles and the picture box name property to picDisplayFiles.

Code attached to the GUI

```
Private Sub Form_Load()
    filSelectFiles.Path = "c:\vb\metafile\business"
    filSelectFiles.Pattern = "*.wmf"
End Sub

Private Sub filSelectFiles_Click()
Dim PartOfPath As String
Dim FullPathToFile As String
    PartOfPath = filSelectFiles.List(filSelectFiles.ListIndex)
    FullPathToFile = filSelectFiles.Path & "\" & PartOfPath
    picDisplayFiles.Picture = LoadPicture(FullPathToFile)
End Sub
```

Description trace for the Form_Load event procedure

Statement	Description
filSelectFiles.Path = "c:\vb\metafile\business"	The Path property of the file list box is available at run-time and, therefore, can only be set at run-time. The path to metafiles is assigned to the Path property during the load event of the form.
filSelectFiles.Pattern = "*.wmf"	The Pattern property returns or sets a value indicating the filenames displayed in a FileListBox control at run-time. Setting the Pattern to *.wmf will only allow metafiles to be displayed in the file list box. The * character acts as a *wildcard* and stands for any legal identifier.

Description trace for the filSelectFiles_Click()event procedure

The following description trace is based on the run-time illustrated in Figure 20.3.

Statement	Description
PartOfPath = filSelectFiles.List(filSelectFiles.ListIndex)	When the user selects an item from the file list box the ListIndex property of FileListBox is altered to reflect the selection. The ListIndex is then used to index the current element of the List string array, the contents of this element (i.e., the name of the metafile) are copied to the string variable *PartOfPath*. Consequently, the string variable *PartOfPath* is assigned answmach.wmf.
FullPathToFile = filSelectFiles.Path & "\" & PartOfPath	The content of the Path property of the file list box, the literal string "\" and the content of the string variable *PartOfPath* are 'joined together' to form the following string: c:\vb\metafile\business\answmach.wmf which is assigned to the string variable *FullPathToFile*.
picDisplayFiles.Picture = LoadPicture(FullPathToFile)	The Picture property of the picture box is loaded with a picture using the LoadPicture function that takes the string variable FullPathToFile as its argument.

Figure 20.3 A typical run-time for the program implementing Specification 20.3.

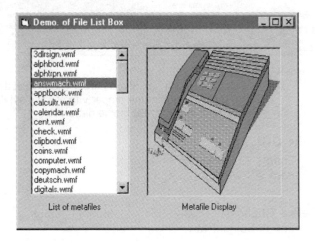

PRACTICAL ACTIVITY 20.3

Implement Specification 20.3.

Directory list box (DirListBox) control ( )

A DirListBox control displays directories and paths at run-time. This control is used to display a hierarchical list of directories. Again (like the list box and file list box) the List, ListCount, and ListIndex properties enable a user to access items in the list.

The implementation of Specification 20.4 will demonstrate the use of the DirListBox control.

> **SPECIFICATION 20.4**
>
> *Amend Specification 20.3 so that it includes a directory list box as part of the GUI.*

Suitable GUI for Specification 20.4

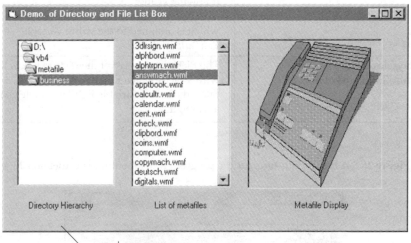

Directory Hierarchy   List of metafiles   Metafile Display

NOTE:
Set the file list box name property to filSelectFiles, the picture box name property tp picDisplayFiles and the directory list box to dirSelect.

Code attached to the GUI

```
Private Sub Form_Load()
    filSelectFiles.Pattern = "*.wmf"
End Sub

Private Sub dirSelect_Change()
    filSelectFiles.Path = dirSelect.Path
End Sub

Private Sub filSelectFiles_Click()
Dim PartOfPath As String
Dim FullPathToFile As String
    PartOfPath = filSelectFiles.List(filSelectFiles.ListIndex)
    FullPathToFile = dirSelect.Path & "\" & PartOfPath
    picDisplayFiles.Picture = LoadPicture(FullPathToFile)
End Sub
```

Description trace for the Form_Load() event procedure

Statement	Description
filSelectFiles.Pattern = "*.wmf"	Setting the Pattern to *.wmf will only allow metafiles to be displayed in the file list box.

Description trace for the dirSelect_Change() event procedure

Statement	Description
filSelectFiles.Path = dirSelect.Path	At run-time double clicking a folder (directory) in the directory list box changes the content of the directory list box (this is best observed when you implement Specification 20.4). It also invokes a directory list box change event. This statement (within this change event) sets the Path property for the file list box. Consequently, the file list box will display the contents of the directory selected from the directory list box. However, it will only display those files that match the Pattern property of the file list box that was set during the form load event (i.e., *.wmf).

Description trace for the filSelectFiles_Click() event procedure

Statement	Description
PartOfPath = filSelectFiles.List(filSelectFiles.ListIndex)	When the user selects an item from the file list box, the ListIndex property of FileListBox is altered to reflect the selection. The ListIndex is then used to index an element of the List string array, the contents of this element (i.e., the name of the metafile) are copied to the string variable *PartOfPath*. Consequently, the string variable *PartOfPath* is assigned answmach.wmf.
FullPathToFile = dirSelect.Path & "\" & PartOfPath	The full path to the metafile to be loaded in to the picture box is constructed from the Path property of the directory list box and file list box, together with the literal string "\". **This statement shows how to synchronise the Path property of both the file list and directory list boxes.**
picDisplayFiles.Picture = LoadPicture(FullPathToFile)	The selected metafile is displayed in the picture box.

PRACTICAL ACTIVITY 20.4

Implement Specification 20.4.

Drive list box (DriveListBox) control ( )

A DriveListBox control enables a user to select a valid disk drive at run-time. This control is used to display a list of all the valid drives in a user's system. A dialogue box can be created that enables the user to open a file from a list of files on a disk in any available drive. Again, like all the other types of list boxes, the List, ListCount, and ListIndex properties enable a user to access items in the list.

The implementation of Specification 20.5 will demonstrate the use of the DriveListBox control.

SPECIFICATION 20.5

Amend Specification 20.4 so that it includes a drive list box as part of the GUI.

Suitable GUI for Specification 20.5

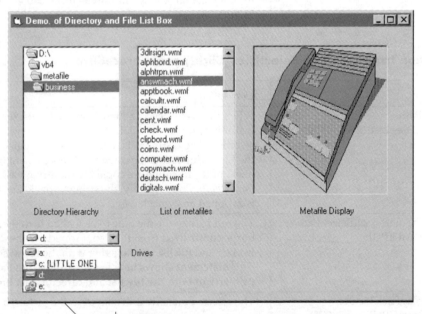

NOTE:
Set the file list box name property to filSelectFiles, the picture box name property to picDisplayFiles, the directory list box to dirSelect and the drive list box to drvSelect.

Code attached to the GUI

```
Private Sub Form_Load()
    filSelectFiles.Pattern = "*.wmf"
End Sub
```

```
Private Sub dirSelect_Change()
   filSelectFiles.Path = dirSelect.Path
End Sub

Private Sub drvSelect_Change()
   dirSelect.Path = drvSelect.Drive
End Sub

Private Sub filSelectFiles_Click()
Dim PartOfPath As String
Dim FullPathToFile As String
   PartOfPath = filSelectFiles.List(filSelectFiles.ListIndex)
   FullPathToFile = dirSelect.Path & "\" & PartOfPath
   picDisplayFiles.Picture = LoadPicture(FullPathToFile)
End Sub
```

There is very little change to the code to accommodate the drive list box. All that is required is the addition of a statement within the drive list change event (shown in bold). This statement, repeated below, synchronises the directory list box with the drive list box.

dirSelect.Path = drvSelect.Drive

The Drive property of the drive list box is copied to the Path property of the directory list box. This results in the directory list box displaying the file system of the selected drive.

PRACTICAL ACTIVITY 20.5

Implement Specification 20.5.

QUESTION 20.3 (DEVELOPMENT)

The project developed during Practical activity 20.5 will crash under certain conditions. One of these conditions is highlighted by Figure 20.4. To reproduce this crash you will need to copy a metafile to the root of your C: directory.

Find out why this crash occurs and correct it.

PRACTICAL ACTIVITY 20.6

For the previous practical activities the picture box displayed metafiles and the Pattern property of the file list box was set as shown below:

filSelectFiles.Pattern = "*.wmf"

Amend the GUI developed during Practical activity 20.5 so that it will *also* allow a bitmap to be loaded into the picture box. This can be achieved by removing the statement above and adding a combo box that will allow for the selection of metafiles or bitmaps. Figure 20.5 shows how the ComboBox should look at run-time.

Figure 20.4 'Screen shot' associated with Question 20.3.

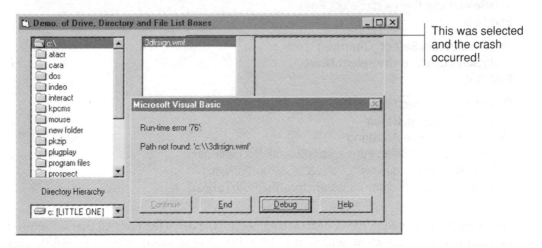

This was selected and the crash occurred!

Figure 20.5 The ComboBox at run-time. This figure is associated with Practical activity 20.6.

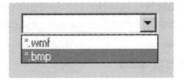

21 The data control (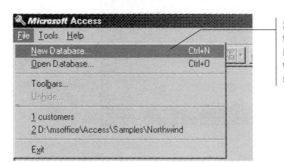)

The data control allows for the creation of applications that display and edit information from many types of existing databases. It also offers an alternative to the direct file access discussed in Chapters 18 and 19.

The data control is *usually* used to access an existing database, therefore, the first thing to do is to build a simple database. The database can be built using Access (or another database, such as, for example, FoxPro or Paradox) or using the data manager supplied with Visual Basic.

A simple database suitable for storing details on the customer of a bank will be built. To allow for comparison with the direct file access, discussed in Chapter 19, the database will consist of a record structure that has the following four fields; Name, Balance, Age and OverDrawn. Access produces relational databases and it is usual to have a field that acts as a primary key. For reasons that will not be discussed here the four fields previously listed are not suitable as a primary key, consequently, an extra field will be added. This field will be called CustomerID and it will act as the primary key.

Building a database table using access

Figure 21.1 illustrates the sequence of steps necessary to build a database table (using Access) capable of storing information in the record structure just described.

Data bound controls

The data control is used to connect a Visual Basic application to an existing database. Bound controls are data-aware controls that are able to access the fields of records within a database table.

Figure 21.1 Building a database table using Access.

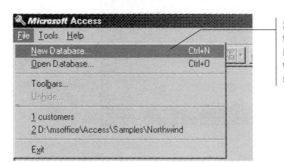

Select *New Database...* from the File menu. Access responds with the dialogue box shown next.

Figure 21.1 (cont.)

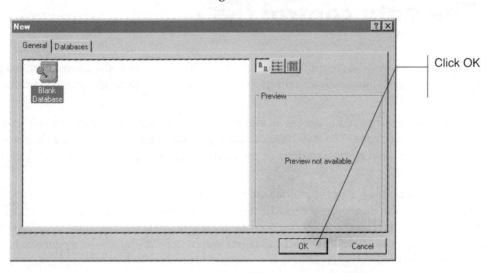

Click OK

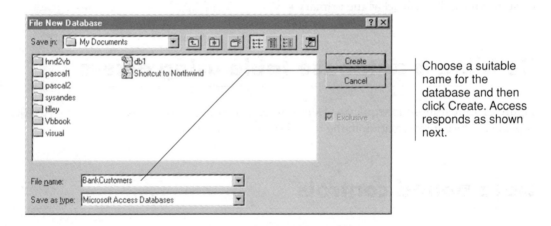

Choose a suitable
name for the
database and then
click Create. Access
responds as shown
next.

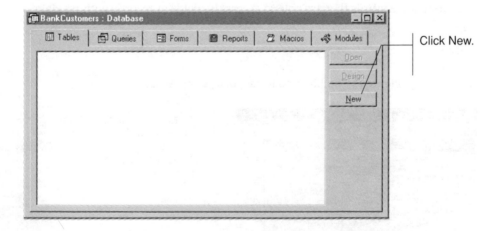

Click New.

Figure 21.1 (cont.)

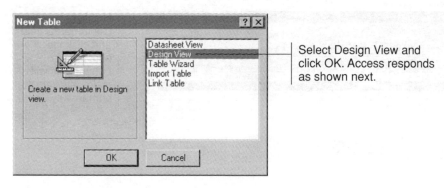

Select Design View and click OK. Access responds as shown next.

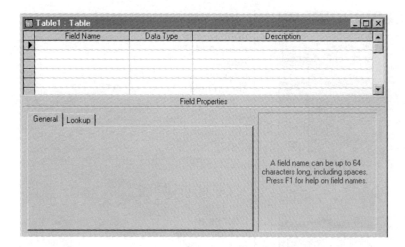

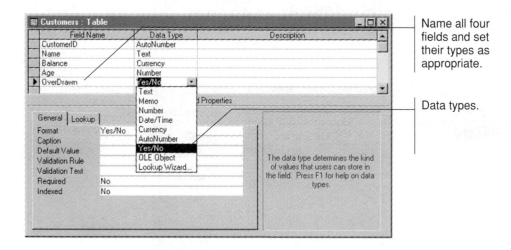

Name all four fields and set their types as appropriate.

Data types.

Figure 21.1 (cont.)

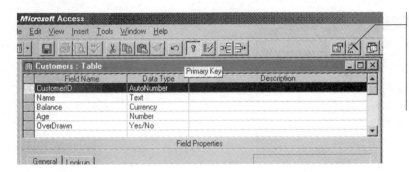

Highlight the Customer ID field and click the primary key button. This will make this field the primary key.

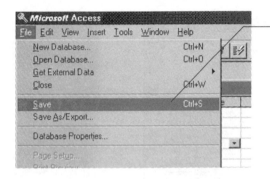

Select *Save* from the *File* menu and Access responds as shown next.

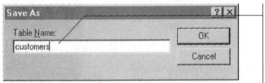

Choose a suitable name and click OK. Access responds as shown next.

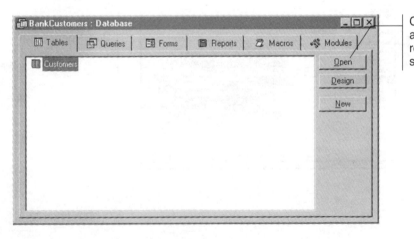

Click Open and Access responds as shown next.

Figure 21.1 (cont.)

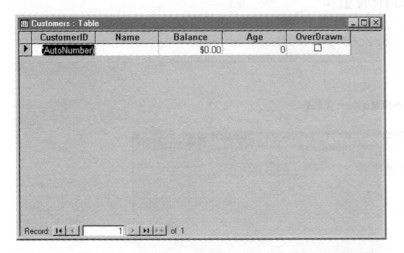

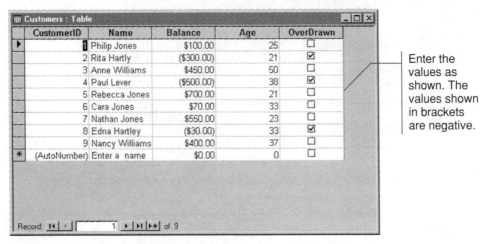

Enter the values as shown. The values shown in brackets are negative.

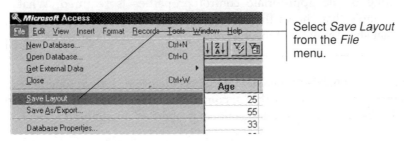

Select *Save Layout* from the *File* menu.

The table is now complete and contains nine records full of data.

A data-aware control is bound to the data control, which in turn, is connected to a database. Consequently, a data aware control is able to 'see' data in the database 'through' the data control.

The implementation of Specification 21.1 will demonstrate the use of data and bound controls.

SPECIFICATION 21.1

Develop a GUI that will display four of the five fields held in the customer's database – do not display the CustomerID field.

Suitable GUI for Specification 21.1

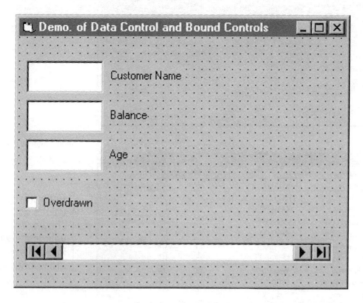

The GUI consists of three text boxes, three labels, one check box and one data control.

 NOTE: *The implementation of Specification 21.1 requires no coding!* Only the correct setting of the appropriate control properties is required. What follows is a table that shows the correct settings and also a sequence of diagrams that show how to set the important properties for database access.

Table 21.1 lists the important controls of the GUI (the labels are not included) together with their setting for properties used to access the customer's database. Not all the property settings are shown in this list, for example, all 'positional properties' are ignored.

Table 21.1 Controls and their property settings.

Control	Property	Setting
Data Control	Name	datCustomers
	Connect	Access
	DatabaseName	D:\My Documents\BankCustomers.mdb
	RecordSource	customers

Table 21.1 (cont.)

Control	Property	Setting
Form1	Name	frmDatabaseDemo
	Caption	Demo. of Data Control and Bound Controls
CheckBox	Name	chkOverDrawn
	Caption	Overdrawn
	DataField	OverDrawn
	DataSource	datCustomers
TextBox	Name	txtName
	DataField	Name
	DataSource	datCustomers
TextBox	Name	txtBalance
	DataField	Balance
	DataSource	datCustomers
TextBox	Name	txtAge
	DataField	Age
	DataSource	datCustomers

Connecting a data control to a database

To connect a data control to a database, perform the sequence of actions illustrated by Figure 21.2.

Once the sequence of events, illustrated by Figure 21.2, has been performed the data control is connected to the BankCustomers database. The next step is to connect data aware controls (i.e., bound controls) to the database.

Figure 21.2 Connecting a data control to a database.

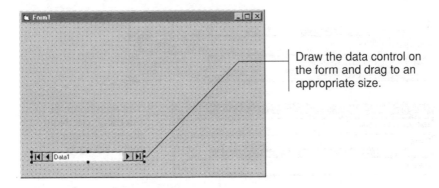

Draw the data control on the form and drag to an appropriate size.

Figure 21.2 (cont.)

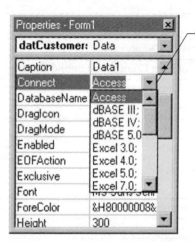

Set the Connect property of the data control to Access. This allows the data control to 'connect up to' a Microsoft Access generated database.

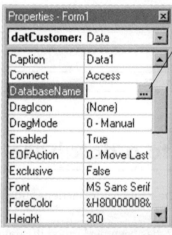

Click here to activate the dialogue box shown next. This property is set to the path of the database to which the data control is to be connected. In this case it will be the BankCustomers database.

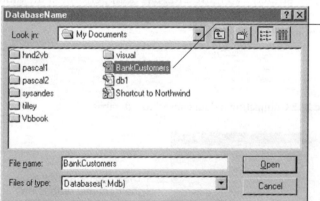

Highlight the database name and select Open. The path of the database will then be entered in the setting box of the property as shown next.

The path name of the database. Note the mdb extension to the file name.

Figure 21.2 (cont.)

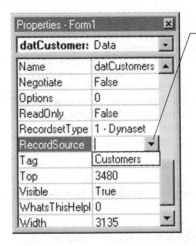

Click here to list the RecordSource available within the database. There is only one table 'inside' the BankCustomer database, consequently, only one is listed in the drop down list, i.e., Customers. Select Customers from the list.

Connecting data aware controls to a database

A number of controls in the Visual Basic toolbox are data aware and they are shown in Figure 21.3.

Figure 21.3 Data aware controls.

The implementation of Specification 21.1 requires the binding of a check box and three text boxes to the BankCustomers database.

To connect a data aware text box control to the BankCustomers database perform the sequence of actions illustrated by Figure 21.4.

Figure 21.4 Connecting a text box to a database.

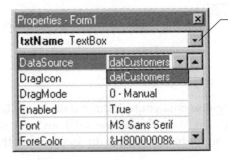

Binding the text box drawn on Form1 to the data control drawn on Form1 is achieved by setting the DataSource property of the text box. Click on the arrow and a drop-down list appears. There is only one data control on Form1, so there will only be one item in the drop-down list. Of course, there can be more than one data control on a form, in which case, there would be more than one item in the list to choose from.

369

Figure 21.4 (cont.)

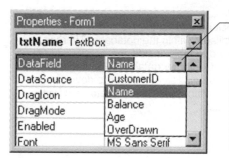

Set the DataField property by clicking on this arrow and a drop-down list appears. This lists all of the fields of the RecordSource to which the data control is connected. Select Name from the list and the text box (txtName) is connected to the second field of the Table, Customers – which is the table 'inside' the BankCustomers database.

Figure 21.5 shows how to set the DataField for the other two text boxes. It is assumed that the DataSource property is already set.

Figure 21.5 Setting the DataField property of text boxes txtBalance and txtAge.

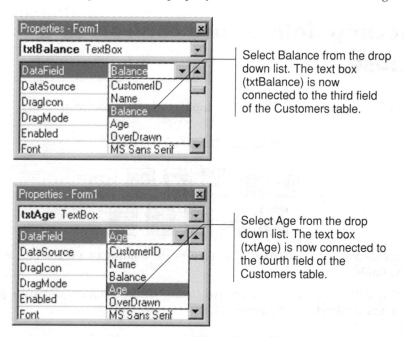

Select Balance from the drop down list. The text box (txtBalance) is now connected to the third field of the Customers table.

Select Age from the drop down list. The text box (txtAge) is now connected to the fourth field of the Customers table.

To connect a data aware Check box control (☑) to the BankCustomers database perform the sequence of actions illustrated by Figure 21.6

PRACTICAL ACTIVITY 21.1

Implement Specification 21.1 using one data control, three data aware text boxes and one data aware check box (i.e., build the GUI and set the properties). **Remember there is no coding required to implement this specification!**

Figure 21.6 Connecting a Check box control to a database.

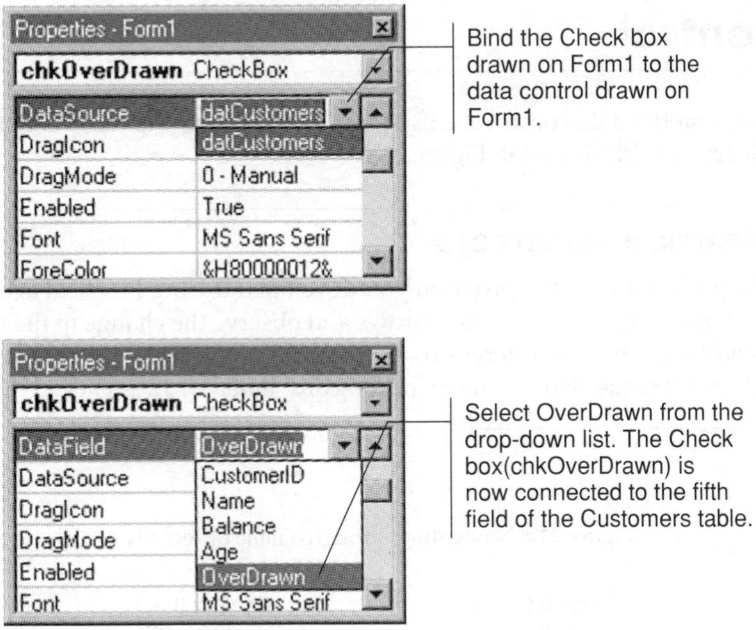

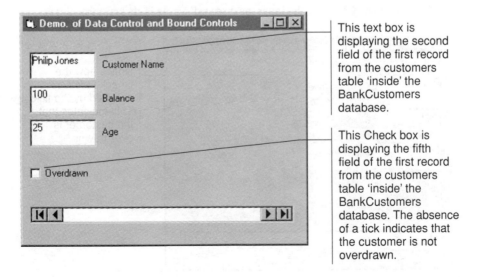

Figure 21.7 shows the GUI immediately after launch, it can be seen that the text boxes and Check box are displaying the first record of the Customers table. Each is displaying a field from this record.

Figure 21.7 The GUI immediately after launch.

371

Navigating through a database using the data control

The four arrows on the data control are used to move through the records in the table. The action of each arrow is illustrated in Figure 21.8.

PRACTICAL ACTIVITY 21.2

Experiment with the program you developed during Practical activity 21.1. Click on the inner and outer arrows and observe the change in the text boxes and Check box as different rows (records) of the table are accessed. Figure 21.9 shows the GUI when the 'next record' inner arrow is clicked three times.

Figure 21.8 Navigating through a table of records.

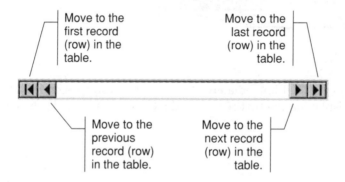

Figure 21.9 The GUI after the inner 'next record' arrow is clicked three times.

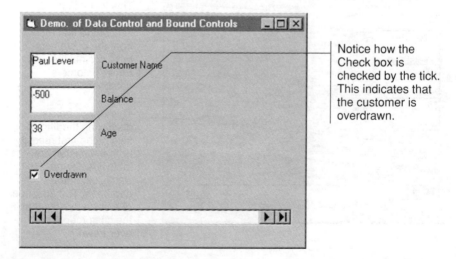

Editing the database

This could not be any simpler. Edit the text in the text box, click the check box, and when any of the data control arrows are used to **move from** the current record the changes are saved. **Again coding has not been necessary!**

PRACTICAL ACTIVITY 21.3

Experiment with the program developed during Practical activity 21.1. Edit the contents of the text boxes and check box and click the next record arrow. Then click the previous record arrow and observe that the changes have been saved.

NOTE: There is no logical connection between the Balance and the OverDrawn field. Consequently, the user must edit both fields, for example, if the customer Philip Jones has his balance changed from 500 to −300 then the Check box must be clicked to indicate an overdrawn balance. Of course, it is possible to arrange for the Check box to alter in sympathy with the entry in the Balance field, it just has not been done here.

PRACTICAL ACTIVITY 21.4

In the Visual Basic directory there is a complete database called *Biblio.mdb*. Build a GUI that will display the records of one of its tables.

HINT: Figures 21.10 to 21.11 offer some guidance.

NOTE: It is usual to have one data control for each table in a database and one data aware control for each field in a record – assuming you wish to connect to each table and field.

PRACTICAL ACTIVITY 21.5

Build a project that displays every table in the *Biblio.mdb*. database.

Have a separate form for each table. **Remember you need to use the Show method to display more than the start up form.**

Record set objects

A record set object represents the records in a base table or the records resulting from running a query. There are three types of Recordset objects.

1. Table-type
2. Dynaset-type
3. Snapshot-type

Table-type Recordset

This is a set of records that represent a single database table in which you can add, change or delete records.

Only the current record of a Table-type Recordset is loaded into memory.

Dynaset-type Recordset

This is a dynamic set of records that represent a database table or the results of a query containing fields from one or more tables. It is possible to add, change or delete records from a dynaset-type Recordset, and the changes will be reflected in the underlying table or tables.

A dynaset-type Recordset has a unique key (like an address that 'points to' the location of the data) for each record that is brought into memory, instead of actual data. As a result, a dynaset is normally updated with changes made to the source data. A dynaset-type Recordset's current record is fetched only when its fields are referenced.

Figure 21.10 Connect the data control to one of the tables in the database.

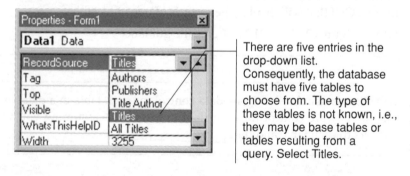

There are five entries in the drop-down list. Consequently, the database must have five tables to choose from. The type of these tables is not known, i.e., they may be base tables or tables resulting from a query. Select Titles.

Figure 21.11 Connecting a text box to a record field.

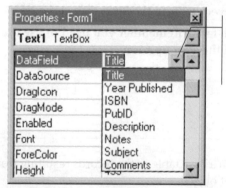

After the text box is bound to the data control and the Titles table, connect it to one of the fields of the Titles table.

Snapshot-type Recordset

This is a static copy of a set of records that can be used to find data or generate reports. This type of Recordset can contain fields from one or more tables in a database but **cannot** be updated.

When a snapshot-type Recordset is created, data values for all fields (except Memo and OLE Object field data types) are brought into memory or the *temp* directory on disk.

Once loaded any changes made to base table(s) – that were used to create the snapshot-type Recordset data – are not reflected in the snapshot. To reload the snapshot-type Recordset with current data, use the Requery method, or re-execute the OpenRecordset method.

Data control RecordsetType property

Figure 21.12 illustrates the three possible settings for the RecordsetType property of the data control.

When a data control is connected to a database it creates a Recordset type that corresponds to the setting of its RecordsetType property.

> **NOTE**: If an application is only going to access one table then set the RecordsetType property to Table-type. This is likely to be the most efficient in terms of speed, memory (RAM) use and in disk space (i.e., the temp directory).
>
> Snapshot-type Recordset objects are generally faster to create and access than dynaset-type Recordset objects because their records are either in memory or stored in TEMP disk space. However, snapshot-type Recordset objects consume more local resources than dynaset-type Recordset objects because the entire record is downloaded to local memory. Also any changes to a snapshot-type Recordset are not saved.

Figure 21.13 illustrates a 'concept' representation of a Recordset. It shows arrows pointing to valid records; the beginning of the Recordset **before the first** record; and the end of the

Figure 21.12 The data controls RecordsetType property.

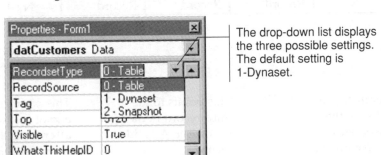

The drop-down list displays the three possible settings. The default setting is 1-Dynaset.

Recordset **after the last** record. A Recordset is associated with a data control. A reference to a Recordset is achieved by the name of the data control and the keyword Recordset 'joined' by a full stop. For example, *Data1.Recordset* refers to the recordset associated with the data control named Data1. Applying a method (e.g., the AddNew method) to the Recordset is achieved as illustrated in Figure 21.13.

Current record

The current record refers to the record in the Recordset object that is used to modify or examine data from the database. At any one time there is only one current record and this record is Visual Basic's 'connection' to the database. It is the contents of the current record that are displayed in the data bound controls, such as text boxes. Navigating through a Recordset changes the current record (i.e., a different record in the Recordset is 'pointed to').

Figure 21.13 A representation of a Recordset.

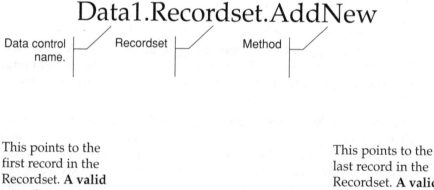

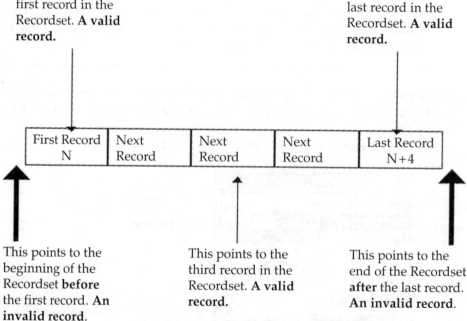

NOTE: Although only one record in the Recordset can be the current record, the Recordset may have no current record. For example, the Recordset may have just been deleted, or the Recordset may have no records or the current record is undefined. When the Recordset has no current record any attempt to operate on the current record results in an error. These errors can be trapped by Visual Basic code and appropriate action taken.

EOF and BOF properties of a recordset

The BOF property returns a value that indicates whether the current record position is *before* the first record in a Recordset.

The BOF property return values are shown in Table 21.2

Table 21.2 The BOF property return values.

Value	Description
True	The current record position is **before** the first record.
False	The current record position is **on or after** the first record.

The EOF property returns a value that indicates whether the current record position is *after* the last record in a Recordset.

The EOF return values are shown in Table 21.3

Table 21.3 The EOF property return values.

Value	Description
True	The current record position is **after** the last record
False	The current record position is **on or before** the last record.

The BOF and EOF return values are determined by the location of the current record pointer.

You can use the BOF and EOF properties to determine whether a Recordset object contains records or whether you have gone beyond the limits of a Recordset as you move from record to record.

If either BOF or EOF is True, there is no current record.

When you open a Recordset that contains at least one record, the first record is the current record and BOF and EOF are False; they remain False until you move beyond the beginning or end of the Recordset (using the MovePrevious or MoveNext method, or by clicking the arrows on the data control). When you move beyond the beginning or end of the Recordset, there is no current record, or no record exists.

Adding records

There are two techniques available for adding a new record to a database, they involve:

1. Using the data controls EOFAction property.
2. Using code in the form of the AddNew method on a Recordset object.

The first technique is discussed next, the second technique is covered later.

The possible settings for the EOFAction property are shown in Table 21.4.

Table 21.4 The EOFAction property and its possible settings.

Setting	Value	Description
vbEOFActionMoveLast	0	**MoveLast** (Default): Keeps the last record as the current record.
vbEOFActionEOF	1	**EOF**: Moving past the end of a Recordset triggers the Data control's Validation event on the last record, followed by a Reposition event, on the invalid (EOF) record. At this point, the MoveNext button on the Data control is disabled.
vbEOFActionAddNew	2	**AddNew**: Moving past the last record triggers the Data control's Validation event to occur on the current record, followed by an automatic AddNew, followed by a Reposition event on the new record.

If the EOFAction property of a data control is set to 0, it is not possible to move past the last record in the Recordset object.

If the EOFAction property of a data control is set to 1, and the move to last record is invoked (by clicking the outer arrow or using the MoveLast method), the current record is positioned to point beyond the last record to the invalid record and the next button on the data control is disabled.

If the EOFAction property of a data control is set to 2, and the user moves past the last record, the data control will automatically create a new record, and allow for data entry into this new record. Any data entered is saved when *moving off* (e.g., clicking a button on the data control) this new current record. If the user moves off the new record without adding data then the new record is removed.

PRACTICAL ACTIVITY 21.6

(a) Experiment with the program implemented during Practical activity 21.1. Change the setting for the data controls EOFAction property and observe the effects.

(b) Set the EOFAction property so that it allows for the addition of a record, then add three more records and enter the appropriate data.

QUESTION 21.1 (DEVELOPMENT)

Use the VB online help to read about the following properties of the data control

  BOFAction   Exclusive   Options   ReadOnly

These are the rest of the data controls, database related, properties.

NOTE: Visual Basic has the same database engine as Microsoft Access; the Jet Engine. The Jet engine provides two separate models for accomplishing most database tasks:

- A *navigational* model that is based on moving through database records.

- A *relational* model that is based on the Structured Query Language (SQL).

The navigational model works with Recordset objects that have properties and methods. SQL works with 'English like sentences' that locate information in the database.

Databases developed with Visual Basic find a use for both models. For example, the relational model (e.g., SQL SELECT statement) may be used to create a small Recordset and the navigation model (e.g., the MoveNext method) will be used to examine specific records one at a time.

Both models are covered in this chapter, starting with the navigational model.

Adding and removing records with code

The *AddNew* method will add a record to a Table-type and Dynaset type Recordset (it does not work with a Snapshot-type Recordset). The data stored in the fields of a new record will be set at their default values (refer to Figure 21.14). The *Delete* method removes the current record from a Table-type or a Dynaset type Recordset (again, this method does not work with a Snapshot-type Recordset).

The implementation of Specification 21.2 will demonstrate how to add and remove records to and from a database table.

SPECIFICATION 21.2

Add two command button to the GUI used to implement Specification 21.1 and attach appropriate code to enable the adding and removing of records to and from a Recordset object.

Figure 21.14 How to set the default value for the fields of a record.

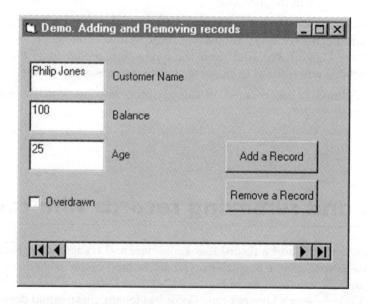

1ˢᵗ Highlight the field.

2ⁿᵈ In design view set the default value here.

GUI for Specification 21.2

Code attached to the command buttons

```
Private Sub cmdAddRecord_Click()
    datCustomers.Recordset.AddNew
    datCustomers.Recordset.Update
End Sub

Private Sub cmdRemoveRecord_Click()
    datCustomers.Recordset.Delete
    datCustomers.Recordset.MoveNext
End Sub
```

Description trace for the cmdAddRecord_Click() event

Statement	Description
datCustomers.Recordset.AddNew	The Recordset associated with the data control datCustomers is increased by one record.
datCustomers.Recordset.Update	Updates the Recordset to include the new addition. The record will contain default values.

Description trace for the cmdRemoveRecord_Click() event

Statement	Description
datCustomers.Recordset.Delete	The current record, within the Recordset object, associated with the data control datCustomers is removed.
datCustomers.Recordset.MoveNext	The Delete method deletes the current record from the Recordset and makes the current record invalid. **MoveNext** is a method that moves to the next record in the Recordset (the MovePrevious could also be used).

PRACTICAL ACTIVITY 21.7

Set the default value of the Name field of the Customers table in the BankCustomers database to the string *Enter a name,* as shown in Figure 21.14. Then implement Specification 21.2 and experiment with the addition and removal of records.

The code to remove the record will work unless the current record is the last record, in which case it is not possible to move to the next record. Under these circumstances an attempt to delete after the deletion of the last record in the Recordset will result in a run-time error, as illustrated in Figure 21.15.

To avoid this run-time error requires a change to the code. This change will involve using the EOF and BOF properties of the Recordset object.

Figure 21.15 A run-time error when an attempt is made to delete an invalid record.

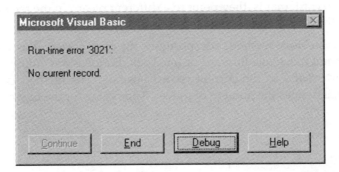

The run-time error experienced during Practical activity 21.7 can be corrected by the following code:

```
Private Sub cmdRemoveRecord_Click()
    If datCustomers.Recordset.EOF = False And datCustomers.Recordset.BOF = False Then
        datCustomers.Recordset.Delete
        datCustomers.Recordset.MoveNext
    End If
End Sub
```

The selection construct will only allow the execution of the code between the *Then* and the *End If* if the current record is valid. The record is valid when EOF and BOF are **both** false.

PRACTICAL ACTIVITY 21.8

Amend the project developed during Practical activity 21.7 so that it avoids the run-time error.

QUESTION 21.2 (DEVELOPMENT)

Use the Visual Basic online help to learn about the following methods:

MoveFirst, MoveLast, MoveNext and MovePrevious.

Also read about the RecordCount property.

PRACTICAL ACTIVITY 21.9

Further amend the project developed during Practical activities 21.7 and 21.8 so that it includes a command button that will display, in a message box, the number of records in the Recordset.

Moving relative to the current position

The move methods, covered by Question 21.2, navigate through the Recordset object. They move the current record, that is, they point to a different record in the record set, it could be the first, the last, the next or the previous record.

Another method, the Move method, also positions the current record in a Recordset object. However, it does not move one forward or one back. It moves any number forward or any number backward *relative* to the current record position. The method is supplied with a number (rows) that defines the number of moves. The syntax for the move method is shown below:

recordset.Move rows[, start]

The Move method syntax has three parts as described in Table 21.5.

Table 21.5 The parts of the Move method.

Part	Description
recordset	The name of the Recordset object whose current record position is being moved.
Rows	A signed Long value specifying the number of rows (records) the position will move. If rows is greater than 0, the position is moved forward (toward the end of the file). If rows is less than 0, the position is moved backward (toward the beginning of the file).
Start	A String value identifying a bookmark. If start is specified, the move begins relative to this bookmark. If start is not specified, Move begins from the current record.

PRACTICAL ACTIVITY 21.10

Further amend the project developed during Practical activities 21.7, 21.8 and 21.9 so that it includes a command button that will move forward a number of places. The number of places to be moved forward can be entered via an InputBox function or another text box.

HINT: The following statement will create a move to a new position in the Recordset.

datCustomers.Recordset.Move RelativePosition

Declare RelativePosition as a Long type variable.

QUESTION 21.3 (DEVELOPMENT)

A Recordset is an object, and like all objects, it has properties. Three useful Recordset properties for navigating through a Recordset are the BookMark property, the AbsolutePosition property and the PercentPosition property.

Use the Visual Basic online help to learn about the BookMark, the AbsolutePosition and the PercentPosition properties.

Finding a record that meets a criterion

The BankCustomers database consists of one table whose records have five fields. It would be useful if all the customers who are overdrawn could be found and displayed by the click of a command button. It would also be useful if the details on an individual customer could be displayed from the entry of their name. The implementation of Specification 21.3 illustrates how records can be found by using appropriate criteria.

SPECIFICATION 21.3

Amend Specification 21.2 so that all the overdrawn customers are displayed in turn on the click of a button.

GUI for Specification 21.3

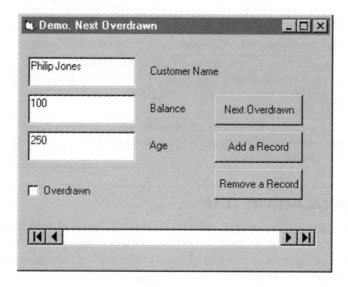

Code attached to the Next Overdrawn command button

```
Private Sub cmdNextOverdrawn_Click()
    datCustomers.Recordset.FindNext "OverDrawn = True"
End Sub
```

The FindNext method is applied to the Recordset object of the data control (i.e., datCustomers.Recordset). The criterion used is shown in the double quotes. When the command button is clicked the Recordset is searched **forward from the current record position** and the next record whose OverDrawn field is set to true (yes) becomes the current record. This current record is displayed in the bound controls (i.e., the three text boxes and the Check box). The next click on the command button will find and display the details on the next overdrawn customer. This will continue until the end of the Recordset. *If the user wishes to view all the overdrawn customers again they will have to move to the beginning of the Recordset (using the outer arrow on the data control) and click the Next Overdrawn command button again.* Alternatively, the GUI could be further amended with the addition of another command button that allows for the previous overdrawn customer to be displayed (this can be achieved using the FindPrevious method).

PRACTICAL ACTIVITY 21.11

Implement Specification 21.3.

NOTE: Make sure that the RecordsetType property of the data control is set to 1-Dynaset – **more on this later.**

Find methods

Visual Basic supports four Find methods and they are:

- The FindFirst method that finds the first record that satisfies the specified criteria.

- The FindLast method that finds the last record that satisfies the specified criteria.
- The FindNext method that finds the next record that satisfies the specified criteria.
- The FindPrevious method that finds the previous record that satisfies the specified criteria.

NOTE: All the above methods work with dynaset-type and snapshot-type Recordsets. To locate records that match a criterion in a table-type Recordset use the **Seek** method.

PRACTICAL ACTIVITY 21.12

Add another Command button to the GUI used to implement Specification 21.3. This button is to display, in turn, all of the Customers who have a balance *over* 100.

HINT: datCustomers.Recordset.FindNext "Balance >100"

Recordset properties and methods

It is worth emphasising that a Recordset is an object that has properties and methods. The sections just covered have shown some of the methods that apply to a Recordset (e.g., MoveNext, MoveLast and FindNext) and some of the properties (e.g., EOF, BOF and RecordCount).

Fields of a Recordset

A Recordset can be divided up into field objects, with each field object representing the entire field of a table. These field objects have properties and methods. The set of all field objects is referred to as the fields collection.

The implementation of Specification 21.4 will demonstrate how to use field objects.

SPECIFICATION 21.4

Further amend Specification 21.3 so that it will produce, on the click of a command button, a brief report, in a text box, on the current customer. For example, a typical report would be:

    Customer Philip Jones aged 25 has a balance of 100 and is in credit.

GUI for Specification 21.4

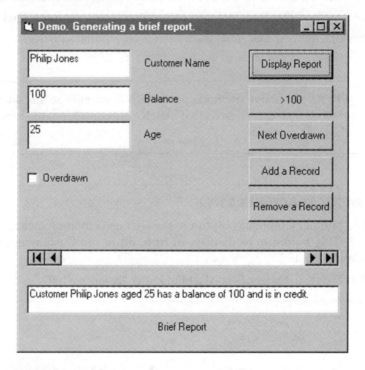

Code attached to the Display Report command button

```
Private Sub cmdReport_Click()
Dim NameString As String
Dim BalanceString As String
Dim AgeString As String
Dim BalanceStateString As String
Dim ReportString As String
Dim Flag As Boolean
    NameString = datCustomers.Recordset.Fields("Name").Value
    BalanceString = datCustomers.Recordset.Fields("Balance").Value
    AgeString = datCustomers.Recordset.Fields("Age").Value
    Flag = datCustomers.Recordset.Fields("OverDrawn").Value
    If Flag Then
        BalanceStateString = " and is overdrawn."
    Else
        BalanceStateString = " and is in credit."
    End If
```

Enter as **one** line.

```
    ReportString = "Customer " & NameString & " aged " & AgeString & "
    has a balance of " & BalanceString & BalanceStateString

    txtReport.Text = ReportString
End Sub
```

This event procedure sets up six local variables, which consist of five string variables and one Boolean variable. Four of the variables are used to store the value of the Recordset **fields** for the current record. How these variables are assigned the values stored in the fields is discussed first. The following statement assigns the value of the Name field of the current record to the NameString variable.

NameString = datCustomers.Recordset.Fields("Name").Value

The **datCustomers.Recordset** part of the assignment statement refers to the Recordset object. The addition of the **.Fields** part identifies the *fields collection*. The further addition of the **("Name")** part identifies Name field. Finally, the **.Value** part (a property) refers to the value stored in the Name field.

This statement can be written in a number of different ways, some of these ways are listed below:

NameString = datCustomers.Recordset.Fields(1).Value *'the one refers to the second field which is the Name field.*

NameString = datCustomers.Recordset.Fields(1) *'the Value property is omitted because it is the default property*

IndexNumber = 1 *' IndexNumber is a Long Type*

NameString = datCustomers.Recordset.Fields(IndexNumber).Value *'an indirect reference by IndexNumber – useful for scanning records using a loop.*

NameString = datCustomers.Recordset(1) *'Fields can be omitted because it is the default collection of the Recordset.*

> **NOTE**: Obviously some of the examples above require less typing, however, it is far better to make your code more readable. Using the 'full name' means more typing but it makes the code easier to debug. Consequently, I recommend that you use the following:
>
> NameString = datCustomers.Recordset.Fields("Name").Value
>
> **OR**
>
> StringVariable = "Name"
>
> NameString = datCustomers.Recordset.Fields(StringVariable).Value

Transactions

A transaction is a recoverable series of changes made to a Recordset object. A transaction is used when you wish to verify any changes before committing the new information to the database. Transactions are controlled by using three methods that work on the **Workspace** object, these Methods are:

- BeginTrans
- CommitTrans
- Rollback

Workspace object

A Workspace object defines a session for a user. It contains an open database and provides mechanisms for transactions. When working with the Jet database engine a default workspace (i.e., DBEngine.Workspaces(0)) is automatically created.

The implementation of Specification 21.5 will illustrate the use of transactions.

SPECIFICATION 21.5

Further amend Specification 21.3 by adding a command button that will clear all the overdrafts, i.e., it sets the Balance field to zero and the OverDrawn field to false.

Code attached to the additional command button

```
Private Sub cmdClearOverdraft_Click()
Dim MyTable As Recordset
Dim MyWorkspace As Workspace
    Set MyWorkspace = DBEngine.Workspaces(0)
    Set MyTable = datCustomers.Recordset
    MyWorkspace.BeginTrans
    Do Until MyTable.EOF
        If MyTable![OverDrawn] = True Then
            MyTable.Edit
            MyTable![OverDrawn] = False
            MyTable![Balance] = 0
            MyTable.Update
        End If
        MyTable.MoveNext
    Loop
    If MsgBox("Save all changes?", vbQuestion + vbYesNo, "Save
    changes") = vbYes Then
        MyWorkspace.CommitTrans
    Else
        MyWorkspace.Rollback
    End If
End Sub
```

Enter as **one** line.

This procedure uses two variables and their declaration is shown below:

```
Dim MyTable As Recordset
Dim MyWorkspace As Workspace
```

The variable MyTable is declared as a Recordset type, this means, that MyTable is able to reference a Recordset object. The variable MyWorkspace is declared as a Workspace type, this means that MyWorkspace can reference the working area for the current database activity.

Description trace of cmdClearOverdraft_Click event procedure

The test assumes that the records are the original seven as shown in Figure 21.1.

Statement	Description
Set MyWorkspace = DBEngine.Workspaces(0)	The variable *MyWorkspace* is set to reference the workspace used by the jet engine.
Set MyTable = datCustomers.Recordset	The variable *MyTable* is set to reference the Recordset object currently 'supported' by the data control.
MyWorkspace.BeginTrans	The BeginTrans method is applied to the Workspace object. This marks the start of the transaction.
Do Until MyTable.EOF	This returns false and the loop is entered.
If MyTable![OverDrawn] = True Then	The *OverDrawn* field of the current record is false (i.e., not overdrawn), consequently, the conditional test is false and the selection construct is not entered (i.e., the statements between the **Then** and **End If** are not executed.
MyTable.MoveNext	The next record in the Recordset becomes the current record.
Do Until MyTable.EOF	Still false so the loop is entered.
If MyTable![OverDrawn] = True Then	The OverDrawn field is True (i.e., the customer, Rita Hartly, is overdrawn), therefore, the code 'inside' the selection construct is executed.
MyTable.Edit	This allows for editing of the current record.
MyTable![OverDrawn] = False	The OverDrawn field is set to false to indicate that the customer is not overdrawn.
MyTable![Balance] = 0	The customer's balance is set to zero.
MyTable.Update	The Recordset is Updated with the changes. **However, these changes have not yet been committed to the database.**
MyTable.MoveNext	The next record becomes the current record. The loop continues until EOF is true. At the end of all the passes the overdrawn customers will have had their Balance field set to zero and their OverDrawn field set to false. What happens next depends upon how the user responds to the MessageBox, as shown in Figure 21.16.

Figure 21.16 The Message Box generated by the event procedure.

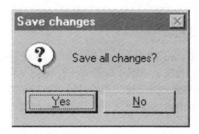

Description trace when the user clicks yes

Statement	Description
If MsgBox("Save all changes?", vbQuestion + vbYesNo, "Save changes") = vbYes Then	This is true, therefore, the statement between the *Then* and *Else* is executed
MyWorkspace.CommitTrans	The CommitTrans method ends the current transaction and saves the changes.

Description trace when the user clicks no

Statement	Description
If MsgBox("Save all changes?", vbQuestion + vbYesNo, "Save changes") = vbYes Then	This is false, therefore, the statement between the *Else* and *End If* is executed.
MyWorkspace. Rollback	The Rollback method ends the current transaction and restores the database in the Workspace object to the state it was in *before* the current transaction began.

Using SQL statements

The Find method, previously discussed, is capable of finding a record **in** a Recordset that matches a criterion. An SQL statement can be used to **generate** a Recordset that meets a criterion.

Specification 21.3 asked to find the next overdrawn customer. This was achieved using the following statement:

datCustomers.Recordset.FindNext "OverDrawn = True"

The statement found the next record in the Recordset where the OverDrawn field was equal to true, that is, the customer is overdrawn. An SQL statement can generate a Recordset of all Customers that are overdrawn. This Recordset can then be navigated using the data control, i.e., each record in the Recordset can be accessed by using the arrows on the data control. The Recordset will *only* consist of all the overdrawn customers. The SQL statement that will produce a Recordset of all overdrawn customers – that would be displayed in all bound controls – is shown below:

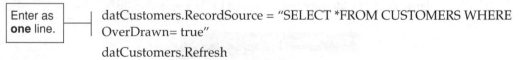

Enter as **one** line.

datCustomers.RecordSource = "SELECT *FROM CUSTOMERS WHERE OverDrawn= true"

datCustomers.Refresh

The original records entered, using Microsoft Access, are shown in Figure 21.17. When the RecordSource property of the data control was set to the value Customers, it generated a Recordset that consists of all the records shown in Figure 21.17. However, the statement above generates a 'new' Recordset object that consists of all the overdrawn customers as shown in Figure 21.18.

Figure 21.17 The original Recordset.

CustomerID	Name	Balance	Age	OverDrawn
1	Philip Jones	£100.00	25	No
2	Rita Hartly	(£300.00)	21	Yes
3	Anne Williams	£450.00	50	No
4	Paul Lever	(£500.00)	38	Yes
5	Rebecca Jones	£700.00	21	No
6	Cara Jones	£70.00	33	No
7	Nathan Jones	£550.00	23	No
8	Edna Hartley	(£30.00)	33	Yes
9	Nancy Williams	£400.00	37	No

Figure 21.18 The 'new' Recordset generated by the SQL statement.

CustomerID	Name	Balance	Age	OverDrawn
2	Rita Hartly	(£300.00)	21	Yes
4	Paul Lever	(£500.00)	38	Yes
8	Edna Hartley	(£30.00)	33	Yes

After the SQL statement has generated the 'new' Recordset, the data control loses the original Recordset. To navigate all the records in the original Recordset will require its generation again. The generation of the original Recordset is achieved by the following SQL statement:

datCustomers.RecordSource = "SELECT *FROM CUSTOMERS

datCustomers.Refresh

Description trace for SQL statement that generated a recordset of overdrawn customers

Statement	Description
datCustomers.RecordSource = "SELECT *FROM CUSTOMERS WHERE OverDrawn= true"	The RecordSource property for the datCustomers data control is assigned a new Recordset that is generated by the SQL statement. The SQL statement appears in double quotes. The word **SELECT** is used to query the database for records that satisfy a specific criteria. The * symbol stands for all records. The word **FROM** is used to name the table from which records are to be selected. The word **WHERE** is used to specify the condition(s) the records must meet to be selected. **OverDrawn= true** is the condition used for the selection, i.e., all the Customers who are overdrawn will be selected.
datCustomers.Refresh	The Refresh method is used to update the bound controls with the records of the newly generated Recordset. The first record in the newly generated Recordset is the current record, consequently, it will be the record that is displayed in the bound controls.

Description trace for SQL statement that generates the original recordset

Statement	Description
datCustomers.RecordSource = "SELECT *FROM CUSTOMERS"	The RecordSource property for the datCustomers data control is assigned a Recordset that is generated by the SQL statement. The SQL statement appears in double quotes. The word **SELECT** is used to query the database for records. The * symbol stands for all records. The word **FROM** is used to name the table from which records are to be selected. In this case the word **WHERE** is *not* used because there is no conditional part to the query -*all* of the records from the Customers table are selected. The data control now has a Recordset that is back to its original values.
datCustomers.Refresh	The Refresh method is used to update the bound controls with the records of the newly generated Recordset. The first record in the newly generated Recordset is the current record, consequently, it will be the record that is displayed in the bound controls.

PRACTICAL ACTIVITY 21.13

Add another command button to the GUI developed to meet Specification 21.4. This button is to generate a Recordset of all overdrawn customers. Once this button has been clicked navigate *back and forth* through the records in the Recordset using the data control arrows. Compare this method of navigation with that offered by the Next Overdrawn command button.

PRACTICAL ACTIVITY 21.14

Add another command button to the GUI that will be used to generate a Recordset of all customers who have a balance greater than 100.

HINT: Use the following SQL statement:

datCustomers.RecordSource = "SELECT *FROM CUSTOMERS WHERE Balance > 100 "

datCustomers.Refresh

PRACTICAL ACTIVITY 21.15

Add another command button to the GUI. When clicked the event procedure attached to this button will use an InputBox() function to ask the user for a value of Age. An SQL statement will then generate a Recordset of all customers at and over this age.

QUESTION 21.4 (REVISION)

After all the additions to the GUI it should look something like Figure 21.19. During execution a user will no doubt click the >100 Recordset command button, the Overdrawn Recordset command button or the Customer Age Recordset command button. Whenever any one of these buttons is clicked a new recordset is generated. How can the user be presented with a means of navigating through all the records in the Customers table (i.e., the original Recordset that contained all the records in the table)?

PRACTICAL ACTIVITY 21.16

Implement your answer to Question 21.4.

Figure 21.19 The GUI after the completion of all the practical activities.

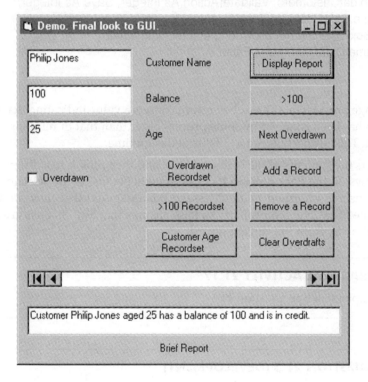

Validate event

The validate event applies only to the data control. It occurs before a different record becomes the current record; before the Update method (except when data is saved with the UpdateRecord method) and before a Delete, Unload, or Close operation.

The heading to a validate event procedure is shown below:

Private Sub datCustomers_Validate(Action As Integer, Save As Integer)

It can be seen that the event procedure has two arguments (parameters) Action and Save.

The Action argument is an integer that indicates the operation causing this event to occur.

The Save argument specifies whether the data in the data aware controls associated with the data control has changed.

The implementation of Specification 21.6 illustrates how the Validate event works.

SPECIFICATION 21.6

Amend the project developed throughout this chapter so that the user cannot edit the Name field of the Customer record.

To implement Specification 21.6 attach the following to the data control Validate event.

```
Private Sub datCustomers_Validate(Action As Integer, Save As Integer)
    If txtName.DataChanged Then
        MsgBox "You are not allowed to edit the Name field."
        txtName.DataChanged = False
    End If
End Sub
```

The DataChange property of the text box returns or sets a value indicating that the data in the bound control has been changed by some process other than that of retrieving data from the current record. This property is not available at design time.

If the user alters the contents of the Name text box and then moves to a different record (e.g., using the arrows on the data control) then the statements inside the selection construct are executed. The user is informed by the Message Box (MsgBox) that they cannot change the field. Setting the DataChanged property to false ensures that any changes are ignored when the user moves away from the current record.

PRACTICAL ACTIVITY 21.17

Implement Specification 21.6

QUESTION 21.5 (DEVELOPMENT)

Use the Visual Basic online help to learn about the Action and Save arguments associated with the Validate event.

---

22 Mouse events

Mouse events enable an application to respond to the location and state of the mouse. The location of the mouse is defined by the x and y co-ordinates of the object receiving the mouse event. The state of the mouse is defined by which button on the mouse is pressed, when a mouse event occurs. Also the status of three keyboard keys can be defined when a mouse event occurs.

The three mouse events are described in Table 22.1.

Table 22.1 Mouse events.

Event	Description
MouseMove	This event occurs whenever the mouse pointer moves to a new point on the screen (i.e. when the mouse is moved).
MouseDown	This event occurs when the user **presses** *any* mouse button.
MouseUp	This event occurs when the user **releases** *any* mouse button.

NOTE: A control can recognise a mouse event when the mouse pointer is over the control. A form can also recognise a mouse event when the pointer is over any part of the form that does not contain a control.

When a user holds down a mouse button over a control (or form) then this control (or form) continues to respond to mouse events until the user releases the button. The control (or form) continues to respond even if the pointer is moved off the control (or form).

When any mouse event occurs it invokes a mouse event procedure that takes four arguments (parameters) as illustrated in Figure 22.1.

Figure 22.1 The parameters passed to a mouse event procedure.

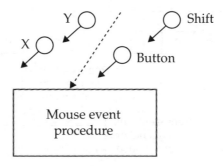

Figure 22.2 illustrates the heading, to all three mouse event procedures, to which a form will respond.

Figure 22.2 The heading of three mouse event procedures.

```
Private Sub Form_MouseDown(Button As Integer, Shift As Integer, X As Single, Y As Single)
Private Sub Form_MouseMove(Button As Integer, Shift As Integer, X As Single, Y As Single)
Private Sub Form_MouseUp(Button As Integer, Shift As Integer, X As Single, Y As Single)
```

The arguments (parameters) to all three mouse events are described in Table 22.2.

Table 22.2 The arguments to mouse events.

Argument	Description
Button	This gives a value that indicates which button on the mouse was pressed when the mouse event occurred.
Shift	This gives a value that indicates which of the following keys on the keyboard were pressed when the mouse event occurred: **SHIFT**; **CNTRL** and **ALT**.
X	This indicates the X co-ordinate of the mouse pointer when the mouse event occurred.
Y	This indicates the Y co-ordinate of the mouse pointer when the mouse event occurred.

The button argument

The button argument is a bit-field argument where each of the three *least* significant bits of an integer variable are used to indicate the state of the mouse buttons. Figure 22.3 illustrates the bits used to represent the state of the buttons.

Table 22.3 shows the value of Button when **one** of the buttons is pressed down.

Figure 22.3 The button argument.

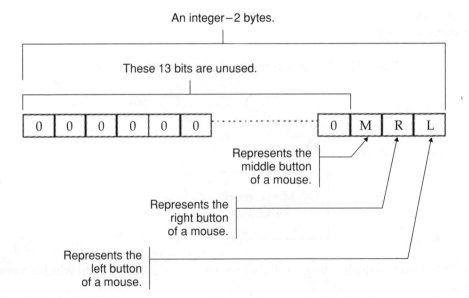

Table 22.3 Possible values for the button argument.

Button pressed	Binary value of the button argument	Decimal value of the button argument
Middle	0000000000000100	4
Right	0000000000000010	2
Left	0000000000000001	1

NOTE: A two-button mouse only has a left and a right button. A one button mouse only has a left button.

With the MouseUp and MouseDown events only one button can be set, therefore Table 22.3 represents the possible values for both these events.

A MouseMove event like the other two mouse events can test for whether one button is being pressed. However, it can also test to see if two or more buttons are being pressed simultaneously. Table 22.4 shows the value of Button for all possible combinations of button presses.

Table 22.4 Combination of button presses.

Button(s) pressed	Binary value of the button argument	Decimal value of the button argument
Left	0000000000000001	1
Right	0000000000000010	2
Left + Right	0000000000000011	3
Middle	0000000000000100	4
Middle + Left	0000000000000101	5
Middle + Right	0000000000000110	6
Middle + Right + Left	0000000000000111	7

NOTE: When a MouseMove event occurs it is possible that no buttons are pressed, in which case, the binary value of the Button argument is 0000000000000000 and the decimal value is 0.

PRACTICAL ACTIVITY 22.1

Attach the code of Figure 22.4 to the MouseDown event of Form1.

- Click the left button and observe the result.
- Click the right button and observe the result.
- Click both buttons and observe the result.

Figure 22.4 The MouseDown event associated with Practical activity 22.1

```
Private Sub Form_MouseDown(Button As Integer, Shift As Integer, X As Single, Y As Single)
    Select Case Button
        Case 1
            Form1.Print "You are pressing the left button"
        Case 2
            Form1.Print "You are pressing the right button"
    End Select
End Sub
```

> **NOTE**: During Practical activity 22.1 when the left button is clicked the string *You are pressing the left button* is displayed on the form. When the right button is clicked the string *You are pressing the right button* is displayed on the form. When both are pressed, **both** strings are displayed. When two buttons are pressed Visual Basic interprets that action as two separate MouseDown events. Consequently, it sets the bit for one of the buttons and displays its message then sets the bit for the other button and displays its message.

> **PRACTICAL ACTIVITY 22.2**
>
> Attach the code of Figure 22.5 to the MouseUp event of Form1.
>
> - Click the left button and observe the result.
> - Click the right button and observe the result.
> - Click both buttons and observe the result. Does it regard this as two separate events?

Figure 22.5 The MouseUp event associated with Practical activity 22.2.

```
Private Sub Form_MouseUp(Button As Integer, Shift As Integer, X As Single, Y As Single)
    Select Case Button
        Case 1
            Form1.Print "You have released the left button"
        Case 2
            Form1.Print "You have released the right button"
    End Select
End Sub
```

> **PRACTICAL ACTIVITY 22.3**
>
> Draw a label on a form and set its name property to lblButtonState. Attach the code shown in Figure 22.6 to the MouseMove event of the form.
>
> - Hold down the left button and move the mouse, observe the result.
> - Hold down the right button and move the mouse, observe the result.
> - Hold down both buttons and move the mouse, observe the result.

Figure 22.6 MouseMove event procedure associated with Practical activity 22.3.

```
Private Sub Form_MouseMove(Button As Integer, Shift As Integer, X As Single, Y As Single)
    lblButtonState.Caption = "The value of the Button argument is " & Button
End Sub
```

The shift argument

The shift argument is an integer that corresponds to the state of the SHIFT, CTRL, and ALT keys. It is very similar to the button argument in the way its represents the state of the keys, as can be seen in Figure 22.7.

Figure 22.7 The shift argument.

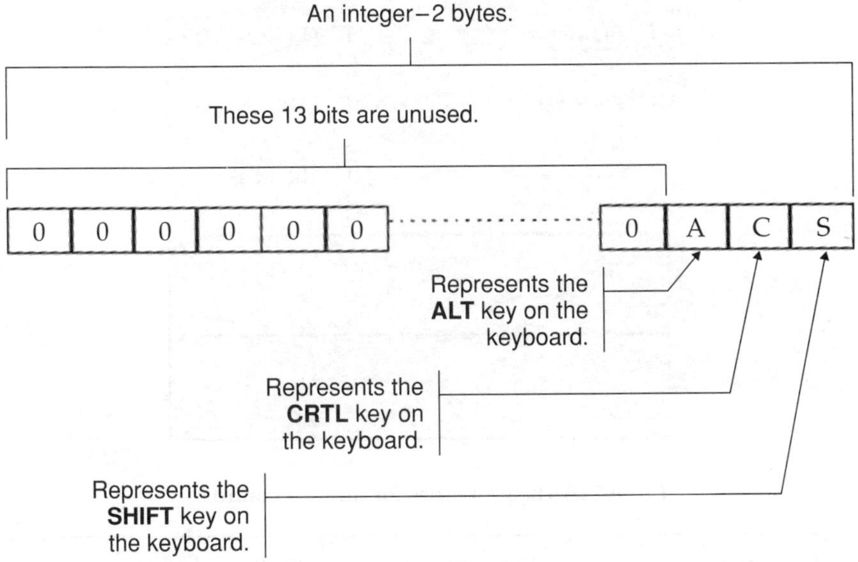

An integer−2 bytes.

These 13 bits are unused.

| 0 | 0 | 0 | 0 | 0 | 0 | - - - - - - - - - - - - | 0 | A | C | S |

Represents the **ALT** key on the keyboard.

Represents the **CRTL** key on the keyboard.

Represents the **SHIFT** key on the keyboard.

The shift argument is a bit field with the least-significant bits corresponding to the SHIFT key (bit 0), the CTRL key (bit 1), and the ALT key (bit 2). The shift argument indicates the state of these keys as shown by Table 22.5.

Table 22.5 Possible values of the shift argument.

Key(s) pressed	Binary value of the shift argument	Decimal value of the shift argument
No keys pressed.	0000000000000000	0
SHIFT	0000000000000001	1
CTRL	0000000000000010	2
SHIFT + CTRL	0000000000000011	3
ALT	0000000000000100	4
ALT + SHIFT	0000000000000101	5
ALT + CTRL	0000000000000110	6
ALT + CTRL + SHIFT	0000000000000111	7

PRACTICAL ACTIVITY 22.4

Build the GUI shown in Figure 22.8. It consists of five check boxes and two labels. Set the properties of the controls according to Table 22.6. Attach the code of Figure 22.9 to the MouseMove event of Form1.

Hold down the mouse buttons and ALT, CTRL and SHIFT keys in numerous combinations and move the mouse. Observe the check boxes and labels.

Figure 22.8 The GUI for Practical activity 22.4.

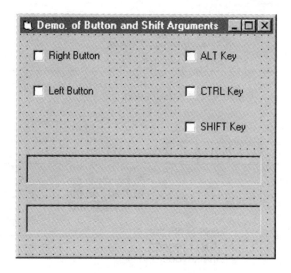

Table 22.6 The properties for the GUI controls.

Control	Property	Setting
Check Box	Name	chkSHIFTKey
	Caption	SHIFT Key
Check Box	Name	chkALTKey
	Caption	ALT Key
Check Box	Name	chkCTRLKey
	Caption	CTRL Key
Check Box	Name	chkLeftButton
	Caption	Left Button
Check Box	Name	chkRightButton
	Caption	Right Button
Label	Name	lblShiftArgument
	BorderStyle	1 'Fixed Single
Label	Name	lblButtonArgument
	BorderStyle	1 'Fixed Single

Figure 22.9 The MouseMove event procedure associated with Practical activity 22.4.

```
Private Sub Form_MouseMove(Button As Integer, Shift As Integer, X As Single, Y As Single)
    chkLeftButton.Value = Unchecked
    chkRightButton.Value = Unchecked
    chkALTKey.Value = Unchecked
    chkCTRLKey.Value = Unchecked
    chkSHIFTKey.Value = Unchecked
    lblButtonArgument.Caption = "The Button argument is " & Button
    lblShiftArgument.Caption = "The Shift argument is " & Shift
    If Button And 1 Then
        chkLeftButton.Value = Checked
    End If
    If Button And 2 Then
        chkRightButton.Value = Checked
    End If
    If Shift And 1 Then
        chkALTKey.Value = Checked
    End If
    If Shift And 2 Then
        chkCTRLKey.Value = Checked
    End If
    If Shift And 4 Then
        chkSHIFTKey.Value = Checked
    End If
End Sub
```

The program is left for you to inspect, however, the **masking** of the arguments is discussed under the following heading.

Testing for a single button and key

For the code of Figure 22.10, if the user holds down the left button and moves the mouse then the string *The left button is pressed* will be displayed on Form1. However, if the user holds down both buttons and moves the mouse the string is not displayed, even though the left button is pressed.

Figure 22.10 A MouseMove event.

```
Private Sub Form_MouseMove(Button As Integer, Shift As Integer, X As Single, Y As Single)
    If Button = 1 Then
        Form1.Print "The left button is pressed"
    End If
End Sub
```

The code shown in Figure 22.11 will display the string regardless of how many buttons are pressed with the left button.

The Button argument has been *And 'ed* with number one to mask off the bit position of the left button. This is illustrated by Figure 22.12.

401

Figure 22.11 A MouseMove event.

```
Private Sub Form_MouseMove(Button As Integer, Shift As Integer, X As Single, Y As Single)
    If (Button And 1) = Then
        Form1.Print "The left button is pressed"
    End If
End Sub
```

Figure 22.12 Masking.

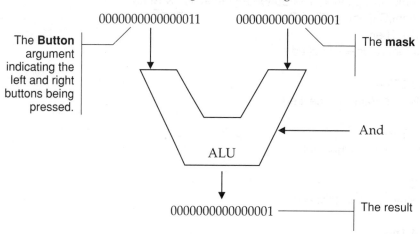

Each bit position of the Button argument is logically *And 'ed* with each bit position of the mask. The And 'truth table' is repeated below, for your convenience.

$0 And 0 = 0 \quad 0 And 1 = 0 \quad 1 And 0 = 0 \quad 1 And 1 = 1$

The event procedure, shown in Figure 22.13, masks for the SHIFT key, the string *The SHIFT button is pressed* will be displayed regardless of whether the CTRL and/or the ALT key is pressed.

Figure 22.13 Masking for the SHIFT key.

```
Private Sub Form_MouseMove(Button As Integer, Shift As Integer, X As Single, Y As Single)
If (Shift And 1) = 1 Then
        Form2.Print "The SHIFT key is pressed"
    End If
End Sub
```

The event procedure, shown in Figure 22.14, masks for the SHIFT and CTRL keys, the string *The SHIFT and CTRL keys are pressed* will be displayed regardless of whether the ALT key is also pressed.

Figure 22.14 Masking for the SHIFT and CNTL keys.

```
Private Sub Form_MouseMove(Button As Integer, Shift As Integer, X As Single, Y As Single)
If (Shift And 3) = 3 Then
        Form1.Print "The SHIFT and CTRL keys are pressed"
    End If
End Sub
```

PRACTICAL ACTIVITY 22.5

Implement the programs shown in Figures 22.10, 22.11 22.13 and 22.14.

Amend the program shown in Figure 22.14 so that the keys SHIFT and ALT are masked and the string displayed is *The SHIFT and ALT keys are pressed.*

The implementation of the following specification will illustrate simple uses for mouse events.

SPECIFICATION 22.1

(a) *Write a program that will move the centre of a picture to the position of the mouse pointer on a MouseDown event.*

(b) *Write a program that will draw a line of random colours from the previous position of the mouse pointer to the new position on a MouseDown event.*

(c) *Write a program that will draw a line marked by a MouseDown and MouseUp event.*

Implementation of Specification 22.1(a)

Draw a picture box on Form1 and set its name property to picBalloon, its AutoSize property to true and it picture property to the balloon bitmap found in c:\vb\bitmaps\assorted.

Attach the following code to the Mouse Down event of Form1.

```
Private Sub Form_MouseDown(Button As Integer, Shift As Integer, X As Single, Y As Single)
    Form1.picBalloon.Move (X – picBalloon.Width / 2), (Y – picBalloon.Height / 2)
End Sub
```

Implementation of Specification 22.1(b)

Set the BackColor property of Form1 to white.

Attach the following code to the MouseDown event of Form1.

```
Private Sub Form_MouseDown(Button As Integer, Shift As Integer, X As Single, Y As Single)
    Form1.ForeColor = RGB(Rnd * 255, Rnd * 255, Rnd * 255)
    Form1.Line -(X, Y)
End Sub
```

Implementation of Specification 22.1(c)

Declare the following variable in the declaration section of Form1.

```
Option Explicit
Dim PreviousX As Single
Dim PreviousY As Single
```

403

Attach the following code to the MouseDown event of Form1.

```
Private Sub Form_MouseDown(Button As Integer, Shift As Integer, X As Single, Y As Single)
    PreviousX = X
    PreviousY = Y
End Sub
```

Attach the following code to the MouseUp event of Form1.

```
Private Sub Form_MouseUp(Button As Integer, Shift As Integer, X As Single, Y As Single)
    Form1.Line (PreviousX, PreviousY)-(X, Y)
End Sub
```

PRACTICAL ACTIVITY 22.6

Implement Specification 22.1 and observe the results.

SPECIFICATION 22.2

(a) Write a program that will draw a randomly coloured circle or square on a form. The circle is drawn on a mouse move if only the left button is held down. The square is drawn for all other states of the mouse.

(b) Amend (a) so that holding down to CTRL key will clear the form when a mouse move occurs. Ensure that holding down the ALT and SHIFT keys will not affect the function of the CNTL key.

Implementation of Specification 22.2(a)

Attach the following code to the MouseMove event of Form1.

```
Private Sub Form_MouseMove(Button As Integer, Shift As Integer, X As     | Enter as
Single, Y As Single)                                                     | one line.
Dim ShapeScale As Single
Dim Colour As Long
    If Form1.Width > Form1.Height Then
        ShapeScale = Form1.Width \ 16
    Else
        ShapeScale = Form1.Height \ 16
    End If
    Colour = RGB(Rnd * 255, Rnd * 255, Rnd * 255)
    If Button = 1 Then
        Form1.Circle (X, Y), ShapeScale \ 2, Colour
    Else
        Line (X, Y)-(X + ShapeScale, Y + ShapeScale), Colour, B
    End If
End Sub
```

Implementation of Specification 22.2(b)

Add the following code to the code shown above.

```
If (Shift And 2) = 2 Then
    Form1.Cls
End If
```

PRACTICAL ACTIVITY 22.7

(a) Implement Specification 22.2 and observe the results.

(b) Amend the program so that all the three keys associated with the SHIFT argument have to be held down to clear the form.

(c) Further amend the program so that holding down the SHIFT key doubles the size of the shapes drawn.

23 Keyboard events

Focus

In the windows environment, at any one time, one of the objects on the screen will have the focus and this will be indicated by the object's appearance. For example, when a command button has the focus, a dotted rectangle appears around its caption, as shown in Figure 23.1

Figure 23.1 A command button and the focus.

This has the focus.

When a Check box has the focus its caption is also surrounded by a dotted rectangle, as shown in Figure 23.2.

Figure 23.2 Check boxes and the focus.

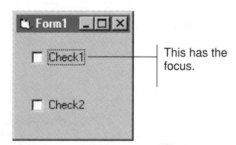

This has the focus.

When a scroll bar has the focus its thumb tab blinks.

The object that has the focus responds to the keyboard input.

There are three keyboard events.

- KeyPress.
- KeyDown.
- KeyUp.

The three keyboard events are described in Table 23.1.

Table 23.1 Keyboard events.

Event	Description
KeyPress	Occurs when the user presses and releases an ANSI key.
KeyDown	Occurs when the user presses a key while an object has the focus.
KeyUp	Occurs when the user releases a key while an object has the focus.

When a KeyUp or KeyDown event occurs it invokes an event procedure that takes two arguments (parameters) as illustrated in Figure 23.3.

Figure 23.3 The parameter passed to a KeyUp or KeyDown event procedure.

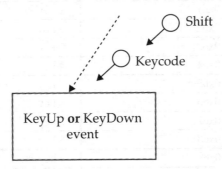

Figure 23.4 illustrates the heading to the KeyUp and KeyDown event procedures, to which a form will respond.

Figure 23.4 The heading of the KeyUp and KeyDown event procedures.

Private Sub Form_KeyUp(KeyCode As Integer, Shift As Integer)
Private Sub Form_KeyDown(KeyCode As Integer, Shift As Integer)

The arguments (parameters) to both these events are described in Table 23.2

Table 23.2 The arguments to two of the keyboard events.

Argument	Description
KeyCode	This supplies a key code, such as vbKeyF1 (the F1 key) or vbKeyHome (the HOME key). To specify key codes, use the constants in the Visual Basic (VB) object library in the Object Browser.
Shift	An integer that corresponds to the state of the **SHIFT**, **CTRL**, and **ALT** keys at the time of the event.

The KeyDown and KeyUp events provide the lowest level of keyboard response. They report the exact physical state of the keyboard itself. For example, when the user presses the *A* key, the Keycode supplied to the KeyDown event is exactly the same as if the user pressed *a*. The *a* and *A* are the same physical key on the keyboard and the KeyCode argument reports that this key has been pressed. Furthermore, if the user presses *1* or *!* on the keyboard the same KeyCode is supplied because it is the same physical key. However, if the user presses the *1* on the Keypad a different KeyCode value, is supplied to the KeyDown event procedure, than when the other *1* is pressed because they are physically different keys.

Key codes for all the letters on the keyboard are the same as the ANSI upper-case codes for the letters. The key codes for the number and punctuation keys are the same as the ANSI codes for the numbers and punctuation.

The key codes for the numeric pad on the keyboard are shown in Table 23.3.

The key codes for the function keys on the keyboard are shown in Table 23.4.

Table 23.3 Key Codes for the numeric pad.

Constant	Value (hexadecimal)	Description
vbKeyNumpad0	0x60	0 key.
vbKeyNumpad1	0x61	1 key.
vbKeyNumpad2	0x62	2 key.
vbKeyNumpad3	0x63	3 key.
vbKeyNumpad4	0x64	4 key.
vbKeyNumpad5	0x65	5 key.
vbKeyNumpad6	0x66	6 key.
vbKeyNumpad7	0x67	7 key.
vbKeyNumpad8	0x68	8 key.
vbKeyNumpad9	0x69	9 key.
vbKeyMultiply	0x6A	MULTIPLICATION SIGN (*) key.
vbKeyAdd	0x6B	PLUS SIGN (+) key.
vbKeySeparator	0x6C	ENTER key.
vbKeySubtract	0x6D	MINUS SIGN (-) key.
vbKeyDecimal	0x6E	DECIMAL POINT(.) key.
vbKeyDivide	0x6F	DIVISION SIGN (/) key.

Table 23.4 Key codes for the function keys.

Constant	Value (hexadecimal)	Description
vbKeyF1	0x70	F1 key.
vbKeyF2	0x71	F2 key.
vbKeyF3	0x72	F3 key.
vbKeyF4	0x73	F4 key.
vbKeyF5	0x74	F5 key.
vbKeyF6	0x75	F6 key.
vbKeyF7	0x76	F7 key.
vbKeyF8	0x77	F8 key.
vbKeyF9	0x78	F9 key.
vbKeyF10	0x79	F10 key.
vbKeyF11	0x7A	F11 key.
vbKeyF12	0x7B	F12 key.
vbKeyF13	0x7C	F13 key.
vbKeyF14	0x7D	F14 key.
vbKeyF15	0x7E	F15 key.
vbKeyF16	0x7F	F16 key.

NOTE: These and other key codes are provided by constants that can be viewed using the object browser. They are specified in VB-Visual Basic objects and procedures under KeyCodeConstants.

The implementation of Specification 23.1 will illustrate a use for the KeyDown event and key code constants.

SPECIFICATION 23.1

An application consists of one form that contains four command buttons. Arrange for the pressing of the F9 function key to quit the application regardless of which control has the focus.

All the four command buttons and the form can respond to a KeyDown event. At run-time one of the command buttons will have the focus and it will respond to the KeyDown event. However, which of the command buttons has the focus when the user presses F9 to quit the application will be unknown. Therefore at first sight it would appear that the End statement (this quits the application) needs to be attached to all the controls on the form. This will work but a better method exists. Set the KeyPreview property of the form to true and place the End statement in the KeyDown event of the form.

Setting the KeyPreview property to true ensures that the form responds to all three keyboard events **before** the control on the form that has the focus. This makes it easy to provide a common response to a specific keystroke.

NOTE: When the KeyPreview property of a form is set to true it does not stop the control that has the focus from responding to the KeyDown event. The control does respond but it does so **after** the form's KeyDown event.

The following code implements Specification 23.1:

```
Private Sub Form_KeyDown(KeyCode As Integer, Shift As Integer)
    If KeyCode = vbKeyF9 Then 'Notice the use of the constant
        End
    End If
End Sub
```

PRACTICAL ACTIVITY 23.1

(a) Implement Specification 23.1, remember to set KeyPreview to true.

(b) Place one command button on a form. Attach the following code to the form's KeyDown event:

    Form1.Print "Form one responding"

Attach the following code to the command button KeyDown event:

    Form1.Print "Command button responding"

Run the program and press a key on the keyboard. Observe the result.

(c) Repeat (b) but this time set the KeyPreview property of the form to false. Observe the different result.

The shift argument

The shift argument is an integer that corresponds to the state of the SHIFT, CTRL, and ALT keys, as can be seen in Figure 23.5.

Figure 23.5 The Shift argument.

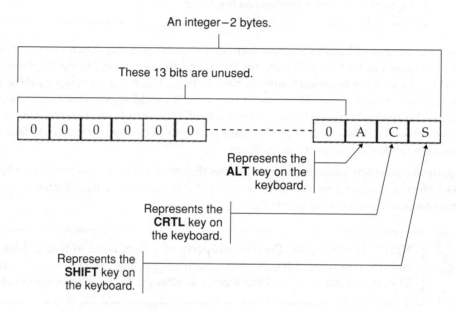

The shift argument is a bit field with the least-significant bits corresponding to the SHIFT key (bit 0), the CTRL key (bit 1), and the ALT key (bit 2). The shift argument indicates the state of these keys as shown by Table 23.5.

> **PRACTICAL ACTIVITY 23.2**
>
> Implement the following amendment to Specification 23.1.
>
> Quit the program when the user presses the following keys together.
>
>   CTRL + ALT + F9
>
> **HINT**: Use a selection construct and consider the following.
>
>   ((Shift And 2) = 2) And ((Shift And 4) = 4) And (KeyCode = vbKeyF9)
>
> Would the above work if the user pressed SHIFT+ALT+CTRL+F9?

When a KeyPress event occurs it invokes an event procedure that takes one argument (parameter) as illustrated in Figure 23.6.

Table 23.5 Possible values of the Shift argument.

Key(s) pressed	Binary value of the shift argument	Decimal value of the shift argument
SHIFT	0000000000000001	1
CTRL	0000000000000010	2
SHIFT + CTRL	0000000000000011	3
ALT	0000000000000100	4
ALT + SHIFT	0000000000000101	5
ALT + CTRL	0000000000000110	6
ALT + CTRL + SHIFT	0000000000000111	7

Figure 23.6 The parameter passed to a KeyPress event procedure.

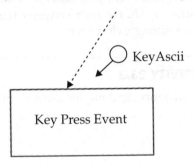

Figure 23.7 illustrates the heading to the KeyPress event procedures, to which a form will respond.

Figure 23.7 The heading of the KeyPress event procedure.

Private Sub Form_KeyPress(KeyAscii As Integer)

The argument (parameter) to this event is described in Table 23.6

NOTE: The KeyPress event occurs when the user presses a key that corresponds to an ANSI character. It, unlike the KeyDown, supplies a different code for *A* and *a*. It does not respond to the pressing of non-ANSI keys, such as the function keys.

It will respond to the ESC key providing there is not a command button on the GUI with its Cancel property set to true. It will also respond to the BACKSPACE key.

Table 23.6 The argument to the KeyPress event procedure.

Argument	Description
KeyAscii	An integer that passes a standard numeric **ANSI** keycode. Keyascii is passed by reference; changing it sends a different character to the object. Changing Keyascii to 0 cancels the keystroke so the object receives no character.

The implementation of Specification 23.2 will show the KeyPress event in action.

SPECIFICATION 23.2

A text box is used to read data from the keyboard. Regardless of the state of the caps lock and the shift key on the keyboard the text box will display the data in uppercase.

The following code implements Specification 23.2

```
Private Sub Text1_KeyPress(KeyAscii As Integer)
    KeyAscii = Asc(UCase(Chr(KeyAscii)))
End Sub
```

KeyAscii is supplied to the KeyPress event procedure as a numeric character code. The **Chr** function converts it to a character, **UCase** then converts this character to upper-case and finally **Asc** converts it back to a numeric character.

PRACTICAL ACTIVITY 23.3

Draw a text box on a form and implement Specification 23.2.

24 The timer ()

A timer is a Visual Basic control that can be drawn onto a form like all other controls. However, the timer does not respond to user-generated events, in fact, it only responds to **one** event, that is, the **Timer Event**. The Timer Event occurs when a pre-set interval of time has elapsed.

Once started a timer works independently and continually regardless of what else the application is doing. The timer effectively supplies a 'regular beat' to an application which responds to each beat by executing an event procedure. For example, upon the receipt of a 'beat' the application can read today's date and, if it is the end of the month, the amount of interest on a customer's account can be calculated. Another example, a clock displayed on the GUI can be updated with the current time. A common use for a timer is in animation. On every 'beat' (timer **event**) a different frame of an animation sequence can be displayed in an image or picture box.

The important properties for a timer control are described in Table 24.1.

Table 24.1 Important properties of the timer control.

Property	Description
Interval	Returns or sets the number of **milliseconds** between calls to a timer control's timer event.
Enabled	When this is set to True the timer starts working, i.e., it responds to the timer events. Setting this property to false stops the timer from responding to timer events.

The implementation of Specification 24.1 illustrates a timer in action.

SPECIFICATION 24.1

Design an application that performs the function of a digital clock.

A suitable GUI is shown here.

The GUI shows a label and timer. The position of the timer is not important because it is **not** visible at run-time. The label has been named lblDigitalClock, the timer has been named

413

tmrDigitalClock. The interval property of the timer has been set to 500 (500 ms = 0.5 seconds). The AutoSize property of the label has been set to True, its BorderStyle to Fixed Single and its font size (found in its Font property dialogue box) to 24.

The following code is attached to the timer event:

```
Private Sub tmrDigitalClock_Timer()
    If lblDigitalClock <> CStr(Time) Then
        lblDigitalClock.Caption = Time
    End If
End Sub
```

NOTE: The interval is **not** guaranteed to elapse on time. The Windows Operating system generates 18 clock ticks per second. So although the interval property of a timer is measured in milliseconds the true precision of an interval is no more than one eighteenth of a second.

Therefore, when using a timer control there is an inherent potential for error. Consequently, always make the interval property one half the desired precision.

The interval property of the timer, for the implementation of Specification 24.1, was set to half a second because the required precision is one second.

Description of the timer event procedure

Time is a function that returns the current system time. This is assigned to the labels caption property. The selection construct is used because there is a chance of two timer events in one second. Consequently, the current time is not assigned to the label if the label is already displaying this current time – this avoids the clock flickering.

PRACTICAL ACTIVITY 24.1

Implement Specification 24.1

Amend Specification 24.1 so that the clock will behave as a digital **alarm** clock. The user enters a time and your computer will beep when this time is reached.

HINT: There is a Beep statement, place it inside a loop.

QUESTION 24.1 (DEVELOPMENT)

The timer is commonly used for computer animation. An example of simple animation is illustrated by one of the sample projects supplied with Visual Basic. This example has the path c:\vb\samples\firstapp\butterf.vbp. Load and run the example and learn how it works.

The design time form for this example is shown in Figure 24.1 and the code window attached to the timer is shown in Figure 24.2.

Figure 24.1 The design time view of the example project.

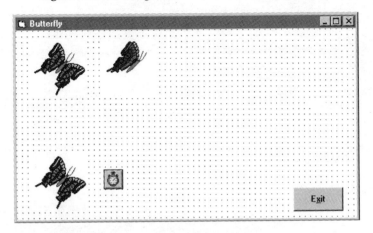

Figure 24.2 The code window for the timer control.

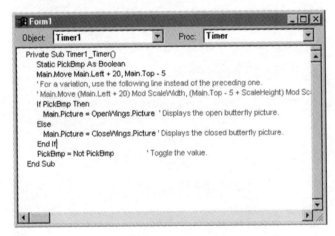

Description of the 'butterfly code'

On a timer event x the butterfly with open wings is displayed, on timer event $x+1$ the butterfly with closed wings is displayed in a slightly different position due to the Move method; on timer event $x + 2$ the butterfly with open wings is displayed in a slightly different position and so on.

The static variable PickBmp is responsible for ensuring a different part of the selection construct is executed every time a timer event occurs (a static variable is able to hold its contents between procedure calls). The value of PickBmp is altered by the statement PickBmp = Not PickBmp on every call, consequently, it toggles between true and false (**note**, I have changed the type of the static variable from Integer to Boolean).

PRACTICAL ACTIVITY 24.2

Redo the program developed during Practical activity 16.16 (in chapter 16) using a timer.

415

Appendix   Fundamental knowledge

This Appendix deals with the fundamental knowledge required by a computer programmer. If you are familiar with computer hardware, the Windows operating system and if you have written programs in another language then you may want to skip this Appendix.

A computer system

A computer system consists of five basic components as illustrated in Figure A.1. Each component is briefly described in the text that follows.

Input devices

A keyboard and a mouse are typical input devices to a computer system. The keyboard supplies the alphanumeric characters requires by an application (program), such as the names and addresses of customers in a bank.

The mouse and its associated cursor are able to activate functions within the application by clicking onto a menu item or button, e.g., activating a spell checker within a word processor – which is an example of a click event.

An application developed with Visual Basic **also** 'sees' the keyboard and the mouse as event generators. These events are used to activate procedures (program code) within the application. Examples of events generated by the mouse are:

- A single click on the mouse button – the **click event** (Click).
- A double click on the mouse button – the **double click event** (DblClick).
- Moving the mouse – the mouse move event (MouseMove).

Each of these events can be 'tied' to a section of code (procedure) within the application and upon occurrence of an event this code is executed. For example if the user clicks the mouse button the code 'tied' to the click event is executed. This code is an example of a click event procedure.

Which particular click event procedure within an application executes is dependent upon the position of the cursor on the Visual Display Unit (VDU). For instance, the cursor may be positioned over the spell check button in which case the spell checker is executed. Alternatively, the cursor may be positioned over the print button in which case a document will be sent to the printer.

Examples of events generated by the keyboard are:

- Pressing down a key on the keyboard – the KeyDown event.
- Releasing a key on the keyboard – the KeyUp event.
- Pressing and releasing a key on the keyboard – the KeyPress event.

417

Figure A.1 A block diagram of a computer system.

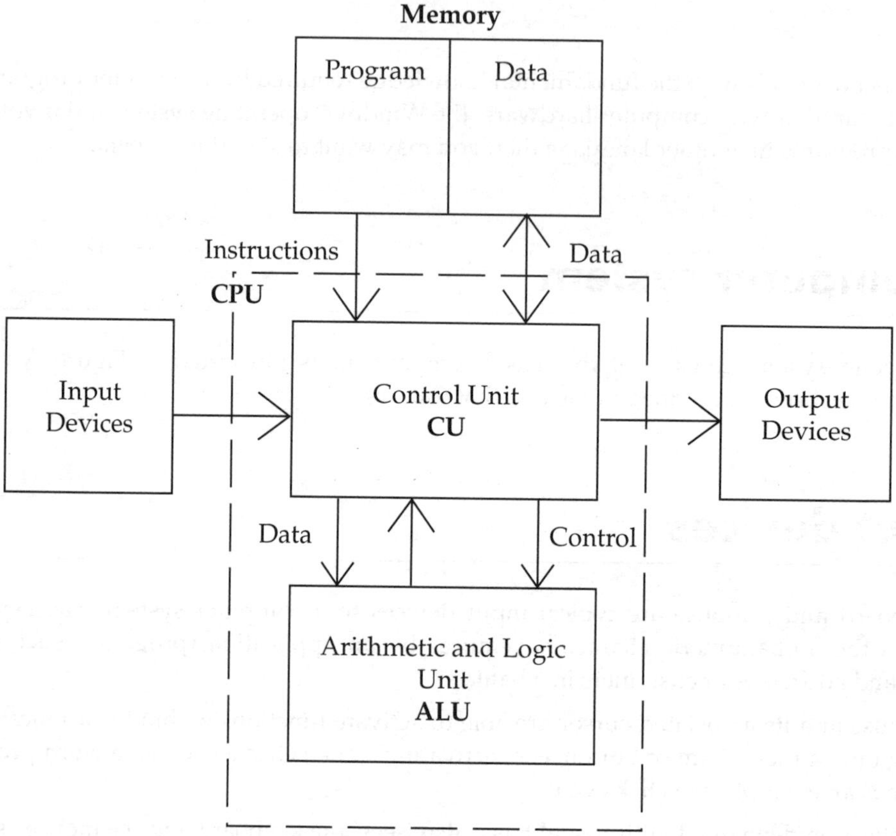

There are many more events available to applications written in Visual Basic and they have been dealt with throughout the book as appropriate. What executes in response to an event depends upon the code attached to an event by the computer programmer. However, it is worth noting that some events may not have associated event procedures, i.e., the programmer has not written any code for the event in question. Conversely, an event procedure may consist of many lines of code performing a complex task.

To summarise, input devices supply data to applications running on the computer system and they can **also** supply events to activate code within the application. This relationship between the application and the input devices is illustrated in Figure A.2.

Output devices

Output devices for computer systems are the Visual Display Unit (VDU), the printer and hard discs. For the development of applications using Visual Basic the most important output device is the VDU. Window applications are graphical in nature and users interact with the graphical view using the mouse and keyboard.

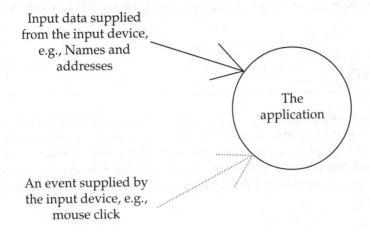

Figure A.2 Relationship between the application and its input devices. The application is represented by the process bubble (circle). The input data is represented by the arrow and the event by the dotted arrow.

Input data supplied from the input device, e.g., Names and addresses

The application

An event supplied by the input device, e.g., mouse click

Memory

Stores the program instructions and the data to be manipulated by the program.

Central processing unit (CPU)

The CPU, under direction from the program instructions, processes the data.

Control unit (CU)

This is a subsystem of the CPU. It is responsible for the issuing of signals that control the movement of data around the system. It also informs the Arithmetic and Logic Unit (ALU) as to the function it is to perform (i.e., add, subtract, logical NOT, compare, etc.). The control unit receives its instructions from the program.

Arithmetic and logic unit (ALU)

This is also a subsystem of the CPU and it is responsible for performing all the arithmetic and logic operations. For example, it will add together data (arithmetic operation) or it will mask incoming data to see if a serial modem line is switched on or off (logical operation).

Call

A **call** is when one segment of code directs the computer system to execute another segment of code.

Program

The program is stored in the computer memory and consists of instructions that dictate the activities performed by a computer system. For applications (programs) developed with Visual Basic, the program instructions are partitioned into smaller segments of code (procedures and functions). These segments of code are executed in response to events generated by the user, events generated by the system, or indirectly by calls from within other segments of code.

Data

Data is stored in the computer memory. It is processed by the computer system hardware components that are in turn controlled by program instructions.

Machine code

The program instructions received by the Control Unit from the program stored in memory are in the language of the machine. This language is referred to as machine code.

Machine code is a low-level language that controls the architecture of the CPU. It opens pathways for the movement of data between the computer system components and it dictates how data is to be processed by the ALU.

There is a vast array of different computer systems available. These systems have CPUs that have different architectures. Every type of CPU has its own language. Consequently, a program in the machine language of one CPU will **not** control the architecture of another CPU type.

Developing software packages in machine code limits their availability to one type of CPU. A programmer experienced in writing programs in one type of machine language requires retraining in the language of another machine. Programs developed in machine code take a long time to produce and are difficult to test and debug.

High-level languages

High-level languages are converted to machine code by a compiler. Compilers are available for each type of CPU. Consequently, a program developed in a high-level language can be used on different types of computer system. Therefore, high-level languages are more **portable** than low-level languages.

Productivity is vastly increased if software is developed in a high-level language rather than machine code. This productivity is achieved because one line of a high-level language is translated into numerous lines of machine code. Also high-level language programs are easier to test and debug than machine code programs.

The main advantage of a high-level language over machine code is that they are problem orientated. This means that a high-level language can represent the solution to a problem in a form that is more understandable to a human.

Machine code programs bear little resemblance to the solution of a problem. This can be best illustrated by the example shown in Table A.1.

Both the machine code and high-level language statement are responsible for the addition of two numbers and the storing of the sum. Obviously, the high-level language is more understandable to a human than the machine code.

Table A.1 Comparison of machine code and a high-level language statement.

High-level language statement	Machine code
Z = X + Y	3E01C60200FF

Assembly language

Low-level programs are actually written in an assembly language and these programs are translated to machine code by an assembler. However, assembly language suffers nearly all the problems associated with machine code. Indeed assembly language is nothing more than symbolic machine code. The relationship between high and low-level languages is illustrated in Figure A.3.

Figure A.3 Comparison of language levels.

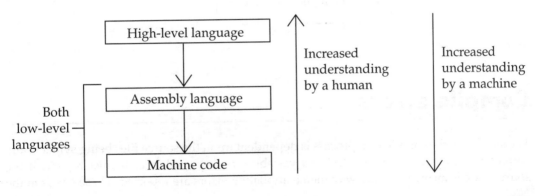

Compilation process

A high-level language, such as Visual Basic, is a collection of files consisting of ANSI codes or binary files (it depends upon how the programmer has set up the system). ANSI codes are 8-bit codes that represent letters, commas, etc. These files are generated using an editor and the Visual Basic interface elements. The Visual Basic development environment consists of objects and their properties, language statements and language constructs, such as sequence, selection and repetition. A Visual Basic statement defines an activity to be performed, such as, read a number from the keyboard.

The Visual Basic files are the input to a program referred to as the COMPILER. The Compiler 'drives' the computer which then 'translates' the Visual Basic files to produce another file that contains the P code (not quite machine code). This P code, in conjunction with the Visual Basic interpreter, will then be used to perform the actions of the program. At the end of a successful compilation process two files exist, the original Visual Basic file (called the source code) and the Executable file (containing the P code). This process is illustrated in Figure A.4

Figure A.4 Compilation process.

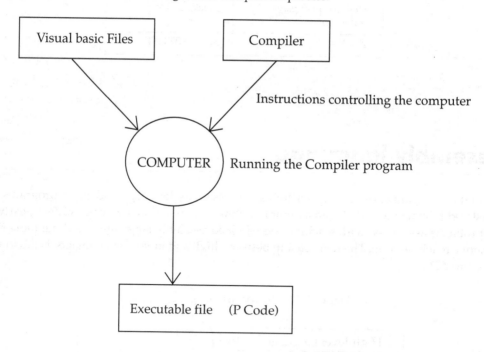

Compile errors

The success of the compilation process is dependent upon the source files being syntactically correct, i.e., correct spelling of declared variables, no keywords words missing, etc. If the source code is incorrect in any way then compilation errors are reported. These errors in the source code are amended by the programmer using an editor. Upon amendment of the compilation errors the Visual Basic files are again compiled. This process may be repeated a number of times until all the errors are removed.

Keywords

Many of the words within a Visual Basic program have a special meaning to the compiler. They, for instance, tell the compiler where the procedures begin and end. Refer to the Visual Basic online help facility for a comprehensive list of KeyWords (refer to the main text on how to use the online help facility).

Run-time

The executable code is the machine representation of the activities defined by the Visual Basic program and with the assistance of the run-time interpreter is used to 'drive' the computer system. The input data is processed to produce the output data and the events activate appropriate procedures within the application as illustrated in Figure A.5.

Figure A.5 The run-time process.

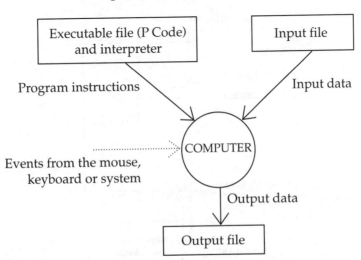

Run-time errors

A successful compilation process does not imply a successful run-time! The executable code, in processing the input data, may attempt to divide by zero. Dividing by zero results in infinity. A run-time error will occur and the action taken by the program will differ depending upon the computer system being used. There are a variety of reasons for run-time errors as you will discover during your study.

Model of a computer system

The advantage of using a high-level language, like Visual Basic, is that it hides the machine from the programmer. A high-level programmer has no concern for the way the computer system architecture actually processes and moves the data around. However, it is useful if a high-level language programmer has a model of a computer system. Such a model will help in visualising the operation of the program and it should give a better insight into the possibilities and limitations of a computer system.

The model is based on the block diagram of Figure A.1. It will be taken for granted that all input to programs will be supplied from the input devices. However, our model will store all input in 'memory boxes'. Likewise all output will be directed to the output devices from 'memory boxes'. All arithmetic and logic operations are performed by the ALU. Our model will assume that operations simply happen. The Control Unit is, obviously, the heart of the CPU, but its control of data movement will again be taken for granted. This leaves us with the model illustrated in Figure A.6. which is simply based upon the memory of a computer system, a memory that is split into two areas, the program and data area. The program area consists of a list of high-level program instructions and the data area consists of memory boxes storing data.

Figure A.6 Model of a computer system.

MEMORY

	BOX 1	BOX 2
INSTRUCTION 1		
	Contents	Contents
INSTRUCTION 2		
INSTRUCTION 3	BOX 3	BOX 4
"		
	Contents	Contents
"		
"	"	
		"
INSTRUCTION N-1	"	
	BOX N-1	BOX N
INSTRUCTION N		
	Contents	Contents

PROGRAM AREA   DATA AREA

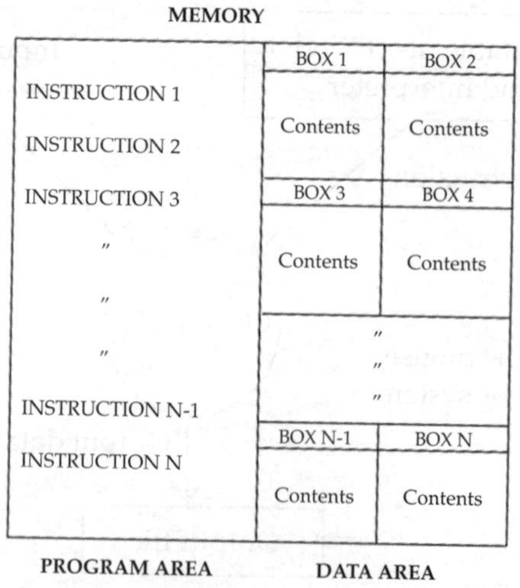

The model will be used to describe the addition of two numbers as illustrated in Figure A.7. The program consists of four instructions and uses three 'memory boxes' (variables).

Figure A.7 The addition of two numbers.

MEMORY

	FirstNumber	SecondNumber
1. Read first number		
2. Read second number		
3. Sum both numbers	Sum	
4. Display the sum		
	"	
	"	
	"	

PROGRAM AREA   DATA AREA

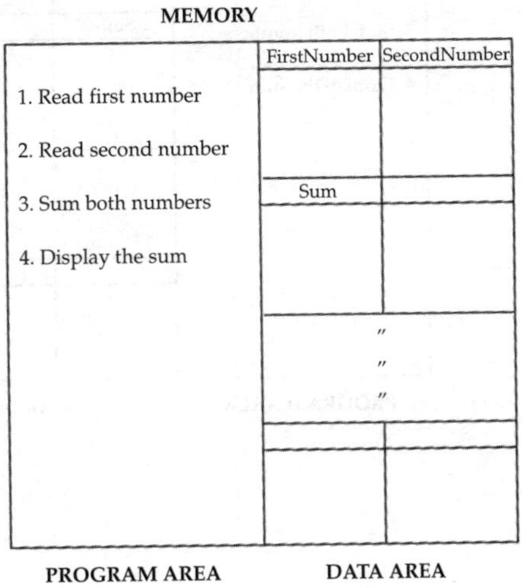

The following sequence of diagrams (Figures A.8 to A.11) illustrates the action of the program shown in Figure A.7. In each diagram the instruction under execution is shown in bold.

Figure A.8 Executing instruction 1. The data from the input device is directed to the memory by the control unit. It is copied to the variable FirstNumber.

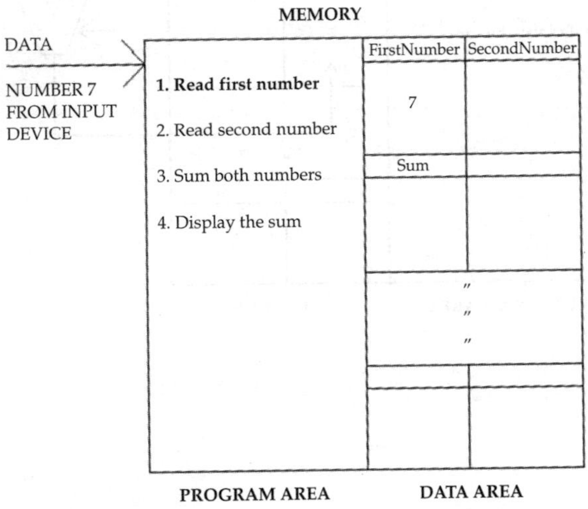

MEMORY

DATA

NUMBER 7 FROM INPUT DEVICE

	FirstNumber	SecondNumber
1. Read first number	7	
2. Read second number		
3. Sum both numbers	Sum	
4. Display the sum		
	"	
	"	
	"	

PROGRAM AREA   DATA AREA

425

Figure A.9 Executing instruction 2. (i.e. SecondNumber)

MEMORY

NUMBER 5

FROM INPUT DEVICE

	FirstNumber	SecondNumber
1. Read first number		
	7	5
2. Read second number		
3. Sum both numbers	Sum	
4. Display the sum		
		"
		"
		"

PROGRAM AREA   DATA AREA

Figure A.10 Executing instruction 3. Here, the control unit directs a copy of the data stored in the memory to the inputs of the ALU. The control unit then issues an addition signal to the ALU. The control unit then directs the output of the ALU to the memory.

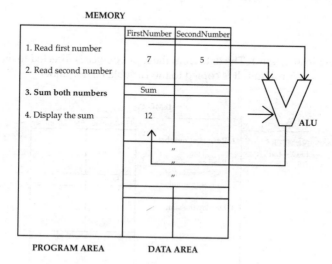

MEMORY

	FirstNumber	SecondNumber
1. Read first number		
	7	5
2. Read second number		
3. Sum both numbers	Sum	
4. Display the sum	12	
		"
		"
		"

ALU

PROGRAM AREA   DATA AREA

Figure A.11 Execution of instruction 4. The control unit directs a copy of the data stored in memory to the output device.

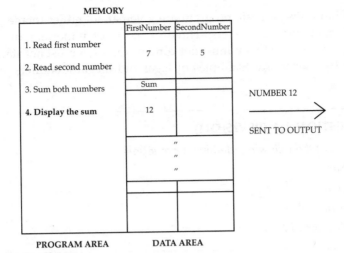

MEMORY

	FirstNumber	SecondNumber
1. Read first number	7	5
2. Read second number		
3. Sum both numbers	Sum	
4. **Display the sum**	12	
	"	
	"	
	"	

NUMBER 12

→

SENT TO OUTPUT

PROGRAM AREA   DATA AREA

Variables and data types

The boxes in the last sequence of diagrams are named: FirstNumber, SecondNumber and Sum. In a Visual Basic program these boxes are referred to as **variables** and their name **identifiers**. Every variable has a particular type. The type, for instance, defines the way in which the data can be processed. Two examples of number types in Visual Basic are integer and single. Integers are used to store whole numbers and singles are used to store numbers with fractional parts. People's names are stored in variables of type string. Both number types can be processed by arithmetic operations such as addition. However, it is nonsense to attempt to **arithmetically** add string variables (how can you add people's names and why would you want to?). The compiler does not allow you to arithmetically add string variables. This is what is meant by a variables type defining the way in which it can be processed.

In the same way that a model has been developed for a computer system, I recommend that you view data types as different size memory boxes. Visual Basic has thirteen standard data types. Three of these types are byte, integer and long. At this stage of your knowledge I recommend you view these types as different size boxes as illustrated in Figure A.12.

Figure A.12 Data types represented as different-size boxes.

Byte

Integer

Long

Identifiers

All variables within a Visual Basic program are given an identifier (name). An identifier is formed from alphanumeric characters. Three of the most important rules regarding the formation of an identifier are that it must not contain spaces, it must not start with a number and it must not be a keyword. Examples of legal and illegal identifiers are shown in the Table A.2.

QUESTION 1.1 (REVISION)

Which of the following identifiers are legal?

1. *Sum*
2. *sum*
3. *3rdNumber*
4. *Product of Numbers*

Table A.2 Legal and illegal identifiers.

Legal identifiers	Illegal identifiers
FirstNumber	Second number
Second_number	2ndnumber
thirdnumber	End

Program style

Most software houses adopt layout rules (styles) for their source code. Adopting a consistent style for Programs is easier on the eye and gives your programs a professional look. The main advantage of a consistent style is that programmers within the same organisation find it easy to debug their colleagues' programs – which is an essential activity when producing code. Figure A.14 shows a program with no style. Compare this program to the program shown in Figure A.13. Both programs will compile and indeed they perform the same function.

Figure A.13 A program with style

```
Private Sub Form_Click ()

Dim FirstNumber As Integer
Dim SecondNumber As Integer
Dim Product As Integer

    FirstNumber = InputBox("Enter a number")
    SecondNumber = InputBox("Enter another number")
    Product = FirstNumber * SecondNumber
    MsgBox "The product of the input numbers is " & Product
End Sub
```

Figure A.14 A program with no style

```
Private Sub Form_Click()
Dim x, y, z
x = InputBox("Enter"): y = InputBox("Enter")
z = x * y: MsgBox "The answer is " & z
End Sub
```

The main difference between Figures A.14 and A.13 is that the statements of Figure A.13 are indented. This indentation is achieved with the tab key (throughout this text there have been programs that show further levels of indentation). Also the variable identifiers have been chosen to reflect their role in the program. For instance, the variable used to store the first number entered at the keyboard is named FirstNumber and not x as in the second program. Using sensible names for variables is the best way to document code. Also the identifier has the first letter of each word capitalised (remember spaces cannot be used in identifiers). Finally every statement appears on its own line. You are advised to adopt a consistent style for all of your programs. For the time being I recommend that you adopt the following rules for code layout.

1. Have only one statement per line.

2. Indent statements using the tab key.

3. Use mixed-case characters for identifiers, ensuring that the first letter in each word is capitalised.

4. Ensure that identifiers reflect the use of the variable within the code.

Programming process

A program is a solution to a problem. In the programming vernacular a solution manifests itself as a program design algorithm. These designs can, for example, be in the form of Nassi Schneiderman charts and Structured English. Once a design (solution) has been found the process of converting the design to code is relatively easy.

The early chapters in this text will show how to convert given designs (solutions) to Visual Basic. Once you have achieved the skill of converting a design to Visual Basic you will have learned much about Visual Basic. However, you will be far from being a programmer. The next step is to derive the designs (solutions) from the given problem (specification).

The process of obtaining a solution to a problem is difficult. However, methodologies for approaching problem solving can be used and with experience the ability in finding solutions (i.e., developing a design) improves.

These methodologies are taught during the text and a number of suitable activities offer you the opportunity to practise your problem-solving abilities.

Figure A.15 The programming process.

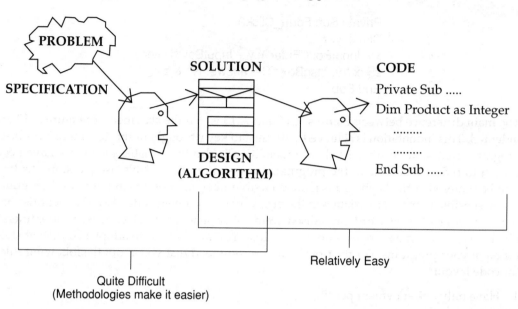

Index